Benjamin Drew

Burial Hill, Plymouth, Massachusetts

Its monuments and gravestones numbered and briefly described, and the

inscriptions and epitaphs thereon carefully copied

Benjamin Drew

Burial Hill, Plymouth, Massachusetts
Its monuments and gravestones numbered and briefly described, and the inscriptions and epitaphs thereon carefully copied

ISBN/EAN: 9783337426071

Printed in Europe, USA, Canada, Australia, Japan

Cover: Foto ©ninafisch / pixelio.de

More available books at **www.hansebooks.com**

BURIAL HILL,

PLYMOUTH, MASSACHUSETTS,

ITS MONUMENTS AND GRAVESTONES

NUMBERED

AND BRIEFLY DESCRIBED,

AND

THE INSCRIPTIONS AND EPITAPHS THEREON CAREFULLY COPIED.

BY

BENJAMIN DREW,

(Author of "Pens and Types.")

" A bit of paper   *   *   *   *
Survives himself, his tomb, and all that's his."

PUBLISHED BY THE AUTHOR.

AVERY & DOTEN, PRINTERS.
Plymouth, Mass.

PREFACE.

The burying-ground of Plymouth is, of course, a place of great interest to the citizens of the town : and visitors from other places feel a sad pleasure in wandering among the tombs of past generations. A few of these tombs contain remains of the original adventurers ; many are occupied by the bodies of their immediate descendants who were imbued with the Pilgrim spirit—worldly enterprise controlled and sanctified by fervid religious faith.

Among the earlier numbers (No. 53, etc.) mention is made of six gravestones bearing dates in the 17th century. As I proceeded in my work I found two others plainly inscribed of the century mentioned, and one next to No. 435 having the face scaled off, so that no inscription is perceptible, but which, judging from its surroundings, is, in all probability, erected at the grave of Nathaniel, son of Nathaniel and Mary Thomas ; his death is said to have occurred in 1697,—there are then but eight or nine bearing date of sixteen hundred and odd years.

These are—

William Bradford, 1657.
John Howland, 1672,
Edward Gray, 1681,
William Crowe, 1683-4,
Hannah Clark, 1687,
Thomas Clark, 1697,
Thomas Cushman, 1691,
Ten children of John and Josiah Cotton, 1699, and the defaced tombstone of Nathaniel Thomas (1697?)

It is well known that the earliest burying-ground of the Pilgrim Fathers was on Cole's Hill. To conceal from the Indians all knowledge of the number of deaths among the new settlers, pains were taken to hide all traces of sepulture. Excavations on the hill sometimes reveal long-hidden tombs ; and on one of these—near the steps which lead to The Rock—has been placed a polished granite slab, on which is engraved in capitals the following inscriptions :

On this hill the Pilgrims who died the first winter were buried. This tablet marks the spot where lies the body of one found October 8, 1883. The body of another found on the 27th of the following month lies 8 feet northwest of the westerly corner of this stone.
                    Erected 1884.

The "unlettered muse" spoken of by Gray has, in many instances, supervised the spelling and punctuation on the tombstones of Burial Hill. The various styles of contracted words and the differences in lettering could not be exactly imitated in ordinary type,—but the author of this work has made as close an approximation to the engraved inscriptions as ordinary type would permit. If other than copied errors are found, I believe they will be trifling, and within negligible limits.
                    BENJAMIN DREW.

INDEX TO BURIAL HILL:

ITS INSCRIPTIONS AND EPITAPHS.

PLYMOUTH, MASS.

[The figures refer to the No. in the body of the book.]

A

ALBERSON Jos'h Warren 621.

ALEXANDER Chas. 27, Charlotte S. 22, Deborah 26, Fanny 23, George 27, Georgeianna 29, John 29, John K. 21, Samuel 25, Samuel L. 23, Silvanus 27, Sophronia 27.

ALLEN Ezra 1324, Geo. 1996, Mary 1323, Mary A. B. 45.

ATHERTON Chas. P. 2094.

ATTWOOD Susana 194.

ATWOOD Abby J. 505, Darius 198 and 200, Elizabeth 195 and 199, Exper 1445, Experience 1367 and 1448, Geo. H. 504, Hannah 1444, Henry R. 1230, Isaac 1230, Joanna 1318, John 1447, John B. 1055, Mehetabel 197, Sarah 1446, Thos. 196, Wm. 1230, (twins) 198, Wm. jr. 1230, Wm. T. 504.

B

BACON Abigail 1259, Betsey 2123, Charles H. 1257, Elizabeth 1303, George 1303, George T. 1333, 1334, 1335, Henry S. 1258, Leverett T. 1333, Mary 1254, 1289, Mary T. 1304, Nathan 1289, 1335, Rebecca 2123, Thomas 1255.

BAGNELL Benjamin 2104, Bethiah 2008, Betsey 2100, Elizabeth 2102, 2104, Lois 2033, Lucy 2103, Lucy E. 2101, Minerva 2034, Richard, 245, 2008, Samuel W. 2009, 2033b, Sarah F. 2033a.

BALLARD Samuel D. 491.

BARDAN Mary 1965.

BARLOW John D. 35.

BARNES (closed tomb) 1764, Anna E. 1099, Annie F. 1100, Benjamin 1800, Betsey T. 1826, Betsey W. 1826, Calvin Carver (two) 1864, Charles Elkanah 2115, Charlie E. 2115, Charlie S. 2117, Charlott 1314, Corban 1316, Corbin 1315, Cynthia B. 39, Eleanor 1864, Elizabeth 1939, 1362, Elizabeth Ishmael 2114, Elkanah 2118, Ellis 786, 2074, Ellis D. 21, Hannah 38, 91, 1788, John 1472, 1470, Jonathan 1487, 1361, Joseph 1940, 1788, Levonzo D. 1307, Mary 1315, 1479, 1786, 2033, Mary A. N. 2073, Mary W. 2025, Mercy 1864, Nathaniel 90, 1788, 1864, Nathaniel jr. 90, Nancy

C. 2074, Rebecca 246, Rebekah 1317, Rosella S. 2075, Sally 1057, Samuel 1803, Sarah 1476. 1791, Susan L. 839, Phebe J. 1038, Phebe 1488, William 1056, 1097, 1785, 1787, William Brewster 787, William E. 790, Willie 11. 1101, William T. 1101b, Winslow (two) 1826, Zacheus, 2024.

BARNS Elizabeth 1434, 1486, Sarah 1477.

BARRY Hattie S. 2083, Maria 2082, Timothy 2082, Timothy jr. 2082.

BARSTOW Sarah R. 1074.

BARTLET Lothrop 568, Margaret 356, Robert 354.

BARTLETT Abby 247, Abigail 138, 353, Amasa 233, Andrew 1186, Angeline 2070, Anna M. 813, Ansel (two) 2051, Augustus 1127, Benjamin 822, 1127, Betsey 364. Betsey L. 105, Caleb 1013, Caroline 1565, Caroline E. 1697, Charles 2069, Charles T. 1344, Cynthia 1552, David 976, Dolly 1757, Dorothy 1578, Eliza Ann 1531, Elizabeth 360, 359, 362, 456, 1691, Elizabeth Thacher 1531, Ephraim 1014, 1019, Experience 2071, Fear 1011, Frederick 574, Hannah 355, 1038, 1521, 748, 2021, Hariot 1201, Henry 248, Bartlett (infant son) 1013, James 1035, 1060, 1327, 1524, James Samson 1340, James Thomas 1339, James T. 1338, Jamima 822, Jane 1326, Jenney 393, Jerusha 396, 843b, John 1030, 1127, 1553, 1565, 1573, 1576, John L. 1574, Jonathan 789, Joseph 358, 575, 1008, 1029, 1121, 1127, [headstone missing; footstone "J. B."] 2076, Lemuel 390, Lewis 1575, Lothrop 391, Lucia 2072, Lucy D. 1128, Lydia 351, Margarett J. 237, Marg'tt 357, Martha 104, Mary 228, 389, 394, 1328, Mary A. 1342, Mary T. 1329, Nathaniel 2d 239, Phebe C. 1813, Polly 976, 2050, Rebecca 1012. 1126. 1330, Rebecca T. 1343, Rebeckah 798, Rebekah 797, (two) 703, Robert 354, Ruth 109, Samuel 361, 457, 458, 1127, Sarah 395, 1028, 1034, Sarah T. 233, Silvanus T. 1337, Silvanus Taylor 1341, Stephen 2071, Susan 1129, 1350, Susan Thacher 1532, Sylvanus 103, Thomas 110, 236, 238, 352, 1690, Truman 2072, William 227, 1125, William Thos. 236, Zacheus 748.

BATES Abby Washburn 1336, Benjamin 72, Benjamin F. 72, 73, David 840. Ebenezer P. 1829, Hira 1309, John 1829, John B. 1336, Martha 72, Thankful 841.

BATTLES Elizabeth 1683, 1684, James W. 418, John 1683, Lydia 1683, Samuel 1199, William 1200.

BAXTER Abner N. 345, Ann E. 345, Charles H. 345, Charles I. 116, James 345.

BISHOP Abigail 844, Catharine 849, Henry 845, John 844, Katie B. 848, Sarah T. 847, William 846.

BOURASSO Hannah D. 497.

BOUTELLE Ann Goodwin 777, Ann L. 795, Caleb 776, Ellen G. 795, Nathaniel G. 795.

BOWRN Mary 251.

BRADFORD Amos 547, Andrew J. 982, Bathsheba 703, 706, Betsey 982, Charles 704, Consider 1601, Cornelius 1435, David 983, David L. 982, Desire H. 982, Ebenezer N. 707, Eleanor 1602. Eleanor Morton 1345, Elizabeth 548, 1428, Hannah 704, 1845, Isaac 547, James 548, 1603, John 11. 1429, Joseph 1432, Lemuel 702, 1433, LeBaron 553, Lydia 1433, 1435, Lydia H. (two) 982. Marcy B. 605, Mary 1430, Nancy 606, Nathaniel (two) 1428, 1431, Rebecca 1428, Ruth 547, Sally 1300, Sally H. 1040. Sarah 412, 553, 1603, Thomas 683, William 547, 606, 610, 1439, 1467, 1602, Zephaniah 1039.

BRAMHALL Grace 219, Joseph 220, 453, Joshua 217, 444, Lucy 1452, Lucy M. 1452, Mary 449, Mary B. 218, Mercy 447, Phebe J. 229, Sarah 445, Silvanus 448.

BRECK Moses 1064, Sarah Tyler 1065.

BREWSTER 741, America 825, Elizabeth T. 745, (three) 747, Ellis 740, Sarah 824, William 746, (three) 747, Wm. & Elizabeth, child of, 744.

BRIGHAM Antipas 1681, Mercy M. 1682, Mercy S. 1681.

BROOKS Betsey 1256.

BROWN Abigail Allen 1387, Alice A. Neal 1698, Ann 1070, Anne Rice 1068, Barnabas A. 1388, Charles (two) 16, Lemuel 1067, 1069, Lucy C. J. 600, Lydia 1387, Lydia Allen 1389, 1390, Margret 1385, 1393, Martha 1393, Mary 1383, 1385, 1391, Nabby 1386, Priscilla 1393, Robert (two) 1384, 1392, 1393, 1394, Sarah 1068, Sarah Palmer 1067, 1068, Sophia 603, William 1385, (two) 1387.

BRYANT Homer 2092, Butler Alma M. 2108.

BUGBEE Aurin 1321, James H. 637.

BULLARD Benjamin D. 1184, Mary 1185.

BURBANK Mary Allen 1793, Betsey 1793, Daniel T. 1796, Ezra 1799, Hannah 1796, John 1795, John jr. 1794, Lydia 1795, Mercy 1801, Nehemiah 1797, Polly 1798, Timothy 1801.

BURGESS George A. 1763, Georgiana 1938, Hannah E. 1750, John 1953, Lucy 826, Susannar 1952, Thomas 1927.

BURGIS Sally 2017.

BURGISS Renslow P. 2018.

BURN Samuel 1282.

BURNS Catharine 128, Ellen 128, Henry 128, James 128, James H. 129, Mary (two) 128, Rose 128.

BURT Edward 1709, Elizabeth 1708, Hannah 899, Laban 899, Thomas B. 1709.

C

CALLAHAN Marge 512.

CALLAWAY Mary Ann 208.

CARVER Betsey 1957, Dorothy 1354, 1355, Eliza 1884, James 1355, Joanna 1957, Joseph 1355, Mary 1800, 1957, Nancy 540, 1957, Nathaniel 1955, 1957, Nathl jr. 1957, Sarah 1956, Stephen 1890, 1957, Theodore S. 1905, innominata 1355.

CASSADY Ann 221.

CASSIDY Bridget 215.

CASWELL Henry 1816.

CHANDLER Hannah 338, 451, Hannah B. 339, John B. 338, John T. 339, Lucy S. 339.

CHASE Abigail 1769, George E. 1768, Henry 1768, John 1769, Samuel R. 1768, Wm. 1768.

CHURCH Joseph 387.

CHURCHALL Ezra 654, Susan A. 654.

CHURCHELL Abigal 1674, Abigal W. 1674, David 1674, Eleazar 1660, Ephraim 1643, 1644, Hannah 1465, John 1464, Mary C. 1661, Nathaniel 1640, Priscilla 1643, Stephen 1570.

CHURCHILL Abigail 2000, Adry Anna 1520, Amelia 666, Asenath 1529, Barnabas 2087, (two) 2089, Bethiah 1466, 1541, Catharine B. 2001, Charles 1999, Charles O. 2149, Daniel 1396, David 2099, Elizabeth 1689, 1707, 2098, Elizabeth C. 5, Elizabeth H. 6, Ienor 1572, Elkanah 1402, 1558, 1665, Ephraim 1658, Esther 1970, Eunice 1131, 1665, Hannah 1659, 1675, Hannah P. 2084, Heman 1687a, Heman, six children of, 1688, Isaac 1379, Isaac jr. 1379, Jane 1687a, Jesse 1674, Job 2084, John (two) 951,

1490, 1539, 1540, Joseph 665, Joseph L. 665, Lemuel B. 1688, Lucy 2099, Lucy Ann 33, Lydia 2080, Lydia A. 1559, Lydia L. 664, Marcia G. 665, Mary 1827, Mary A. 1687b, Mary E. 2003, Mary L. 1889, Mercy 667, Nancy 1540, 1542, 2003, Olive 951, Rebecca 1377, Rebecca P. 2002, Rufus and child, 1130, Ruth 1889, 1933, Sally 1325, 2085, Sally C. 1971, Samuel 1706, Sarah 1378, 1634, 2088, Sarah and an infant son 1705, Seth 2097, 2009, Silvanus 7, Solomon 1689, Susan 1932, Thomas 1975, twins 5, William 1379, William C. 5, William C. (2d) 5, Wilson 1931, Zacheus 1666.

CLARK Abigail 884, Eliza H. 1071, Ella M. 677, Hannah 634, John 1072, John T. 674, Mary 645, 1073, Nathaniel 884, Rebecca T. 675, Samuel 646, Thomas 633, Zoheth 676.

CLARKE Elisabeth 1511.

COAL Isaac 955.

COB John 1881, Marcy 1880.

COBB Cornelius 60, Ebenezer 1882, Elizabeth 63, Ephraim 949, 950, Francis 724, Grace 59, 61, (innominata) 801, Isaac E. 62, Job 58, 66, John 802, 803, Josiah 801, Lemuel 919, 970, Margaret 950, Mary 805, Patience 67, Ruth 57, Sarah 806, Susanna 279.

COLE Caroline E. 1547, Cyrus 333, Deborah B. 1547, Ephraim 1365, 1369, James 1353, Jane R. 1547, Rebecca 2141, Sally 1548, Samuel 1138, 1372, 1366, 1549, Sarah (1st and 2d) 1365.

COLGAN John 183, Thomas 183.

COLLIER Mary A. 417.

COLLINGS Lois 180.

COLLINGWOOD John B. 1049, 2125, Joseph 1047, Martha T. 1050, Nellie F. 1050, Rebecca W. 1048, Susan 2125, Thomas 1051, William and Eleanor, 4 children of, 2126, Willie D. 1050, Willie L. 1050.

COLLINS Gamaliel 181, James 179, Lois 182, Mary 177, 178.

COOK Caleb 158, Marcy 292.

COOPER Emeline P. 1172, Esther 1166, George 1121, 1170, George W. 1123, Hannah 1320, 1440, 1442. John 1441, Joseph 1168, Lucy 1167, Lucy T. 1171, 1172b, Mary B. 1169, Mary C. 1122, Richard 1319, 1443, Sylvia 1929, 1930.

CORNISH Thos. E. 2122, Zoraday T. 498.

COTTON David B. 476, Hannah 416, 472, Joanna 470, John 473, John, 3 children of, 430, 2144, Josiah 415, 478, 1566, Josiah, 7 children of, 414, Josiah, sons of, 430, 2144, Lydia 477, 1657, Martha 531, Mary 482, Priscilla 475, Rachel 479, Rosseter 481, Rossiter M. 480, Temperance 1568, Theophilus 530, Thos. 480, Ward 426, William C. 480.

COURTIES Elisabeth 1489.

COVENTON Elizabeth 1087.

COVINGTON Mary 1942, Sarah 1943, Thomas 1944.

COWEN Ann T. 1646, Mary Ann 1647, Robert 1645, 1647.

COX Elias 941, 942b, 1410. Eliza O. 942a, James 1417, Mary 1272, Nancy H. 1416, Patience 1412.

CRAIG David N. 1061.

CRANDON Benjamin 838, Jane 834, Mary D. 833, Ruth 832, Sarah 836, Sukey 837.

CROADE Deborah 261.

CROMBIE Deborah 528, 537, Fanney 538, James 539, Kimball 536, William 527, 534, Zeruiah 535.

CROSWELL Andrew 1455, 1459; David 1420, Joseph 1422, Mary 1456, Rebecca 1421, Rebekah 1458, Sarah 1457.

CROWE William 403.

CRYMBLE [broken] 912, Holms 913.

CURRIER Daniel 654, Ezra C. 654, Freddie A. 654, Susan E. 654, Winnie S. 654.

CURTIS James 1478, ——— les 1025, Mary 1454, Nathl 1907, Zacheus 1906.

CUSHING Nathan G. 2143.

CUSHMAN Mary 54. Robert 54. Thomas 53, 54.

D

DARLING Martha 446.

DAVEA Pricilla 2146.

DAVEE Robart 1887, Sarah 1886, Thomas 1860.

DAVIE Deborah 1823, Deborah C. 2061, Ebenezer 2063, Elizabeth 1824, 1870, Fanny E. 1900, George 2063, Harriet F. 1899, Harriot 2147, Harriot E. 214, Ichabod 1821, Isaac 1117, Jane 1859, Joanna 1820, 1825, John 2059, John L. 2060, Lydia 2062, Nancy 1822, Priscilla 2060, Rhoda C. 1118, Robert 1870, 1901, Sarah 1819, Thomas 1859.

DAVIS Eliza 1077, John and Betsey B., 2 children of, 1818, John R. 1817, Mercy 556, Rebecca 558, Samuel 555, Thomas 557, 560, (tomb) 2095, Wendell 554, William 559.

DEACON Daniel 800, Polly T. 800, Susan A. 800.

DELANO Anonyma 2138, Henrey 2138, Lydia 1985, Penelope 2137, Salome 2137, Sarah 804.

DELENO Abigail 1873, Bathsheba 1874.

DEVINE James T. 36, Peter J. 37.

DICKSON John 1181, John jr. 1180, Phebe 1182, Ruby P. 1146, Samuel 1183, Samuel R. 1147.

DIER Hannah 1373.

DIKE Anthony 881, Parney Y. 1994, Phebe S. 1090, Rebecah 1993, Russell R. 1090, Simeon 1954, Thomas 880, Wm. P. G. 1995.

DILLARD Benjamin 1945, Mercy 1947, Nancy 1948, Polly 1946.

DIMAN Abigail B. 2132, Abigail N. 2132, Daniel 1613, David 2132, David (2d) 1607, David (3d) 1606, Elisabeth 1608, Elizabeth 1116, 'annah 1611, Hattie A. 1269, Josiah 1359, 1425, Josiah (2d) 1427, Lizzie G. 1269, Lois 1605, 1614, Margaret H. 909, Maria S. 1270, Mary 1612, Polly 910, Polly S. & 2 children 1485, Sarah N. 2133, Sophia 1426, Susanna 1427, William G. 1269.

DITMAR Valentine 1308.

DOGGET Mrs. ——— 1026.

DOGGETT June 2106.

DOTEN Abigail 1187, Betsey P. 657, Charles A. 656, Daniel 1949, David 977, Ebenezer 708, Esther 658, Hannah 973, Hellen 657, Isaac 924, 975, Jabez 972, Jabez & Hannah, 4 children of, 972, Jain 363, James 1888, 1892, James 2128, Jerusha 1207, Joseph 1893, 1934, Lewis 658, Louisa S. 657, Lydia 2128, Martha 925, Martha Torrey 974, Mary 971, 1811, Mary W. 1052, Mercy 1810, Nathaniel 1809, Polly and infant 984, Prince 1814, Prince and Susan, 3 children of, 1810, Ruth 69, Sally 1949, Susan 1815, Thomas 1206, William 363, 977.

DOTEY Ansel 709.

DOTY Joanna 911, Nathaniel 911, Ruth 1153.

DREW Abbot 627, Addie 630, Atwood 1516, Atwood and Lydia, 5 children of, 1515, Bathsheba 1802, Benjamin 562, Benjamin (3d) 566, Betsey Churchill 628, Charity S. 1719, Charlotte A. 631, David 1560, David and Sally, 3 children of, 1562, Deborah 561, Desire 562, Ebenezer 564, Elizabeth 462, 563, 1474, George II. 1514, Hannah 1469, Helen A. 1628, Isaac 464, James 1451, John 1020, John C. 1655, Joseph 463, Leman L. 1656, Lemuel 461, Lemuel Mrs. and 2 children 1450, Lydia 1517, 1686, Lydia W. 1657, Malachi 565, Mary 1475, Nicholas II. 632, Rebekah 1685, Sally 235, 1561, Sarah 629, Simeon 562, Sophia 567, Sophia B. 567, Sophia B. (2d) 567, Susan II, Allen 2056, William 367, 401, 1473.

DUNBAR John D. 532, Nancy 533.

DUNHAM Abigail T. 999, Abraham 1712, Abraham T. 1713, Benjamin F. 1346, Elijah 1711, Elisha 1237, Elizabeth 1001, Elizabeth C. 1712, Eunice 1710, George 886, Nancy 886, Patience 1713, Sally 1830, Silvanus 1041, Sylvanus 1941, William 1000.

DURFY Peleg 1368.

DYAR John 1374.

DYER Bethiah 529, Charles 529, Hannah 1375, Mary 465.

DYKE Mary 882.

DYRE Hannah 413.

E

EDDY Ann E. 443a, Ann Eliza 443b, George 443a, Henry F. 870, Seth W. 1306, Willie O 1306.

EDWARDS Polly 140.

ELLIOT Clarissa and infant son 337, Mercy C. 336, Samuel 2107.

ELLIOTT Susan L. 1536.

ELLIS Betsey 1667, George S. 1347, Lydia 1910, Mary H. 1347, Nathaniel 1911, 1912, Rebecca 1911, Samuel 1909.

ERLAND Edwin F. 2159, Henry 106, Sally C. 107.

F

FARMER Phebe 856a.

FARRELL Andrew and 5 sailors 222.

FAUNCE Abigail 1668, Elizabeth 1671, Hannah and 2 children 281, Jerusha 253, John 280, 1648, Mary 1263, Nathaniel 1649, Sarah 1669, Thadius and Mary A., 3 children of, 655, Thomas 1653, Zilpah 1670.

FIELD Charles 1225.

FINNEY Alfred C. 125, Betsey E. 2154, Elizabeth 934, 1583, Ephraim and Phebe, twin children of, 1696, Ezra 1723, Harrison 936, Harrison K. 935, Kate C. 935, Leavitt 506, Lewis 934, Mary A. 507, Mary E. 508, Nancy 1585, Pelham 2035, Pelham and Mary A., 4 children of, 2035, Phebe 1695, Rebekah 1557, Thomas 1584, (tomb) 1764, William 123, William (2d) 124.

FISH Thomas 1702.

FISHER Richard 1059.

FLEMMONS Charles R. 1851.

FOBES Marcy 1844.

FOSTER Elisha 1300, Gershom, 1772, Hannah 1247, 1771, Job 1251, John 1770, John jr. 1773, Lemuel 1246, Lois 1777, Mercy 1832, Nathaniel 1831, Samuel 1248, Seth 1246, Susannah 1832, Thomas 1250, Thomas and Lois, 6 children of, 1777.
FRANK Antoine 1590, Samuel A. 1589.
FREEMAN Abner B. 133, Elizabeth 348, Frederick R. 349.
FULGHUM Joseph 647, Joseph (2d) 649, Luraina 648.
FULLER Rebecca 796.

G

GALE Elizabeth 1253, Noah 1252, Rebekah 1252.
GAMMONS Deborah 842.
GARDNER Fanny H. 843a.
GIBBS Thomas H. 978.
GODDARD Abigail O. 1579, Ann E. 1806, Benjamin 1806, Beulah 2011, Daniel 2011, Daniel jr. 2111a, Daniel (3d) 2112, Grace H. 1579, John 1579, John and Mary, 3 children of, 1979, Lemuel S. 2011, Lucy 1807, Lydia, 1979, 2111b, Mary 1198, 1979, 2112, Mary S. 2010, Polly 1979, Rufus 1197, William 1196, William (2d) 1196.
GOODWIN Abigail P. 1973, Anna 294, 651, Anna L. 662, Charles P. 1972, Desire 1972, Edwin J. 769, Hannah 592, 773, Hannah J. 593, Heverland P. 1972, Heverland P. (2d), 1972, Isaac 1113, John A. 1113, Lazarus 297, 775, Lewis 660, 663, Lucretia 1267, Lucy 433, Lydia 296, 768, Lydia C. 1113, Mary A. 769, Molly 772, Molly I. 774, Nancy 588, Nathaniel 295, 767, 771, 2162, Roby 293, Ruth 770, Simeon S. 1113, Thomas 1972, Timothy 434, William 1113, William jr. 1113.
GOULD Drusilla 1093.
GRANVILLE Rebecca D. 673.
GRATON Alwin M. 889, Charles A. 887, Mary D. 889.
GRAY —— 411, Edward 653.
GREEN Clarissa A. 1348, Marcia C. 871, William C. 871.
GRIFFIN Granvill and Rebecca D., 3 children of, 672, Oliver W. 1284.

H

HALL Eber 732, Elizabeth 732, Joanna A. 2120, John T. 731, Mary 732, Nathan T. 956, Reuben 511, Sally 956.
HAMMATT Abraham 373, 375, 377, John H. 372, Lucy 378, Priscilla 374, Sophia 375.
HAMROSA John H. 34.
HARLOW A. B. and B. J. (twins) 1376, Albert 120, Amaziah and Ruth R., 5 children of, 111, Amaziah 115, Ansel H. 903, Barnabas L. 1401, Bathsheba 902, Benjamin 263, 264, 266, Betsey 160, 161, 262, 265, Catherine 1555, David 509, Deborah 1767, Desire 168, 171, Eliza S. 2146, Elizabeth 166, Elizabeth A. 173, Elizabeth F. 1401, Ellis J. 1987, 1988, Experience 467, Ezra 1903, George 120, Hannah 172, 176, 510, 1400, 1788, Henry 117, Horace 526, Ichabod 120, James 92, Jesse 165, 174, 175, John 71, 159, 162, 187, 425, Josiah 83, Lazarus and Sarah, 2 children of, 192, Lewis 1400, Lewis and Betsey, 4 infants of, 1401, Lewis O. 1401, Lot 298, Lucy 114, 1804, Lydia 1904, Mary 187, 298, Mercy 93, 94, 268, 2066, Nancy 118, 249, Noah 169, Patience 120, Priscilla 865, Rebecca 1902,

Rebecca H. 2110, Rebekah D. 469, Remember 95, 96, 97, Sally 191. Sally and 3 children 1554, Samuel 68, 95, 119. Sarah 164, 2064, Seth 2065, Silvanus 167, 170, Stephen 298, 1315, William 267.

HATCH Phila H. 15.

HATHAWAY Allen 2096.

HAYWARD Beza 1222, Beza jr. 1223, Charles L. 1235, Edward W. 1226, Elizabeth A. 1224, Experience 1221, G. W. and J. A. (twins) 1227, Mary W. 1229, Penelope P. 1228.

HEDGE Abigail 1351, Barnabas 1363, Mercy 1364, (tomb) 2095.

HEMMERLY George D. 1381, William 1382, William K. 1380.

HILL Elisabeth 945, Mary 1692.

HOBART Betsey 1543, Priscilla 2153.

HODGE Betsey H. 1537, Michael 1538.

HOLBROOK Amelia 2151, Bethiah 1704, Eliphalet 1728, 2151. Jeremiah 1703, Peggy 466, Sally 1717.

HOLLIS Abigail 1724, Elizabeth O. 1726, Henry 1725.

HOLMES Abigal 829, Abner 821, Adoniram J. 873b, Albert 1148, Albert and Jerusha T., 3 children of, 1106, (anonymous) 823, Ansel 1311, 1312, Antoinette 1152, Barnabas 680, Bathsheba 820, Bathsheba J. 897, Benjamin 660, Bethiah 1414, Betsey 1765, Betsey and 3 children 1865, Betsey C. 685, Cephas A. 918, Chandler 1833, 1837, Chandler jr. 1780, David C. 915, Eleazer 1840, 1842, 1869, Eleazer and Betsy, 2 children of, 1839, Elener 922, Elizabeth 685, Ellis 1774, Esther 1834, 1843, Esther P. 888, Esther P. (2d) 888, Eunice 1983, Franklin B. 1153, Frederic 1753, Gershom 920, Grace 1775, Hannah 901, 1845, 1868, Harrie W. 493, Henry 831, Henry S. 1987, I. and R., 3 children of, 1781, Ichabod 1779, Ichabod jr. 1852, Ichabod S. 1833, Irving B. 492, Jeremiah jr. 854, Jerusha T. 1106, Joanna 788, 1885, John C. 1415, Joseph 872, 877, 890, Joseph and Eliza, 3 daughters of, 1410, Lemuel D. 684, Lewis 1866, Lois 388, Louisa 917, Lydia 893, 2160, Marcy 1871, Mariah 668, Martha 831, 1911, Mary 855, 895, Mary and infant 821, Mary B. 823, Mary E. 684, Mary S. 850a, Mary T. 689, Massena F. 1313, Mehitable 1835, Mercy 892, Miriam C. 1312, Mrs. 2049, Nancy 854, 1729, Nancy and Rufus 1413, Nathan 876, (N?)athan 1883, Nathaniel 873a, 1872, Nathaniel jr. 685, Nathll 921, Patience C. 874, Peter 855, Phebe 914, 1836, Polly 684, 901, 1775, 1790, Polly and infant 1841, Rebekah 1778, Reuben 900, Richard 828, 883, 892, 921, Ruth 875, Ruth G. 671, Ruth G. (2d) 671, Sarah 820, Sarah M. 1982, Samuel N. 688, Susan C. 670, Susan W. 1838, William 898, 901, William R. 896, William S. 891, Zephaniah 1413.

HOSEA Hannah 341, Daniel 342.

HOVEY James 728, Keturah 1217, Lydia 729, Mary 730, Rachel 1217.

HOWARD Eleanor 1739, Eunice 1928, James 1741, James H. 1742, John 1739, John W. 1740.

HOWES Ebenezer 326, Hannah 1571, Meriah 323, 327, Moriah 325, Sarah 324.

HOWLAND Consider 379, 381, 385, Deborah 1397, Elizabeth 373, Emma M. 188, Hannah 383, Jacob 19, Joannah 384, John 207, 376, 2161, Joseph 366, 382, Martha 651, Nathaniel 650, Patience 207, Ruth 380, Thomas 386, Thomas S. 385.

HOYT Betsey 1722, Betsey M. 1734, Crosby 1722, Curtis 8, Curtis F. 9, Israel 1734, Moses and 2 sons 1721, Ruth 1735.

HUESTEN Hannah 1082, Mary 1085, Nancy H. 1084, Nathaniel 1083, William 1086.

HUTCHINSON Adaline 937, Deborah 938, George W. 937, Robert 938.

J

JACKSON Abraham 1580, Anna 519, 524, Betsey M. 487, Caroline
750, Charles 601, Cornelius S. 835, Daniel 599, Desire 762, Edwin
584, Elizabeth 756, 759, Esther 520, Experience 766, Ezra T.
760, Frederick 749, 761, Frederick W. 522, F. W. 523, Hannah
757, 1005, Harriet 785, Harriet O. 1581, Hezekiah 755, Horace
1582, Jacob 474, Jacob and Joann, 4 children of, 474, Joann
474, John T. 486, Lucy 602, 753, 763, Lydeay 587, Lydia 591, Maria
T. 483, Mercy 521, 764, Meriah M. 484, Nancy 588, Nancy B.
835, Nath 1301, Rebecca 598, Ruth 1302, Salome 758, Samuel
765, Sarah 586, 590, 595, Sarah M. 596, Thomas 585, 589, 597, 752,
754, Thos. jr. 594, William 518, Wm. M. 603b, Woodworth 485.
JACOBS John 1059.
JENNINGS Mary 471.
JEWETT Wm. H. 1058.
JOHNSON Betsey 853, Daniel jr. 1502, Joseph 852, Joseph jr. 852,
Lucy S. 2047, Patience 86, Wm. A. 201.
JONES Harriet T. 209.
JORDAN James 1091.
JOYCE Asa 682b.
JUDSON Abigail 346, Abigail B. 347, Adoniram 347, Adoniram
(2d) 347, Ann H. 347, Ann H. (2d) 347, Ellen Y. 347, Elnathan
347, Emily C. 347, Maria E. B. 347, Roger W. 347, Sarah B. 347.

K

KEEN Lydia 550, Margaret 561, Wm. 549.
KEITH Betsey M. 1733.
KEMPTON Abigail W. 1596, Elizabeth 1594, Ephraim 1654, John
1595, John and Elizabeth, 6 children of, 1594, Mary 923, Obed
2090, Obed W. 2090, Oliver 939, Sally 939, 940, Sarah 1597, Zach.
and Sarah, 4 children of, 1598.
KENDALL Elizabeth 319, James 318, Sarah 319.
KENDRICK Albert B. 985, Asa N. 2129, Charlotte F. 963, Deb-
orah 987, Elizabeth F. 963, Hattie B. 986, James 986, Mary B.
963, Mary E. 989, Reuben R. 963, Sally K. and infant 988.
KENNEDY Mary J. 156b.
KEYES Lydia (two) 1149.
KIKERT A. M. E. 127.
KING (anonymous) 1962, Isaac B. 2155, John 1961, John jr. 1960,
Nath'l 2052, Polly 1961.

L

LANMAN Jane 2109, John E. (two) 1141, Mary 990, Peter 991,
Sam'l 992, Sarah 827.
LAPHAM Elisha 1751, Eliza A. (two) 1751.
LEACH Abigail 1124, David 1036, Ebenezer 1124, Finney 1031,
Finney and Mercy, 4 children of, 1032, Marcia 1037, Robert
B. 1032.

LeBARON Bartlett 143, Francis 147, Isaac 144, 148, Isaac and Mary D., 4 children of, 148, Joseph 145, Lazarus 155, Lidia 154, Lydia 142, 153, Margaret 152, Mary D. 148, Sarah 149, Wm. 150, 151.

LeBARRAN Francis 146.

LEMOTE Abigail 1637, Math. 1636, Mathew 1491, 1638, 1639, Marcy 1636, Mercy 1492.

LEONARD Abigail 1016, Anna 1495, Daniel 1493, Eph'm B. 1017, Mary 1494, Rebekah 1018, Sally 1727, Susanna 1017, Thomas 1727.

LEWIS Hannah 1449, Philip 300, Thomas 300, William 739.

LINCOLN Lorrain H. 335.

LITTLE Eph'm 636, Sarah 278, Thos. 277.

LOBDELL Hannah 82.

LOTHROP Bathsheba 290, David 290, Ellen 1498, Experience 652, Freeman 1501, Hannah 1500, Isaac 1484, 2152, Lucy 1499, Melatiah 1496, Nath'l 1497, Polly 291.

LOTHROPS Thos. 1483.

LOVELL Leander 1332, Mercy B. 1331.

LUCAS Catherine H. and 3 ch'n 781, Deborah 659, Hannah 784, Hannah C. 625, Isaac J. 780, Isaac J. jr. 778, Levi 783, Mary A. 779.

LUCE Crosbe 953, Crosby 954, Betsey 954, Seth 957, 2081.

LUMBER Elizabeth 1063, Leuis 1063.

LYNCH Mehitable P. 839.

M

MAGEE Monument 244.

MANTER Lucy B. 1290, Wm. and Lucy B., 4 children of, 1291.

MARCY Abbigail 517, Charlott 516, Joseph 515, 571, Lucy 569, 573, Mary 572, Stephen 570, Thos. J. 572.

MARSH Lillis G. 224, Marcy 223, Thos. 223, Warren 223.

MARSHAL Bartlett 1408, Hannah 1408, Ruth 1407, Sam'l 1408.

MARSON Samuel 1154.

MATHEWS Desire 1078, Thos. 1078.

MAY Bathsheba 282, 287, Iohn 286, John 283, 288, Sarah 285, Thos. 289, Wm. 284.

McCARTER Henry 1081, Nancy 1081.

McGLATHLIN Lovica T. 1600, Robert 193, Seth 1132.

MENDIL Moriah 1627.

MILLER Henryetta 1591.

MITCHELL Joseph 2105, Mary 2105.

MOORE Rebecca W. 76.

MOREY Cornelius 2022, Mary E. 2022, Mary E. and Wm. T. 1986, Wm. 943.

MORSE Nancy E. 1812.

MORTON Abigail 1854, Barnabas 1852, 1855, Benjamin 1777, Betsey 1465, Catharine B. 1041, Dorcas (two) 1745, Edward 1981, Eleanor 1984, Eleazer and Jemima and 8 children 1693, Elisha 1621, Elizabeth 1462, 1652, Elizebeth 1610, Eph'm 1618, George 1402, 1526, 1615, Hannah 1856, Henry 1678, Jacob T. 1694, James 1518,

1677, James and 5 children 1406, Jemima 1693, Joanna 1626, John 1463, 1619, John B. 1522, John L. 1522, Joseph 1617, Joseph 99, 1777, Josiah 1609, Lemuel 905, Lilly R. 1523, Lucia W. 1043, Lydia 1684, Marcy 100, Mary 906, 1461, 1519, 1525, Mary B-C. 1119, Mary Edwards 1977, Mary Ellen 1978, Mercy 1676, 1679, Nathanael 1651, Nathaniel 1544, 1624, Osborn 1989, Perez 98, Polly 1527, Rebecca 1623, Rebekah 1404, 1482, Reliance 1620, Sally 1522, Sarah 907, 908, 1545, 1980, 1981, Seth 1042, 1676, 1680, Silas 1460, Susan B. 2156, Thomas 1616, Thos. and Thos. 1546, Wm. 1678, William H. 2157, Zepheniah 1650.

MURDOCH Thomas 622.

MURDOCK John 623.

N

NELSON A. and M. 690, Bathsheba 701, Charles 714, 2127, Charles and Lucy, daughter of. 714, Ebenezer 694, 696, 699, 705, Elisha 697, George 710, Hannah 698, Lemuel 691, Lewis 699, Lucy 712, Lydia 693, 705, Martha T. 713, Ruth 692, 695, 911, Sarah W. 334, Thomas 690, William 700.

NICHOLS Rizpah 1991, Susanna 1990.

NICKERSON Ambrose E. 964, Betsey 965, Charles H, 965, Joan B. 968, John and Lydia, 4 children of, 1861, John jr. 1862, Maria A. 966, Maria H. 966, Mary B. 966, Sophronia A. 24, Warren M. 966, William 969, William T. 967.

NICOLSON Daniel 313, Elizabeth 308, Hannah 307, 314, James 309, Lucy M. 311, Samuel 310, Sarah 310, 312, Thomas 314.

NOONNEN John 624.

NYE Ann H. 422, Betsey 422, Wm. C. 422.

O

OSGOOD John 157.

OSMENT Mary 1371.

OTIS Abigail 1579, Barnabas jr. 243, Hannah 1569, John 1565, Henry 1903, Polly 240.

P

PAINE Stephen 271, John S. and dau. 1746, Deborah and infant 1747, Hannah 271, Susan W. 1748.

PALMER Nancy K. 1232.

PATY Betsey 1967, Cordelia 1969, Deborah 1915, Elvira 1969, Ephraim jr. 20, Eph'm jr. and Sarah C., 4 children of, 20, Ephraim 1966, George W. 1966, 1969, Hannah C. 2055, Jean 2054, Jerusha 1936, John 1916, Martha 1968, Meriah 1917, Seth 1969, Silvia 1917, Thomas 1935, 1937, (tomb) 1976.

PAULDING Catherine 1730, Father and 5 children 1349, James P. 2048, Nancy D. 2053.

PEARSON Abia 1699, Stephen 1701, William 1700.

PEIRCE America 10, Margaret D. 10.

PECKHAM Sarah 1736.

PERKINS Elizabeth J. 1410, George 1205, Hannah 1204, Joann
1309, Joshua and Betsey (Hobart), 3 children of, 1543, Pella
1204, Pella M. 1410, Priscilla 1410, William 1204.

PERRY Caroline A. 3, 132, John 1133, 1138, John M. 930, Lewis
1136, (two) 1138, Lewis F. 1720, Lewis W. 1720, Mary B. 1134,
Rhoda 1133, Ruth 1137, Sarah 1135.

PHILLIPS Elizabeth 1370.

PIERCE Ann E. 944, Betsey 2036, Dorcas 2158, Eliza C. 2124,
Ignatius 2036, Lucretia 2093, Lucy 2037, Mary and infant 1828,
Mary Ann 944, Phineas 1622, 2158, Rebecca J. 1622, 2158, Su-
sanna W. 2038, William N. (1st & 2d) 2039.

PLASKET Joseph 681, Tabitha 682a.

POPE Mary 2080, Thomas 2057, 2058, 2079.

PRATT Elener B. 1732, Joshua 1732, Mary A. and 3 children
1731.

PULSIFER (anonymous) 421, Bethiah 420, Joseph 419.

PURINGTON Jerome W. and Mary E. 1752.

R

RANDALL Elizabeth 450, Enoch 830 b.

RAYMOND Betsey 815, Charles 1092, Eunice 1787, George 1088,
1143, George LeB. 1142, Harvey H. 1010, Lydia 1144, Priscilla
1089, Samuel 1737, Samuel B. 51, William T. 1009.

REED Hezekiah B. 44, Lemuel 738, Lydia 1914, Nathan 1563, Rebecca 1564.

REIDLE Catherine 1550, Mary 1551.

REMOND Ellen M. 50.

RICHMOND Abbigal 2028, Alpheus and Alpheus jr. 2028, Ellen
1151, Mary B. 609, Saloma 2020, Solomon 607, Solomon H. 608,
William 2019, 2020, Wm. H. 1150, 1151.

RICKARD Anselm 979, 980, Bathsheba 1372, Cynthia 980, Elijah
926, Freeman W. 927, Georgie 929, Giles 1857, Henry 423, Lothrop 1027, Lucy 926, Margaret 979, Mary 1022, William and infant son 1002, Zilpah 424.

RIDER Abigail 617, 1004, Abner 1808, Anna 885, A., 2 sons of, 981,
Benjamin 615, Hannah 1743, John 997, Joseph 613, 618, 619,
Joseph jr. 815, Lydia, 995, Mary 998, Patience 613, Seth 1743,
Southworth 794, Tilden 620, William 616, 996.

RING Eleazar 408, William 407, 409.

RIPLEY Anna 717, Elizabeth 716, 723, Leavitt 721, Levi 1599, Nancy 718, Nancy W. 715, Nathaniel 722, Nehemiah 725, Polly 719,
1599, William P. 720.

ROBBINS Adoniram 343, Albert R. 350, Amasa 43, Ann C., Ann
G., Ann G. C. 1754, Betsy 1744, Chandler 315, 1588, Charles 1285,
Ebenezer 948, Eben'r and Eunice, 4 children of, 948, Edward
343, Eunice 948, Experience 1754, Frank C. 41, Frankie L. 40,
George F. and infant dau. 1140, Hannah 317, Jane 316, 392,
Jesse 1744, Josiah 1754, Josiah A. 1754, Josiah A., children of,
2142, Lemuel 1587, Lemuel F. 1278, Lemuel S. 1556, Lewis F.
343, Lucia 1288, Lucia R. 1286, Lucia W. 1287, Margaret 1586,
Margaret H. 1958, Mary 1285, 1587, (obelisk) 1281, Pamelia 343,
Pella M. (two) 1754, Rebecca J. (two) 1754, Rufus 1586, Sally
1178, Sally C. 399, 1744, Samuel 397, Sarah 398, Sarah B. 1279,
1280, Sarah T. 1908, Thomas S. 42.

ROBERTS Robert 1075, Sarah and dau. 1075, Silvanus H. 1076.

ROBERTSON Mary 1749.

ROGERS Abigail 1766, Elizabeth 1920, Ellis 274, Emma F. 273, Ichabod 1919, Irene H. 275, Jane 1789, Jane F. 1789, John 1919, 1923, Lydia H. 1926, Lucretia 1268, Melinda 276, Nancy B. 1922, Polly 1924, Rebecca 1918, Silvanus 1789, William 1921, William H. 1925, William jr. 1919.

ROLFE Horace H. 513, Mary A. 513, Mary T. 514.

RUSSELL Abigail 1423, Betsey 1760, Betsey F. 1757, Bridgham 1758, Elizabeth B. 1756, James 1436, 1437, John and Mary and 2 children 1357, Mary W. 2140, Russell Mercy 1761, Rebecca 1759, 1762, Thomas 1358, 1437, Sarah F. 1755, William S. 1236.

RYAN Lizzie 134.

RYDER Lucy D. 819, Merrick 818, Samuel 1006.

S

SAMPSON Albert L. 334, Alice B. 1104, Benjamin 269, Caroline 1165, Elizabeth 1783, George 611, George S. 231, Isaac and Isaac jr. 1784, Mary A. 230, 1105, Patience 611, Phylander 334, Ruth 1163, Samuel 1103, Sarah E. 334, Solomon 1139, Zabdiel 1164, Zabdiel and Ruth, 2 children of, 1162.

SAMSON Benjamin 270, Hannah 272, Sarah 1471, Simeon and Deborah, 5 children of, 1115, George 612, Isaac 1120, Jemima 405, Simeon 1114.

SAUNDERS Thomas S. 1398.

SAVERY Elizabeth 1155.

SAWYER Joshua 1092.

SEARS Bartlett 1673, Bathsheba 1672, Belinda T. 743, Daniel H. 742, Eunice B. 1877, Harriet N. 1875, Hiram R. 1876, James and Almira, 5 children of, 1863, Mary A. 1876, Rebecah 1878, Willard 1867, William 1879.

SEARSON Sarah 226.

SEYMOUR Horace 1738, Naomi 1738.

SHADE Caroline 1296, Maryetter 1295.

SHAW Betsy and infant dau. 1112, Elizabeth 1107, Esther 1110, Helen M. 502, Ichabod 726, 1107, 1111, James R. 2150, Julia S. 503, Marcia 1109, Mary 1107, Priscilla 726, Rebecca B. 1107, Southworth, 727, 1108, William H. 112.

SHERMAN Cynthia T. 2113, Samuel 1409, Sarah 402, William and Elizabeth 1782.

SHURTLEF William 1297.

SHURTLEFF Jabez 1299, Lydia 1298, Thankful 1276.

SHURTLIFF Mary 1274, female relative of James [broken gravestone] 1275.

SIMMONS Abigail 2026, Augustus F. 2007, Beulah 2012, George 2004, Gershom 52, Iraetta 52, Joann W. 2006, Lemuel 2014, 2026, Lorenzo 2005, Lydia W. 52, Mercy 2004, Moses 2007, Priscilla and infant 2015.

SMITH Henry 2068, Mehitable P. 839.

SNOW George F. 17, Leonard 18, Maria 18.

SOMES Lucia 1436.

SOUTHWORTH Edward 1273, Ruth D. 1273.

SPEAR Ida L. 12.

SPINKS Sarah 2013.

SPOONER Allen C. 13, Ebenezer 442, Ephraim and Elizabeth, 4 children of, 604, Lucy W. 14, Nath'l 14, Sarah 440, Susan L. 13, Thomas 250, 441, (tomb) 2095.

STANDISH Lydia A. 1079, 1080.

STEPHENS Augusta F. 1046, Edward 1662, 1664, Eleazer 1630, Elisabeth 1629, Emma E. 1045, Hannah 1633, Mary D. 1044. Mrs. — 1663, Nancy 1642, Sarah 1631, Susanna 1632, (tomb) 1764, William 1046, 1641.

STETSON Bradford 1438, John 406, Mary 55.

STEWARD Bethiah 2077, George 11, H. O. and B., 3 children of, 2078.

STRAFFIN George and Geo. jr. 2027, Mary S. 2027, Robert 2027.

STURTEVANT Hannah 404, Jane 82, Joseph 1848, Joseph and 3 children 1850, Lucy 79, 1846, Mercy and Mercy A. 1849, Sarah 77, 81, Thankful 1847, William 80, William W. 78.

SULLIVAN James 184.

SWAN Chas. T. 1231.

SWIFT Annabella 122, Jabez 126, Jacob 121, Lucy B. 126, William 113.

SWINBURN Elon S. 410, Keziah D. 225.

SYLVESTER Abigail 1189, Elsey 1260.

SYMMES Elizabeth 961, Hannah 576, 577, 583, Isaac 578, 580, Joanna 579, 581, Lazarus 962, Mary 962, Mary H. 1262, Nancy 582, Nath'l 1260, William A. 1261.

T

TALBOT George W. 1898, Jerusha (two) 1895, Jerusha T. 1894, Robert D. 1897, Samuel 1896.

TAYLOR Edward 1356, Jacob 1023, 1024, James 141, Jemima 1023, William 1216.

THACHER Catharine 1534, Eliza and Elizabeth 1531, James 1533, 1535, Mary 1530, Sukey 1535.

THOMAS Deborah and child 1858, Hope 436, Jane 210, John 437, Joseph 206, Luce 429, Mary 203, 205, 431, Mercy 202, 204, Nancy 210, Nath'l 211, 429, 438, 2148, Nathll and Nathll 435, Priscilla 212, (tomb) 2095, William 202, 432.

THOMPSON Elizabeth 439, Louisa 2121.

THOMSON Geo. D. 322, Irene 321.

TILLSON Anna H. 2016, Edmund 1468, Elizabeth 452, 454, 1468, Hamblin 370, Maria 371, Perez 455, Susan B. 369.

TINKHAM Rebecca 1528.

TOLMAN Isaac 427.

TORREY Betsey 254, (infant) 256, John 258, 259, Joseph 137, Joshua 252, Mary 255, 260, Meriah 257, Sally 1891.

(TOWN) tomb 1764.

TRASK Jerusha 1592, Joseph 1593, Thomas 1593, William 1593.

TRIBBEL Bathsheba 1053, John and Bathsheba, 5 children of, 1053, Joseph 1951, Mary 1179, Sarah 1950, Thomas 1179.

TRIBBLE Augustus 1716, Betsey 1203, Francis 1203, Gideon H. 1715, Hiram 867, Isaac 1714, 1718, Joseph jr. 1193, 1195, Lois 1714, Maria P. 869, Maria T. 868, Mary 1193, Robert F. 1193, Sarah 1195, Thomas 867, 2113, William 1193, 1202, William T. 867, Winslow M. and 3 children 1054.

TRIBELL Sarah 1194.

TUFTS Charles 328, Charles II. 329, Cordelia B. 329, Elizabeth 306, Emma C. 331, James W. 330, Jonathan 305, Mary J. 330, Priscilla 303, 304, Sarah 301, Sarah E. 332, William D. 302.

TURNER David 792, 1238, 1239, 1241, 1245, Eleazar S. 1209, Elizabeth 1210, Elizabeth H. 994, Jesse 994, Jesse H. 993, Lothrop 1212, Lydia P. 1243, Martha L. 791, Meroa 1242, Patience 1233, Patience C. 1208, 1234, Rebecca 1240, Ruth 1241, Susannah 1211.

Y

VIRGIN Abigail 1174, John 1173, 1175, William II. (1st and 2d) 1177.

W

WADSWORTH Charles 1293, George E. 1292, Sarah E. 1294.

WAIT Mary 156a.

WAITE Mart * * 1322.

WARD John 1007.

WARLAND Sarah 1066.

WARREN —— 2042, Benjamin 84, David 75, Elizabeth 2043, Esther 85, George 459, George W. 46, Georgiana M. 344, James 2040, 2041, 2046, Jane 88, Lois 89, Mercy 2040, 2044, Patience 74, 87, Penelope 2045, Sally 46, Sally C. 47, (tomb) 2095.

WASHBURN Bathsheba 213, Hannah J. 782, Lydia 214, Margaret J. 552, Olive and infant 108, Priscilla (two) 460.

WATERMAN Bethiah 70, Hannah 65, John and Hannah, 8 children of, 65.

WATSON Abigail 1504, Benjamin 1190, Benjamin M. 1165, B. M. and L. B., 3 children of, 1266, Charles L. 1214, Edward W. 1218, Eliza A. 1219, Elizabeth 1191, 1506, 1507, 1509, Elkanah 1214, Eunice 1219, George 1503, 1505, 1512, Daniel 1510, Harriet L. 299, John 1220, 1481, 1508, Jonathan S. 1267, Lucia 1215, 1220, Lucretia B. 1264, Patience 1213, Phebe 1513, William 1192, William jr. 1190, Winslow 299.

WEBSTER Erwin 30, Harriet 2147, Manly M. 32, Olin E. 31.

WESGATE Lydia A. 626.

WEST Samuel 1305.

WESTON Ann M. 496, Betsey 959, Clara 489, Coomer 494, 641, Elijah J. 1604, Elizabeth 542, George 2, George and Mary, 3 children of 2, Hannah 495, 543, Harvey 1992, Hattie 489, Jane L. 1015, Johnny C. 1604, Lewis 549, 959, Lewis and Betsey, 4 children of, 959, Lewis and Eliz'h, 2 children of, 960, Lucy 546, 1, 544, 1998, Mary 2, 638, 640, Mary T. 541, Nancy C. 540, Patty 642, Priscilla 1176, Prudence 643, Sally C. 1992, Sarah E. 1992, Sarah N. 542, Susan 958, Susan S. 490b, Thomas 642, William 1, 490a, 638, 639, William L. 438.

WESTRON Mary 644.

WETHRELL Anna 814, Anna M. 856b, Elizabeth 809, Harriot 808, Isaac 807, 812, John M. 856c, Joshua 863, Lucia 811, Nancy 866, Rebecah 857, Sarah 811, Thomas 810, 858, 859, William 807.

WHITE Cornelius 1157, Elizabeth 1159, 1480, Experience 1160, Gideon 1157, Hannah 1158, Joanna 1156, Thomas 1161.

WHITING Asa A. 501, Elizabeth 1033, Ephraim 1033, Joseph B. 799, Levi 1963, Mary 1964, Mary M. 2148, Sophia B. 1776.

WHITMARSH Sarah 365.

WHITTEN Albertina L. 931, Edward W. 878, Elisha C. 879, Emeline A. 932, Harriet B. 1635, Joseph W. 878, Lewis H. 933, Lydia M. 678, Mary H. 678, 679, Samuel 1635, Willie B. 678.

WILLIAMS Eliza 2030, Eliza A. 2029, 2032, John (two) 2029, John B. 2031, Mary 242, Nancy 186.

WITHERELL Hannah 1525.

WITHERLY Hannah 862, Lemuel 861.

WITTE Hans 185.

WOOD Betsey 735, Betsey S. 737, Eleanor 736, Eliab 733, Huldy 946, Nath'l 947, Perses 734.

WRIGHT Elisabeth A. 1095, Sally 500.

Z

ZAHN Luise 1418.

THE OLD FORT ON BURIAL HILL. (1621).

BURIAL HILL:
ITS INSCRIPTIONS AND EPITAPHS.

PLYMOUTH, MASSACHUSETTS.

Copied by BENJAMIN DREW.

" A bit of paper, even a rag like this,
Survives himself, his tomb, and all that's his."—BYRON.

Every stone that we look upon, in this repository of past ages, is both an entertainment and a monitor.—Plain Dealer, Vol. 1, No. 42.

No. 1.
[Blue slate, 3 1-2 ft. high,—good condition.]

To the memory of Lucy Weston Consort of Capt. Harvey Weston who died July the 19, 1818 aged 22 years 11 months & 5 days

> It is finished, yes
> The race is run
> The battle is fought
> The victory is won.

Also to the memory of William their Son who died Novr 26, 1817, aged three months & 12 days

> So fades the lovely Blooming Flower
> Frail Smiling Solace of an hour
> So soon our transient Comforts fly
> And pleasure only Blooms to Dye.

No. 2.
[White marble, about 4 feet high. Good condition.]

In memory of CAPT. GEORGE WESTON who died Nov. 28, 1844, aged 54 years. MARY his wife died Oct. 23. 1863, aged 72 years 3 mo's. Also LYDIA M. died Oct. 2. 1831: aged 17 years. JAMES H. died Feb. 2. 1830: aged 1 year & 3 mos. GEORGE died Feb. 3. 1823: aged 5 days. Children of Geo. & Mary Weston.

No. 3.
[White marble, curtain drapery at top. Fair condition.]

CAROLINE A. WIFE OF NELSON P. PERRY, & DAUGHTER OF JUDSON & ALMIRA RICE, BORN MAR. 5, 1831, DIED SEPT. 5, 1853. *A beloved wife, an affectionate daughter, and a true friend; may she find rest in heaven.*

I

No. 4.

[Small, white marble, in good condition.]

Almira Judson, daughter of Judson & Almira Rice died April 27, 1840 aged 5 y'rs 4 mo.

She was too promising a flower
To bloom upon this earth.

No. 5.

[Blue slate. Good condition. Weeping willow and urn.]

In memory of ELIZABETH C. dau. of Silvanus and Elizabeth H. Churchill, who died Aug. 27, 1850, Æ 11 y'rs 1 mo.

Also, 4 infant sons William C. 1822. William C. 1829. Twins 1833.

No. 6.

[A purple, close-grained slate; good condition.]

In memory of Elizabeth H. Churchill Died June 22, 1876. Æ. 77 y'rs 9 mo's.

He raiseth up the soul and lighteneth the eyes;
He giveth health, life, and blessing.

No. 7.

[Similar to No. 6.]

In memory of Silvanus Churchill Died March 2, 1878, Æ. 81 y'rs 8 mo's.

I will bind up that which was broken, and strengthen that which was weak.

No. 8.

[White marble, on granite base; good condition.]

In memory of Curtis Hoyt, Died Aug. 3, 1860. Aged 42 y'rs.

I am the resurrection and the life.

No. 9.

[White marble; figure of a broken flower-stalk. Somewhat dis colored; but otherwise in good condition.]

Curtis F. son of Curtis & Harriet Hoyt, who died July 1, 1852, Æ. 2 y'rs 8 mo.

Because thy smile was fair
Thy lips and eyes so bright!
Because thy cradle care
Was such a fond delight;
Shall love with weak embrace
Thy heavenward flight detain?
Not angel seek thy place
Amid yon cherub train.

No. 10.

[Originally white marble; now gray, discolored. Inclined backward.]

AMERICA PEIRCE Died May 8, 1845; aged 75 years.

MARGARET DREW his wife died Sept. 13, 1806; aged 35 years.

No. 11.
[Wood; letters fading out.]
GEORGE STEWARD DIED FEB. 13, 1861 AGED 28 YEARS.

No. 12.
[White marble; stem and leaves. This stone was first set in a block of freestone, which broke; the stone is now set in the ground.]
Ida Lizzie dau. of Thomas & Elizabeth R. SPEAR died Jan. 23, 1860.

No. 13.
[Very conspicuous, white marble, about 6 feet in height. Is somewhat injured at the base in consequence, it is said, of having been thrown down in a gale, some years ago.]
Allen C. Spooner, Born March 9, 1814, died June 28, 1853.
Susan L. Spooner Feb. 25, 1814, May 5, 1880.

No. 14.
[White marble set in freestone; somewhat inclined, otherwise in good condition.]
NATHANIEL SPOONER died at sea, March 9, 1817: aged 31 years.
LUCY W. SPOONER, his wife, whose remains lie beneath, died in Plymouth, April 29, 1860; aged 77 years.

No. 15.
[White marble: about 3 ft. high; is in good condition.]
Our Mother,—Gone Home. PHILA H. Wife of Dr. Isaac Hatch, Died May 14, 1865; aged 56 years, 9 mo.

No. 16.
[White marble; about 3 feet high; is discolored and somewhat moss-grown.]
CHARLES BROWN, died Sept. 20, 1846, in the 25th year of his age, Also, CHARLES, Son of Charles & Charlotte Ann Brown, died Jan. 29th, 1853, aged 5 y'rs & 11 Mo.
Why am I left alone?

No. 17.
[White marble, in good condition.]
GEORGE F. SNOW DIED July 22, 1867, Aged 31 y'rs 3 mo's.
Therefore be ye also ready; for in such an hour as ye think not the son of man cometh.

No. 18.
[White marble, in good condition.]
Father & Mother LEONARD SNOW Died March 7, 1874, Aged 76 y'rs 5 mo's.

MARIA, his wife Died Sept. 30, 1870.   Aged 72 y'rs 11 mo's.
"When Christ who is our life shall appear, then shall we also appear with him in glory."

No. 19.
[White marble, in good condition.]

Father & Mother.   JACOB HOWLAND Died June 3, 1876, Aged 82 y'rs 4 mos.
SALLY, His wife Died Jan. 20, 1884, Aged 88 yrs 4 mos.

No. 20.
[White marble, in good condition.]

Capt. EPHRAIM PATY, Jr. Died in California, July 24, 1849.   Aged 43 y'rs.   WILLIE A. Died Feb. 30, 1847 Aged 13 mo's 12 d's.   SARAH C.   Died Aug. 19, 1850. Aged 14 y'rs 9 mo's.   WILLIE A.   Died Sept. 5, 1850.   Aged 13 mo's. 23 d's.   LIZZIE E. Died July 11, 1860.   Aged 19 y'rs 7 mo's.   Children of Capt. Ephraim. Jr. & Sarah C. Paty.

NOTE.—The date "Feb. 30" in the above, is given as cut on the marble.

No. 21.
[White marble, in good condition.]

JOHN K. ALEXANDER CO. E. 29 Mass. Vols. Died at Fredericksburg Va. May 12, 1864, Aged 28 y'rs.
And underneath the evergreen,
Away from grief and care,
Alone beneath its leafy screen,
They laid a loved one there.

No. 22.
[White marble, in good condition.]

CHARLOTTE S. Wife of SAM'L L. ALEXANDER DIED April 9, 1887, Aged 83 years.
At Rest.

No. 23.
[White marble, in good condition.]

SAMUEL L. ALEXANDER Died Sept 21, 1869, Aged 63 y'rs.

No. 24.
[White marble, in good condition.]

SOPHRONIA ALEXANDER Nickerson, Died Sept. 4, 1869, Aged 50 y'rs 4 m's, 12 days.
"Meet me in Heaven."

No. 25.
[White marble, in good condition.]

SAMUEL ALEXANDER Died March 30, 1871, Aged 91 y'rs, 2 m's, 23 days.
"Blessed are the dead who die in the Lord."

No. 26.

[White marble, in good condition.]

In Memory of DEBORAH, wife of Samuel Alexander, died Dec. 20, 1853. Aged 68 y'rs 8 months.
"There is rest in Heaven."

No. 27.

[Dark blue slate; weeping willow and urn. Good condition.]

In memory of Four Children of Mr. Samuel Alexander and Mrs. Deborah, his wife, viz Silvanus P. Alexander died August 14, 1816; aged one year and 7 months. Sophronia Alexander died June the 3, 1818; aged one year and 3 months. George Alexander died Sep 14, 1824; aged 9 months. Charles Alexander died Aug 19, 1826; aged Eight months and 21 days.

No. 28.

[Dark slate; weeping willow and urn. Good condition.]

Erected to the memory of MISS FANNY ALEXANDER Daughter of Samuel and Deborah Alexander who Departed this life January 25, 1829; aged 16 years and 4 months.

Not beauty worth nor friends fond love could save
The lovely victim from the cruel grave.
Like a fair flower that faids in earliest bloom
In life's bright morn she meet her early tomb.

Oh! fare thee well, dearest—thy spirit though gone
Shall live in this desolate bosom alone
Till it burst in the splendor of weakness forgiven
And gloryous shine in the lustre of heaven.

No. 29.

[Dark slate; weeping willow and urn. Good condition.]

In memory of JOHN ALEXANDER. who died Dec. 5, 1842, Æt. 32 y'rs 27 ds. Also his daug. Georgeianna, Æt. 14 mo.

No. 30.

[White marble set in granite base, with brimstone; is 4 feet in height; in good condition.]

ERVIN WEBSTER M. D. Passed onward Aug. 28, 1856, aged 28 years, 2 months & 28 days.

No. 31.

[Small, beautiful white marble; set in granite with brimstone; is in good condition.]

OLIN E. Son of Dr. Ervin & Harriet W. Webster; passed onward Aug. 28, 1856, aged 4 years 1 mo. & 20 days.

No. 32.

[Small, beautiful white marble; set in granite with brimstone; is in good condition.]

MANLY M. Son of Dr. E. & Harriet W. Webster died May 28th 1855, Æ. 3 Mon. & 22 d's.

No. 33.

[Blue slate, lying on its side edge, against a tree.]

LUCY ANN'died Jan.y 17, 1839, aged 1 year. Daughter of Rufus and Lucy W. Churchill.

With equal voice, in unknown worlds
Old men and babes appear.

No. 34.

[A wooden cross; inscription in capitals.]

John H. Hamrosa Died Dec. 30th, 1864 Aged 1 month.

No. 35.

[A wooden cross; inscription in capitals.]

John B. Barlow Died Jan' 8th 1864 Aged 2 yrs' & 3 months.

No. 36.

[A wooden cross; inscription in capitals.]

James T. Devine Died May 3, 1864 Aged 2 yrs. 5 mos. 24 days.

No. 37.

[A wooden cross; inscription in capitals.]

Peter J. Devine Died Feb. 13th 1867. Aged 9 mos. 5 days.

No. 38.

[White marble; in good condition.]

HANNAH BARNES.

No. 39.

[White marble; in good condition.]

CYNTHIA B. BARNES.

No. 40.

[White marble; in good condition.]

Frankie L. Son of T. S. & E. T. Robbins, Born Feb. 15, 1846, Died Dec. 20, 1847.

"Weep not for those
Who sink within the arms of death
'Ere yet the chilling wintry breath
Of sorrow o'er them blows."

No. 41.

[White marble; in good condition.]

Frank C. Son of T. S. & E. T. Robbins. Passed away

June 14, 1866. Aged 17 y'rs 11 mo's.

Loving and loved—his life is ours,
Was like the sunshine from above
His sudden call from unseen powers,
Makes him immortal in our love.

No. 42.
[White marble; in good condition.]

THOMAS S. ROBBINS Died May 16, 1861, Aged 43 y'rs 4 mo's 16 days.

He suffered many weary years,
"To him the grave no victory had,
and death no sting."

No. 43.
[White marble; in good condition.]

In memory of AMASA ROBBINS, who died Jan. 28, 1856, aged 33 yrs. 10 mons.

"The casket lies
beneath the sod, but Heaven claims the gem.

No. 44.
[White marble; set in freestone, with brimstone; inclined.]

HEZEKIAH B. REED, Died Feb. 15, 1839. Æ. 42 y'rs 8 mo. Also his infant daughter EUNICE.

"Our life is ever on the wing"
And death is ever nigh."

No. 45.
[White marble; set in freestone. Good condition.]

In Memory of MARY A. B. wife of Ira Allen, & dau. of David & Sally C. Warren, died Dec. 31, 1859, aged 29 y'rs 1 mo. 16 ds.

No. 46.
[White marble; left its feeble socket, and is now firmly set in the ground.]

GEORGE W. Died May 2, 1826, Aged 4 days. SALLY Died Nov. 6, 1837. Aged 1 year 8 mo. & 19 days. Children of David and Sally C. Warren.

No. 47.
[White marble, in granite; the whole mass inclined.]

SALLY C. Wife of David Warren, Died Feb. 15, 1877, Aged 75 y'rs 9 mo's, 6 days.

No. 48.
[At top, broken chain with legend "Parted below; united above."
White marble, set in granite. Good condition.]

Priscilla Whiting, the affectionate wife of Edward Hathaway, Born in Bucksport, Me. October 22, 1818, Died June 29, 1842 ; Æ. 23 yrs & 9 mos.

Farewell dear wife, untill that day more blest,
When if deserving, I with thee shall rest;
With thee shall rise, with thee shall live above,
In worlds of endless bliss and boundless love.

No. 49.

[White marble; good condition.]
"Oh for a touch of a vanished hand
And the sound of a voice that is still."

LUCY N. [MORTON] the beloved wife of Edward
Hathaway Born in Carver, Aug. 15, 1821, Died Aug. 11,
1883, Æ. 62 yrs 11 mos 47 days.

"Turn those dear eyes,
Once so benignant to me, upon mine,
That open to their tears such uncontrolled
And such continued issue. Still awhile
Have patience; I will come to thee at last.

A few more prayers, a few more tears,
And the long agony of life will end,
And I shall be with thee. If I am wanting
To thy well being, as thou art to mine,
Have patience; I will come to thee at last."

No. 50.

[White marble; in good condition. 50 and 51 are inclosed.]

ELLEN M. daughter of Samuel E. & Caroline Remond
sweetly fell asleep with Jesus, May 25, 1862. Æ. 10 yrs
8 mos & 2 dys.

Thy gentle spirit passed away
'Mid pain the most severe
So great we could not wish thy stay
A moment longer here.

No. 51.

[White marble; good condition.]

SAMUEL B. RAYMOMD Died April 3, 1873.   Aged
43 y'rs 5 mo's. 23 days.

Husband thou art gone to rest,
Thy sins are all forgiven,
And saints in light have welcomed thee,
To joy the shares of heaven.

(So on the stone; my reasons for following inscriptions literally
are given in the preface.)

No. 52.

[White marble; 4 ft. high (only approximate heights are mention-
ed-—the object being to facilitate finding any particular monument);
in good condition, save being slightly inclined.]

In memory LYDIA W. SIMMONS Died Feb. 6, 1864,
Aged 37 y'rs 10 mo's. GERSHOM SIMMONS, Died
May 21, 1869, Aged 54 y'rs. IRAETTA, their dau.
Died Apr. 22, 1862, Aged 1 y'r 7 mo's.

No. 53.

[The noted Cushman gravestone of 1691; one of the Six bearing
date in the 17th century. The other Five will be particularized when

their sites are reached. This Ancient Landmark was removed by the descendants of Elder Thomas Cushman, to make room, as they say, "for a more enduring memorial." The original gravestone of "purple Welsh slate" is as fresh in appearance as if it had just left the hand of the engraver. The new monument is more showy, but whether it will be "more enduring" than the humbler Welsh slate is a question of time,—a question which the descendants of Elder Cushman, some thousand or more years hence, may be able to solve. The inscription on the purple Welsh slate is as follows,—all in capital letters:]

Here lyeth buried ye body of that precious servant of God Mr. Thomas Cushman, who after he had served his generation according to the will of God, and particularly the church of Plymouth for many years in the office of a ruleing elder fell asleep in Jesus Decemr. ye 10, 1691 & in ye 84. year of his age.

This stone placed at the grave of Elder Cushman by the First Church in Plymouth, was removed to this situation in 1858, to make room for a more endureing memorial which now exactly occupies its original position.

No. 54.

[The Cushman Monument. This is a granite column, 25 feet in height. There is a bronze tablet inscribed with capital letters, on each of the four sides of a square member supporting the obelisk. The tablet on the northerly side is as follows:]

ROBERT CUSHMAN❧

Fellow-exile with the Pilgrims in Holland,
Afterwards their chief agent in England.
Arrived here -IX- November, -MDCXXI,
With Thomas Cushman his son:
Preached -IX- December,
His memorable sermon on "The Danger of self-love
And the sweetness of true friendship:"
Returned to England -XIII- December,
To vindicate the enterprise of Christian emigration;
And there remained in the service of the Colony
Till -MDCXXV,
When, having prepared to make Plymouth
His permanent home,

[Second tablet—West side:]

He died, lamented by the forefathers
as "their ancient friend.—who was
as their right hand with their friends
the adventurers, and for divers years
had done and agitated all their business
with them to their great advantage."

"And you, my loving friends, the adventurers
to this plantation, as your care has been first
to settle religion here before either profit
or popularity, so, I pray you, go on. ——
I rejoice ——that you shall be repaid
with your riches, and I trust you shall be repaid
again double and treble in this world, yea,
and the memory of this action shall never die."
DEDICATION OF THE SERMON,

[Third tablet—South side:

THOMAS CUSHMAN,

Son of Robert, died -X- December, MDCXCI,
Aged nearly -LXXXIV- years.
For more than -XLII- years he was
Ruling Elder
Of the First Church in Plymouth,
By whom a tablet was placed to mark his grave
On this spot,
Now consecrated anew by a more enduring memorial.

MARY,

widow of Elder Cushman and daughter of Isaac Allerton,
Died -XXVIII- November, MDCXCIX, aged about -XC- years,
The last survivor of the first comers in the Mayflower.

[Fourth tablet—East side:]

Erected
by
The descendants of
Robert Cushman
In memory of their Pilgrim Ancestors,
XVI- September, MDCCCLVIII.

No. 55.

[Small blue slate; at top, human head under curtains; the stone has the pyramidal outline, much in vogue here, about the beginning of the present century.]

In memory of Mary Stetson Daughter of Mr. Hervey Stetson & Mrs. Mary his wife who died Aug 10 1805 aged 1 year 1 month

No. 56.

[Blue slate; symbol; somewhat moss-grown, but legible.]

Here lyes ye body of Priscilla Holmes who deceased August ye 8th 1735 in ye 21st year of her age.

No. 57.

[Blue slate; in good condition.]

In memory of Mrs. Ruth Cobb wife of Mr. Job Cobb died July 22 1817 in the 70 year of her age.

No. 58.

[Blue slate; good condition.]

In memory of Mr. Job Cobb died Dec. 13, 1835, in the 91st yr. of his age.

No. 59.

[Blue slate; weeping willow and urn. Good condition.]

In memory of Mrs. Grace Cobb wife of Mr. Cornelius Cobb who Died May 3, 1811 in the 59 year of her age.

No. 60.

[Blue slate; 4 ft. high; willow and urn. Good condition.]

In memory of MR. Cornelius Cobb who died Feb. 4, 1830, aged 82 years and 7 months.

"An honest man the noblest work of God."

No. 61.

[Blue slate; urn. Good condition.]

In memory of Miss Grace Cobb Daughter of Mr. Cornelius Cobb & Mrs. Grace his wife who Died Octr 20th 1804 in the 24th year of her age.

No. 62.

[Blue slate; willow and urn. Good condition.]

To the memory of Isaac Eames Cobb who was born Jany 19, 1789, and died Jany 14, 1821.

Possess'd he talents ten, or five or one
The work he had to do that work was done
Improv'd his mind, in wisdom's ways he trod
Reluctant died, but died resigned to GOD.

No. 63.

[Blue slate; willow and urn. Good condition.]

To the memory of ELIZABETH COBB widow of ISAAC E. COBB who was born July 27, 1797, and died August 28, 1821.

She is not dead, but sleeps to rise
An heir of glory in the skies,
With spirits pure, from flesh set free
T' enjoy a bless'd eternity.

No. 64.

[Small, blue slate; laminæ separating; symbol. Some moss, but inscription can be read without much difficulty.]

Here lies buried Benjamin Son of Mr Cornelius Holms & Mrs Lydia his wife who died Augst ye 7th 1760 aged one year 7 months & 24 days.

No. 65.

[Blue slate; symbol; indications of cleavage of laminæ, parallel to face of stone.]

In memory of Mrs Hannah Waterman ye wife of Mr John Waterman who Died May ye 4th 1767 In ye 54th yr of her Age, & of 6 of their Sons & 2 Daughters by her [*Stone broken off at lower left hand corner.*] all Died in their ...... y their Son Elka died ...... cia August ye 31st 175‖‖ ...... year of his Age.

No. 66.

[Like 65.]

[All capitals.] In memory of Mr Job Cobb who died June ye 8th 1767 in ye 45th year of his age.

No. 67.

[Like 65.]

In Memory of Mrs PATIENCE COBB, widow of JOB COBB who died July 26 179. aged 70 years

No. 68.

[Like 65.]

Here lies Interred the Body of Capt. Samuel Harlow who departed this Life January ye 17th 1767 in ye 41st year of his age.

No. 69.

[Stone somewhat defaced; full of flaws; symbol.]

Here lies buried ...... Mrs. Ruth Doten wife of Mr. James Doten who deed Mar ye 29 1752 in ye 24th year of her age.

No. 70.

[A small stone nearly half covered with earth near N. W. corner of Cushman Monument; cherub mostly scaled off.]

In memory of Mrs. Bethiah Waterman who died Sept ye 19th 1769 Aged 18 years.

No. 71.

[Blue slate; well preserved; cherub. Good condition.]

Here lies buried Mr John Harlow who Deed Janry ye 30th, 1771, Aged 87 years 1 month & 28 days

No. 72.

[White marble; discolored; inclined.]

BENJ. BATES DIED Dec. 24, 1868, Aged 60 y'rs. MARTHA, his wife Died May 29, 1869. Aged 58 y'rs. BENJ. F their son Died June 17, 1867, Aged 30 y'rs 10 mo's, 29 days.

Gone but not forgotten.

No. 73.

[White marble; discolored; more inclined than 72.]

BENJAMIN F. BATES Co. E. 29 Mass. Regt. Died June 17, 1867 Aged 30 y'rs 10 mo's 29 days.

No. 74.

[Light blue slate, in good condition; cherub.]

In Memory of Miss Patience Warren Daughter of Capt Benjamin Warren who died Novr 23, 1780, aged 74 years.

Hark from the tombs a doleful sound,
My ears attend the cry
Ye living men come view the ground
Where you must shortly lie.

No. 75.

[Blue slate; a tomb engraved at top, with flowers in bloom above it. Good condition.]

In memory of David Warren Son of Capt David Warren and Mrs Sally his wife who died Sept 12th 1802 aged 2 years 4 months.

'Tis God who lifts our comforts high
Or sinks them in the grave
He gives and blessed be his name
He takes but what he gave

No. 76.

[White marble, surface roughened and stained; urn; fair condition.]

REBECCA W. MOORE wife of Rev. Josiah Moore, and the last of the daughters of William Sturtevant, Esq. died of consumption, at Duxbury, April 7th, 1838, aged 33 years.

No. 77.

[White marble; rough and discolored.]

In memory of SARAH, daughter of William & Sarah Sturtevant, who died July 1st, 1833 ; aged 33.

No. 78.

[Blue slate; weeping willows and urn. Good condition.]

In memory of William W. son of William & Sarah Sturtevant, who died June 13, 1794 Aged 2 years and 4 mon's.

No. 79.

[Blue slate; inscription within figure of urn. Good condition.]

In memory of Lucy Sturtevant Daughter of Capt. William Sturtevant and Sally his wife who died August 7th 1807 aged 4 years and 11 months.

No. 80.

[Blue slate. Inscription within fig. of urn; moss grown, and slightly inclined.]

To the memory of William Sturtevant Esqr who Departed this life December 15 1819, aged 38 years.

No. 81.

[Inscribed in urn-shaped space. Cracked diagonally, nearly through centre.]

To the memory of Mrs. SARAH STURTEVANT, widow of William Sturtevant, Esq.r departed this life Dec.r 5, 1838, aged 69 years.

No. 82.

[White marble; rough; disintegrating.]

In memory of JANE, daughter of William and Sarah Sturtevant, who died Nov. 8, 1832 ; aged 38. Also of her sister HANNAH, wife of Thomas J. Lobdell, who died and was entombed at Boston, Oct. 3, 1818 ; aged 22.

No. 83.

[Low, blue slate; cherub; good condition.]

To the memory of Josiah Harlow son of Capt. Zephaniah Harlow & Patience his wife who died Novr 10th 1795 in the 16th year of his age.

No. 84.

[Light blue slate; cherub; good condition.]

Here lyes buried the body of Capt Benjamin Warren
Died May ye 30th 1746 in ye 76th year of his age.

No. 85.

[Blue slate; laminæ separating; cherub. Moss grown.]

Here lies Buried Mrs Esther Warren wife of Capt
Benjamin Warren who decd Novr ye 1st 1770 aged 88 years.

No. 86.

[Blue slate; cherub wingless, rudely sculptured. Good condition.]

Here lies buried Mrs Patience Johnson ye wife of Mr.
Josiah Johnson who decd Feby ye 1st 1767 aged 38 years.

No. 87.

[Blue slate; urn and weeping willow; pyramidal outline; mossy,
but sound.]

This Stone is Erected in memory of Mrs Patience Warren Consort of Mr. Benjamin Warren, who died April 15,
1819 in the 69 year of her age.

Blessed are the dead
That die in the LORD.

No. 88.

[Dark blue slate. Urn. Good condition.]

In memory of Mrs. JANE WARREN Consort of Mr.
Benjamin Warren who died Feby 28th 1797 in the 59th
year of her age.

See me behold me moulding into dust
As you see me so certainly you must.

No. 89.

[Blue slate, thick, substantial. Urn. Good condition.]

In memory of Mrs Lois Warren Consort of Majr Benju
Warren Deceasd Novr 19th 1809 In the 57th year of her
Age.

No. 90.

[White marble set in a base or socket of reddish stone, which here
and elsewhere in this work, I shall term freestone. The cement of
No. 90 is crushed, and the stone much inclined backward,—i. e.
liable to fall with the face upward.]

NATHANIEL BARNES died Feb. 20, 1854, aged 60
years. His daughter BETSEY G. ELLIS died Dec. 9,
1848 : aged 27 years. NATHL. BARNES Jr. died Feb.
7, 1854, aged 25 years.

No. 91.

[White marble, in base of same material. Good condition.]

HANNAH, Widow of Nathaniel Barnes, Died Aug.
12, 1878, Aged 83 y'rs 7 mo's, 23 days.

At Rest.

No. 92.
[Low, blue slate. Cherub. Good condition.]

In memory of James Harlow son of Mr. Samuel & Mrs Mercy Harlow Died Decr ye 26 1757.

No. 93.
[Low blue slate. Cherub. Top somewhat marred.]

In memory of Mercy Harlow, Daur of Mr Samuel & Mrs Mercy Harlow, who died Sept 29 1750 Aged 13 Months & 11 days

No. 94.
[Blue slate. Crossbones above a winged skull. Good condition.]

In memory of Mrs MERCY HARLOW the wife of Mr Samuel Harlow who departed this Life July the 4th 1762 in the 34 year of her Age.

No. 95.
[Blue slate; over 4 ft. in height. Weeping willow and urn. Inscription in urn-shaped space. Good condition.]

In memory of Capt. Samuel Harlow who died at Charlestown South Carolina in 1796, aged 51 years. Also Mrs. Remember Harlow, wife of the above, who died December 26, 1829, aged 79 years.

No. 96.
[Low blue slate; symbol. Moss-grown, but quite sound.]

In memory of Remember Daughtr of Capt. Samuel Harlow & Remember his wife Born Augst ye 4th 1775 died Novbr ye 20th 1775

No. 97.
[Part of symbol scaled off,—otherwise like 96.]

In memory of Remember Daughter of Capt. Samuel Harlow & Mrs Remember his wife Born Novr ye 12th 1770 Died June ye 27th 1775

No. 98.
[Purplish slate. Slightly inclined backward. Somewhat moss grown, but quite sound.]

Here lyes ye Body of PEREZ MORTON Son of Mr Joseph Morton Junr & Mrs Anna his wife Who died Nov. 16, 1748 in ye 9 year of his age.

No. 99.
[Thick, compact, blue slate. Symbol. Good condition.]

Here lyes Buried ye Body of Mr JOSEPH MORTON who departed this life Feb ye 24 1754 in ye 71st Year of his Age

No. 100.

[Low, wide, purple slate. Symbol. Good condition.]

Here lyes ye Body of Mrs MARCY MORTON Wife to Mr Joseph Morton Who Departed this Life Octor ye 8 : 1756 : in ye 72 Year of Her Age

No. 101.

[Light blue slate; about 3 ft. high (heights given in this work are only approximate). Festoons. Mossy, but in good condition generally.]

Here rest the remains of Dea'n JONATHAN DIMAN who resigned his mortal Life in hopes of Glory Febry 25th 1797 in the 85 year of his age.

No. 102.

[Light blue slate, very thick and sound. Symbol.]

In memory of Mrs HANNAH DIMAN wife of Deacon Jona Diman who departed this Life July ye 6th 1778 in ye 65th year of her age.

No. 103.

[Blue slate. Weeping willow and urn. Good condition.]

Sacred to the memory of Mr Sylvanus Bartlett who Deceased Nov. 16 in the year 1811 aged 92 years.

No. 104.

[Blue slate. Weeping willow and urn. Good condition.]

Sacred to the memory of Mrs Martha Bartlett wife of Mr. Sylvanus Bartlett who deceased Dec. 31 1809 aged 83 years.

No. 105.

[Blue slate. Weeping willow and urn. Good condition.]

Betsey L. Bartlett Consort of Mr. Jesse Bartlett Born Dec 25 1781 and died Sept. 23, 1806 By this event her Husband is deprived of his best friend Three children of an affectionate Parent A Mother of her only .Child.

Farewell those Happy days that once I knew
Adieu my friend I bid a long Adieu
Till we united shall that hand adore
That parted lovers on this Earthly shore.

No. 106.

[This No. and 107 are inclosed with iron fence. 106 is white marble, over 4 feet in height; at top rose twig in a wreath. The monument is set in a freestone base; inclined backward; cement crumbled.]

Henry Erland Born in Devonshire Eng. Mar. 7, 1798 Died Sept. 6, 1853.

His virtues will embalm his memory.

No. 107.
[Thick white marble block, set in or upon granite. The whole mass inclines backward.]

Sally C. Erland, Widow of Henry Erland, Died Sept. 30, 1873, Aged 78 y'rs 3 mo's 13 days.
Entered into rest.

No. 108.
[On path, N. of Cushman monument. Purplish slate. Symbol. Good condition.]

To the memory of Mrs. Olive Washburn wife of Mr. Abiel Washburn with an infant in her arms who died Octr 14 1794 in the 30 year of her age.

No. 109.
[Blue slate. Festoons. Good condition.]

In memory of Mrs Ruth Bartlett wife of Mr Thomas Bartlett who died Octr 14th 1802, in the 22 year of her age.
Weep not for me, but weep for yourselves.

No. 110.
[Dark blue slate. Urn with flowers on either side. Good condition.]

To the memory of Thomas Bartlett son of Mr. Thomas & Mrs. Ruth Bartlett who died Septr 9th 1802 aged 1 year 2 months 11 days.
That once loved form now cold & dead,
Each mournfull thought imploys
And nature weeps his comforts fled
And withered all his joys

But ceas fond nature dry thy tears
Religon pints on high
And ever lasting spring appears
And joys that never die.

No. 111.
[White marble; moss grown: disintegrating.]

JOHN W. died Aug. 5, 1857, Æ. 15 y'rs 8 mo. ALSO PHEBY ANN died Oct.15, 1824, Æ. 1 y'r 5 mo. ANN died May 22, 1828, Æ. 3 y'rs 7 mo. MARY A. died March 12, 1833, Æ. 6 y'rs. WILLIAM M. died March 19, 1835, Æ. 1 y'r 2 mo. Children of Amaziah and Ruth R. Harlow.
Dearest children thou hast left us,
Here our loss we deeply feel,
But 'tis God that hath bereft us,
He can all our sorrows heal.

No. 112.
[White marble in marble socket. Good condition.]

Wm. H. Shaw Co. E. 32 Mass. Regt. Died Aug. 6, 1865, Aged 35 years.

2

No. 113.

[White marble in marble base. Good condition.]

WILLIAM SWIFT, Co. E. 29 Mass. Regt. Died Feb. 18, 1878, Aged 52 years.

No. 114.

[Blue slate, shivered and broken. Symbol minus one wing.]

In memory of Mrs. Lucy Harlow wife of Mr. Amaziah Harlow who died March 6 1796 in the 42 year of her age.

No. 115.

[Blue slate. Urn. Fair condition.]

In memory of Mr. Amaziah Harlow who Departed this Life December 15 1802 in the 55th year of his Age

No. 116.

[White marble, inclosed in palings. Wreath at top. Stone inclines to left.]

CHARLES IRVING Son of J. D. & E. B. Baxter fell asleep Aug. 8, 1861 ; aged 1 year 7 months & 12 days.
Our dearly beloved one will not be forgotten.

No. 117.

[Blue slate. Good condition.]

Erected to the memory of Mr. Henry Harlow who died July 15, 1833, in the 51 year of his age.

No. 118.

[Similar to 117,—but the lamina on which is the inscription, seems porous, and allows a growth of moss.]

Erected to the Memory of Miss NANCY HARLOW who died Feb. 3, 1849, in the 55 year of her age.

No. 119.

[Blue slate. Good condition.]

Erected to the memory of SAMUEL HARLOW who died Nov. 30th, 1849, aged 73 years.

No. 120.

[Blue slate, placed horizontally. Good condition.]

ICHABOD HARLOW died April 19, 1828, aged 17 yr.s PATIENCE HARLOW, died Sept. 15, 1840, aged 61 yrs. GEORGE HARLOW died Aug. 2, 1825, aged 2 yr.s. ALBERT HARLOW died May 12, 1833, aged 25 yr.s.

No. 121.

[White marble, weathering rough. No. 321, which was, within my recollection, perhaps the most beautiful monument on the Hill, shows that all monuments of that material must perish within a few years.]

Erected in memory of JACOB SWIFT died Nov. 1st 1854, Aged 43 years and 5 mon.

No. 122.

[White marble. Not yet 40 years old, but I found some difficulty in making out the epitaph.]

ANNABELLA, daughter of Jacob & Deborah S. Swift, died Feb. 27, 1853, aged 17 months.

Ere sin could blight or sorrow fade,
Death came with friendly care,
The opening bud to Heaven conveyed,
And bade it blossom there.

No. 123.

[White marble. Sound.]

WILLIAM FINNEY DIED April 13, 1869, Aged 61 y'rs 6 mo's.

No. 124.

[White marble. Sound. Has been removed from a broken stone socket, and set in the ground.]

CAPT. WM FINNEY, died at sea April 4, 1821, aged 37 years. And his wife MARTHA, died Aug. 4, 1856, aged 69 yrs. 8 mos.

No. 125.

[White marble. Sound.]

ALFRED C. FINNEY, a member of Co. E. 5th Reg. Mass. Vols. died at Newbern, N. C. March 13, 1863; Æ. 21 years 6 mo. 24 days.

Drop a kind tear for the Soldier that's gone,
For 'tis manly to weep for the brave.

No. 126.

[White marble, set in granite. Good condition.]

FATHER & MOTHER. JABEZ SWIFT Died March 14, 1865, Aged 47 y'rs 6 mo's. LUCY B. his wife Died July 2, 1874, Aged 54 y'rs 10 mo's.

Loved ones, we shall meet and rest
'Mid the holy and the blest.

No. 127.

[Blue slate, handsome and compact. Weeping willow and urn.]

In memory of Mrs. A. M. E. Kikert. who died June 10, 1853, Æt. 44 Y'rs.

No. 128.

[White marble obelisk: in good condition. A cross on E. side. On West side:]

JAMES BURNS.   MARY, wife of James Burns, died April 17 1867, Aged 54 years.

Requiescant in peace. Amen.

[On North side:]

ELLEN Aged 11 yrs. CATHARINE, Aged 9 yrs. HENRY, Aged 7 yrs. MARY, Aged 5 yrs. ROSE,

Aged 3 yrs. Children of James & Mary Burns. Drowned at Manomet Point Nov. 20, 1848.

No. 129.

[Grayish white marble in excellent condition, but slighily inclined.]

In honor of James H. Burns, Locomotive Fireman, killed at his post of duty, during the inundation of Rowley Marshes Nov. 15, 1871.

Son of James & Mary Burns. 21 y'rs. 6 mo's.

Erected by the Eastern R. R. Co.

No. 130.

[This and the two following numbers are inclosed with chain fence. White marble, in good condition. Nos. 130 and 131 are out of perpendicular.]

PELEG FAUNCE Dea. First Baptist Church, Died Oct. 3, 1878, Aged 80 years.

In hope.

· No. 131.

OLIVE FAUNCE, wife of Peleg Faunce, Died March 22, 1877, Aged 77 years.〜〜〜*At rest.*

No. 132.

CAROLINE A. PERRY, Daughter of Peleg & Olive Faunce, Died March 2, 1882, aged 48 years 9 mos.

With Christ.

No. 133.

[Low, white marble, disintegrating rapidly.]

Abner B. Son of Nathl & Betsey D. Freeman, Died Sep. 1838, aged 3 years.

No. 134.

[Low, white marble. Fair condition.]

LIZZIE RYAN, Aged 2 yrs & 8 mon. died Aug. 1st, 1853.

No. 135.

[Blue slate, broken and much worn. Inclined. Symbol.]

ELIZABETH Dau. to Deacon Heaviland & Mrs. Elizabeth Torrey his wife decd Novbr ye 2d 1731 aged 7 months.

No. 136.

[Purple slate, seamed and cracked. Symbol.]

Heaviland son to Deacon Heaviland & Mrs Elizabeth Torrey his wife decd July ye 17th 1752 in ye 17th year of his age.

No. 137.

[Low, hard, blue slate. Inclined and moss-grown. Symbol.]

In Memory of Joseph Son to Mr. William Torrey & Mary his wife who died April ye 25th 1757 aged 18 months & 4 days.

No. 138.

[Light blue slate. Seams and flaws. Symbol.]

In memory of Mrs ABIGAIL BARTLETT wife of Mr Solomon Bartlett who died Sept. 11, 1788, aged 40 years.

No. 139.

[Dark blue slate. Piece broken off.]

In memory of Mrs Mary Torrey daughter of the late Deacon John Torrey who died Sept 19th 1801 in the 45th year of her age.

No. 140.

[Thick, low, blue slate; moss-grown; fair condition. Symbol.]

In Memory of Polly Daughter of Mr John & Mrs Lydia Edwards who died Sept 11, 1791 aged 5 years & 3 months.

No. 141.

[Compact blue slate. Ornamental sculpture at top. Good condition.]

In memory of JAMES P. Son of Philip & Nancy Taylor, who died Oct. 6, 1833, aged 11 years & 6 mons.

So fades the lovely blooming flower
The smiling solace of an hour
So soon our transient comforts fly
And pleasure only blooms to die.

No. 142.

[Blue slate, good condition. Flaming urn.]

In memory of Lydia, widow of Bartlett LeBaron, who died Jan. 1st, 1823, Aged 66 years.

Blessed are the dead
which die in the Lord.

No. 143.

[Blue slate. Some moss. Fair condition. Urn.]

To the memory of Mr BARTLETT LE BARON who departed this life June 24, 1806 aged 67 years.

No. 144.

[White marble. Moss. Inclined forward.]

ISAAC LE BARON, Born Jan. 1743; Died Dec. 1819. His wife MARTHA HOWLAND, Born Dec. 1739; Died June 1825.

No. 145.

[Thick, wide, light blue slate. Laminæ separating. Surface seamed. Moss-grown and inclined. Symbol.]

Here lies buried Doctr Joseph Lebaron who decd May ye 11 1761 in ye 59th year of his age.

No. 146.

[Compact purple slate, about 20 inches high. Small fig. of hour-glass at top, under which is the symbol (cherub?) of the winged head, sculptured far better than usual. Low down on the right, under the ornamental border, is the number 24,—supposed to indicate the price of the stone. This Dr. Lebarran is the hero of "The Nameless Noble-man." The orthography of the name and occupation indicates that the sculptor was a pupil of the "unlettered Muse" spoken of by Gray.]

Here lyes ye body of Mr. FRANCIS LE. BARRAN phytician who departed this life Augst ye 18th 1704, in ye 36 year of his age.

No. 147.

[Blue slate, somewhat broken and moss-grown, but easily read. Inclined.]

Here lyes ye body of Francis Lebaron who decd Augst ye 6th 1731 in ye 31st year of his age.

No. 148.

[Thick, firm, granite block, 4 1-2 feet high.]

In memory of Isaac LE BARON Born March 11, 1777, Died Jan. 29, 1849, Of Mary Doane his wife Born July 19, 1787, Died June 18, 1863. And of their children Isaac Francis, Born Oct. 29, 1814, Died June 28, 1816. Frederic, Born Feb. 28, 1816, Died July 5, 1861. Mary Jane Born Aug. 12, 1817, Died Nov. 28, 1855. Isaac, Born Dec. 6, 1819. Died Dec. 24, 1853.

No. 149.

[Blue slate. Slightly inclined. Stone in good condition.]

In memory of Mrs SARAH Le BARON wife of Wil-liam Le Baron Esq. died Oct. 29th 1796 aged 46 years.

No. 150.

[Blue slate. Good condition.]

This Stone is erected in memory of Wm LEBARON Esqr. who deceased at Fairhaven and their intered the 23 day of October in the year of our LORD one thousand eight hundred & sixteen aged 65 years.

No. 151.

[Blue slate. Laminæ opened somewhat. Inclined.]

In memory of The decd Children of Mr. William & Mrs Sarah LeBaron Viz William decd Nov. 8, 1778 aged 9 days William decd Oct. 21 1780 aged 17 months.

No. 152.

[Similar to 151.]

In memory of Margaret Daughter to Doctr Lazarus & Mrs Lydia Lebaron Born July ye 5th 1755 Died Novı ye 20th 1756

No. 153.
[Similar to 151.]

In memory of Mrs Lydia Lebaron wife to Doctr Lazarus Lebaron who decd Octr ye 28th 1756 in ye 37th year of her age.

No. 154.
[Similar to 151.]

Here lyes buried ye body of Mrs Lidia Lebaron wife to Doctr Lazarus Lebaron who decd May ye 29th 1762 aged 44 years, 4 mos & 22 days .

No. 155.
[Very light-colored blue slate. Very wide and thick. Somewhat moss-grown, but can be read without much difficulty.]

In memory of Doctor Lazarus Lebaron who departed this life Sept 2d 1773 Ætatis Suæ 75
> My flesh shall slumber in the ground
> Till the last trumpet's joyful sound.
> Then burst the chains with sweet surprise
> And in my Saviour's image rise.

No. 156 a.
[Blue slate. Laminæ separating. Weather-worn.]

Here lyes ye body of Mrs Mary Wait wife to Mr Return Waite She Decd Sept ye 26th 1737 in ye 69th year of her age.

No. 156 b.
[Blue slate; a small stone. Good condition. Willow.]

Mary Jane dau. of Mr. John & Esther Kennady who died Sept. 21, 1822, aged 14 months.
> So fades the lovely blooming flower
> Frail, smiling solace of an hour,
> So soon our transient comforts fly,
> And pleasure only blooms to die.

No. 157.
[White marble. Good condition.]

JOHN OSGOOD Died Jan'y 31, 1854, Æ. 25 y'rs 9 mo. & 3 days

No. 158.
[Blue slate. This stone is very much broken and decayed. The tens in the year of the date cannot be made out.]

Here lyes ye body of Mr. Caleb Cook who decd Febry ye 13th 17—½ in the 72d year of his age.

No. 159.
[White marble, taken from fragile, broken socket and set in the ground.]

OUR FATHER. JOHN HARLOW Born Sept. 15, 1777, Died Sept. 5, 1864.

No. 160.

[Blue slate. Weeping willow and urn. Moss-grown. Inclined.]

Mrs. Betsey Harlow Consort to Mr. John Harlow was born Feb. 22d 1780 and died Nov. 22d 1806

This stone an unvailing tribute of affection Is erected by her Husband to her memory.

With her was crowned my earthly bliss
Home was my joy and happiness
But oh! how soon death's arrow flies,
On Christ alone my hope relies.
We yet may meet above.

No. 161.

[Purplish slate. Weeping willow and urn. Good condition.]

In memory of BETSEY, consort of John Harlow Junr who died Sept. 22, 1835, in her 44 year. Also Mary L. aged 1 year & 10 mo's. and John H. aged 7 mos. Children of the above.

A husband's care, a husband's love,
Could not save her from the grave;
With thy children sweetly rest,
And learn the wisdom of the blest.

No. 162.

[Purplish slate. Urn. Good condition.]

In memory of John Harlow son of Mr John Harlow & Mrs. Betsey his wife who deed August 1814 aged 7 months & 3 days

Frail though endear'd the tie
The stronger band of grace
Shall last when
Death itself shall die

No. 163.

[A wooden slab without lettering.]

No. 164.

[Thick, compact, purplish-blue slate. Weeping willow and urn. Good condition.]

To the memory of Mrs. Sarah Harlow widow of Cap, Jesse Harlow who died November 22, 1828 aged 65 years.

No. 165.

[Blue slate. Symbol, under which are festoons hanging over an urn.]

This stone is erected to the memory of Capt Jesse Harlow who died Aug. 20, 1809 aged sixty nine

No. 166.

[Similar to 165.]

This stone is erected To Perpetuate the memory of Mrs ELIZABETH HARLOW Consort of Capt Jesse Harlow who Departed this life January 27th 1805, in the 65 year of her age

No. 167.

[Blue slate. Symbol. Moss-grown. Good condition.]

To the memory of Mr. Silvanus Harlow who Died augst 14 1799 In the 62 year of his age

No. 168.

[Blue slate. Urn. Good condition.]

To the memory of Mrs Desire Harlow wife of Mr Silvanus Harlow who died Octr 8th 1796 aged 58 years

How happy they thats gone to rest]
For they shall be forever blest.

No. 169.

[Low, blue slate. Symbol. Moss-grown. Fair condition.]

Here lies buried Noah Son to Mr. Silvanus Harlow & Mrs Desire his wife who decd August ye 23d 1767 Aged 5 weeks

No. 170.

[Similar to 169.]

In memory of Silvanus son of Capt Silvanus Harlow and Mrs Desiah his wife who died Sept 5th 1775 Aged 11 years

No. 171.

[White marble. Weeping willow and urn. Winged figures in upper corners, blowing trumpets. Urns in lower corners. Rapidly disintegrating.]

Sacred to the memory of Miss DESIRE HARLOW who was born Sept 27 1797, and died May 12, 1821.

Dear hon'd spirit if angels e'er bestow
A thought on what is acted here below,
With pitying eye this weak attempt survey
The last sad tribute which thy friend can pay

No. 172.

[White marble like 171. Weeping willow and urn.]

In memory of Mrs. HANNAH the virtuous and amiable consort of Silvanus Harlow, who after a distressing illness of 6 months, which she bore with unexampled fortitude untill exhausted nature compelled her to say I must give up. Departed this life Nov. 1, 1836 aged 48 yrs & 10 ds.

Crop'd like a flower she wither'd in her bloom
And flattering life had promis'd years to come
The years she lived in virtue's path she trod
But now her spirit sought to meet her God
In realms of bliss, where joys eternal reign
Devoid of care and uncontroll'd by pain.

3

No. 173.

[Same kind of marble as 171. Figure at top, a square surmounted with three cones—a mausoleum?]

In memory of ELIZABETH A. wife of Silvanus Harlow. Born Oct. 28, 1812, Died June 4, 1850, Æ. 37 y'rs 7 mo. & 7 ds.

> We mourn who loved her here
> And who that knew her ne'er could fail to love
> Yet we would dry the tear
> And strive to meet her in the world above.

Also their dau. Elizabeth A. died Jan. 13, 1842, Æ. 3 weeks & 2 ds.

> With chasten'd heart we'l strive to bear
> Submissive to God's will
> Tis he that gives, tis he that takes
> And we will bless him still.

No. 174.

[Low; blue slate. Symbol. Side of stone broken off.]

In Memory of Jesse son of Mr Jesse Harlow   Mrs. Hannah his wife died July 10, 1788   4 months & 19 days.

No. 175.

[Firm, blue slate. Good condition.]

To the memory of Mr. Jesse Harlow This Stone is Erected who died August 4. 1810 aged 50 years In this death his wife Lost an agreeable Companion his children an affectionate Parent

> Make Christ your Friend who never dies
> All other Friends are vanities
> Make him your Life your all
> Prepare for Death that solemn call

No. 176.

[Light blue slate, 2 1-2 feet high. Weeping willow and urn. Moss-grown; otherwise in good condition.]

This stone is Erected As an unavailing tribute of respect and humanity By the Children To Mrs. HANNAH, wife of Mr. Jesse Harlow, who Departed this life November 18, 1836, Aged 72 years & 6 months.

> Her husband knew her worth
> Her children knew it well.

No. 177.

[Purplish-slate. Moss-grown. Inclined.]

In memory of MISS MARY COLLINS died June 14th, 1846, aged 60 years.

No. 178.

[Blue slate. Good condition.]

In memory of MRS. MARY COLLINS wife of *James Collins* who died May 28th, 1840, aged 83 years.

No. 179.

[Blue slate. Slightly inclined. Good condition.]

In Memory of *Capt.* JAMES COLLINS died Feb. 17, 1839, aged 90 years.

No. 180.

[Blue slate. Signs of cleavage. Symbol.]

Here lies buried ye body of Mrs Lois COLLINGS wife of Mr JAMES COLLINGS, with an Infant in her arms who died March ye 1st 1787 in ye 28th year of her age.

No. 181.

[Blue slate, solid. Good condition.]

In Memory of Capt GAMALIEL COLLINS the first adventurer in the whale fishery to the Falkland Islands who died April 1, 1786, in ye 44 year of his age.

No. 182.

[A closed-grained, purple stone,—of which kind a few have been erected in recent years.]

In memory of LOIS COLLINS born May 20, 1787, died Aug. 23, 1862, Æ. 75 years 3 mos. & 3 days.

No. 183.

[White marble set in freestone; the whole inclines backward.]

THOMAS COLGAN, Born in Kings Co. Ireland, Nov. 6, 1825, Died Sept. 11, 1871. JOHN, Son of Thomas & Ann Colgan Died Dec. 12, 1861, Aged 4 y'rs.

May they rest in peace.

[On the reverse of No. 183 is a cross above the letters I H S.]

No. 184.

[White marble. Covered, like many others, with what appears to be minute vegetation.]

(A cross at top.)

In memory of James Sullivan who died in Plymouth, Oct. 6, 1855, aged 22 y'rs.

A native of County Cork, Ireland, Parish of Castletownsend.

No. 185.

[White marble. Slightly inclined.]

HANS WITTE, Died Jan, 10, 1866, Aged 46 yrs. 9 mos. 26 ds.

No. 186.

[Firm, blue slate; inclined backward.]

In memory of NANCY WILLIAMS, a faithful (African) servant in the family of Rev. F. Freeman, died Nov, 31, 1831, aged 25 years.

"Honor and shame from no condition rise,
Act well your part,—there all the honor lies." |

No. 187.

[Blue slate. Laminæ separating. Part of the stone is broken off, carrying with it two figures of a date; but the deficiency is supplied by an inscription on the footstone, to wit: "J. H. 1780 M. H. 1779." Surface of stone cleft its whole length in centre.]

In Memory of JOHN HARLOW who Decd March 10th 17 in ye 73d year of his age. Also In Memory of Mrs MARY HARLOW his wife who Decd April 2d 1779 in ye 64th year of her age.

No. 188.

[Square marble column: good condition.]

EMMA M. Dau. of S. S. & R. M. Howland Died Sept. 12, 1867, Aged 15 y'rs 12 ds.

Affection lives beyond death's dark and withering will.
(By the side of the above is a small stone inscribed:)

EMMA. GONE FROM US THE CHILD WE LOVED.

No. 189.

[Low, blue slate; Laminæ separating; inclined. Symbol.]

In Memory of 2 children of Mr Crosbe Luce & Mrs Elizabeth his wife Viz Elkanah died Nov. 5, 1779 aged 1 year 3 months & 11 days Crosbe born June 25 1780 died the same day.

No. 190.

[Low, compact, blue slate. Good condition. Symbol.]

In Memory of Elizabeth Daughter of Mr Crosbe Luce & Mrs Elizabeth his wife who died Angst 5, 1787 in ye 7th year of her Age.

No. 191.

[Blue slate. Piece broken from top, not injuring inscription.]

In memory of Mrs Sally Harlow Consort of Capt Lazarus Harlow who died Jany 11 1810 in the 56 year of her age.

Prepare me Lord for thy right hand
Then come the Joyful day
Come Death and come celestial band
To bear my soul away.

No. 192.

[Blue slate. Moss-grown. Inclined. Symbol.]

In Memory of 2 children of Mr Lazarus Harlow & Mrs Sarah his wife, Viz Lazarus died Octr 3 1782 aged 14 months. Gracy died April 21, 1790 aged 6 weeks.

No. 193.

[White marble, in broken socket. Inclined. Discolored.]

ROBERT McLAUTHLIN Co. B. 14 Mass. Regt. Died Oct. 13, 1864 Aged 20 y'rs 6 m's. 3 days.

No. 194.

[Dark blue slate. Good condition. Symbol.]

Here lies Interd Mrs Susanna Attwood & her Infant in her armes Wife to Mr Wait Attwood died Feb. 2 1785 in the 35 year of her Age

No. 195.

[Blue slate. Good condition. Weeping willow and urn.]

Consecrated to the Memory of Mrs. ELIZABETH ATWOOD, amiable Consort of Capt. Thos Atwood. died April 11, 1813 : in the 31st Year of her age.

"The seasons as they fly,
Snatch from us in their course, year after year
Some sweet connection some endearing tie.

No. 196.

[Compact blue slate. A square at top, surmounted by three pyramids,—probably figure of mausoleum. Good condition.]

Erected to the Memory of CAPT. THOMAS ATWOOD, who departed this life April 28, 1831 in the 65 year of his age.

No. 197.

[Blue slate. Seams running downward on face of stone. Weeping willow and urn. Fair condition.]

Erected to the MEMORY of Mrs MEHETABEL, wife of Capt Thos Atwood. who died Jan. 11, 1809, In the 58 year of her age. In early life her feeble constitution gave painful premonition of her early exit. She however unexpectedly passed the meridian of life, discharging in a very laudable manner, filial, parental & conjugal duties. At length the seeds of death were planted in her vitals—she sickened, languished & expired in hopes of a blessed immortality.

Short is our longest day of life,
And soon its prospect ends
Yet on that day's uncertain date
Eternity depends.

No. 198.

[Blue slate. Urns. Badly cleft on the right.]

Erected in MEMORY of TWIN DAUGHTERS of Capt THOS ATWOOD and MEHETABEL his Wife, Born Nov. 2, 1802 ; Died Nov. 4, 1802. Also, In MEMORY of Darius, Son of Capt THOS Atwood and MEHETABEL, his wife, who Died Jan. 23, 1809, Aged 2 Mo & 8 days.

Here, here they lie! oh! could I once more view
Those dear remains take one more fond adieu
Of th' work of God, their beautious clay, which here
In infant charms so lovely did appear
As tho' in nature's nicest model cast,
Exactly polish'd, wrought too fine to last
By the same hand that wrought, again shall they arise
To bloom more gay, more lovely in the skies.

No. 199.

[Blue slate. Moss-grown; otherwise good condition.]

In memory of our Mother, ELIZABETH, widow of the late Thomas Atwood, Born in Truro, June 30, 1778, Died in Fairhaven, Nov. 2, 1866. Aged 88 y'rs 4 mo's 3 d's.

No. 200.

[Blue slate. Figure of broken bough. Some moss; otherwise in good condition.]

Erected in Memory of DARIUS, Son of Capt. Thos Atwood, & Mrs. Elizabeth his wife died Oct. 8, 1813 : aged 11 Months & 12 days.

No. 201.

[Wooden slab.]

WM. A. JOHNSON. DIED 1854.

No. 202.

[Blue slate. A fissure, near right hand corner, extends downward nearly to middle of monument.]

WILLIAM THOMAS, M. D. Died Sept. 20, 1802, Aged 84 years. MERCY, Daughter of Wm & Mercy Thomas Died Nov. 1776, Aged 17 years.

No. 203.

[Purple slate intersected with parallel gray veins. Symbol. Good condition.]

Here lies buried the body of Mrs Mary Thomas the wife of Doct William Thomas aged 26 years Died April ye 25th 1749.

No. 204.

[Light blue slate. Symbol. Good condition.]

Here lies Interr,d ye body of Mrs MERCY THOMAS ye wife of Doctor WILLIAM THOMAS who departed this life August ye 3d AD. 1769 in ye 44th year of her age

No. 205.

[A stone similar to 204; broken horizontally ; upper moiety gone.]

MARY THOMAS, Widow of Dr. William Thomas Died Dec. 4, 1806, aged 74 years

No. 206.

[Blue slate. Good condition.]

JOSEPH THOMAS, born Jany 8th 1755, died August 10, 1838 ; Captain of Artillery during the War of the Revolution.

No. 207.

[Blue slate. Many cracks across the face, and laminæ separating. Symbol.]

This Stone is erected to the Memory of Mrs PATIENCE HOWLAND who departed this Life July 23d 1774 in ye 52

year of her Age. She was widow of Capt JOHN HOW-
LAND who died on the Florida shoar AD. 1750 in ye 39th
year of his age

No. 208.

[White marble, weathering rough. Set in freestone socket; the
whole inclined backward.]

In memory of OUR MOTHER MARY ANN. widow of
George W. Callaway. Died Apr. 20, 1870, Aged 65
y'rs. 9 mo's. 16 days.

Though I walk through the valley of the shadow of death I will
fear no evil; for thou art with me: thy rod, and thy staff they comfort me.

No. 209.

[Similar to 208, and set in same block of freestone.]

In memory of MY MOTHER. Harriet T. widow of
Samuel J. Jones, died Dec. 19, 1867. Aged 62 years. &
2 mo's.

Beloved, and lamented.

No. 210.

[White marble, tending to the condition of 321.]

JANE, widow of Nathaniel Thomas died Dec 22d
1851, in her 81st y'r. *Also*, NANCY, their Daughter
died Jan. 18th, 1821, aged 18 years.

No. 211.

[Solid purplish slate. Good condition. Urn, with flame issuing
from it.]

In memory of Nathaniel Thomas, born Nov. 22, 1756;
and died March 21, 1838.

No. 212.

[Blue slate. Moss-grown, but otherwise in good condition.]

In memory of Mrs PRISCILLA THOMAS Consort of Mr
Nathaniel Thomas, who died Decr 6th 1795 aged 36
years

No. 213.

[Blue slate, low. Cleft downward to the word "who."]

In Memory of Mrs Bathsheba Washburn wife of Mr
Benjamin Washburn who died July 13 1788 Aged 26
years.

No. 214.

[Blue slate; not in very good condition. Symbol.]

In Memory of Mrs LYDIA WASHBURN wife of Mr JOHN
WASHBURN who died May ye 12th 1782 in ye 47th year
of her Age.

No. 215.
[A wooden cross.]
BRIDGET CASSIDY Born Jan. 2d, 1864 Died Feb. 19, 1865 Aged 1 Yr. 1 Mo. 17 Ds.

No. 216.
[White marble. Broken flower stem at top. The material does not weather so well as could be desired.]
MARY A. wife of Lewis Hall, died Apr. 27, 1860, Æ. 43 years & 6 mos.
Blessed are the dead who die in the Lord.

No. 217.
[Blue slate, in fair condition for so old a stone. Symbol.]
In Memory of Joshua son of Mr Joseph Bramhall & Mrs Remember his wife who died March ye 5th 1779 Aged 3 Months & 8 Days.

No. 218.
[Similar to 217.]
In Memory of Mary Bennet Daughter of Mr Joseph Bramhall & Mrs Remember his wife who decd July ye 20th 1781 Aged 1 year & 4 days.

No. 219.
[Blue slate. Sound and firm. Symbol.]
In Memory of Grace Daughter of Mr Joseph Bramhall & Mrs Remember his wife who died March 13 1788 aged 6 months and 13 days.

No. 220.
[Blue slate. Sound; little moss. Urn at top.]
In memory of Mr JOSEPH BRAMHALL who Departed this life September 17th 1805 in the 62d year of his age.

No. 221.
[White marble, set in freestone. Inclined.]
[A cross engraved with I. H. S.]
In memory of ANN wife of JOHN CASSADY, who died July 20, 1860; in her 77th year.

No. 222.
[Blue slate, 6ft. high. Urn under festoons. Cleft from top downward into two nearly equal parts.]
ANDREW FARRELL, of respectable connexions In IRELAND, Aged 38 years, Owner & Commander of the Ship Hibernia, Sailed from Boston Jany 26, And was wrecked on Plymouth Beach Jany 28 1805. His remains

With five of seven seamen Who perished with him are
here interred.

O piteous lot of man's uncertain state!
What woes on life's eventful journey wait—
By sea what treacherous calms; what sudden storms;
And death attendant in a thousand forms.

No. 223.

[Blue slate. Good condition. Figure of tomb at top.]

THOMAS MARSH, died Sept. 16, 1835 : Aged 61
y,rs. WARREN son of the above died at Sea August
25, 1828 : aged 21 y,rs. MARCY, dau,tr of the above
died Sept,r 3, 1813 ; Aged 9 mo,s.

No. 224.

[Blue Slate. Sound. Inclined. Urn.]

To the m · y of Lillis Gill Marsh Daughter of Mr
Thomas Marsh And Mrs Marcy his wife who died Octr
1st 1806 Aged 15 months.

No. 225.

[White marble on granite base. Good condition. This, and No. 410
are inclosed in the same wooden fence.]

KEZIAH D. Wife of ROBERT SWINBURN Died
Mar. 26, 1882 Aged 77 y'rs. 4 mo's. & 11 d'ys.

[On the reverse side:]

Mother "Dear Wife and Mother."

To us you have done your duty,
Now lie here and rest,
It was God's will to take you from us,
For he knew what was best.   R. S.

No. 226.   ·

[White marble; discolored: weathering rough. Figure of rose at top.]

In memory of SARAH. wife of Robert Searson, and
daughter of Dennis & Sarah Deleany Born June 6, 1832,
Died May 3, 1863.

I will remember thee love, when many have forgot; and may you
rest in peace with God.

No. 227.

[Blue slate. Good condition.]

In memory of Capt William Bartlett who departed this
life April 19, 1807 in the 79 year of his age.

No. 228.

[Dilapidated stone, dropping to pieces.]

In memory of rs Mary Bartlett wife of Mr William
Bartlett who died July 16, 1785 in ye 56 year of her age.

No. 229.

[Blue slate. Good condition. Weeping willow and urn.]

Sacred to the memory of Phebe J. Bramhall, A native

of Virginia & wife of Benjn Bramhall Jun who died August 27, 1817, Aged 21 years.

Possess'd of an amiable disposition, She
endeared herself to all around her
"but"
Weep not for her in her Spring time she flew
To that land, where the wings of the soul are unfurl'd
And now, like a star beyond evening's cold dew
Looks radiantly down on the tears of this world.   .

No. 230.

[White marble; weathering rough. Urn.]

Sacred to the memory of MARY ANN SAMPSON wife of Schuyler Sampson, and Daughter of Amasa. and Sarah Bartlett: who died September 3rd, 1825, aged 26 years, 11 months, and 24 days.

"The virtuous are truly happy."

No. 231.

[Similar to 230.]

GEORGE SCHUYLER son of Schuyler and Sarah T. Sampson, died Nov'r 22, 1833 ; aged 2 mo. & 24 ds.

"This lovely bud so young, so fair,
Call'd hence by early doom,
Just came to show how sweet a flower
In paradise would bloom.

No. 232.

[White marble. Moss-grown.]

LITTLE CHARLIE

[On the reverse:]

Son of J. A. & N. E. Dunham, died Oct. 5, 1857, aged 8 mo. 17 ds.

No. 233.

[White marble. Moss-grown.]

Amasa Bartlett, Born June 23, 1763, Died March 3, 1835. Sarah Taylor, Relict of *Amasa Bartlett*, Born June 29, 1767, Died April 13, 1849.

No. 234.

[Blue slate. Good condition. Weeping willow and urn.]

In memory of Mr. Heman Holmes, who died May 8th 1810 aged 45 years and 10 months.

Those who loved the living,
And lament the dead,
Pay their last tribute
To thy gentle shade.

No. 235.

[Blue slate. Good condition. A low stone. Symbol.]

To the memory of Sally Drew Daughter of Mr Lemuel Drew & Mrs Sally his wife who died July 27 1800 Aged 2 years & 9 months.

No. 236.

[Blue slate. Two symbols (winged faces—"cherubs.") Good condition.]

Thomas Born July 18th 1799 died Novr 9th 1800 William Thos Born April 14th 1801 died Sepr 24th 1801 Children of Capt Thomas & Mrs Margret J. Bartlett his wife and hear lies Enterred.

> Surely life is, as a vapour that appeareth
> For a little time and vanisheth away.

No. 237.

[Purplish slate. Flaming urn. Good condition.]

In memory of MARGARET JAMES, wife of Capt. Thomas Bartlett, who died Oct. 23d, 1840, aged 65 years.

No. 238.

[Like preceding, out is inclined.]

In memory of CAPT. THOMAS BARTLETT who died Dec. 30, 1849, in the 80th year of his age.

No. 239.

[White marble set in freestone.]

In memory of NATHANIEL BARTLETT 2D DIED June 23, 1862, aged 56 years & 6 mos.

No. 240.

[Blue slate, 4 ft. high. Moss-grown on surface (probably a soft or porous lamina). Otherwise in good condition.]

In memory of Mrs. Polly Otis, the amiable Consort of Mr. Barnabas Otis, who departed this life April 25th 1831, in the 77 year of her age.

> Yes thou art gone, and we no more
> Shall hold sweet converse here below;
> But now we trust a brighter shore
> Is thine beyond the bound of woe.

No. 241.

[Dark blue slate. Inclined. Stone in good condition.]

This Stone is erected to the memory of Henry Otis the second son of Barnabas Otis and Polly his wife who died in the Island of Martinico July 26th AD. 1802, aged 15 years 5 months and 20 days.

No. 242.

[Dark blue slate. Good condition. Weeping willow and urn.]

Sacred to the memory of Mrs. Mary Williams wife of Mr. Elias Williams and Daughter of Mr. Barnabas Otis & Polly his wife died at King & Queen County, Virginia Oct. 3, 1813 aged 23 years and was there interred & in

March 1817 her remains were taken from that place and brought to Plymouth and here deposited.

> Too good the miseries of this world to share
> The hand of mercy took her from our sight
> Releas'd from this abode of grief and care
> Her gentle spirit sought the realms of light.

No. 243.

[Blue slate. In good condition, save being moss-grown.]

Sacred To the memory of Mr. Barnabas Otis, Junr who Died at Sea May 18 1812 Aged 27 years from inclination he commenced traversing the Ocean in early life and was attended by a series of uncommon misfortunes and disasters on that element until his death.

> Cold is that breast where pure affection flow'd.

No. 244.

[The Magee monument. The erection of this obelisk is in the highest degree creditable to the public spirit of Stephen Gale, Esq. It is to be regretted, however, that he was not fortunate in the selection of marble as the material for a structure intended to be a permanent memorial of the disastrous shipwreck of the brig Gen. Arnold. The condition of No. 321, and of other marbles which have been erected in later years, is convincing evidence that marble (I speak of such as is generally found in Plymouth cemeteries) is wholly useless for monumental purposes. On the south and west sides of the Magee monument, clefts are apparent in the squared block, the principal one striking the name of Magee.]

(The inscription on the northeasterly side is:)

In memory of Seventy two Seamen who perished in Plymouth harbour on the 26, and 27, days of December 1778. on board the private armed Brig, Gen. Arnold, of twenty guns, James Magee of Boston, Commander, sixty of whom were buried on this spot

(On the northwesterly side:)

Capt. James Magee died in Roxbury, February 4, 1801 ; aged 51 years.

(Southwesterly side:)

> "Oh! falsely flattering were you billows smooth
> When forth, elated, sailed in evil hour,
> That vessel whose disastrous fate, when told,
> Fill'd every breast with sorrow and each eye
> With piteous tears."

(Southeasterly side:)

This monument. marks the resting place of sixty of the seventy two mariners, "who perished in their strife with the storm," and is erected by Stephen Gale of Portland Maine, a stranger to them, as a just memorial of their sufferings and death.

No. 245.

[White marble, set in granite. Good condition, save slightly inclined.]

RICHARD BAGNELL Died March 4, 1868, Aged 67 years.

LYDIA, his wife Died Dec. 10, 1885, Aged 85 years.

No. 246.

[Very thick blue slate. Good condition. Weeping willow and urn.]

In memory of MRS. REBECCA BARNES Consort of Mr Benjamin Barnes Jr who died June 10, 1826, in the 55 year of her age.

No. 247.

[This monument and the two following were inclosed in a wooden paling, which is now in a ruinous state. The material of the gravestones is white marble,—not enduring.]

MISS ABBY BARTLETT Died Jan. 22, 1867 Aged 72 y'rs 6mo's

"There is rest in Heaven."

No. 248.

[Stone broken across; the upper portion placed upright in the ground, perhaps covering an epitaph. The essentials—name and dates—are visible.]

HENRY BARTLETT Died at sea March 14, 1817 Aged 48 years.

No. 249.

MISS NANCY HARLOW Died Nov. 17. 1848. Aged 86 y'rs.

No. 250.

[Blue slate; laminæ separating, admitting water. Cracked on surface. Symbol. The inscription can easily be read.]

In Memory of Thomas Spooner son of Mr Thomas Spooner & Mrs Deborah his wife who was drown'd near Clarks Island June 21st 1768 aged 12 years

No. 251.

[Blue slate, in a rather shattered condition. Symbol.]

In Memory of MARY BOWRN Who Deed Sept ye 21st 1748 in ye 27th year of her Age.

No. 252.

[Blue slate. Height 3 1-2 ft. (Heights are given [approximately] in some cases, as an assistance in finding any particular stone). Good condition, Symbol.]

Sacred to the Memory of DEA. JOSHUA TORREY who departed this life Dec. 22, 1838, aged 71 years.

In faith and hope he trod the heavenly way
To meet his Saviour in the realms of day

No. 253.

[Blue slate. 3 1-2 ft. Good condition. Weeping willow and urn.]

JERUSHA, wife of Charles L. Faunce, died Dec. 5th, 1840, aged 26 years.

She hath gone to that radiant shore,
Where the bowers are mansions of rest;
Where weeping for ever is o'er,
And the spirit for ever is blest.

No. 254.

[Blue slate. 4 ft. Good condition. Urn.]

Erected to the memory of Mrs. Betsey Torrey wife of Col. John Torrey who died April 15, 1810 aged forty seven years.

She pin'd in thought.

No. 255.

[Blue slate. Small piece broken from top; otherwise in good condition. Symbol.]

To the memory of Mary Torrey daughter of Col. John & Mrs. Elizabeth Torrey who died March 2d 1803 aged 3 months & 21 days.

No. 256.

[Blue slate. Small stone; laminæ opened; part of face scaled off.]

r John Mrs Elizabeth wife who died Oct. 10, 1784 aged 3 days.

No. 257.

[Blue slate, in crumbling condition.]

To the Memory of Mrs MERIAH TORREY, wife of Mr John Torrey who decd July ye 20th 1782 in ye 25th year of her age.

Her Life agreeable Her Death Triumphant
Through Her Saviour.

No. 258.

[Low, blue slate. Several fissures on surface, Symbol.]

In Memory of John son of Mr John Torrey & Mrs Meriah his wife who died Oct. ye 7th 1779 Aged 1 year 4 Months & 19 days.

No. 259.

[Blue slate, very thick and solid. Symbol.]

In Memory of JOHN TORREY *Esqr* who departed this Life Decemr ye 16th 1776 in ye 60th year of his Age.

In Faith he dy'd in Dust he lies
But Faith foresees that Dust shall rise
When Jesus with almighty word
Calls his dead Saints to meet the Lord.

No. 260.

[Blue slate; somewhat dilapidated. Symbol.]

In Memory of Mrs MARY TORREY wife of DEA-CON JOHN TORREY who departed this Life Decr ye 31st 1774 in ye 43d year of her Age.

No. 261.

[Purplish slate. Abounds in clefts and fissures. Symbol.]
(All capitals.)

In memory of MRs Deborah Croade, ye consort of Mr John Croade, and daughtr of ye late Honble Nathl

Thomas Esqr who died in ye 73d year of her age June ye 14th 1741.

No. 262.

[This and the two following Nos. are inclosed with wooden paling. 262 is white marble in freestone socket. A crack across top of stone is traceable some distance downward. White marbles look well when new; but they soon become rough, and in a few years the legends on them become illegible. See 321, and others.]

BETSEY, wife of Nathaniel Harlow, DIED April 23, 1866, Aged 77 years.

Heaven is my home.

No. 263.

[Blue slate. Uninjured. Inclined. Symbol.]

In memory of Mr. Benjamin Harlow who died November 18th 1816 aged 34 years.

Friends and physicians could not save
My mortal Body from the Grave
Nor can the Grave confine me here
When Christ the son of God appears

No. 264.

[White marble: similar to 262. A discoloration of base is perhaps caused by rust from a dowel-pin.]

BENJAMIN HARLOW died Aug. 18, 1846, Aged 35 years.

"Blessed are the pure in heart;
for they shall see God."

No. 265.

[Similar to 264.]

BETSEY HARLOW DIED March 27, 1866, Aged 53 years.

"Blessed are they that mourn for they shall be comforted."

No. 266.

[Low, blue slate. Laminæ separating. Part of face scaled off. Symbol. Corner of stone broken off.]

memory of   enjamin son of Seth Harlow and Sarah his wife who died Octr ye 17th 1775, Aged 11 years.

No. 267.

[Blue slate. Face uninjured, but lines of cleavage well developed. Symbol.]

Here lies Buried Mr. William Harlow who Decd April ye 11th 1751 in ye 59th year of his age.

No. 268.

[Low, blue slate. Cleft diagonally across left part of surface. Symbol.]

Here lies buried Mrs Marcy Harlow Widow to Mr William Harlow who decd Janury 21st 1772, in ye 77th year of her Age.

No. 269.
[Low blue slate. Good condition.]
(Capital letters.)
In Memory of Benjamin Son to Mr Ebenezer Sampson & Mrs Hannah his wife who decd June ye 21st 1759 in ye 19th month of her age

No. 270.
[Similar to 269.]
In Memory of Benjamin Samson son to Mr Ebenezer Samson & Mrs Hannah his wife who decd Septr ye 5th 1761 in ye 16th Month of his Age.

No. 271.
[Good condition for white marble.]
HANNAH PAINE, Widow died Jan. 3, 1832, Æ. 80 years.

Also her Husband Stephen Paine, died at Liverpool, N. S. 1794, Æ. 48 y'rs.

No. 272.
[Blue slate. Fair condition. Symbol.]
In Memory of Mrs Hannah Samson wife of Mr Ebenezer Samson who died May 13 1702 in ye 72 year of her age.
No Pain, nor Grief no anxious Care nor Fear
Invade these sacred Bounds; No mortal Woes
Can reach or vex the pious Sleeper here
May Angels gently watch her soft repose

No. 273.
[This and the three following Nos. (273-276) are white marble inclosed with wooden fence. 273 is set in freestone socket. Is cleft from the base upward thro' the four lines of the epitaph.]
EMMA FRANCES, dau. of Ellis & Melinda Rogers, died March 6, 1865, Aged 16 y'rs 4 m's, & 6 days.
Our dear one is gone to the land where no care
Can ever approach her or trouble her there
Her Saviour has called her to enter the fold
Prepared for the righteous as promised of old.

No. 274.
[White marble in freestone socket.]
ELLIS ROGERS, Died Nov. 27, 1873. Aged 64 y'rs. 6 mo's.

No. 275.
[Cemented in granite base. Good condition.]
IRENE HARLOW, Dau. of Ellis & Melinda ROGERS, Died Aug. 16, 1880, Aged 25 yrs. 4 mos. 24 das.
Resting, sweetly resting.

No. 276.

[Granite base. Good condition.]

MELINDA Widow of ELLIS ROGERS, Died Sep. 13, 1882, Aged 67 yrs. 5 mos. 24 ds.

At Rest.

No. 277.

[Purplish slate. Pieces scaled off, but the cherub symbol and inscription are uninjured.]

(All capitals.)

Here lyes buried ye body of Mr Thomas Little Practitioner in Physick & Chyrurgery Aged 58 years Decd Decemr ye 22 1712

No. 278.

[Similar to 277, but the symbol is mostly gone.]

(In capital letters.)

Sarah Little Daugr to Charles & Sarah Little Aged 17 mo decd January ye 3d 1714.

No. 279.

[Blue slate. 3 ft. high. Good condition. Urn.]

Sacred To the memory of SUSANNA COBB wife of John K. Cobb who died Feby 20th 1809 in the 26 year of her age.

Here lies entomb'd within this house of clay
The mortal part of an engageing wife
Whose virtue shone amid the blaze of day
Whose kind affection ended with her life.

No. 280.

[Blue slate. Good condition. Fig. of mausoleum.]

Sacred to the Memory of CAPT. JOHN FAUNCE, who departed this life. June 19, 1831 : aged 46 years.

Gone to the resting place of man
His long his silent home
Where ages past have gone before
Where future ages come.

No. 281.

[Similar to 280.]

Sacred to the memory of HANNAH, consort of Capt. John Faunce, who departed this life May 19, 1850 : aged 40 years. Also two children

OLIVE JANE, died Nov,r 12, 1825 : aged 15 mon,s.

OLIVE JANE, died May 20, 1829 : aged 8 mon,s.

"Her end was full of peace,
Fitting her uniform piety serene,
T'was rather the deep humble calm of faith,
Than her high triumph.

No. 282.

[Blue slate. Many clefts and seams. Symbol uncommonly large.]

In Memory of Mrs Bathsheba May, ye widow of Mr John May who decd may ye 20th 1770 Aged 45 years.

4

No. 283.

[Blue slate. Good condition. Symbol.]

In Memory of Mr John May who decd Sept ye 4th 1769 Aged 46 years & 8 months.

No. 284.

[Low, blue slate. Inclined, broken and moss-grown.]

In Memory of William Son of Mr John May & Mrs Bersheba his wife who decd Augst ye 4th 1762 aged 13 days

No. 285.

[Blue slate; sound, but inclined and moss-grown.]

In Memory of Sarah May, Dautr of Mr John May, & Mrs Bersheba his wife, who Decd Sept ye 13th 1761 aged 2 years & 4 days.

No. 286.

[Low, blue slate, right hand corner at top broken off. Symbol. The capital N's in 286 and 287 have the diagonal line running in the wrong direction—imitated in first line of 286.]
(In capitals.)

Here lyes the body of IOII ʍ MAY who died August ye 7th 175 in ye 2d year of his age.

No. 287.

[Blue slate. Laminæ separating. Two clefts across face of stone. Symbol.]

IN Memory of BATHSHEBA MAY who died July ye 31 1753 IN ye 5 year of her age a Daughtr Mr JOHN MAY & Mrs BATHSHEBA his wife

No. 288.

[Blue slate. Laminæ cleaving apart. Cleft thro' at top. Symbol.]

IN MEMORY OF Mr JOHN MAY WHO DIED IUNE ye 3d 1754 IN ye 67th YEAR OF HIS AGE

No. 289.

[Blue slate. Good condition, but slightly inclined. Urn]

To the memory of Thomas May son of Mr John May & Mrs Mercy his wife who died Octr 1798 aged 18 years

No. 290.

[Blue slate. 3 ft. Sound. Weeping willow and urn.]

Consecrated to the memory of Mr David Lothrop who died November 1804 in the 56 year of his age. Also his Consort Mrs Bathsheba Lothrop who died Oct 1, 1817. in the 63 year of her age.

.No. 291.

[Blue slate. Good condition. Urn.]

In memory of Miss Polly Lothrop Daughter of Mr

David Lothrop and Mrs Bathsheba his wife who died July
12, 1809 in the 52 year of her age.

No. 292.

[Blue slate. Broken. Moss-grown.]

Here lyes ye body of Marcy Cook who decd Feby ye
8th 1714-5 in ye 30 year of her age

No. 293.

[Blue slate. Quite sound, but moss-grown. Symbol.]

Here lyes buried Roby Son of Nathani Goodwin &
Mrs Lydia his wife who died Decmr ye 5th 1761 Aged 4
months & 14 days.

No. 294.

[Low, blue slate. Slightly inclined. Some moss, but in fair condition. Symbol.]

Here lies buried Anna Daftr to Mr Nathaniel Goodwin
& Mrs Lydia his wife who Decd July ye 14th 1766 Aged
11 months 3 days.

No. 295.

[This monument is of a very different material from any previously
mentioned. In some respects it resembles sandstone; but some
specimens afterward met with, presented a laminated appearance.
The color is, in my opinion, a mixture of yellow and red. Similar
stones I shall designate by the name "Goodwin." A few inches
above the ground is a cleft extending nearly across the stone. The
surface of 295 is rough and moss-grown. At the top is a heraldic device, or coat-of-arms,—three lozenges above a shield on which is a
lion apparently walking along with an air of unconcern.]

Here lies buried the Body of Mr Nathaniel Goodwin
who departed this Life ye Twenty third day of May one
Thousand seven hundred and seventy one. In ye Forty
eight year of his age.

No. 296.

[Very thick, blue slate. Good condition. Urn.]

In memory of Mrs LYDIA GOODWIN Relict of Mr NA-
THANIEL GOODWIN Died March 24th 1801 aged 76 years

No. 297.

[Blue slate. Fractures at top. Otherwise in good condition.]

In memory of LAZARUS GOODWIN Esq. who died June
27th 1795 aged 42 years.

No. 298.

[Blue slate. 4 1-2 ft. Sound. Weeping willow and urn.]

In memory of Deac. Lot Harlow died Sept. 10th 1832
aged 64 years. Mary, Relict of Deac. Lot Harlow died
Sept. 21st 1832, aged 62 years. Stephen Harlow. their
son died Dec. 23d 1831, aged 25 years.

44   BURIAL HILL:

No. 299.

[White marble. Disintegrating. Cleft near upper right corner.]
HARRIET L. WATSON Died in Boston Mar. 24,
1853 Æ. 68 yrs.
>Grant unto her Oh Lord we beseech thee eternal rest.

Her husband WINSLOW WATSON Died at sea Dec.
17, 1816 Æ. 30 yrs.
>Their affectionate children
>Place this stone to their memory.

No. 300.

[Purple slate, with veins of lighter color across face. Top presents two semi-circles, each with symbol. Two inscriptions side by side.]

Here lyes buried the body of THOMAS LEWIS Son of Capt Philip & Mrs Martha Lewis who died April 6th Anno Domini 1732 in ye 22d Year of his Age.

Here lyes buried ye Body of Capt PHILIP LEWIS of Boston Who Died April 6 Anno Domini 1732 in ye 56 Year of his Age.

No. 301.

[Purplish-blue slate. Sound. Urn.]
In memory of MISS SARAH TUFTS who died April 18, 1844, aged 49 years

No. 302.

[Blue slate. A fissure at top threatens to remove about one-eighth of the stone, with part of the name. Urn.]
In memory of William Drew Tufts Son of Jona & Priscilla Tufts, Born Nov. 9 1791 Died at the Island of Cuba March 29 1811 aged Nineteen years.
>Green as the bay tree, ever green,
>With its new foliage on,
>The young, the healthful have I seen,
>I pass'd, and they were gone.

No. 303.

[White marble. set in reddish stone (which I term "freestone") base, with brimstone for cement. Weathers rough. Urn.]
In memory of Priscilla Tufts. Died April 9, 1870, Aged 73 years.

No. 304.

[Blue slate. Sound. Weeping willow and urn.]
In memory of MRS. PRISCILLA TUFTS, wife of MR. JONATHAN TUFTS, who died August 20, 1820, aged 55 years.

No. 305.

[Blue slate. Good condition, but slightly inclined. Weeping willow and urn.]

In memory of Mr Jonathan Tufts, who died January 19, 1821, aged 74 years.

No. 306.

[Blue slate. Lines of cleavage between laminæ are apparent, but the stone is yet in fair condition. Symbol.]

Here lies buried the body of Mrs Elizabeth Tufts wife of Mr Jonathan Tufts, who departed this Life Jany 12th 1786 Aged 39 years.

No. 307.

[Blue slate. Cleft on face threatens to remove about one-third of it. Portion of face scaled off.]

In Memory of Mrs Hannah Nicolson wife of Capt James Nicolson who died Sept. 24 1780 aged 75 years.

No. 308.

[White marble. Once very beautiful.]

In memory of ELIZABETH daughter of Thomas Nicolson born in Plymouth. July 11, 1777, died in Boston April 20, 1855 Æ. 77 years.

No. 309.

[Blue slate. Split across face, nearly in the middle, and at the right. Symbol.]

Here lies buried the Body of Capt. James Nicolson who departed this life August ye 4 1767 Aged 68 Years 1 Month & 7 days.

No. 310.

[White marble. On marble block which rests on granite. Base of monument cleft upward, several inches, in two places,—probably by expansion of dowel-pins, or freezing of water about them.]

IN MEMORIAM SARAH [Brinley] wife of Samuel Nicolson : Born in Boston May 23, 1798 ; Died in Cambridge Sept. 9, 1861.

Beloved and lamented.

SAMUEL NICOLSON Son of Thomas & Hannah [Otis] Nicolson. Born in Plymouth, Dec. 22, 1791, Died in Boston, Jan. 6, 1866.

No. 311.

[Similar to 308.]

In memory of LUCY MAYHEW daughter of Thomas Nicolson, Born in Plymouth, July 28, 1778, Died in Boston, Jan. 21, 1858.

No. 312.

[Blue slate. Cracked diagonally, nearly through central portion. Symbol.]

In Memory of Mrs SARAH NICOLSON, Consort of Capt THOMAS NICOLSON, who died Octr 24th 1788, in ye 36tn year of her age

No. 313.

[Blue slate. Tall, thick, and having the pyramidal outlines, which were in vogue here a while before and after the opening of the present century. Sound. Inscription within figure of urn.]

The remains of Mr Daniel Nicolson, who was born March 11, 1796, and who died March 6, 1815 are here Intered.

No. 314.

[White marble. Similar to 310, but is in better condition.]

In memory of CAPT. THOMAS NICOLSON who died and was buried in the island of Guadaloupe February 9, 1798 ; in the fiftieth Year of his age. Also of HAN-NAH, his wife, daughter of John Otis of Barnstable ; who died in Boston, June 22, 1844, and whose remains are here interred.

No. 315.

[This No. is blue slate, standing a few feet from the monument which "marks where the watch house was erected in 1643." Good condition. Festoons of curtains with tassels form an upper border.]

This Stone Consecrated to the memory Of the Revd Chandler Robbins D D was erected By the inhabitants of the first Religious Society in Plymouth As their last grateful tribute of respect For his eminent labors In the ministry Of JESUS CHRIST Which commenced January 30th 1760 And continued till his death June 30th 1799 Ætatis 61 When he entered into the everlasting rest Prepared for the faithful embassadors Of the most high God.

Ah come heaven's radiant Offspring hither throng
Behold your prophet your Elijah fled
Let sacred simphony attune each tongue
To chant hosannas with the virtuous dead

No. 316.

[Similar to 315.]

This Stone consecrated to the memory of Madam JANE ROBBINS consort of the late Revd Dr ROBBINS who languished from his death 30th June 1799 till 12th September 1800 when in the 60th year of her age She commenced her inseparable union with her much beloved

Husband and her God is erected by the Piety of her afflicted children.

Unfading Hope when Life's last embers burn,
When soul to soul, and dust to dust return,
Heav'n to thy charge resigns the awful hour
Oh, then thy Kingdom comes immortal Power.

No. 317.

[Blue slate,—purplish. Piece broken from top, taking part of the symbol. Otherwise in good condition.]

Here lies ye Body of HANNAH ROBBINS Daur of the Revd Mr CHANDLER & Mrs JANE ROBBINS. Decd July 17th 1766 Aged 10 months

No. 318.

[White marble. On granite base, with lead. Good condition. Hand holding a sickle whose edge is against a stalk of grain.]
"The Reapers are the Angels."
"As a shock of corn in his season."

REV. JAMES KENDALL, D. D. Ordained 1 Jan. 1800. Died 17 March 1859. Aged 89 years. For sixty years Minister of the First Parish in this town.

No. 319.

[Blue slate. 6 ft. Good condition.]

Consecrated to the Memory of Mrs Sarah Kendall, amiable consort of Reverend James Kendall Who departed this life Feby 13th 1809, In the 33d year of her age ; Leaving to her surviving friends The best consolation, —The remembrance of her virtues In life ; Her pious calmness, christian resignation & triumphant hope In death.

"Blessed are the dead who die in the Lord ; yea, saith the Spirit ;
For they rest from their labors, and their works do follow them."
Revelation.

Also their Infant Elizabeth, who died Dec. 14th 1808, aged 13 days.

"It is not the will of your Father which is in heaven
"That one of these little ones should perish."
Christ.

No. 320.

[Blue slate. Moss-grown. Weeping willow and urn.]

In memory of Lydia, youngest daughter of Reverend James Kendall who died March 21, 1810, aged three years.

Suffer the little children, and forbid them not, to come unto me ; for of such is the kingdom of heaven.

No. 321.

[When a boy I much admired what was then a most beautiful white marble monument, and whenever I crossed the hill, was accustomed to go out of my way to see it. Instead of the Medusa-like head supplied with wings, or even a questionable "cherubic" face, this presented drapery of curtains, arranged in gracefully curving folds. On my return to Plymouth two or three years ago, I sought for this stone unsuccessfully, and supposed it had been removed to Oak Grove. Some time after, I happened to be on Burial Hill at an hour in the morning when the sun's rays threw the incised letters into shadow, when, lo! the familiar name and brief inscription reappeared, though scracely legible. The only words on the stone which can be read at any time are the two in the epitaph "may endure"—which have no possible reference to white marble. A V-shaped portion is gone from the top at centre; the monument is gray, and wasting away, grain by grain. It is to be regretted that this same material, apparently from the same quarry, has been so extensively employed here. Eighty years is a longer period than white marble can be expected to endure; it is but seventy years since my boyish fancy was charmed with the beauty of 321,— now unread and unobserved.]

Miss Irene Thomson died January 3, 180 [0 or 9?] Aged 53 years

Weeping may endure for a night, but joy cometh in the morning.

No. 322.

[Fine, blue slate. Cleavage has removed about one-half of the thickness of the stone. The front portion appears compact and sound.]

In memory of Mr George D. Thomson Attorney at Law who died April 2, 1798 aged 24 years.

Till the great Rising Day this Dust must lie
Which loudly speaks Reader prepare to die.

No. 323.

[This No. and the following to 327 inclusive, a row of low blue slates, are monuments of the Howes family. All are legible, though moss-grown. All have the cherub, or winged symbol, and three have the crossbones supraposed.]

In Memory of Miss Meriah Dautr of Mr Jeremiah & Mrs Hannah Howes who died Decr 2d 1776 in ye 15th Year of her Age.

No. 324.

[Inscription wholly in capitals, except superior letters. Low, blue slate.]

Here lies the body of Sarah Howes Daughter of Mr Jeremiah Howes & Mrs Moriah his wife who decd Decer ye 1 th 1756 in her 6th year of her age.

No. 325.

[Low, blue slate—inscription in capitals.]

Here lies the body of Moriah Howes Daughter of Mr Jeremiah Howes & Mrs Moriah his wife who decd May ye 31st 1755 in her 13th year of her age.

No. 326.

[Capitals; a low, blue slate.]

Here lies the Body of EBENEZER HOWES Son of Mr Jeremiah Howes & Mrs Moriah his wife who decd Novemr ye 7th 1757 in the 16th year of his age.

No. 327.
[Broken and somewhat defaced.]

r lies ye body of Mrs Meriah Howes ye wife of Mr Jeremiah Howes who departed this life Febry ye 14th 1757 in her 45th year of her age

No. 328.
[This No. and the following to 332 inclusive, are inclosed in a low granite border. 328 is directly on a marble block which rests on a granite base. Good condition, except the marble block on which the monument rests.]

Charles Tufts, Born July 29, 1803, Died Jan 22, 1871.
"Blessed are the dead which die in the Lord."

No. 329.
[White marble. Discolored.]

CORDELIA B. wife of Charles Tufts, died June 20, 1840: Aged 32 Years. CHARLES HENRY, Son of Charles & Cordelia B. Tufts, died July 15, 1841; Aged 2 years.

No. 330.
[Fine, blue slate. Willow, carved on left side of stone, spreads its branches over the whole inscription. Good condition.]

JAMES W. died Feb. 10, 1830, aged 2 months. MARY JANE, died Aug. 20, 1833 aged 13 months. Children of Charles & Cordelia B. Tufts.

No. 331.
[White marble. Discolored.]

EMMA CORDELIA daughter of Charles & Cordelia B. Tufts died Mar. 19, 1859, aged 22 y'rs.

No. 332.
[Similar to 331.]

Sarah Elizabeth. daughter of Charles & Cordelia B. Tufts, died July 3, 1859, aged 24 years.

No. 333.
[Blue slate. Good condition. Weeping willow and urn.]

In memory of Cyrus Cole, son of the Rev. Timothy & Susan Cole, who died Sept. 28, 1832, aged 4 weeks.

No. 334.
[White marble, weatherworn. Inscription scarcely legible.]

In memory of Sarah W. Nelson Daughter of Stephen S. and Esther Nelson who died Mar. 6, 1821 aged 3 years 3 months and 24 days

Sweet flower soon nip'd
Be ye also ready

5

No. 335.

[Blue slate. Sculptured as in 330. Cracked diagonally from upper right to lower left hand corner.]

LORRAIN H. Dau. of Luke P. & Stella Lincoln died May 31, 1834, aged 1 year & 8 mon.

No. 336.

[White marble. Granite base. Good condition.]

Mercy C. wife of Samuel Elliot died July 8, 1878, Aged 71 yrs.

No. 337.

[Blue Slate. Good condition.]

CLARISSA, wife of Samuel Elliot, died Jan. 27, 1835, aged 39 years. Also an Infant Son.

No. 338.

[White marble, 4 feet in height. Good condition.]

ERECTED to the memory of JOHN B. CHANDLER, who died March 4, 1846, aged 61 yrs.

———

Also his wife HANNAH, died Nov. 5, 1845, aged 58 yrs.

———

Into thine hand, O GOD of truth,
Our spirits we commit.

No. 339.

[Blue slate. Weeping willow and urn. Good condition.]

In memory of 3 Children of Mr. John B. Chandler and Mrs. Hannah his wife viz. John T. Chandler died December 11th 1820 aged 6 months and 21 days Lucy S. Chandler died December 29th 1820 aged 5 years 11 months and 13 days Hannah B. Chandler died January 13th 1821 aged 4 years 6 months and 13 days

Their souls are gone to Heaven we trust,
God called them home he thought it best.

No. 340.

[Blue slate. Stone nearly square. Good condition.]

In memory of PHYLANDER SAMPSON, who died May 18, 1847, Æt. 36 years. Also two children of Phylander and Sarah A. Sampson, Sarah E. died April 18, 1845, Æt. 4 y'rs 3 mo. Albert L. died May 6, 1845, Æt. 6 y'rs 2 mo.

Calm be the spot where their forms now repose,
May the friends who so loved them revisit the grave,
And feel though the cold sod their ashes enclose,
They live in the presence of him who can save.

No. 341.

[Blue slate. Cleft across the middle of surface lamina.]

In Memory of Hannah Hosea Wife of Mr. Daniel Hosea who decd March ye 17th 1773 in ye 24th year of her age. Daughtr of Dean Joseph Bartlett

No. 342.

[Low, blue slate. Surface slightly abraded. Fair condition.]

Here lies buried Daniel Son to Mr Daniel Hosea & Mrs Hannah his wife Born Jany 29th 1769 decd Sept ye 27th 1777

No. 343.

[Blue slate, 4 ft. high. Good condition.]

Erected In Memory of PAMELIA, wife of SAMUEL ROBBINS, Jr. who died Sept,r 5, 1833 : age 50 yr,s. Also their sons, Edward, died Nov,r 5, 1802 aged 5 mos. Adoniram died March 16, 1815 : aged 6 mos. Lewis F. died Feb,y 14, 1824 Aged 11 mos.

No. 344.

[Small, square white stone; material, that of Miss Irene Thomson's monument (No. 321), and, like that, rapidly disintegrating, and very difficult to read. Some words or sculpture may have been in what is now a wide vacant space at top; but all that is legible begins with a small "d."]

·died Aug 4th 1832 Georgiana Minerva daughter of C. J. & C. W. Warren, aged 14 years.

Here sleep, sweet daughter, all alone;
With aching hearts we leave thee,
To the our sorrows are not known,
Nor can our absence grieve thee.

No. 345.

[White marble. Top checked. Discolored.]

In memory of JAMES BAXTER, who died Dec. 11, 1843, aged 52 years. And three of his children. Abner Morton died Aug. 29, 1826, aged 3 ; Charles Homer died Aug. 29, 1843, aged 8 ; Ann Elizabeth died June 29, 1844, aged 5 years.

No. 346.

[In a railed inclosure with with 347. White marble. 5 ft. high. Discolored. Weeping willow and urn.]

Sacred to the memory of MRS. ABIGAIL widow of the late Rev. Adoniram Judson who died Jan. 31, 1842, aged 82 years.

Her hope was in the Gospel of our Lord and Saviour Jesus Christ. She felt the balm and efficacy of those leaves which are for the healing of the nations.

A guilty weak and helpless worm,
On thy kind arms I fall
Be thou my guide and righteousness
My Jesus and my all.

52

No. 347.

[A large slab of white marble, placed horizontally on six columns resting on freestone, and inclosed by a neat white fence. Good condition.]
Sacred to the memory of Rev. ADONIRAM JUDSON, who died Nov. 28, 1826, Æ. 75. A faithful and devoted Minister of Christ.
ELNATHAN JUDSON, M. D. who died at Washington City May 8, 1829, Æ. 34 years. ANN H. JUDSON, his dau. died May 30, 1832, Æ. 7 years. ELLEN YOUNG, his wife, died Nov. 25, 1832, Æ. 30 y'rs. ANN H. JUDSON, Missionary to Burmah, who died at Amherst, B. E. Oct. 24, 1826, Æ. 37 yrs ROGER W. JUDSON, died May 4, 1816, Æ. 8 yrs. MARIA E. B. JUDSON, died April 24, 1827, Æ. 2 yrs. 3 mo. SARAH B. JUDSON. Missionary to Burmah, who died in the port of St. Helena, Sept. 1, 1845, Æ. 42 y'rs. ADONIRAM JUDSON, D. D. Missionary of the American Baptist Missionary Union to the Burman Empire, who died at Sea, April 12, 1850, Æ. 62 years. EMILY C. widow of Adoniram Judson D. D. & Missionary to Burmah, died June 1, 1854, Æ. 37 y'rs. ABIGAIL BROWN JUDSON, born in Malden, March 21, 1791, died in Plymouth, Jan. 25, 1884.

No. 348.

[White marble. Moss-grown on upper part. Weathering rough. Weeping willow and urn.]
In memory of ELIZABETH, wife of the Rev. Frederick Freeman, who died March 12, 1833, aged 33 years, Leaving her husband and five children to deplore their loss and cherish the dear remembrance of her worth.

Her children rise up, and call her blessed; her husband also, and he praiseth her.

No. 349.

[Low, white marble. Rough. Weeping willow and urn.]
Frederick Russel son of F. & E. Freeman died Feb. 1, 1825, aged 17 days.

No. 350.

[White marble, cemented in marble base. Good condition, but slightly inclined.]
ALBERT R. ROBBINS Co. E. 29 Mass. Reg't. Died Mar. 5, 1864 Aged 22 y'rs 5 m's 23 days.

No. 351.

[[Blue slate. Moss-grown. Symbol, resembling winged skull.]
Here lyes ye Body of Mrs Lydia Bartlett wife to Mr Benjn Bartlett SHE decd October ye 21st 1739 in ye 37th year of her age.

No. 352.

[Blue slate; part of inscription gone.]

Here lies buried the body of Thomas Bartlett who departed this life Sept ye 28th 17 in ye 71st year of his age.

No. 353.

[Blue slate; figures denoting age broken off. Full of clefts and falling to pieces. About one half of the symbol remains.]

Here lies buried the Body of Mrs Abigail Bartlett ye wife of Mr Thomas Bartlett who departed this life march ye 14th 1765 in ye   year of her Age.

No. 354.

[Purple slate. Fissure on left hand part of surface, but in fair condition otherwise. Symbol.]

Here lyes ye body of Mr Robert Bartlet died January the 3d 1718 in ye 55th year of his age.

No. 355.

[Light blue slate. Laminae separating. Moss-grown. Symbol.]

Hannah dautr to Samuel & Mrs Elizabeth Bartlett his wife decd April ye 21st 1739 aged 8 months & 6 days

No. 356.

[Purple slate. Inclined, but in good condition for so old a monument. Symbol.]

Here lyes buried ye body of Margaret dautr to Mr Samuel & Mrs Elizabeth Bartlet decd April ye 25th Anno 1729 Aged 1 year & 3 days

No. 357.

[Blue slate. Cleavage lines opening. Moss-grown. Face of stone unbroken.]

Here lyes ye body of Margtt daugtr of Samll Bartlett Esqr. & Elizath his wife born April ye 13th 1737 decd Decbr ye 31st 1739.

No. 358.

[Low, thick, light blue slate. Broader at top than at the ground. Good condition. Symbol.]

Here lyeth buried ye body of Joseph Bartlett who departed this life April ye 9th 1703 in ye 38th year of his age

[The footstone of 358 is about twenty feet from the headstone, in a N. E. direction, and on the other side of the concrete walk. It bears the following inscription:]

J.   B.

Thousands of years after blest Abell's fall
Twas said of him being dead he speakth yet
From silent grave methinks I hear a call
Pray fellow-mortall, don't your death forget
　　　You that your eyes cast on this grave
　　　Know you a dying time must have.

No. 359.

[Dark blue slate, as good as new. Symbol.]

Here lyes buried the Body of ELIZABETH BART-
LETT the daughter of Samuel Bartlett Esqr & Elizabeth
his wife. born Augt 25th 1725 : died Septr 30th 1746.

No. 360.

[Purplish slate, handsomely wrought. Symbol under crossbones.]

Here lyes buried the Body of Mrs ELIZABETH
BARTLETT the virtuous wife of SAMUEL BARTLETT
Esqr and daughter to the Honble ISAAC LOTHROP
Esqr (Decd) & ELIZABETH his wife departed this life
Novr the 1st 1745, in the 41st year of Her age and lies
inter'd by 3 of her Children only one child surviving.

No. 361.

[Broad, light blue slate. Defaced a little, and slightly inclined.
Symbol under crossbones.]

Here lies buried ye Body of Samuell Bartlett Esqr who
departed this Life March ye 25th 1769 Aged 72 years

No. 362.

[Dark blue slate. Good condition, but slightly inclined. Symbol.]

In Memory of Mrs ELIZABETH BARTLETT Relict of SAM-
UEL BARTLETT *Esqr* who died March 29 1793 in ye 77 year
of her age.

No. 363.

[Fine, blue slate. Good condition. Weeping willow and urn.]

In memory of Mr William Doten who died Octr 12,
1813, in the 63 year of his age Also his wife Mrs Jain
Doten died May 14 1813 in the 58 year of her age.

No. 364.

[Thick, blue slate. Four feet in height. Good condition. Weeping
willow and urn.]

Erected to the memory of Mrs. Betsey Bartlett, wife of
Mr. Eleazer S. Bartlett who died May 9, 1832, in the 25th
year of her age.

> My soul, my body I will trust
> With him who numbers every dust,
> My Saviour faithfully will keep
> His own, their death is but a sleep.

No. 365.

[Fine, blue slate. Good condition. Figure of mausoleum,—a square
structure, surmounted by three pyramids.]

Erected to the memory. of Miss SARAH WHIT-

MARSH, of Boston. who died Sept. 19th, 1841, in the
64th. y.r of her age.

She was beloved by all who knew her
worth.

No. 366.

[Thick, blue slate. Solid, but moss-grown.]

In memory of Mr JOSEPH HOWLAND who Died Septr
6th 1806 in the 56 year of his age.

No. 367.

[This and No. 368 are white marble in freestone sockets. Inclosed
with iron fence. Good condition.]

WILLIAM DREW, Born Sept. 21, 1779, Died Dec.
16, 1839.

No. 368.

[Described with preceding No.]

PRISCILLA WASHBURN, wife of William Drew,
Born Dec. 7, 1786, Died Sept. 21, 1858

No. 369.

[This No. and 370, 371, are white marble, and are inclosed with a
wooden fence. 369 discolored in spots.]

SUSAN BRADFORD wife of HAMBLEN TILLSON
departed this life December 11, 1837 in the 58th year of
her age.

No. 370.

[Similar to 369.]

HAMBLIN TILLSON departed this life August 16,
1830, in the 70th year of his age.

No. 371.

[White marble. Good condition.]

MARIA TILLSON, Daughter of Hamblin & Susan B.
TILLSON, Born July 24, 1822, Died Sept. 23, 1856.

Rest with the loved ones above.

No. 372.

[Small, white marble. Weatherworn. Very difficult to read.
Moss-grown.]

John Howland Son of William & E. P. Hammatt of
Howland, in the State of Maine, was born 11 Oct. 1824,
and died 15 August, 1825

(Footstone reads "J. H. 1825.")

No. 373.

[Same defaced condition as 372.]

Abraham Son of William Hammatt & Esther P. his

wife was born 21st January A. D. 1811 and died 16th
April following.

Of such is the Kingdom of God.
(Footstone reads "A. Hammatt 1811.")

No. 374.

[Thick, blue slate. Has broken in two, and the upper part is set in
the ground; of course the inscription is partly out of sight. For the
nonce, I removed a portion of the earth in front, and found the
legend to begin as follows:]

Sacred to the memory of Mrs. Priscilla Hammatt widow
of Capt Abraham Hammatt

No. 375.

[Dark blue slate. Good condition. Symbol.]

In This sacred spot Are deposited the remains of Capt
Abraham Hammatt who died of a malignant Fever October 12th 1797 *Ætatis* 47 And of his daughter Sophia
who on the fst December following Fell a victim to the
same Disease *Ætatis* 13.

Hers was the mildness of the rising Morn
And his the radiance of the risen day.

No. 376.

[Tall and wide, blue slate. Fair condition, save a cleft from the
ground upward. When Bradford's manuscript history of Plymouth
Plantation was discovered in England in the year 1855, the statement
on this stone that Elizabeth Howland "was the dau tr of Gov. Carver" was shown to be erroneous. She was the daughter of John
Tilley, one of the Mayflower Company. The correction should be
made, lest the thought "Here lies the body" be exchanged for "Here
lies the stone."

Here ended the Pilgrimage of JOHN HOWLAND and
ELIZABETH his wife. She was the dau.tr of Gov.
Carver. They arrived in the Mayflower, Dec. 1620.
They had 4 Sons and 6 dau.trs from whom are descended
a numerous posterity. "1672 Feb.y 23. John Howland
of Plymouth deceased he lived to the age of 80 yr.s. He
was the last man that was left of those that came over
in the ship called the Mayflower that lived in Plymouth."

Plymouth Records.

[By the side of No. 376 is a wooden slab on which are the words:]

The grave of John Howland.   Died Feb. 25, 1672.

No. 377.

[Light blue slate. Flawy. Slightly inclined backward. Human
figure carved at top.]

This Stone is erected to the Memory of Capt. Abraham
Hammatt, who departed this Life June 23d and in the
year of our Lord 1774 Ætatis 55.

No. 378.

[Blue slate. Thick, firm, but moss-grown. Slightly inclined forward. Urn.]

To the memory of Mrs. Lucy Hammatt Relict of the late Capt. A. Hammatt who died April 30th 1803 Ætatis 77.

Composed in suffering, and in joy sedate,
Good without show, for just discernment great.

No. 379.

[Blue slate. Good condition. Symbol.]

In memory of Mr. Consider Howland who departed this life Augt 8th 1759 aged 60 years.

No. 380.

[Blue slate. Good condition. Draped curtains with tassels.]

In memory of Mrs Ruth Howland Relict of Mr Consider Howland who departed this life Jan. 11 1775 aged 61 years.

No. 381.

[Low, blue slate. Mossy and slightly defaced. Symbol (partly gone).]

Consider Son to Consider and Mrs Ruth Howland died Febry ye 16th 1742-3 Aged 7 years & 16 days

No. 382.

[Blue slate. Cracked, and laminæ opened. Symbol.]

Joseph Son of Mr Consider & Mrs Ruth Howland He died May ye 11th 1742 Aged 3 mo & 3 days

No. 383.

[Blue slate. Fair condition for so old a monument. Symbol,—above which the words "Sic transit mundi."]

To the memory of Mrs Hannah Howland who died of a Languishment, January ye 25th 1780 Ætatis 26.

For us they languish, & for us they die
And shall they languish shall they die in vain.

No. 384.

[Low, blue slate, moss-covered. Symbol.]

In memory of Joannah Howland who departed this life feby 29 1799 aged 62 years

No. 385.

[Blue slate. Sound, but moss-grown. Symbol.]

In memory of Thomas Southworth Howland who departed this life Octr 15th 1779 aged 45 years In memory of Consider Howland who was lost at sea Octr 1780 aged 35 years.

No. 386.

[Blue slate. Broken; defaced; moss-grown.]

Capt.   THOMAS HOWLAND

DECD   1739

No. 387.

[Low, thick, blue slate (South of concrete walk). About 1-4 broken off, and gone, from right hand side,—remainder cleft downward through middle. Symbol.]

Here lyes ye body of Joseph Church Aged 25 years Died October ye 13 1707

No. 388.

[Low, blue slate. Weatherworn. Symbol.]

Lois Dautr to John & Lois Holmes his wife died Septbr ye 11th 1736 aged 20 months

No. 389.

[Blue slate. Good condition. Weeping willow and urn.]

In memory of Mrs Mary Bartlett who died November 5, 1810 aged 89 years and 9 months.

No. 390.

[Thick, blue slate. Sound. Symbol.]

To the memory of Mr Lemuel Bartlett who departed this life May 29 1792 Ætatis 77

> With silent steps he meekly trac'd the way
> To the bright realms of love his wish'd abode
> Nor did he ask a moment's longer stay
> When the last summons called his soul to god.

No. 391.

[Low, purple slate. Good condition. Symbol.]

Here lyes ye body of Lothrop Bartlett son to Samuel & Elizabeth Bartlett, aged 6 weeks Decd Sepr ye 27 1723.

No. 392.

[White marble. Discolored. Moss-grown. Inscription fading out, as it were.]

Sacred to the memory of JANE, wife of Frederick Robbins who died Oct. 11, 1841, aged 88 yrs 1 mo. and 11 days.

Hannah Harlow, dau. of the above died May 27, 1838, aged 1 yr & 11 days.

> When the Christian's race is run.
> Tho' low she slumbers in the ground,
> Her virtues, like the setting sun,
> Shall shed a heavenly lustre round.

No. 393.

[Low, blue slate. Good condition. Symbol.]

Jenney Daur to Mr John & Mrs Sarah Bartlett died Septr 16th 1749 in ye 10th year of her age.

No. 394.

[Blue slate. Very little moss upon it. Symbol.]

Here lyes ye body of Mary Bartlett daur to Mr John & Mrs Sarah Bartlett who died Augt 16th 1748 in ye 18th year of her age.

No. 395.

[Blue slate. Bad condition,—it being cracked and broken. Part of symbol remains.]

Here lies ye body of Sarah Bartlet wife to John Bartlet Decd Seper ye 28th 1731 in ye 30th year of her age.

No. 396.

[Low, dark colored stone, protected by an iron hood.]

Jerusha Bartlet Dautr to John & Sarah Bartlet his wife decd July ye 9th 1732 in ye 9th year of her age.

No. 397.

[This No. and Nos. 398 and 399 are similar blue slates, side by side, each 4 1-2 ft. high. All are in good condition, save that 397 and 399 are moss-grown. Each has the figure of weeping willow and urn.]

In memory of CAPT. SAMUEL ROBBINS who died July 27, 1838, aged 86 years.

No. 398.

[See No. 397.]

In memory of SARAH, wife of Capt. Samuel Robbins, who died Dec. 31, 1834, aged 76 years.

No. 399.

[See No. 397.]

Sacred to the memory of Miss SALLY C. ROBBINS dau'r of Capt. Samuel & Mrs. Sarah Robbins. She deceased by a fall from a chaise, Aug. 14, 1828, aged 25 years, 5 mo's and 10 days.

Our home is in the grave;
Here dwells the multitude; we gaze around,
We read their monuments, we sigh and while
we sigh, we sink.

No. 400.

[Low, blue slate. Upper and right hand portions chipped off.]

In memory   4 children of Mr
Samuel & Mr   viz Samuel died
Sepr 28 1777   Isaac died Sepr 14,
1783 aged 5   died Sepr 25, 1786
aged 1 year   1791 aged 9 months
& 19 days.

No. 401.

[Blue slate. 3 1-2 feet high. Good condition.]

In memory of Mr. WILLIAM DREW 2d Died Nov.r 7, 1829, aged 45 y.rs.

Our life how short! a groan, a sigh;
We live—and then begin to die;
But oh! how great a mercy this,
That death's a portal into bliss.

No. 402.

[Blue slate. 3 ft. Good condition.]

MRS. SARAH SHERMAN Died Dec. 20, 1861, aged
76 y'rs 1 mo. 2 days.

No. 403.

[Purple slate. Sound. Protected by an iron hood. Symbol. (Next
in age to the oldest stone on the hill.)]

HERE LIES BURIED YE BODY OF MR WILLIAM
CROWE AGED About 55 YEARS WHO DECD JAN-
UARY 1683-4.

No. 404.

[Purple slate. Sound. Symbol.]

Here lyes ye body of Mrs Hannah Sturtevant aged
about 64 years decd in March 1708-9.

No. 405.

[Purple slate. Good condition. Protected by metallic hood. Symbol.]

Here lyes buried the body of Mrs Jemima Samson wife
to Mr Lazarus Samson decd July ye 20 1731 in ye 27th
year of her age

No. 406.

[Thick, blue slate. Fair condition, but laminæ are separating.]

Here lies buried Mr John Sturtevant who died February 4th 1752 Aged about 92 years & 5 months

No. 407.

[Blue slate. Weatherworn. Somewhat broken and defaced.]

Here lyes ye body of William Ring who decd sum time
in April 1729 in ye 77th year of his age.

No. 408.

[Blue slate. Quite sound. Inclined. Symbol.]

Here lyes ye body of Eleazar Ring who decd Feby ye
3d 1734 in ye 31st year of his age.

No. 409.

[Blue slate. Weatherworn. Symbol. This and the two preceding Nos. are on or near the northern line of the site of the Watch-
house of 1643.]

Here lyes ye body of William Ring who decd Decbr ye
25th 1728 in ye 31st year of his age

No. 410.

[White marble. Fair condition. Is inclosed in the same paling
with 225.]

In memory of Elon S. Daugh'r of Robert & Keziah D.
Swinburn, who died July 27, 1855, Aged 10 y'rs and 6
d'ys. Also an infant Son.

For thee this heart shall beat,
For thee these tears shall flow;
And thy fond name I'll repeat
When sad with many a woe.

No. 411.

[Slate. Face of stone much scaled off. (Absence of words is indicated by space.) Symbol.]

Gray Dautr to   & Jo
a   Gray His Wife   March
17th 1703-4   ye   year of   her age.

No. 412.

[Blue slate. At top the words:]

Memento mori.

[Under which is the symbol,—a winged face.]

In memory of Mrs Selah Wife of Mr Pelham Bradford. She died Novr 29th 1801 Aged 22 Years 1 month & 7 Days

No. 413.

[Blue slate. Right upper corner of face of stone slivered off. Symbol.]

Here lyes ye Bod   of Mrs. Hannah Dyr   who decd Octor ye 27th 1731 Aged about 22 1-2 She was late wife to Captn Willm Dyer formerly wife to Captn Tomson Phillips who was drowned at sea Decbr ye 16th 1729

[Footstone, large; is inscribed:]

Mrs Hannah Dyre Decd 1731

No. 414.

[Slate. Broken and defaced.]

Samuel H   Josiah ye   n John Cotton   Josiah Anonymus Edward Josiah Edward Richard Roland 7 sons of Josiah Cotton who died between ye year 1712 & 1734

No. 415.

[Slate. Weatherworn. Crossbones over symbol.]

Here lyes the Body of The Honble JOSIAH COTTON ESQ. Who Died August 19th 1756 Aged 76 years and 7 months

(The footstone reads:)

The Honble JOSIAH COTTON Esqr 1756

No. 416.

[Slate. Crossbones over symbol—a winged skull.]

Here lyes ye Body of Mrs HANNAH COTTON Wife of JOSIAH COTTON Esq. Who Died May 27th 1756 Aged 69 years and 1 month.

No. 417.

[Dark blue slate. Good condition. Weeping willow and urn.]

In memory of Mary Atwood Collier daughter of Ezra & Mary S. Collier who died August 28, 1826: Aged 10 months & 5 days.

Of such is the kingdom of heaven.

No. 418.

[White marble. Very fair condition.]

Jane Wight Dau. of Bradford L. & Nancy Battles, died Sept. 4, 1840, Aged 4 years and 5 months.

No. 419.

[Blue slate. Similar in form to 146 and 358. Fissures opening. Symbol.]

Joseph Son   Mr Abiel & Mrs Bethiah Pulsifor his wife departed this life Decr 28th 1733 Aged 3 weeks

No. 420.

[Blue slate. Weatherworn. Moss-covered. Left upper corner broken. Symbol.]

e lyes inteid ye body of Mrs Bethiah Pulsifer wife to Mr Abiel Pulsifer who died Sepbr ye 25th 1736 Aged 21 years 3 months and 7 days

No. 421.

[Blue slate. Broken at top. Part of wing of the cherub symbol remains. The surface in which is the inscription, does not appear to be at all abraded. The grave is a very short one; evidently that of a young child. I think that neither the name of the child, nor the word "son" or "daughter" was ever engraved on the stone; and there is an unoccupied space after the word "Aged" The footstone has at the right the letter "P." There is no initial for a Christian name.]

		TO
Mr		s
AbIAL	&	MR
BETHIAH		PULΓIFER
		d
HIS	WIFE	DEC
	e	th
JANUARY	y	6
		6
I	7 5	5
AGED		

No. 422.

[White marble, set in freestone. Good condition. This stone is unique in the omission of dates and ages. The persons named were well known to elderly people now living,—1897.]

Father & Mother. William C. Nye. Betsey Nye. Ann H. Nye.

Arise, let us go to our Father.

No. 423.

[White marble. Slightly inclined; otherwise in good condition.]

Henry Rickard, Died Dec. 18, 1867, Aged 36 y'rs 10 mo's 20 days.

No. 424.

[White marble, set in granite. Good condition.]

Zilpah, wife of Henry Rickard, Died May 8, 1880, Aged 50 y'rs 9 mo's. 18 days.
Divided below. United above.

No. 425.

[Blue slate. Good condition. Symbol.]

To the memory of Capt John Harlow who died June 29th 1775 aged 44 years.

No. 426.

[Light blue slate. Badly cracked. Moss-grown. Inclined backward. Symbol.]

Here lyes the body of ye Re7d Mr Ward Cotton late Minister of ye Gospel at Hampton who died at Plymouth Novr ye 27 1768 aged 57 years 2 Months & 8 days.

No. 427.

[Blue slate. Dilapidated. Cleft from top downward. At top, a rude carving of the human figure.]

In memory of Isaac Totman who died March ye 20th 1740 Aged 13 months & 9 days Son of Mr Simeon & Mrs Sarah Totman.

No. 428.

[Blue slate. Part of wing of symbol gone. Inscription scaled off, except the beginning of lines.]

Her   th   Hann   to Mr   Decd   in the

No. 429.

[Low, wide, blue slate. Symbol.]

Here lyes buried ye Bodyes of NATHANIEL & LUCE THOMAS Children to Nathaniel Thomas Esqr & Elizabeth his wife NATHANIEL Born Oct 17th 1742 Dyed June 10th 1743 LUCE Born Decmr 5th 1743 Dyed 18th Instant.

No. 430.

[A high, broad stone, of very dark purple slate, about one-third of the face, on the right, split off and gone. At top, a portion of the symbol remains. The engraving, as on all the most ancient stones, is in capital letters. This stone is remarkable as being one of the six old monuments bearing dates in the 17th century:]

Here lyes   ter   children   z   Sons of   r
John Cotton died in th   of the   pel Ministry
town in   Carolina Sepr   169   where he had

succe　　　and 7　　　　R　　Sons　　　f Josiah Cotton
Esqr who deceas'd　　in their infancy.

[A copy of the whole inscription, as originally cut on the stone No.
430, has been kindly furnished the author by EDGAR F. RAYMOND,
Esq., who often saw the monument when it was in fair condition. It
is as follows:]

Here lyes interred ten children viz three sons of Revd
Mr John Cotton who died in the work of the gospel ministry at Charlestown in South Carolina Sept 18th 1699
where he had great success and seven sons of Josiah Cotton Esq who deceas'd in their infancy

No. 431.

[Small, blue slate.　Part broken off, on the right, but inscription entire.　Symbol.]

Mary ye daughter of Nathaniel Thomas Esqr & Mary
his wife died ye 3 of April 1744 in ye 5 year of her age

No. 432.

[Small, low, blue slate.　Edges marred.　Over the symbol are two
letters, the first of which appears to be a "W," the second a "G."]

William son of Nathaniel Thomas Esqr & Mary his
wife dyed ye 23 of iune 1714 in 11 day of his age.

No. 433.

[White marble.　3 ft. in height.　Weeping willow and urn.]

In memory of Mrs. Lucy Goodwin, who died January
28, 1818, in the 68th year of Her age.

No. 434.

[White marble.　3 ft. high.　Willow and urn.]

In memory of Mr. Timothy Goodwin, who died January 24, 1817, in the 70 year of his age

No. 435.

[Blue slate.　Fair condition.　Symbol.]

Here lyes buried 2 sons to Mr. Nathaniel & Mrs Hope
Thomas his wife ye 1st decd Jany 26 1726-7 aged 23 mons
21 days ye 2d son decd Feby ye 27 1726-7 aged 31 days.

(The footsone reads:)
Nathll Thomas & Nathll Thomas

No. 436.

[Purple slate.　Good condition.　Handsome border.　Symbol.]

Here lyes ye body of Mrs Hope Thomas wife to Mr
Nathaniel decd May ye 3d 1728 in ye 26 year of her age.

No. 437.

[Blue slate.　Piece 1-2 inch thick split off the face, taking upper part
of inscription.　Symbol.]

Here lyes inter'd the body of John Thomas Esqr who
died Aug. ye 7th 1737 in ye 41st year of his age.

No. 438.
[Blue slate. Good condition. Symbol.]

Here lyes interr,d the body of the Honourable Nathaniel Thomas Esqr who departed this life February the 24th 1738 in the 75th year of his age

No. 439.
[Blue slate. Cleft, and partially defaced. Symbol.]

In memory of Elizabeth Thompson formerly wife to Thomas urdoch decd She departed this Life Febry ye 24th 1779 in ye 75th year of her age.

No. 440.
[A Goodwin stone. Bust of woman, with arms folded.]

Here lies interrd the Body of Sarah Spooner who deceased January ye 25th AD. 1767 in ye 72d year of her Age ☞She was widow to Thomas Spooner.

No. 441.
[Thick purple stone, 3 ft high. Head and shoulders of male figure.]

Here lies Buried ye Body of Mr Thomas Spooner who Departed this life Decembr 19th Anno Domini 1762 in the 68th Year of his Age

No. 442.
[Blue slate. Much crumbled, and split. Part of inscription gone. Remains of one wing of symbol.]

Here lyes th   body of Ebenez   Spooner who d Febry the 3d 1717-8 about ye 52d year of his age

No. 443 a.
[Blue slate. Sound and compact.]

ANN ELIZABETH died July 24th, 1836 aged 3 y'rs & 7 Mon. GEORGE, died April 19th, 1839 aged 3 y'rs & 5 Mon. Children of John & Betsy Ann Eddy.

No. 443 b.
[White marble. Granite base. Good condition.]

Ann Eliza Daughter of John & Betsey Ann Eddy Died Dec. 31, 1863, aged 16 yrs 9 mo. 16 days.

No. 444.
[Blue slate. Moss-grown. Symbol.]

In memory of Mr Joshua Bramhall who decd Janury ye 21st 1763 In ye 80th year of his Age

No. 445.
[Blue slate. Cracked, and laminæ separating. Symbol.]

In memory of Mrs Sarah Bramhall widow of Joshua Bramhall who departed this life Decr 15th 1778 in ye 97th year of her Age

6

No. 446.

[Blue slate. Appears sound and compact. Urn.]

In memory of Mrs Martha Darling wife of Jonathan
Darling & Daughter of Joshua Bramhall who Departed
this life January the 7th 1779 in the 63 year of her age

Why flow my tears why should I
Not rejoice
At their deliv'rance from this cumbrous
Clay
I soon shall meet them hear their
Gentle voice
Welcome my soul to ever lasting day.

No. 447.

[Low, wide, blue slate. Urn, with flowers in bloom on either side.]

To the memory of Mrs MERCY BRAMHALL relict of Mr
SILVANUS BRAMHALL who died March 21 AD. 1798 aged
77 years

No. 448.

[Blue slate. Shaky. Broken across, diagonally. About one-fourth
of stone gone.]

In Memory of Mr SILVANUS   who departed this
March ye 14th 1779 in ye   year of his Age

No. 449.

[Low, blue slate. Cracked and moss-grown. Symbol.]

In Memory of Mrs Mary Bramhall who decd Decembr
ye 21st 1775 in ye 49th year of her age wife of Mr Silvanus Bramhall

No. 450.

[Blue slate. Inscription difficult to read. Stone moss-grown, and
in bad condition otherwise. Symbol.]

Here li   ied Eliza   wife of M   ough
Randall & Daughter of   Edmond T.   who died
July ye 22d 1749 in ye 23 year of her age

(Footstone reads:)

Mrs Elizabeth Randall

No. 451.

[Purple slate, with bluish veins. Superficially cut. Symbol.]

Here lies buried the body of Mrs HANNAH CHANDLER
wife of Capt Reuben Chandler Died Febry 25th 1750 in
in the 28th year of her age

No. 452.

[Blue slate. Fair condition. Somewhat moss-grown.]

Elizabeth Daughtr of Mr Perez Tillson & Elizabeth his
wife And Grand daughter of Capt Thomas Doty Died
Octr 26th N. S. 1753 in ye 7th year of her age

No. 453.

[Blue slate. Moss-grown. Symbol.]

Here Lies Buried Mrs SARAH BRAMHALL who Died January 26 1754 in ye 25th year of her age Relict to Capt JOSEPH BRAMHALL who died at Jamaica Janury ye 26 1758 in his 36th year.

No. 454.

[Wide, blue slate, nearly 3 ft. high. Crossbones over symbol (a winged skull).]

Here lyes Buried Mrs ELIZABETH TILLSON ye wife of Mr PEREZ TILLSON The only Daughter of COLL. THOMAS DOTY who died November 8th 1756 in ye 32d year of her age

No. 455.

[Low, blue slate. Moss-grown. Symbol.]

In Memory of Mr Perez Tillson, Who decd Sept ye 3 1767 in ye 42d year of his Age.

No. 456.

[Low blue slate. Laminæ of surface scaling off. Symbol.]

In Memory of Mrs Elizabeth Bartlett widow of Mr Samuel Bartlett who died Sept 19th 1783 in ye 48th year of her Age

No. 457.

[Blue slate. Good condition. 3 ft. high. Symbol.]

In Memory of Mr SAMUEL BARTLETT who departed this life April 7th 1780 in ye 54th year of his Age

No. 458.

[Thin, blue slate. Good condition. Symbol.]

Here lies buried the Body of Lieut. Samuel Bartlett who died March the 9th 1750 in the 59th year of his Age

No. 459.

[White marble in freestone socket. Good condition.]

GEORGE WASHBURN Son of George and Priscilla Washburn Died in Montgomery, Alabama, Sept. 4, 1853, Aged 25 y'rs & 6 mo.

The only son of a Widow'd Mother.

No. 460.

[Similar to preceding. Inclines backward.]

PRISCILLA WASHBURN, Daughter of George and Priscilla Washburn, Died December 31, 1863, Aged 33 y'rs & 11 mo.

PRISCILLA, Wife of George Washburn Died March 7, 1883, Aged 81 y'rs.

No. 461.

[Blue slate. 4 1-2 feet high. Cracked across the whole width about eight inches above the ground. Weeping willow and urn.]

Erected in memory of DEA. LEMUEL DREW, who with faith patience and Submission with the will of God, died May 24, 1825 : aged 80 years & 6 mo,s. SARAH, dau,tr of Lemuel & Elizabeth Drew, Died March 20, 1829 : aged 47 y,rs & 7 mo,s.

We have fought a good fight, we have finished our course, we have kept the faith.

No. 462.

[Blue slate. 4 ft. in height. Good condition. Face of stone carved to represent a large urn, in which is the inscription.]

To the memory of ELIZABETH DREW, wife of DEAC. LEMUEL DREW, who died November 4, 1815, aged 67 years and 48 days

No. 463.

[Low, blue slate. Seamed and cracked. Symbol.]

In Memory of Joseph Son of Mr Lemuel Drew & Mrs Elizabeth his wife who died March 4th 1780 aged 2 years 3 months & 17 days.

No. 464.

[Blue slate. Nearly 4 ft. high. Good condition. Urn.]

In memory of ISAAC DREW, who departed this life March 2d, 1844, aged 54 years & 6 mon.

No. 465.

[Blue slate. Slightly cut. Moss-grown. Difficult to read. Urn.]

Consecrated to the Memory of Mrs Mary Dyer who died April 17th 1805 aged 47 years

One thing is needfull And Mary hath chosen that Good part which shall not be taken away from her.

No. 466.

[Blue slate. 3 ft. high. Cracked through diagonally. Weeping willow and urn.]

Consecrated to the memory of Mrs PEGGY HOL-BROOK wife of Mr Jeremiah Holbrook who departed this life August 28th 1811 aged 26 years

Her amiable Disposition endeared her to her friends and died lamented by all who knew her

Though harsh the strike and most severe the rod
Cease mourner cease it was a strike from God

No. 467.

[Blue slate. Seamed and cracked. Symbol.]

Here lies buried Experience Daughr of Capt Jabez Harlow & Mrs Experience his wife who decd Sept ye 17th 1769 aged 13 years 4 Months & 18 days

No. 468.

[Blue slate. Upper part broken off and gone. Letters very large.]

of Capt JABEZ HARLOW who died March ye 8th A D 1773 in ye 40th year of her Age

No. 469.

[Blue slate, 1 foot high. Broken badly. Part of surface gone.]

Here lies   Rebekah D   Mr Jabez   wife   May ye aged 6 years 4 months & 4

No. 470.

[Blue slate. 3 1-4 ft. high. Appears compact, but is cracked diagonally across, which threatens about one-third of the monument. Weeping willow and urn.]

Erected to the memory of Miss JOANNA COTTON Daughter of JOHN COTTON Esqr and Hannah his wife who died Novemr 2, 1822 aged 62 years.

No. 471.

[Blue slate. Seams spreading open. Face cleft across. Symbol.]

In Memory of Mrs MARY JENNINGS, wife of Mr JOSEPH JENNINGS who died Aug. 3, 1793 in ye 43d year of her age. Also in memory of t   children, viz 3 Sons & 1 Daughter who died in infancy

No. 472.

[Blue slate. Crack on the right does not extend into the lettering. 3 ft. high. Symbol.]

This Monument is erected To the memory of Mrs HANNAH COTTON who Died May 25th 1800, in the Seventy-third year of her age.   Relict of JOHN COTTON, *Esqr*.

"Blessed are the dead which die in the LORD
"From henceforth yea saith the Sperit
"That they may rest from their labours
"And their Works do follow them."

No. 473.

[Blue slate. Thick, compact. Well cut; the cherub or symbol much elaborated.]

To the Memory of JOHN COTTON, *Esqr* formerly a Minister of the Gospel at Hallifax (which Employ was ever his greatest Delight) who died Novr 4 A D 1789, in ye 78 year of his Age.

'Tis Heaven's irrevocable Decree
That the great, the good, the pious shall fall,
In the dark Grave undistinguished to lie,
Till the last Trumpet rends the azure sky;
When the Virtuous immortal shall rise,
To Glory and joys above the starry skies;
The Vicious to pain, dishonour, contempt,
In realms below the splendid Firmament.

No. 474.

[White marble slab, in a neat white paling.]

JACOB JACKSON, born January 1, 1794, died October 27, 1857.

JOANN HOLMES, His wife born January 23, 1803, died January 2, 1879. ·

MARCIA, born December 16, 1840, died August 2, 1842.

ANDREW, born March 7, 1839, died July 9, 1845.

SOPHIA GORDON, born March 15, 1833, died September 20, 1845.

Children of Jacob & Joann Jackson. Also LAVANTIA, born June 14, 1831, died September 23, 1851.

No. 475.

[White marble. 4ft. high, nearly. Fair condition. This No. and the following to 479 inclusive are inclosed in an iron railing.]

PRISCILLA COTTON, widow of Josiah Cotton, born Sept. 30, 1760, died Oct. 4, 1859

No. 476.

[Blue slate. Good condition. Urn.]

In memory of David Barnes Son of Josiah & Rachel Cotton who died April 27 1795 Aged seven months

Dear babe sleep their in the dust
Till the Saviour says arise with the just

No. 477.

[Light blue slate. Some seams. Moss-grown. Bust of female.]

In the Memory of the amiable Mrs LYDIA COTTON Consort of Josiah Cotton Esqr who died Novr 1st 1787 in ye 39th year of her Age

'Tis God who lifts our comforts high,
Or sinks them in the grave,
He gives and blessed be his name,
He takes but what he gave.

No. 478.

[Blue slate. Firm and compact. Pyramidal outlines, in vogue here about the beginning of this century. Urn.]

Sacred to the memory of JOSIAH COTTON Esq. formerly settled in the ministry at Wareham who was called from this transitory scene April 19, 1819 aged 71 years.

He delivered the poor that cried,
And those that had none to help them,
And caused the widow's heart to sing for joy.
Job 29-15

No. 479.

[Blue slate. 3 1-2 feet in height. Urn.]

I
am erected
by
Josiah Cotton Esqr
in remembrance of *Rachel* his pious and Virtuous Wife,
who died Janury 17th 1808 aged 50 years.

In belief of Christianity I lived,
In hope of a glorious Resurrection I died.

No. 480.

[Blue slate, 4 1-2 feet in height. Good condition. Weeping willow
and urn.]

Capt Thomas Cotton, Born January 17th 1785 Died in
Havana June 9th 1819.
Rossiter M. Cotton, Born July 11th 1798, Died Jackson
Co. Louisiana, Oct. 4th 1817.
William C. Cotton, Born April 17th 1804, Died August
23, 1805.
Children of Rossiter & Priscilla Cotton.

No. 481.

Blue slate; good condition; pyramidal outline; urn under drapery.]

In memory of Rosseter son of Rosseter Cotton Esq. &
Mrs Priscilla his wife who died January 30 1796 Aged 2
Years

No. 482.

[Light blue slate; good condition; symbol.]

In memory of Mary Daughter of Dr. Rosseter & Mrs
Priscilla Cotton who died Augt 6 1791 aged 13 months
& 6 days

No. 483.

[Blue slate; 483 to 487 inclusive, inclosed in iron fence; 483 in good
condition.]

MARIA T. JACKSON Died May 18, 1856. aged 52
years

No. 484.

[Blue slate; crack thro' the stone, destined probably to throw off
about one-fifth of it; weeping willow and urn.]

To the memory of Mrs Meriah M. Jackson the wife of
Mr Woodworth Jackson who died December 25 1816
aged 37 years

No. 485.

[Blue slate; good condition; weeping willow and urn.]

In memory of Woodworth Jackson who died Novr 10,
1821 aged 47 years

No. 486.

[Blue slate; good condition; weeping willow and urn.]

In memory of John T. Jackson son of Woodworth &
Meriah Jackson Decd who died Feb. 4, 1825 aged 11 years

No. 487.

[Blue slate; good condition; weeping willow and urn.]

In memory of Betsey M. Jackson Daughter of Woodworth and Meriah Jackson who died June 10, 1827 aged
26 years

No. 488.

[White marble; good condition, save an upward crack where it is
dowelled to the plinth.]

William L. Weston, died Oct. 31, 1869, Aged 21 y'rs
6 mo's 15 days

(The reverse:)

·OUR WILLIE.

"Thy will be done on earth as it is in Heaven."

No. 489.

[White marble; good condition.]

Our HATTIE, Aged 7 years.

Little CLARA, Aged 3 years 8 mo's.

Children of William & Susan S. WESTON, died Feb. 22,
1860.

Treasures in Heaven.

No. 490 a.

[White marble; good condition.]

WILLIAM WESTON born July 19, 1819, died Oct.
18, 1884.

No. 490 b.

[White marble, new and beautiful. On marble plinth, with granite
base.]

. SUSAN S. wife of William Weston Born Oct. 7, 1819
Died May 26, 1888.

No. 491.

[White marble, set in granite.]

SAMUEL D. BALLARD, died Sept. 27, 1868, Aged
41 y'rs 8 mo.

I know he waits beside the gate,
For us to come, our child and me;
He'll meet us when life's day grows late
And we, too, cross the billowy sea.
Yes, we shall meet in the land above,
For heaven is light and God is love.

No. 492.

[492 and 493 inclosed in wooden paling; 492 white marble block; good condition.]

(On summit:)

IRVING.

(On obverse:)

IRVING B. Son of H. & F. M. Holmes Died Jan 21, 1876, Aged 3 y'rs 4 mo's.

(On reverse, an engraved rose-twig,—bud and leaves.)

No. 493.

[Low, white marble; marble plinth; freestone base.]

HARRIE W. Son of H. & F. M. Holmes, Died April 10, 1867. Aged 1 year 4 mo's 14 days.

'Tis Jesus speaks: " I fold," says he,
These lambs within my breast;
Protection they shall find in me,
In me be ever blest.

No. 494.

[494-497 inclusive, white marble; good condition.]

Capt. COOMER WESTON, died July 7, 1870, Aged 85 y'rs 8 mo's.

No. 495.

· HANNAH WESTON, died March 22, 1868, Aged 82 y'rs 4 mo's.

No. 496.

ANN M. WESTON died Aug. 3, 1881, Aged 68 y'rs 2 mo's.

No. 497.

HANNAH D. BOURASSO, Died Feby. 20, 1882, Aged 73 y'rs. 3 mo's. 19 d'ys.

No. 498.

[White marble; granite base; inclined backward.]

OUR MOTHER, Zoraday T. Wife of Capt. T. E. Cornish, died Nov. 10, 1866, Aged 61 y'rs.

No. 499.

[White marble; small ornament at top broken and loose; otherwise good condition; it has but one word, beneath which is a carved bouquet.]

ALICE.

No. 500.

[White marble, granite base; good condition.]

SALLY, Wife of Capt. Joseph Wright, Died March 21, 1866, aged 63 y'rs 7 mo.

No. 501.

[White marble, granite base; good condition.]

ASA A. WHITING DIED April 29, 1868 aged 55 y'rs 9 mo's.

"The gift of God is eternal life."

No. 502.

[This and 503 are white marble blocks, set in granite; both injured near dowels at base; both inclined.]

HELEN M. SHAW, died June 29, 1868, Aged 18 y'rs. 1 mo. & 7 days

(On reverse:)

HELEN.

No. 503.

JULIA S. SHAW, died Nov. 29, 1867. Aged 17 y'rs. 6 mo's. & 7 days.

No. 504.

[White marble; do. plinth; freestone base.]

WILLIAM PERLEY, Died May 26, 1868, Aged 18 y'rs 1 day.

GEORGE HERBERT, Supposed to have been lost at sea, Aug. 2, 1867, Aged 14 y'rs 11 mo. 1 day.

(On reverse:)

WILLIE & GEORGE Sons of Capt. Wm. & Sarah J. Atwood.

No. 505.

[White marble; rose-twig at top.]

ABBY JANE Daughter of Capt William & Sarah Jane Atwood, died Feb. 22, 1849, aged 6 Mon.

No. 506.

[White marble; granite base. On the very top the word:]

FATHER.

(On face:)

LEAVITT FINNEY died June 3, 1885, Aged 72 y'rs 4 mo's 29 days.

No. 507.

[White marble; granite base. On the very top the word:] ·

MOTHER.

(On face:)

MARY A. Wife of Leavitt Finney died Aug. 5, 1880, Aged 65 y'rs 8 mo's, 29 days.

No. 508.

[White marble; at present in fair condition.]

In memory of MARY ELLEN, dau. of Leavitt & Mary W. Finney, who died April 20, 1849, Æ. 3 y'rs 11 mo's.

'Tis God who lifts our comforts high,
Or sinks them in the grave,
He gives and blessed be his name,
He takes but what he gave.

No. 509.

[White marble, on granite base; and with No. 510, inclosed with a wooden fence.]

OUR FATHER. IN MEMORY OF DAVID HARLOW who died July 22, 1859, Æ. 60 years 6 mos.

Dear as thou wert, and justly dear,
We will not weep for thee;
One thought should check the starting tear,
It is that thou art free.

No. 510.

[White marble; granite base.]

HANNAH, dau. of David & Eliza S. HARLOW, died March 2, 1865, Æ. 26 years 7 mo's.

Lone are the paths and sad the hours,
Since thy loved spirit's gone,
But oh! a brighter home than ours
In heaven is now thine own.

No. 511.

[White marble; not firm in the ground.]

REUBEN HALL, Died Aug. 30, 1867, Aged 53 y'rs 4 mo's.

Dear Husband, dear father now sweetly at rest,
United forever with those that are blest,
Now an angel in heaven before the white throne,
Praise God for His goodness in taking thee home.

We miss that sweet smile and loving caress,
So fondly bestowed on those you loved best,
But that smile is now sweeter and that love is more strong,
And the angels in chorus have joined your glad song.

No. 512.

[White marble, on granite base; top in form of a Gothic arch, with hand, the index finger pointing upward.]

MARGE CALLAHAN, died Feb. 25, 1868, Aged 61 y'rs.

My work is with my God.

No. 513.

[Blue slate. Moss-grown; weeping willow and urn.]

Erected to the memory of Mr. Horace H. Rolfe, who died at Charleston, S. C. Feb.y 24, 1831, Aged 30 years.

Blessed are the dead who die in the Lord.

Also Mary Augusta Rolfe died Nov. 1, 1831, aged 2 years & 4 months.

Of such are the kingdom of Heaven.

No. 514.

[Blue slate; good condition, except being inclined,—leaning against No. 513. Weeping willow and urn.]

Erected to the memory of Mrs. Mary T. Rolfe, who died July 30, 1829, aged 26 years, wife of Horace H. Rolfe.

Blessed and holy is he that hath part in the first resurrection; on such the second death hath no power.—Rev. 20—6.

No. 515.

[Blue slate; about 4 ft. high; inscription within figure of urn, under curtains. Good condition.]

Erected In memory of Mr. Joseph Marcy who died March 6, 1817 in the 26 year of his age.

No. 516.

[Same as preceding.]

Erected In memory of Mrs. Charlott Marcy wife of Mr. Joseph Marcy who died Decr 7th 1816 in the 24th of her age.

No. 517.

[Same description as 515.]

Erected In memory of Mrs. Abbigail Marcy wife of Capt Charles Marcy who died June 17th 1816 in the 26th year of her age.

No. 518.

[518 to 525 blue slate, in good condition, inclosed with iron fence. 521 to 525 have the pyramid form. At top of 518 urn with flame.]

WILLIAM JACKSON Esqr Born July 14, 1763, Died Oct.r 22, 1836, aged 73.

Here rests an affectionate Parent, a sincere friend and Christian.

No. 519.

[Scroll at top has the legend,—ET EGO IN COLUMBIA VIXI.]

To The Memory Of Mrs. ANNA JACKSON Obiit July 20, 1794 Aged 28 years.

Death is the privilege of human nature,
And life without it were not worth our taking
Thither the poor, the unfortunate, and Mourner
Fly for relief & lay their burdens down.

No. 520.

[Flaming urn.]

The remains of MRS. ESTHER JACKSON, wife of Wm Jackson Esqr Rest here. Decd June 1st 1836, Aged 71.

No. 521.

[Urn at top.]

To the memory of Mrs MERCY JACKSON Consort of Wm
JACKSON *Esqr* Obiit Septr 24th 1802 Aged 39 years.

No. 522.

[Urn.]

Frederick Wm Jackson born July 21, 1796 died Aug.
16, 1796.

No. 523.

F. W. Jackson Obiit March 23, 1799 Aged One year 7
days.

Heaven knows What man
He might have made, But we
He died a most rare boy.

No. 524.

[Stone inclined to right.]

In memory of Anna Jackson Daughter of Wm & Mercy
Jackson Obiit 27th Novr 1802 Aged 3 years

No. 525.

In memory of Wm. R. Jackson son of Wm & Mercy
Jackson Obiit 12th Octr 1802 aged one year.

No. 526.

[Granite border around lot; marble monument, set on granite base;
ornamental sculpture above inscription.]

HORACE, Son of Ivory L. & Rebecca B. Harlow,
Died Nov. 29, 1870, Aged 23 y'rs 3 mo's.

———

(On reverse side:)

WE SHALL MEET BEYOND THE RIVER.

HORACE.

No. 527.

[Blue slate. Condition good.]

To the memory of Capt WILLIAM CROMBIE who died
Febry 9, 1804, in the 40th year of his age.

No. 528.

[Blue slate; urn; large piece broken from upper part of stone.]

To the memory of Mrs DEBORAH CROMBIE Consort of
Capt WILLIAM CROMBIE, who died Janry 3d 1800 in the
32 year of her age.

No. 529.

[Fine, blue slate, about 4 feet high.]

Cap CHARLES DYER died at Sea March 1786 : aged
46 yr,s BETHIAH, his wife died June 8, 1837 : aged 87

yr,s. Their son CHARLES, died May 7, 1822: aged 46 yr,s.

No. 530.

[Light blue slate; moss-grown; diagonal cracks passing nearly through the centre. Symbol (winged head), with representation of clouds above it.]

To the Memory of Col. THEOPHILUS COTTON who departed this Life Febry ye 18th 1782

" The firm Patriot there
" Who made the welfare of Mankind his care
" Shall know he conquered.

No. 531.

[Blue slate; good condition. Urn.]

In memory of Martha Cotton Relict of Colo. Theophilus Cotton Esqr who died April 10th A. D. 1796 aged 79 years

Many years I liv'd
Many painfull scenes I pass'd
Till God at last
Call'd me home

No. 532.

[White marble; surface roughened.]

In memoriam JOHN D. DUNBAR ESQ. died Feb. 10, 1810, Aged 42 years

No. 533.

[533—535 tall; blue slate; pyramidal; good condition. 533, urn under curtain.]

In memory of Mrs NANCY DUNBAR Consort of JOHN D. DUNBAR Esqr Deceased May 3d 1804 in the 33d year of her age.

No. 534.

[Weeping willow and urn.]

In memory of Deac. WILLIAM CROMBIE who lived and died in the good man's hope the 26th of Novr, 1814, in his 83 year.

An honest man's the noblest work of God.

No. 535.

To the memory of Mrs ZERUIAH CROMBIE Consort of Dean WILLIAM CROMBIE who died May 1st 1803 in the 66th year of her age.

No. 536.

[Blue slate, seamed and shaky.]

In memory of Mr KIMBALL CROMBIE who died July 23, J79J aged 24 years

No. 537.

[Blue slate, firm and solid, though moss-grown.]

In Memory of Mrs DEBORAH wife of Mr KIMBALL CROMBIE, who died Novr J7, J789 aged 2J years

No. 538.
[Blue slate; pyramidal; good condition. At top bust of female under curtain. drapery. The epitaph is from Young's Night Thoughts, "Narcissa."]

Fanney Crombie daughter of Mr Calvin Crombie & Mrs Naomi his wife Departed this life June 25th 1804 in the 8th year of her age.

> As young as beautiful! and soft as young!
> And gay as soft! and innocent as gay!

No. 539.
[Blue slate; pyramidal; good condition. Urn, curtained.]

In memory of James Crombie Son of Mr Calvin Crombie & Mrs Naomi his wife died Oct. 9 1803 aged 1 year 10 months.

No. 540.
[Blue slate—beautiful specimen; leans to the right. Urn.]

NANCY CARVER Dau. of Benj. & Joanna Weston, died March 18, 1842, in the 27 y,r of her age.

> Could our fond gaze but follow where thou art,
> Well might the glories of this world seem naught,
> To the one promise given the pure in heart.

No. 541.
[Light blue slate. Good condition. Urn.]

To the memory of Mary Tilden daughter of Benjn & Joanna Weston Born March 1, 1813 & died Novr 22, 1815.

> God in his holy word has said
> Children were for his kingdom made.

No. 542.
[Fine, blue slate. Good condition.]

ELIZABETH born Feb,y 28, 1822, died Jan,y 2, 1823. SARAH NYE born Feb,y 15, 1830, died Dec. 18, 1837, Children of Benjamin & Joanna Weston.

> Thou art gone to the grave we no longer behold thee;
> Nor tread the rough paths of the world by thy side:
> But the wide arms of mercy are spread to enfold thee;
> And sinners may die for the sinless has died.

No. 543.
[Low, blue slate, slightly inclined. Urn.]

In Memory of Hannah Daughter of Mr Lewis Weston & Mrs Lucy his wife who died Feby 9 1788 aged 1 year 4 months & 9 days.

No. 544.
[Fine, blue slate; sound; slightly inclined.]

Erected in memory of MISS LUCY WESTON, who died Jan. 1, 1848, in the 63 yr. of her age.

No. 545.
[Blue slate; sound; moss-grown.]

To the memory of Mr. Lewis Weston who Departed this life Sept the 28th 1798 in the 45th year of his age.

No. 546.
[Fine, solid, blue slate; slightly inclined.]

In memory of MRS. LUCY WESTON, who departed this life Oct. 16, 1840, in the 84th year of her age.

Blessed are the dead who die in the
LORD.

No. 547.
[Blue slate; apparently sound, but face nearly covered with mosses. Urn.]

To the memory of Mr William Bradford who died in Roxbury Jany 14 1794 aged 44 years. Also of Mrs Ruth Bradford his wife who died May 22, 1813 aged 60 years Also of two of their children viz Amos who died in Martinico Aug. 3, 1794 aged 17 years Aud Isaac who died March 16 1806 aged 21 years

No. 548.
[Low, blue slate. Good condition, but inclined. Symbol.]

In Memory of 2 Children of Mr William & Mrs Ruth Bradford Viz Elizabeth died Novr 15 J787 aged 7 weeks. James died Decr 28 J788 aged 7 weeks & 6 days

No. 549.
[Blue slate. Good condition. Weeping willow and urn.]

Erected In memory of Mr. WILLIAM KEEN, who died Feb. 18, 1825, aged 69.

This modest stone what few vain marbles can,
May truly say—Here lies an honest man.

No. 550.
[Fine, blue slate, sound, erect, but threatened by a higher monument (of white marble) within striking distance, and inclined towards it. Urn.]

In memory of Lydia Widow of the late William Keen Died Dec. 7,1839. Aged 72 years

But no, I would not call the hence—
For thou art with the blest,
And oh, may I prepare to be
A sharer in thy rest.

No. 551.
[Blue slate. Laminæ separating. Moss-grown. Half of symbol scaled off.]

In Memory of Mrs Marcy Warren widow of Mr. WILLIAM KEEN who departed this Life April 26th J78J in the 66th year of her age

No. 552.

[Thick, compact, blue slate. Good condition. Weeping willow and urn.]

Consecrated to the memory of Margaret J. Washburn, who died June 4, A. D. 1823, in the 32 year of her age.

Rest gentle spirit rest, thy toils are o'er,
The place that knew thee knows thee now no more
Cease mourner cease! sweet consolation dies
We part--but 'tis to meet in happier skies.

[NOTE (by the author).—It is obvious that "dies" has, on the stone, been unfortunately substituted for "cries." But I have not, as previously remarked, felt at liberty to vary words or phrases.]

No. 553.

[White marble; about 4 1-2 feet high, and 2 1-2 wide. Good condition, save somewhat roughened.]

Here are interred in adjoining graves, the remains of SARAH BRADFORD relict of LeBaron Bradford of Bristol, Rhode Island. Born June 29, 1754, Died Nov. 10, 1821, and of their son LeBaron Bradford Born 1780, Died Nov. 1846.

No. 554.

[White marble. Weathering rough (by which phrase I mean that, owing probably to climatic changes, disintegration of the stone is going on, particles falling off, leaving the surface rough. The final not long deferred result, of course, must be obliteration.]

'In memory of HON. WENDELL DAVIS, who died at Sandwich, Dec. 30, 1830, aged 54 years, and is here interred.

No. 555.

[White marble; similar description as preceding.]

To the memory of SAMUEL DAVIS A. M. who died July 10, 1829, in the 65th year of his age.

From life on earth our pensive friend retires;
His dust commingling with the pilgrim sires;
In thoughtful walks their every path he trac'd,
Their toils, their tombs, his faithful page embrac'd,
Peaceful, and pure, and innocent as they,
With them to rise to everlasting day.

[NOTE (by the author). The above epitaph, which does exact justice to its subject, and which is as well-expressed as it is just, is, as I am informed by Hon. Wm. T. Davis (see "Ancient landmarks of Plymouth,") from the pen of John Davis, author of the celebrated ode, "Sons of renowned sires."]

No. 556.

[Blue slate. Laminæ separated. Mossy, but perfectly legible. Cross-bones and two symbols at top.]

In Memory of Mrs MERCY DAVIS wife of Capt Thomas Davis who departed this life Sept ye 20th J779 in ye 45th year of her Age Also their Son stillborn J8th

No. 557.

[Blue slate. Laminæ opened. Is cracked on the face, and somewhat moss-grown; but it will probably outlast the neighboring marbles.]

To the Memory of Capt Thomas Davis who departed this life March 7, 1785 in the 63d year of his age and here lies interred.

No. 558.

[White marble. See No. 554.]

In memory of Rebecca Davis, relict of Hon. William Davis, Born December 30, 1762, Died April 1, 1847.

No. 559.

[White marble. See No. 554.]

In memory of Hon. William Davis, Born July 15, 1758. Died January 5, 1826.

No. 560.

[White marble. See No. 554.]

In memory of Thomas Davis, son of William and Rebecca Davis, Born April 3, 1791, Died September 14, 1848.

No. 561.

[Blue slate. Laminæ separating. Part of symbol broken off.]

In Memory of Mrs. Margaret Keen widow of Mr. William Keen who departed this Life April 26th J78J in ye 66th year of her age

No. 562.

[Blue slate. 4 1-2 feet high. Good condition. Mausoleum.]

Sacred to the memory of Mr BENJAMIN DREW, who died Dec. 22, 1820, Aged 82 yr,s. Also DESIRE, daughter of Benjamin & Elizabeth Drew, who died Nov,r 15, 1815; aged 39 yr,s, and SIMEON, their son, who died Nov,r 1, 1815; Aged 37 yr,s.

What though this sad this gloomy hill contains
Of relatives and friends the loved remains
Yet in our breasts let cheerful hopes arise
Again to meet in "mansions" of the skies.

[NOTE (by the author). The above epitaph was written by Mr. Benjamin Drew (b. 1767) a son of the decedent. The same Mr. Drew was once requested to write an epitaph on Mr. Barnabas Holmes (No. 680) his brother-in-law, who attained the ripe age of 81 years. Mr. Drew wrote the following:

By temperance taught, a few, advancing slow,
To distant fate by easy journeys go.
Calmly they lie then down like evening sheep,—
On their own woolly fleeces softly sleep.

—but objection arose to these lines on the ground that Mr. Holmes had, at some time in his life, been a mutton-dealer! Accordingly Mr. Drew threw them aside, and penned the epitaph now on the monument No. 680.]

No. 563.

[Blue slate. Sound, but moss-grown. Urn.]

To the memory of Mrs Elizabeth Drew wife of Mr Benjamin Drew who died Dec. 6, 1798 aged 60 years.

No. 564.

[White marble, set in granite with lead. Good condition.]

EBENEZER DREW Died Jan. 6, 1851, aged 77 y'rs.
DEBORAH, his wife, Died April 15, 1844, Aged 72years.

No. 565.

[Similar to preceding No.]

MALACHI DREW Died Feb. 22, 1853, Aged 78 y'rs.

No. 566.

[Low, blue slate. Good condition. Symbol.]

In memory of Benjamin Drew 3d, Son of Benjamin Drew Junr and Sophia his wife Deceased July 8th 1802 aged 1 year 7 months and 2 days.

[NOTE (by author). The family of which the above named decedent was a member, lived at the corner of High and Spring streets, and, in common with the residents of the neighborhood, were obliged to procure water from the spring at the foot of the hill. To save this trouble they dug a well on the north side of High street, near the house formerly occupied by Capt. Zacheus Barnes, and but a short distance from the boundary of Burial Hill. Soon after beginning to use the well-water, typhoid fever broke out among the children of the vicinity, eight of whom, including this Benjamin Drew, 3d, died. The well was then abandoned.]

No. 567.

[White marble, set in granite socket with lead. Good condition.]

SOPHIA, Aug 29, 1802 Aug 19, 1803
SOPHIA B. Oct. 8, 1803 Nov. 2, 1806
SOPHIA B. Sept. 28, 1807 Sept. 2, 1821
Children of Benjamin & Sophia [Bartlett] Drew.
Thy shaft flew thrice, and thrice my peace was slain.

No. 568.

[Low, blue slate. Face of stone scaled off at top. Symbol.]

In Memory of Lothrop Bartlet Son of Samuel Bartlett Esqr & Mrs Elizabeth, his wife Born August ye 7th J755 Decd June ye J8th J756

No. 569.

[Blue slate. 4 feet in height. Good condition. Urn.]

Erected to the memory of MRS. LUCY MARCY; wife of the late Dr. Stephen Marcy, who died June 13, 1842 aged 83 years

"Servant of God! well done,
Rest from thy long employ,
The battle fought, the victory won,
Enter thy Master's joy.

No. 570.

[Dark blue slate. Good condition. Urn.]

To the memory of DOCTR STEPHEN MARCY who died March 24th 1804 aged 45 years.

No. 571.

[Low, blue slate. Good condition. Symbol.]

In Memory of Joseph Son of Dr. Stephen Marcy & Mrs Lucy his wife who died Octr 16. 1790 aged J year & 9 months.

This little one did quit this drooping house of clay,
And God will restore it in the appointed day.

No. 572.

[Blue slate. Good condition, but inclined. Symbol.]

In memory of 2 Children of Doctr Stephen & Mrs Lucy Marcy. 1st a son Thomas J. Marcy who died Aug. 17th 1801 aged 1 year & 3 months 2d a daughter Mary who died Augst 19th 1801 aged 2 years & 11 months.

No. 573.

[Beautiful white marble, on granite block. Good condition.]

LUCY MARCY, died Feb. 20, 1887, aged 92 y'rs 9mo's.

No. 574.

[Low, blue slate. Laminæ separating. Two clefts down the whole face of stone. Symbol.]

In memory of Frederick son of Mr Joseph & Mrs Mary Bartlett his wife who died July 27th 1782 aged J year 2 months & 27 days

No. 575.

[Low, blue slate. Good condition, save moss-grown. Symbol.]

Here lies buried Joseph Son to Mr Joseph Bartlett & Mrs Mary his wife who decd March ye 26th 1773 aged 1 Month & 11 days

No. 576.

[Blue slate. Good condition, save being moss-grown. Symbol.]

In Memory of Mrs Hannah Symmes wife of Mr Isaac Symmes who died Decr 17th 1783 Æt. 35th

No. 577.

[A Goodwin stone (see No. 295). Weatherworn. Symbol.]

To the memory of Mrs Hannah Symmes the wife of Mr Isaac Symmes who died Octbr Jst J773 Æt. 3J

No. 578.

[Low, blue slate. Moss-grown. Inclined. Symbol.]

Here lies buried the Body of Jsaac Son to Mr Jsaac & Mrs Hannah Symmes who departed this life Novbr ye Jst J767 aged 5 Months

No. 579.

[Low, blue slate. Fair condition. Symbol.]

In Memory of Joanna Daughter of Mr Isaac & Mrs Joanna Symmes who died Decr 27th J789 aged 5 years 2 months & J3 days

No. 580.

[Blue slate. 5 feet high. Good condition. Weeping willow and urn,—inscription on the urn.]

Died Mr Isaac Symmes Augst 27. J79J. in ye 48. year of his age.

No. 581.

[Blue slate. 6 feet high. Appears to be cleft through at about midway of the height; and again, about a foot lower. Weeping willow and urn. Inscription on the urn.

JOANNA Relict of Isaac Symmes, died Dec. 14, 1834, in the 81st year of her age

No. 582.

[Dark blue slate. Sound. Weeping willow and urn.]

In Memory of NANCY SYMMES died March 15, 1858, Æt. 71 y'rs 4 mo. & 13 days

Say why should friendship grieve for those
Who safe arrive on Canaan's shore,
Released from all their hurtfull foes
They are not lost but gone before.

No. 583.

[Blue slate. Good condition. Festoons.]

Here lies inter'd the body of *Miss Hannah Symmes* eldest Daughter of *Mr Isaac & Mrs Hannah Symmes* who at the early period of 28 years after being long exercis'd with bodily pain with christian fortitude yielded her spirit to its benevolent Author. Born Jany 30, 1766, Died March 27, 1794.

No. 584.

[Blue slate. Good condition. Symbol.]

In Memory of Edwin Son of Mr Thomas Jackson 3d & Mrs Sarah his wife who died April 20, J790 aged 22 days

Of such is the kingdom of Heaven.

No. 585.

[Low, blue slate. Fair condition. Symbol.]

In Memory of Thomas son of Mr Thomas Jackson 3d & Mrs Sarah his wife who died Decr 24, 1788 aged 31 days

Can the human heart remain untouched
With tender feelings when an Infant dies.

No. 586.

[Low, blue slate, moss-covered, and inclined. Symbol.]

In Memory of Sarah Daughtr To Mr Thomas Jackson Jun & Mrs Sarah his wife Ye Child Born April ye 22d 1759 Decd Octr ye 3d 1759

No. 587.

[Low, blue slate. Moss-grown. Symbol.]

Here lies buried Lydeay Daughter of Mr Thomas Jackson Junr & Mrs Sarah his wife was born Janry ye J6th J767 Decd June ye J2th J767

No. 588.

[Low, blue slate. Fair condition. Symbol.]

In Memory of Nancy Daughter of John Goodwin and Mrs Fear his wife who died Janry 17th 1780 aged 1 month & 5 days

No. 589.

[Blue slate. Festoons and Symbols.]

To the Memory Of THOMAS JACKSON *Esqr* This Monument Is erected Obiit September 19, 1794, Aged 67 years

The spider's most attenuated thread
Is cord, is cable, to man's slender tie.

No. 590.

[Similar to 589.]

To The memory of Mrs SARAH JACKSON Relict of THOMAS JACKSON Esq. Obiit Octr 27th 1811 Aged 78

Although spared to life's utmost verge
The tender parent died too soon
For those who still survive

No. 591.

[White marble, originally in freestone socket, now set in the ground. Moss-grown.]

In memory of LYDIA JACKSON dau. of Thomas Jackson Esq. & Sarah his wife born April 8, 1768, died March 27, 1849.

The mortal remains are deposited here, but the spirit has returned to God who gave it.

No. 592.

[Purplish slate. Good condition. Symbol.]

Here lies Buried the Body of Mrs HANNAH GOODWIN. the wife of Mr John Goodwin and daughter of Mr THOMAS and Mrs SARAH JACKSON who departed this life March 8th AD. 1777 ; in the 22d Year of her Age.

A Soul prepar'd Needs no delays
The Summons comes the Saint obeys
Swift was Her flight & short the Road
She clos'd Her Eyes & saw Her God
The Flesh rests here till Jesus comes
And claims the Treasure from the Tomb

No. 593.
[White marble. Taken from stone socket and set in the ground.]
In memory of HANNAH J. GOODWIN, daughter of John & Hannah Goodwin, who died Sept. 6, 1855, Aged 81 years.

No. 594.
[Blue slate. 5 feet high. Good condition.]
In memory of MR. THOMAS JACKSON, JR. who died August 8, 1837 ; aged 80 years.

No. 595.
[Similar to 594.]
In memory of MRS. SARAH JACKSON, widow of Thomas Jackson, Jr. who died Sept,r 27th, 1837 aged 76 years.

No. 596.
[This and the Nos. following to 603 b. inclusive are inclosed with iron railing. No. 586 is blue slate, sound, but inclined. Festoous.]
To The memory of Sarah May Jackson This Monument is erected by Her afflicted Parents Mr Thomas Jackson, *Jun.* and Mrs Sarah his Wife died Septr 26 1797 Aged 3 years 11 Months

No. 597.
. [White marble, granite base. Good condition, but inclined.]
THOMAS T. JACKSON Born Sept. 11. 1798. Died Jan. 4. 1876.

No. 598.
[Dark slate. Height, 4 1-2 feet. Good condition.]
In memory of REBECCA, Consort of Daniel Jackson, deceased January 24th 1851, aged 90 years & 10 Months.

No. 599.
[Blue slate. 4 feet high. Good condition.]
In memory of MR. DANIEL JACKSON who died Nov. 4, 1829 aged 68 years.

No. 600.
[White marble. Inclined;—cement having crumbled.]
LUCY COTTON JACKSON Wife of Charles Brown, Died Feb, 9, 1868, aged 69.

> How sweet to think of peace at last,
> And feel that death is gain.

No. 601.
[Blue slate. Good condition. Inscription within figure of an urn.]
To the memory of *Mr. Charles Jackson* who departed this life August 8, 1818, aged 48 years.

No. 602.

[Similar to preceding.]

To the memory of *Mrs Lucy Jackson* widow of the late *Charles Jackson Decd* who departed this life October 15, 1818 aged 50 years.

No. 603 a.

[White marble. Good condition.]

MARY SOPHIA BROWN aged 21 died Dec. 19, 1842.
"Blessed are the pure in heart."

No. 603 b.

[Low, blue slate. Pyramidal form. Good condition. Symbol.]

To the Memory of Wm. Morton Son to Mr Daniel Jackson & Mrs Rebecca his Wife died July 9th 1801 Æ. 4 years & 6 mo.s

No. 604.

[Blue slate. About one-fourth of surface lamina gone from right side of stone.]

Here lyes buried   4 Children of Mr Eph Spooner & Mrs Elizabeth   Viz Jst A Son born April 1st lived 20 hours 2d Elizabeth   April J7th J767 aged J year   Months & J2 Days 3d Ephraim   decd Decr 2d J769 Aged 2 years & 7 Months 4th Ephraim decd Augt 4th 1775 Aged 4 years & 4 Months

No. 605.

[This No. and those following to No. 610 inclusive are inclosed in wooden palings. No 605 is blue slate; upper part of inscription broken off.]

To the   of Mary B.   daughter of M William & Mrs Anna Bradford who died Sept 17th 1802 aged 1 year & 1 month & 1 day

No. 606.

[White marble, 3 1-2 feet; set in freestone; the whole mass inclined, as if falling backward. Bas-relief figure of obelisk.]

WILLIAM BRADFORD Born June 1, 1775, Died July 25, 1816, Æ 41. Also his wife NANCY, Born Jan'y 28, 1775, Died Jan'y 27, 1843, Æ. 68

No. 607.

[Blue slate. Good condition. Flaming urn.]

Sacred to the Memory of Mr. SOLOMON RICHMOND, who died Oct. 16th 1849 : aged 58 y.rs.

No. 608.

[Blue slate. Good condition. Weeping willow and urn.]

In memory of Solomon Hinkley Son of Solomon Richmond and Anna his wife who died July 20, 1826, aged one year eight months and twenty seven days

No. 609.

[Blue slate. Weeping willow, cut across by a cleft in the stone.]

MARY B. dau. of Solomon & Anna Richmond died Aug. 14, 1840, aged 7 mo. & 3 ds.

No. 610.

[Blue slate. Good condition. Urn between scrolls.]

In memory of William son of William and Elsey Bradford who died May 12, 1829, aged 3 years 3 months and 9 days.

Boast not thyself of tomorrow
For thou knowest not what a
day may bring forth.

No. 611.

[Blue slate. 5 feet high. Good condition, but slightly inclined. Figure of three cones on a square base, which I have denomiated "Tomb" or "Mausoleum."]

In memory of GEORGE SAMPSON, who died Nov. 9, 1826, in the 52 year of his age Also of PATIENCE, his wife, who died Oct. 18, 1835, in the 58 year of her age.

No. 612.

[Blue slate. Good condition, but inclined. Urn between blown roses.]

To the memory of George Samson son of Mr George & Mrs Patience Samson who died Sepbr 15th 1803 aged 1 year 7 months & 6 days

Uncertain life how swift it flies
Swift as an hour how short the bloom
Like springs gay verdure once did rise
Cut down ere night to fill the tomb.

No. 613.

[Blue slate. Fair condition, but moss-grown. Symbol.]

To the memory of Mr Joseph Rider who died March 19, 1794, aged 65 years

No. 614.

[Blue slate. Good condition; but little moss. Symbol.]

In memory of Mrs PATIENCE RIDER wife of Major BENJAMIN RIDER who died June J8, J79J in ye 42d year of her age

Why do we mourn departing friends,
Or shake at death's alarms,
'Tis but the voice that Jesus sends,
To call them to his arms

No. 615.

Blue slate. A cleft diagonally across stone, scarcely touches the inscription. Symbol.]

To the memory of Majr BENJAMIN RIDER who died Octbr 12th 1804 aged 71 years

(The footstone has symbol and date of death.)

8

No. 616.

[Blue slate. Good condition. At top, figure of a man standing behind roof of a low brick structure, his right hand resting upon, or holding a scroll, or something of the sort.]

Here lyes Interr,d the body of Mr WILLIAM RIDER who departed this life June the 29th A D. 1772 In the 49th year of his age

(The footstone has symbol, name, and year.)

No. 617.

[Blue slate. Right corner (i. e. the part opposite spectator's right hand) of face of stone slivered off. Symbol.]

Here lies bur   Mrs Abigail Rider ye widdow of Mr Joseph Rider Daughtr to Capt Benjamin Warren Decd who departed this life Decmr ye 5th J766 in ye 67th year of her age

No. 618.

[Blue slate. Considerable portion of face of stone scaled off. Part of wing of symbol remains.]

lyes buried   body of JOSEPH RIDER who departed this life July ye 18th 1737 aged 46 year   Job ye vii : 8. 9. 10

No. 619.

[Blue slate. Moss-grown. Cleft down the face. Symbol.]

Joseph son to Joseph & Abigail Rider his wife decd July the 5th 1728 Aged 8 weeks & 3 days

No. 620.

[Blue slate. Fair condition, but moss-grown. Symbol.]

Tilden son to Mr Joseph & Mrs Abigail Rider his wife aged 1 year 4 mo 23 days Died June ye 30th 1737

No. 621.

[Blue slate. Surface seamed, but in fair condition. Symbol.]

In memory of Josh Warren Alberson son of Mr Jacob Alberson & Lydia his wife who was born June 25 1778 Decd the same day •

No. 622.

[Blue slate, wider than high. Good condition. Symbol.]

Here lyes inter'd the body of Mr Thomas Murdoch son of John Murdoch Esqr who Departed this Life on the 30th day of September 1751 and in the 50th year of his age

No. 623.

[Light blue slate. Good condition. Symbol under crossbones.]

In Memory of Mr John Murdock who Decd Sept ye 17th 1756 in ye 65th year of his age

No. 624.

[White marble. 3 1-2 feet in height. Inclined. Urn in relief.]

JOHN NOONNEN Died Dec. 31, 1848, Aged 52 y'rs.

& his son William H. Died March 19, 1855, Aged 19 y'rs 2 mo.

'Tis God who lifts our comforts high,
Or sinks them in the grave;
He gives, and blessed be his name,
He takes but what he gave.

No. 625.

[Purplish blue slate. Moss-grown and inclined, but quite sound. Symbol.]

To the memory of Hannah C. Lucas Daughter of Mr Lazarus & Mrs Nancy Lucas who died Octr 7th 1802 aged 2 years & 28 days

No. 626.

[Blue slate. Good condition. Urn.]

In memory of Lydia Ann Daughter of Charles & Lydia Wesgate who died Nov. 14, 1833, aged 5 yrs & 3months.

Our daughter rests beneath this sod,
Our hearts are with her there,
Her spirit it hath gone to God,
To dwell forever there.

No. 627.

[White marble, on granite base. Good condition. This and Nos. following to 632 inclusive are inclosed in wooden palings.]

ABBOT DREW Died Dec. 3, 1881, Aged 80 yrs. 8 ms. 13 ds.

No. 628.

[Marble, on same base as 627. Good condition.]

BETSEY CHURCHILL wife of Abbot Drew, Died March 2, 1843, Aged 43 yrs.

No. 629.

[White marble, on same base as preceding No. Good condition.]

SARAH DREW, wife of Abbot Drew, Died May 18, 1872, Aged 54 yrs. 1 mo.

No. 630.

[White marble on granite base. Good condition.]

ADDIE Dau. of Abbot & Betsey DREW Died Feb. 15, 1879, Aged 37 yrs. 6 ms. 10 ds.

No. 631.

[White marble on granite base. Good condition.]

CHARLOTTE A. Dau. of Abbot & Betsey DREW, Died July 5, 1843, Aged 5 yrs. 10 ms. 13 ds.

No. 632.

[White marble in freestone base. Good condition, but slightly inclined.]

Sacred to the memory of NICHOLAS H. DREW, who
died Oct. 21, 1847, aged 41 years.

"The righteous hath hope in his death."

Thou hast gone to thy rest dear Husband
Whilst I am left to mourn:
And travel on in sorrow
And trouble here alone.

But again I hope to meet thee
When the ills of life are fled
And in Heaven I hope to greet thee
Where no farewell tear is shed.

No. 633.

[One of the six bearing date in the 17th century. It is, as Mr.
Davis informs us, (see "Ancient Landmarks") of purple Welsh slate.
It is in good condition, is handsomely carved, and is protected by a
hood of galvanized iron. Symbol. The inscription is in capital letters.]

Here lyes ye body of Mr Thomas Clark aged 98 years
departed this life March ye 24th 1697.

(The footstone bears the symbol, and the words:)

Mr. Thomas Clark 1697.

[It was in 1889 that I copied the inscriptions on Burial Hill. Since
then I have inserted a few from such new monuments as came under
my observation. Among these is the following, copied from a metallic plate secured to a huge boulder recently placed on the grave of
Thomas Clark. On said plate this name is spelled "Clarke," which
forbids us to suppose that the spelling reform, of omitting silent letters, caused Mr. Clark's de (s) cendants to leave out the letter S in
two words of the inscription.]

(All in capital letters on the plate.)

Here lies buried ye body of Mr. Thomas Clarke, aged
98. Departed this life March 24, 1697. Thomas Clarke
came to Plymouth from England in the ship Anne 1623.
He married Susan Ring of Plymouth, 1634. Their children were Andrew, James, William, Susanna, Nathaniel
and John. From whom decended a numerous posterity.
He married his second wife Mrs. Alice Hallett Nichols of
Boston, in 1664. He lived for some years in Boston, and
also in Harwich of which town he was one of the original
proprietors. He died in Plymouth, having lived in the
reigns of six British sovereigns and the Com'th.

This stone is erected to his memory by his decendants
A. D. 1891.

No. 634.

[Another of the six 17th century monuments. Blue slate, cleft
downwards from the top, separating about one-third of the stone.
Stone is inclined. It has no moss, and the inscription is perfectly
clear and plain. The lettering, as on many of the oldest stones, is in

capital letters, which in this work I have not deemed it advisable to endeavor to imitate. Symbol.]

Here lyes ye body of Mrs Hannah Clark wife to Mr William Clark Decd Febry ye 20th 1687 in the 29th year of her age

No. 635.

[Blue slate. Compact, and in good condition. Symbol.]

Here lyes ye body of Nathl Clark Esqr Decd Janry ye 31st 1717 in the 74th year of his age

No. 636.

[Purplish striated slate, very thick. 3 feet wide by 2 1-2 feet high. Handsomely wrought. Good condition. Symbol.]

Here lyes buried the body of Reverend Mr Ephraim Little Pastor of the Church of Christ at Plymouth, Aged 47 years 2 m. & 3 d. Deceased Novr ye 24th 1723

No. 637.

[Granite block. 4 feet high, 6 or 8 inches thick.]

Rev. James H. Bugbee, Preacher of the Gospel of Christ, Pastor of the First Universalist Society in Plymouth, Died May 10, 1834, aged 31 years.

No. 638.

[Blue slate. 3 1-2 feet high. Good condition. Two urns at the top. North of preceding, and 4 or 5 feet from concrete walk.]

Erected to the memory of WILLIAM WESTON, who departed this life Decem. 28th. 1838, aged 82 years. Also MARY his wife, departed this life March 7th. 1843, aged 83 years.

No. 639.

[Blue slate. Cleft upward, near the ground. Weeping willow and urn.]

In memory of Capt William Weston who died June 27, 1820, in the Ninetieth year of his age.

No. 640.

[Blue slate. Moss-grown. Symbol.]

Erected to perpetuate the memory of Mrs MARY WESTON who died July 28th 1805 in the 69th year of her age.

Can storied urn or animated bust
Back to its mansion call the fleeting breath?
Can honor's voice provoke the silent dust,
Or flattery sooth the dull, cold ear of death?

No. 641.

[Purplish slate. Inclined at an angle of 45°. Moss-grown. Symbol.]

To the memory of Capt COOMER WESTON who died at Martha's Vineyard (and is there interred) January 10th A. D. 1796 In the 34th year of his age

That hardy virtue which adorn'd thy bloom
Friendship recalls and weeps upon thy tomb
There sad remembrance drops a silent tear
And chaste affection stands a mourner there

No. 642.

[White marble. Weathering rough. Moss-grown.]

In memory of Mrs Patty Weston, who died May 27, 1841, aged 78 years. Thomas Weston, son of Capt. Coomer and Mrs Patty Weston, died at St. Pierres, Martinique, Dec. 10, 1808, aged 20 years.

No. 643.

[Blue slate. Surface cracked in all directions. Symbol.]

Here lies buried Mrs Prudence Widow to Mr Thomas Weston who died Janry ye 4th 1766 In ye 59th year of her age

No. 644.

[Low, blue slate. Split into two nearly equal parts by cleft parallel to surface. Symbol. The inscribed part is sound, and the lettering as clear as when first cut. There is probably an error in the spelling of the surname.]

Here lyes buried the body of Mrs Mary Westron wife to Mr Thomas Westron Aged about 28 years Decd Febry ye 13th 1730

No. 645.

[Blue slate. Laminæ separating. Surface cleft from top nearly to the ground. Symbol.]

Here lyes Buried Mrs Mary Clark ye widow of Mr Samuel Clark who died Octr ye Jst J765 in ye 73d year of her age

No. 646.

[Light blue slate. Sound, but moss-grown. Symbol.]

Here lies buried Mr. Samuel Clark who died April ye 2d 1763 aged 76th years

No. 647.

[Blue slate. Inclined. Quite sound, but moss-grown. The words:]

Memento Mori

(appear above the symbol.)

In Memory of Mr Joseph Fulghum who Departed this Life June 14 1764 Aged about 44 years

No. 648.

[Blue slate. Fair condition, but moss-grown. Symbol, with words as in No. 647.]

In Memory of Mrs Luraina   wife of Capt Joseph Fulghum who Departed this Life Novr 28th 1778 In the 53d year of her age

No. 649.

[Blue slate. Somewhat defaced. Symbol.]

In Memory of Joseph Son of Capt Joseph & Mrs Luraina Fulghum who Departed this Life Febry 6th 1768 Aged JJ Years & 8 Days

No. 650.

[Light blue slate. Good condition, save some moss. Crossbones above symbol,—which last is a winged skull.]

Here lyes buried the body of Mr Nathl Howland died Decr ye 20th 1746 in the 76th year of his age.

No. 651.

[Light blue slate. Apparently sound, but surface much moss-grown. Symbol.]

Here lyes ye body of Martha Howland aged about 46 years Decd Augt ye 11th 1718.

No. 652.

[Purplish slate. Good condition. Symbol.]

Here lies buried the body of Mrs EXPERIENCE LOTHROP the wife of Capt BENJAMIN LOTHROP died Sepr 5th 1748 in the 47th Year of her Age.

No. 653.

[Dark compact slate. The oldest monument on Burial Hill,—considering which circumstance, it may be said to be in excellent condition. It probably has the usual cherub or symbol,—if so, it is concealed by the iron hood which protects the edges of the stone from water and frost. It is a few feet from a small elm, now (1891) 6 or 8 inches in circumference, at one foot above the ground; and by its side is a wooden slab, bearing the legend, "The Grave of Edward Gray, June, 1681."]

Here lyeth ye body of Edward Gray   ent
Aged about 52 years & Departed this life ye last of Ivne 1681

No. 654.

[White marble obelisk on granite base. Eight feet in height. Good condition, save fissures on the marble member between obelisk and granite base.]

(On N. side.)

EZRA CHURCHALL Died April 11, 1832 in his 28th year. SUSAN A. his wife died Oct. 18, 1878, Æ. 70 y'rs 3 m's. 7 d's.

(On the W. side.)

DANIEL CURRIER

SUSAN E. wife of Daniel Currier & daughter of Ezra & Susan A. Churchall died April 18, 1864, Æ 31 y'rs & 11 d's.

> Although her earthly sun has set,
> Its light shall linger round us yet,
> Pure—radiant—blest!

(On S. side.)

FREDDIE A. Died March 20, 1858, Æ. 15 mo's.
WINNIE S. Died Jan. 28, 1862 Æ. 7 mo's & 16 d's.

EZRA C. Died Sept. 1, 1862, Æ 7 y'rs 4 mo's & 22 d's. Children of Daniel & Susan E. Currier.

> Treasure's to these parents given
> Planted on earth to bloom in Heaven.

No. 655.

[White marble. Weathering rough.]

WILLIAM H. died Aug. 2, 1842 ; aged 1 y'r & 4 mo. CHARLES B. died Oct. 4, 1849 : aged 5 mo's & 15 d's. JAMES S. died Feb. 2, 1854 : aged 14 y'rs & 6 mo's. Children of Thadius & Mary A. Faunce.

> By angels borne they fly to rest,
> We know 'tis well nay more 'tis best
> When we our Pilgrim path have trod
> We hope to meet them all with God.

No. 656.

[White marble. Weathers rough. Set in stone socket.]

CHARLES A. Son of Edward & Salina Doten, Died March 23, 1872, Aged 23 y'rs 2 mo's.

No. 657.

[Purplish blue slate. Good condition.]

BETSEY P. died Oct. 25, 1851, in her 19th y'r. HELLEN died Sept. 4th, 1847, aged 7 years. LOUISA S. died Sept. 12th, 1847, aged 3 years. Children of Edward & Salina Doten.

> Tis the blest hope that they shall meet
> And with their friends shall Jesus greet—
> That lamb-like sacrifice.

No. 658.

[Blue slate, 4 feet high. Good condition, but has some moss.]

ESTHER DOTEN, widow of Edward Doten, died Jan. 27, 1843, aged 67 years. Also their Son LEWIS, died Feb,ry 27, 1839, aged 26 years.

No. 659.

[Blue slate. Good condition, but inclined. Urn.]

In memory of Deborah Lucas Daughter of Mr Alden Lucas and Mrs Deborah his wife Died July 24th 1810 aged 1 year & 8 days

> This infant's soul has begat her clay,
> We hope to heaven has wing'd away.

No. 660.

[Blue slate. Five feet in height. Good condition. Urn, with flame issuing from its top.]

Erected in memory of CAPT. LEWIS GOODWIN who died April 26, 1836, aged 53 y.rs. Also of Lorenzo ; son of

Lewis and Anna Goodwin, who died Oct. 1, 1818, aged 2
Mon.

> What is our life:—'tis but a moment lent:
> A transient lease of earthly troubles given.
> And what is death:—tis but a summons sent
> To call us from this tenement to Heaven.

No. 661.

[Similar to 660. Seam across face, about a foot above the ground.]

Erected in memory of Mrs. ANNA GOODWIN, wife
of Capt. Lewis Goodwin, died Aug. 7, 1838, in the 59 y.r
of her age.

> Cease then to murmur; know that God is just;
> And learn this truth· for, it is his decreeing;
> That dust must mingle with its mother dust
> The Spirit flies to him who gave it being."

No. 662.

[Blue slate. Good condition. Leafy branch.]

Erected To the memory of Anna Lewis Goodwin
Daughter of Capt Lewis Goodwin and Mrs Anna his wife
who Departed this life September 26 1808 aged three
months and 26 days.

> So fades the lovely, blooming flower
> Frail, smiling solace of an hour,
> So soon our transient comforts fly,
> And pleasure only blooms to die.

No. 663.

[Similar to 662.]

Sacred to the memory of Lewis Goodwin Son of Capt
Lewis Goodwin and Mrs Anna his wife who was Born and
Died September the 2d 1809

> Life is a Span a fleeting hour
> How soon the vapour flies
> Man is a tender transient flower
> That in the Blooming Dies.

No. 664.

[White marble on granite base. Good condition.]

Lydia L. Churchill died April 28, 1875, Aged 81 y'rs.

No. 665.

[Blue slate. Five feet in height. Figure in relief, of a vessel in a
storm. A seam or crack extends from near centre of top downward
thro' the figure, and then curves to the right, clearing the inscription.]

Erected in memory of JOSEPH CHURCHILL, who
sail'd from Boston Nov. 1836, in the Brig Plymouth
Rock of Plymouth, Bound to Rochelle in France, and supposed Foundered at Sea aged 54 years. Also to his Children JOSEPH LEWIS died at Sea on board the Brig
Androscoggin of Portland Aug. 1842, aged 37 yrs.
MARCIA GOODWIN, died May 2, 1839, aged 22 yrs.

9

No. 666.

[Fine, blue slate. Good condition. Urn.]

In memory of Amelia Churchill Daughter of Capt
Joseph Churchill and Mercy his wife died Sepr 12th 1807
aged 7 months & 5 days

> The infant's bloom with morning Smile
> Did but the parents hearts beguile
> Ended in death now pale She lies
> And fills the parents hearts with Sighs.

No. 667.

[Blue slate, 3 1-2 feet in height. Is cleft in its whole length, from
top to ground, and again at left of centre. Weeping willow and
urn.]

In memory of Mrs MERCY CHURCHILL wife of Mr
Joseph Churchill who died October 2, A D. 1822 in the
42 year of her age   Also in memory of their Children
Edward who died January 8, 1809 aged one year. George
who died Octr 21, 1811 aged 3 months   Charles Thomas
who died September 13, 1825, aged 4 years & 5 months.

No. 668.

[Purplish blue slate. Good condition, but slightly inclined. Urn.]

In memory of MARIAH, widow of Benjamin Holmes.
who died April 13, 1850, Æ. 75 y'rs 4 mo's.

> Thrice happy souls who've gone before,
> To their inheritance Divine
> They labor sorrow sigh no more
> But bright in endless glory shine

No. 669.

[Blue slate. Moss-covered. Inclined. Urn.]

In memory of BENJAMIN HOLMES, died May 7,
1836, aged 61 years.

> Unveil thy bosom, faithful tomb,
> Take this new treasure to thy trust,
> And give these sacred relics room
> To slumber in thy silent dust.

No. 670.

[Purplish blue slate. Good condition. Urn.]

In memory of SUSAN C. wife of Ichabod T. Holmes,
who died April 14, 1847, Æt. 31 y'rs 4 mo's.

> Her soul has gone to Heaven we trust,
> God call'd her home he thought it best.

No. 671.

[Blue slate. Fair condition. Weeping willow and urn.]

In Memory of RUTH G. Born Sept. 26, 1852, Died
Feb. 22, 1856, Ruth G. 2d Born March 2, 1856, Died
Sept. 12, 1856, Children of Ichabod T. & Ruth Holmes.

No. 672.

[White marble. In free, or sand, stone socket. Roughened by climatic influences, which I term in this work "weathering rough." Is inclosed with No. 673 in a white fence.]

GRANVILL S. Died Dec. 20, 1852, Aged 19 y'rs. 5 mo's. EDWARD P. Died March 18, 1854, Aged 16 y'rs. 7 mo's. REBECCA J. Died Oct. 10, 1851, Aged 10 mo's. Children of Granvill & Rebecca D. Griffin.

Gone but not forgotten.

No. 673.

[White marble in freestone base. Good condition.]

Rebecca D. wife of GRANVILLE GRIFFIN Died April 9, 1881, Aged 72 years, 24 days.

Gone but not forgotten.

No. 674.

[Low, firm, blue slate. Festoons.]

In memory of John T. Clark, Son of John Clark 3d & Abigail his wife who died Augt 20, 1823, aged 2 years

No. 675.

[Purple slate. Very compact.]

REBECCA THOMAS wife of Zoeth Clark, Died Oct. 13, 1843, Aged 77 years.

No. 676.

[Blue slate. Good condition. Weeping willow and urn.]

In memory of Mr. ZOHETH CLARK, who died June 12th 1826; in the 60th year of his age.

'Tis done he sleeps the sleep of death,
Nor will he wake again,
Till the last trumpet's awful voice
Shall rend the grave in twain.

No. 677.

[White marble. Weathering rough, but now in fair condition for that material.]

ELLA MARIA only daughter of Zoeth & Rebecca M. CLARK, Died Dec. 17, 1865, Aged 14 y'rs. 4 m's. & 1 day.

And lo! above the dews of night
The vesper star appears
So faith lights up the mourners heart
Whose eyes are dim with tears
Night falls but soon the morning light
Its glorie shall restore
And thus the eyes that sleep in death
Shall wake to close no more.

No. 678.

[White marble column on freestone base; the whole mass inclined, and in danger of falling.]

Whitten

(On east side:)

LYDIA M. wife of CHARLES WHITTEN Jr. called home Apr. 20, 1860; Æ. 30 years.

Thou still art dear, though numbered with the dead.

(On west side:)

MARY H. died Sept. 12, 1853, Æ. 3 mos.
7 ds. WILLIE BRADFORD died Sept. 4, 1859, Æ. 3
months & 2 days.

No. 679.

[Low, white marble. Moss-grown. At top, figure resembling a
butterfly.]

In memory of MARY H. Dau. of Charles & Lydia N.
Whitten who died Sept. 12, 1853, Æ. 3 mo. 7 ds.

No. 680.

[Blue slate. Four and one-half feet high. Good condition. Urn.]

Erected In memory of Mr. BARNABAS HOLMES,
who died March 20, 1837, aged 81 years.

By temperance governed, and by reason taught,
The paths of peace and pleasantness he sought;
With competence and length of days was blest,
And cheered with hopes of everlasting rest.

No. 681.

[Blue slate. Good condition. Symbol.]

In Memory of Mr. JOSEPH PLASKET who died August 1, A. D. 1794 in the 48 year of his age

All ye that doth behold my stone
Consider how soon I was gone
Death does not always warning give
Therefore be careful how you live
Repent in time, no time delay
I in my prime was called away.

[NOTE (by the Author). The above epitaph was written by Mrs.
Tabitha Plasket (said to have been a school teacher), the wife of the
decedent. She also penned the epitaph for herself (see No. 682 a.),
which is remarkable for a certain independence of spirit. Its first
line corresponds with a remark made, near the close of her life, by
Miss Harriet Martineau, and which is doubtless shared by many
aged people.]

No. 682 a.

[Blue slate. Good condition. Weeping willow and urn.]

In memory of Mrs. Tabitha Plasket who died June 10,
1807 aged 64 years.

Adieu vain world I have seen enough of the
And I am careless what thou say'st of me
Thy smiles I wish not;
Nor thy frowns I fear,
I am now at rest my head lies quiet here.

. No. 682 b.

[Blue slate. Four feet in height. Seamed half across surface, near
the ground.]

In memory of Mr. ASA JOYCE who died Nov. 5, 1826 :
aged 57 years. Mrs. LUCY JOYCE his wife died July 2,
1852, aged 81 years.

Blessed are the dead who die in the Lord.

No. 683.

[Low, blue slate. Seam on face. Urn.]

In memory of Thomas Bradford Son of Mr Thomas Bradford & Mrs. Mary his wife died Jenury 7 1804 aged 1 year.

No. 684.

[White marble, veined, set in freestone socket. Good condition, save being inclined.]

LEMUEL D. HOLMES, Died June 4, 1873, Aged 75 y'rs 4 mo's. POLLY his wife Died Sept. 13, 1866, Aged 65 y'rs 1 mo. MARY E. their dau. Died Dec. 30, 1832, Aged 4 y'rs 2 mo's.

No. 685.

[White marble. Weathering rough.]

NATHANIEL HOLMES Jr. died Aug. 29, 1805; in the 31st year of his age. ELIZABETH HOLMES, his widow died Jan. 30, 1860 Æ. 86 yrs 7 mos & 8 days. BETSEY C. HOLMES, their daughter died Feb. 26, 1848: in the 48th year of her age

No. 686.

[Blue slate. Good condition, but inclined. Weeping willow and urn.]

Erected To the memory of Mrs. Lucy T. Gleason wife of Mr. James G. Gleason died November 23, 1818, aged 18 years.

Calm be thy rest Till the last trump shall sound,
And then awake to sing the Glorious song
Worthy the Lamb.

No. 687.

[White marble in stone socket with brimstone for cement. The whole mass inclined.]

PHEBE, wife of James G. Gleason, died Oct. 10, 1860; aged 70 y'rs, 1 mo. 5 d'ys.

Dear is the spot where loved ones sleep,
And sweet the strain which angels pour;
O, why should we in anguish weep?
They are not lost—but gone before.

No. 688.

[Marble, mottled or veined. This and the next No. are set on one and the same granite base.]

SAMUEL N. HOLMES Died July 10, 1840, Aged 84 y'rs 8 mo's.

He rests from his labors.

No. 689.

[Similar to 688. Both in good condition.]

MARY T. HOLMES Died Oct. 21, 1871, Aged 95 y'rs 5 mo's 19 days.

Blessed are the dead which die in the Lord.

No. 690.

[Blue slate. Three urns at top indicate three names on stone; but this is broken and so set in the ground, that only the first name can be read.]

THOMAS NELSON died Feb. 17, 1832 aged 66 years. AB

(The footstone has three lines, of two initials each :)

T. N. | A. N. | M. N.

·No. 691.

[Blue slate. Good condition. Symbol.]

To the memory of Mr. LEMUEL NELSON who died Octr 30th 1801 in the 30th year of his age.

No. 692.

[Blue slate. Good condition. Weeping willow and urn.]

In memory of Miss Ruth Nelson who died September 13, 1823 in the 64th year of her age.

No. 693.

[Blue slate. Three and a half feet in height. Good condition.]

In memory of LYDIA, widow of Ebenezer Nelson, who died Oct 21st, 1851, aged 87 years

No. 694.

[Blue slate. Seams across face, below the inscription. Weeping willow and urn.]

Erected to the memory of MR. EBENEZER NELSON who died Febr 14. 1829 ; in the 73 year of his age.

E   N

No. 695.

[Blue slate, Good condition. Symbol.]

To the memory of Mrs Ruth Nelson wife of Mr Ebenezer Nelson who died April 29th 1803 aged 69 years.

No. 696.

[Blue slate. Fair condition, but moss-grown. Weeping willow and urn.]

To the memory of Mr. EBENEZER NELSON who died June 29 1809 in the 86 year of his age.

No. 697.

[Blue slate. Good condition, but inclined. Figure of an eye, with rays darting from it; below it, clouds; and on either side a head with wings (commonly called "cherub," but which I have in this work called a symbol.)]

To the memory of Mr Elisha Nelson Son of Mr Ebenezer Nelson & Mrs Ruth his Wife he died Ocr the 6 1797 in the 22d year of his age

No. 698.

[Low, blue slate; of pyramidal form. Fair condition. Symbol.]

To the memory of Mrs Hannah Nelson Daughter Of Mr Ebenezer Nelson & Mrs Ruth his wife Died December 20 1798 In 29 year of her age.

No. 699.

[Blue slate. Fair condition. Weeping willow and urn.]

Sacred to the memory of two Children of Mr Ebenezer Nelson Junr & Mary his wife. Ebenezer born and died January 16, 1814. Lewis born Januy 3, 1818, died April 18, 1820, aged two years three months & 15 days.

No. 700.

[Blue slate. Good condition. Weeping willow and urn.]

Sacred to the memory of Mr. William Nelson, who died October 9, 1820. in the 53 year of his age.

God my Redeemer lives
And often from the skies
Looks down and watches all my dust
Till he shall bid it rise.

No. 701.

[Blue slate. Moss-grown. Has met, apparently, a fate similar to that of No. 690. Weeping willow and urn. Several seams on face of stone, one cutting through the first word.]

Sacred to the memory of Bathsheba Nelson Consort of William Nelson died Sept. 12, 1829 aged 56 years

No. 702.

[White marble. Four feet in height. Weathering rough. Set in a socket of dark-colored stone (frequently met with and which I term "freestone"). Whole mass much inclined, and in danger of falling. Weeping willow and urn.]

LEMUEL BRADFORD died March 1, 1855, aged 66 years.

Calm be the spot where his form now repose,
May the friends who so loved him revisit his grave
And feel though the cold sod his ashes enclose,
He lives in the presence of one who will save.

No. 703.

[Similar to 702, but not so dangerously inclined.]

BATHSHEBA BRADFORD wife of Lemuel Bradford died Jan. 22, 1861 ; Aged 68 yrs 10 mos. & 12 days.

Dear as thou wert—and justly dear,
We will not weep for thee
One thought shall check the startling tear,
It is, that thou art free.

No. 704.

[Blue slate. Has a seam on surface, indicating a short life for this handsome monument. Urn.]

Erected to the memory of CHARLES BRADFORD Lost at Sea Sept. 1846, Aged 25 yrs. & 8 Mon. Also

HANNAH E. BRADFORD, Died March 23d. 1854. Aged 21 yrs.

> Our Saviour summons us away,
> A brighter world to view
> Although a while behind you stay,
> Weep not, weep not for us.

No. 705.

[Purplish shade of blue slate. Good condition. Weeping willow and urn.]

Died June 20, 1833, Aged 15 yrs & 7 Mon. EBENEZER NELSON. Died Sept. 13, 1826, Aged 2 years, LYDIA NELSON, Children of Lemuel & Bathsheba Bradford.

No. 706.

[Blue slate. Seam near top; good condition otherwise.]

Erected to the Memory of BATHSHEBA BRAD-FORD, Dau.tr of Lemuel & Bathsheba Bradford, died Jan.ry 15, 1837, in the 22 y.r of her age

> Ah, art thou gone, is thy short journey o'er
> O lovely child, shall we not see thee more
> Thy soul has gone to everlasting rest
> To dwell with Christ and be forever blest;
> We'll not repine nor wish thee back again,
> To this dark world of trouble and of pain
> Nor will we murmur at the hand divine
> That took our daughter, Lord, for she was thine.

No. 707.

[White marble on granite base. Fair condition. Ornamental work at top, surrounding the letter " B."]

EBENEZER N. BRADFORD, Killed on Rail Road at Copetown, Canada, Jan. 28, 1870.

> He giveth his beloved sleep.

No. 708.

[Low, blue slate. Laminæ separating. Symbol.]

In memory of Ebenezer son of Mr Samuel Doten & Mrs Eunice his wife who died April 28th 1785 Aged 4 Months & 3 Days.

No. 709.

[Lower fragment of a blue slate monument. Upper portion missing.]

Ancel s n of Mr Samuel Dotey & Mrs Eunice his wife who died June 7, J79J aged J year & 7 months

No. 710.

[Blue slate. Good condition. Weeping willow and urn; star on each side.]

Departed this life Sept. 30, 1829, aged 34 years Mr. George Nelson.

———

> Gone to the resting place of man,
> His long his silent Home,
> Where ages past have gone before
> Where future ages come.

No. 711.
[Blue slate. Good condition. Weeping willow and urn.]
In memory of Ruth Nelson Daughter of George Nelson and Ruth his wife Died Sept 27, 1826, aged 6 months.

Lovely babe thy days are ended
All thy painful days below,
And thy spirit has ascended,
Where living pleasures ever flow.

No. 712.
[White marble on granite. Good condition.]
LUCY, wife of Charles Nelson, Died Nov. 6, 1874, Aged 69 y'rs 11 mo's.

No. 713.
[White marble, on freestone base. Good condition. Ornamented sculpture at top.]
Martha T. Dau. of Charles & Lucy NELSON died Sept. 8, 1865, Aged 25 yrs. 7 mo's.

Rest, blessed spirit, rest,
Life's fitful fever's o'er
Earth's circle numbers one the less
But Heaven one seraph more.

No. 714.
[White marble. Fair condition, but weathering rough.]
In memory of CHARLES son of Charles & Lucy Nelson, died Dec 31, 1852, in his 20th year.

He died in hope, he died in faith,
A life of suffering o'er;
He smiling met the shafts of death
And lives to die no more.

Also an Infant daughter.

No. 715.
[White marble, weathering rough. Urn. (This and the following Nos. to 723 inclusive are inclosed in wooden fence.)]
Nancy Winslow Daughter of Mr William P. Ripley Born June 1, 1815, died March 15, 1819, aged 5 years & 9 months.

No. 716.
[White marble. Roughened surface. Cleft several inches downward from summit. Urn.]
Consecrated in memory of Mrs ELIZABETH RIPLEY, Consort of Mr WILLIAM P. RIPLEY, who died Dec. 19, 1822, in the 31 year of her age.

Forgive, blest shade the tributary tear
That mourns thy exit from a world like this;
Forgive the wish that would have kept the here
And stay'd thy progress to the seats of bliss.

No. 717.

[White marble. Nearly four feet high. Disintegrating.]

This Stone is Consecrated To the memory of Mrs. Anna Ripley widow of Mr. Wm. P. Ripley who departed this life Aug. 14, 1813, in the 38 year of her age

Blessed are the dead which die in the Lord.

No. 718.

[White marble, set in freestone. Cement crumbling away. Stone much inclined; weathering rough.]

NANCY RIPLEY, wife of William P. Ripley, Died Aug. 16, 1862, Aged 83 years.

She trusted in the mercy of the Lord, and now rejoices in his Salvation.

No. 719.

[White marble. Rough.]

Erected By Mr. Wm. P. Ripley In remembrance of Mrs POLLY RIPLEY his Amiable Wife Who Died May 5th 1808 in the 30th year of her age

The virtuous are truly happy.

No. 720.

White marble, weathering rough. In a semicircle at top are the words:]

"Having a desire to depart, and to be with Christ."

[Then the inscription:]

Sacred to the memory of DEA. WILLIAM P. RIPLEY, who died Nov. 10, 1842 ; aged 67 years.

A friend of the oppressed and enslaved.

The poor will cherish his memory. The widow and the fatherles shall call him blessed.

His life was gentle, and serene his mind.
His morals pure, his every action just,
A husband dear, and as a parent kind;
As such he lies lamented in the dust,
While weeping friends bend o'er the silent tomb,
Recount his virtues, and his loss deplore.
Faith's piercing eye darts through the dreary gloom,
And hails him bless'd where tears shall flow no more.

No. 721.

[White marble, weathering rough. Urn.]

In memory of LEAVITT RIPLEY who died Sept. 17, 1807 in the 21st year of his age

The all surrounding heav'ns, the Vital air
Is big with Death.

No. 722.

[Blue slate, compact and solid. Weeping willow and urn.]

In memory of Capt. NATHANIEL RIPLEY who died October 23, 1821, in the 80 year of his age

No. 723.

[Blue slate. Good condition. Urn.]

This Stone Consecrated to the memory of Mrs Elizabeth Ripley Consort of Capt Nathaniel Ripley who died may 15, 1801 in the 55 year of her Age.

No. 724.

[Blue slate. Good condition. Weeping willow and urn, with rose twigs on each side.]

In memory of Francis Cobb Son of William Cobb Esq & Elizabeth his wife Died Oct. 8, 1804 aged 3 years 7 months.

No. 725.

[Light blue slate. Three feet high. Somewhat marred. Laminæ separating. Symbol.]

In memory of Mr NEHEMIAH RIPLEY who departed this Life April ye 8th 1775 in ye 75th year of his age

No. 726.

[Blue slate. Good condition. Two urns.]

In Memory of Mr. ICHABOD SHAW, who died Aug. 25, 1821, aged 87 y.rs. Also PRISCILLA his wife who died July 24, 1824 aged 84 y.rs.

No. 727.

[A Goodwin stone. Moss-covered and difficult to read. Symbol.]

Here lyes Interr'd ye Body of SOUTHWORTH Son to ICHABOD SHAW & PRISCILLA his wife, he died Sept ye 9th Day AD. 1772, Aged 7 months and 6 Days

No. 728.

[Blue slate. Laminæ separating to some extent, but in fair condition. Symbol.]

In memory of JAMES HOVEY Esq. who decd Jany ye 7th 1781 in ye 72d year of his Age

No. 729.

[Blue slate. Badly cleft and seamed.]

Here lies Buried ye Body of Mrs Lydia Houey late wife of James Houey Esqr & Daughter of ye late Deen John Atwood decd She died Febry ye 23d 1771 In ye 56th year of her age

No. 730.

[Blue slate. Laminæ separating. Face entire, excepting the symbol, which has lost the greater part of its wings.]

Here lyes Buried ye body of Mrs Mary Hovey late wife of James Hovey Esq She died on ye 2d day of June A D. J774 in the 44th Year of her Age.

No. 731.

John T. Hall June 6, 1819, Sept. 21, 1885

I shall be satisfied, when I awake with thy likeness.

No. 732.

EBER HALL, Lost at sea, Oct. 11, 1820, aged 29 y'rs.
ELIZABETH, his wife died Sept. 12, 1851 aged 61 y'rs.
MARY their dau. died Dec. 15, 1813, aged 8 mo's & 26 d's.

No. 733.

ELIAB WOOD died June 14, 1842, in the 57 year of his age.

For our hearts shall rejoice in him because we have trusted in his holy name.

No. 734.

PERSES, wife of Eliab Wood died Oct. 5th, 1824, in the 38 year of her age

Let thy mercy, O Lord, be upon us, according as we hope in thee.

No. 735.

BETSEY, wife of Eliab Wood died Oct. 23, 1839, in the 49th y.r of her age.

No. 736.

In memory of Mrs. Eleanor Wood wife of Eliab Wood died Jann 28, 1828 ; aged 35 years   Also their Son Isaac L. Wood died June 26 1828 aged 5 months.

No. 737.

In memory of BETSEY S. wife of Eliab Wood Jr. who died June 13, 1841 aged 25 years.

No. 738.

LEMUEL REED born April 25, 1819, died Nov. 20, 1844.

No. 739.

In memory of Mr. William Lewis who died July 15, 1806 in the 30 year of his age

My flesh shall slumber in the ground
Till the last trumpet's joyful sound,
Then burst its chains with sweet surprise,
And in my Saviour's image rise.

No. 740.

[Blue slate. Pyramidal outline. Four feet in height. Good condition. Weeping willow and urn.]

In memory of Capt ELLIS BREWSTER, who died at Sea, August 27, 1817 in the 49 year of his age.

No. 741.

[Blue slate. Top and right-hand corner gone.]

Capt Ellis Brews   and Mrs Nancy   wife died Dec 13 180   aged 4   years

He listen'd for a while to hear
Our mortal griefs then tun'd his ear
To angel harps and songs and cried
To join their notes celestial sigh'd and dyed.

No. 742.

[White marble mottled. Has left a granite base, and is set in the ground. Marble in sound condition.]

Daniel H. Sears, Died Sept. 1 1882 Aged 71 y'rs, 5 mo's, 12 days.

(On the reverse the word:)

FATHER.

No. 743.

[White marble similar to preceding. Has left a marble plinth which was on a freestone base, and is set in the ground.]

Belinda T. wife of Daniel H. Sears, Died Oct. 21, 1832, Aged 38 y'rs 2 mo's, 15 days.

(On reverse:)

MOTHER

No. 744.

[Low, blue slate, top and right side broken off, taking part of inscription.]

of Capt. Willia   Mrs Elizabeth Br
who died Sept 22d 180   aged 3 years 6 months & 22 days

Hush weeping parents & ye kindred dear
Weep not for us nor shed a mournful tear
Our bodys sleep within the silent dust
Our souls redeem'd are happy with the just.

No. 745.

[Very small, low, blue slate. Good condition. Symbol.]

To the memory of Elizabeth Taylor Brewster daughter of Capt William & Mrs Elizabeth Brewster who died Sept 25, 1802 aged 17 days

No. 746.

[Blue slate. Good condition. Symbol.]

In memory of William Brewster Son of Capt William Brewster & Mrs. Elizabeth his wife died April 5th 1804 aged one year 5 months & 17 days

The father and the children dead
We hope to heaven their souls are fled
The widow now alone is left
Of all her family bereft.
May she now put her trust in God.
To heal the wounds made by his rod.

No. 747.

[White marble. Set in the ground, in front of its former stone socket or base.]

WILLIAM BREWSTER, Born Dec 27, 1770, Died Jan. 12, 1804 ELIZABETH T. BREWSTER, Born Oct. 30, 1769, Died Dec. 31, 1854 Also their Children Elizabeth T. Born Aug. 31, 1796, Died June 7, 1798. William Born March 1, 1799, Died Sept. 22, 1802. Elizabeth T. Born May 8, 1801 Died Sept. 25, 1802. William Born Oct, 23, 1803 Died April 4, 1805.

No. 748.

[A handsome granite column in iron inclosure. Inscription, on bronze tablet, in capital letters.]

Dr. ZACHEUS BARTLETT born Sept. 20, 1765, died Dec. 25, 1835.

———

HANNAH BARTLETT born Aug. 24, 1777, died June 21, 1858.

No. 749.

[White marble. In stone socket. Inclined.]

FREDERICK JACKSON, Born May 19, 1791 : Died June 27, 1857.

No. 750.

[Blue slate. Good condition. Urn.]

CAROLINE JACKSON, died June 5, 1841, aged 48 years.

No. 751.

[Blue slate. Good condition. Weeping willow, mausoleum, and urn.]

In memory of Sarah. widow of the late Thomas Jackson who died Jan. 30, 1846 in her 70th year.

No. 752.

[Blue slate. Good condition. Weeping willow over tomb, or mausoleum.]

In memory of MR. THOMAS JACKSON who died Nov. 10, 1840 aged 86 years

No. 753.

[Blue slate. Good condition. Urn, with lily on each side.]

To the memory of Mrs LUCY JACKSON wife of Mr. THOMAS JACKSON, who died Nov. 10, 1804, Aged 39 years

The sainted partner, and the friend sincere
The tenderest parent—traveller—slumbers here
Smote by the storm, with blooms and verdure crowned
So falls the tree, and spreads a fragrance round.

No. 754.

[Light colored blue slate. Crossbones, under which are two symbols (or "cherubs").]

In Memory of Capt THOMAS JACKSON who departed this Life July ye J0th J775 Aged 7 years.

[The unit figure of the age is marred. It seems to be "5."

No. 755.

[Blue slate. Compact. Moss-grown. Symbol.]

Here lies buried Capt Hezekiah Jackson who decd Febry ye 6th J768 In ye 30th year of his Age.

No. 756.

[Blue slate. Laminæ separating. Surface somewhat seamed. Symbol.]

In Memory of Mrs ELIZABETH JACKSON wife of Mr NATHANIEL JACKSON who departed this Life Octr ye 27th J775 aged 28 years

No. 757.

[Light blue slate. Laminæ separated. Surface seamed and cleft. Crossbones and two symbols, similar to 754.]

In Memory of Mrs HANNAH JACKSON widow of Capt THOMAS JACKSON decd who departed this Life Jany ye 21st 1778 Aged 70 years

No. 758.

[A Goodwin stone. Covered with moss. Is about 15 inches high. Symbol.]

Here lies buried the body of Salome Daughter of William Hall Jackson & Deborah his wife who departed this life ye 27th of July AD 1769 aged 10 Months & 2 Days

No. 759.

[Low, blue slate. Fair condition. Symbol.]

In memory of Elizabeth Daughter to Mr Samuel & Mrs Experience Jackson his wife decd July ye 3J J763 aged JJ days.

No. 760.

[Low, blue slate. Laminæ separating. Symbol, injured.]

In Memory of Ezra Thayer Jackson son of Mr Thomas Jackson 2d & Mrs Lucy his wife who died Novr 23d J783 Aged 25 days

What did the Little hasty Sojournr find so forbidding & disgustful in our upper World to occasion its precipitant exit.

No. 761.

[Low, blue slate. Sound and compact. Symbol.]

In Memory of Frederic son of Mr Thomas Jackson and Mrs Lucy his wife who died March J5, J788 aged J year & 5 days

O! happy Probationer! accepted, without being exercised!—It was thy peculiar Privilege not to feel the slightest of those Evils, which oppress thy surviving kindred.

No. 762.

[Low, blue slate. Good condition. Symbol.]

Died Augst 22d 1788 Desire Jackson Daughter of Mr Thomas Jackson & Mrs Lucy his wife aged 2 months & 13 days

No. 763.

[Low, blue slate. Good condition. Symbol.]

Died Septr 10th 1796 Lucy Jackson Daughter of Mr Thomas Jackson & Mrs Lucy his wife aged 1 year 3 months & 9 days.

No. 764.

[White marble. Disintegrating rapidly. Urn.]

In Memory of MERCY JACKSON died Octr 13th 1799 aged 29 years.

> At thy Command she meekly yields
> Her body to the dust
> Jesus, she trusts alone in thee
> And knows in whom she trusts.

No. 765.

[Blue slate. Over 4 feet in height. Good condition, except two seams on surface laminæ. Figure of obelisk at top, in relief.]

Consecrated to the memory of Mr SAMUEL JACKSON who departed this life March 27th 1805 in the 74th year of his age.

> Let Earth dissolve, yon ponderous orbs descend
> And grind us into dust the soul is safe
> The man emerges, mounts above the wreck
> A towring flame from nature's funeral pyre.

No. 766.

[Blue slate. Good condition; save moss-grown. Urn.]

In memory of Experience Jackson relict of Samuel Jackson who died August 23 1808 aged 72.

No. 767.

[White marble, standing in a broken stone base. Marble in fair condition.]

Erected In memory of NATHANIEL GOODWIN, died Feb. 13, 1857: in his 87th year.

No. 768.

[White marble. Weathering rough.]

Erected in memory of LYDIA GOODWIN, Consort of NATHIEL Goodwin died Aug. 29, 1842, in her 74th year.

No. 769.

[White marble, 4 feet in height. Good condition.]

Erected in memory of MARY ANN. dau. of Nath.l & Lydia Goodwin. died April 7, 1832, aged 26 y'rs & 6

mo. Also their Son Edward J. Goodwin, died in Havana
March 16, 1828, aged 24 y'rs. & 6 mo.

No. 770.

[Blue slate. Moss-grown, but sound and compact. Two symbols.]

In memory of Mrs. RUTH GOODWIN, widow of Genl
Nathl Goodwin who died Feb. 10, 1825, Aged 79 years

No. 771.

[Blue slate. 4 1-2 feet high. Several seams entirely across the surface. Urn at top. Inscription in large figure of urn.]

To the memory of Genl Nathl Goodwin who departed
this life March 8th 1819 aged 70 years

No. 772.

[Very thick, blue slate. Laminæ separating. Moss-grown. Crossbones, with two symbols beneath.]

To the memory of Mrs MOLLY GOODWIN wife of
Nathaniel Goodwin Esqr who departed this Life Octr ye
22d AD 1779 Ætatis 30 years.

No. 773.

[Low, blue slate. Good condition, but moss-grown. Symbol.]

To the memory of Hannah Daughter of Nathl Goodwin and Molly his Wife who died May ye 5th 1772
Ætatis 8 Days

No. 774.

[Low, blue slate. Moss-grown. Fair condition. Urn.]

To the memory of Molly I. Goodwin daughter of Mr
Thomas & Mrs Abigal Goodwin of Portland who died
Augst 24, 1798 aged 15 months

No. 775.

[Low, blue slate. Fair condition. Symbol.]

In Memory of Lazarus son of Nathl Goodwin Esqr and
Mrs Molly his wife who died July ye 29th 1778 Ætatis 6
Days

No. 776.

[Purple slate, sound and compact. Set in granite base, with a cement which appears to be crumbling. Weeping willow and urn.]

In memory of Dr Caleb Boutelle, who died Sept. 2,
1819, aged 35 years.

"He that believeth on me, though he were dead, yet shall he live."

No. 777.

[Similar to 776.]

In memory of Ann Goodwin Boutelle, who died Oct. 2,
1874, aged 89 years

"Jesus said unto her I am the resurrection & the life."

10

No. 778.

[White marble. Discolored. Open book in relief.]

In Memory of ISAAC J. LUCAS, Jr. Born Feb. 20, 1830, Died Oct. 17, 1858, Aged 28 y'rs 8 mo.

Mark the perfect man, and behold the upright: for the end of that man is peace. Ps. 37.,37.

No. 779.

[White marble. Seamed slightly. Fair condition.]

MARY A. LUCAS, Wife of Isaac J. Lucas Jr. Died Apr. 8, 1861 : aged 28 years, 5 mos.

No. 780.

[White marble. Four feet high. Set in freestone base. Whole mass inclined. Stone itself in good condition.]

ISAAC J. LUCAS Born July 3, 1797, Died Dec. 20, 1877, Aged 80 y'rs 5 mo's 17 days.

Trusting in Jesus.

No. 781.

[White marble, in stone socket. Good condition.]

CATHERINE HOWLAND Wife of Isaac J. Lucas, Born July 17, 1800. Died Jan. 18, 1865, Æ. 64 yrs 6 mos. Also three children Catherine H. Lewis F. & George W.

No. 782.

[White marble. Weathering rough. Has left a broken socket, and is set in the ground.]

HANNAH J. WASHBURN daughter of Isaac J. & Catherine Lucas, Died October 17, 1863 ; Æ. 36 years 6 mos.

No. 783.

[White marble. Rough and moss-grown. Square and compasses and "G" at top. Figure of an obelisk, having before it "Psalm" and after it "verse 1." This marble is rapidly disintegrating.]

Erected for the memory of Captn LEVI LUCAS who died April 6, 1814, Æt. 46.

Behold how good and how pleasant it is for brethren to dwell together in unity.

No. 784.

[Blue slate. Broken diagonally across. Upper moiety gone, but an inscription remains.]

To   e memory of Mrs. HANNAH LUCAS wife of Capt Levi Lucas who died Octr 6 1801 in the 29th year of her age

No. 785.

[Low, blue slate. Laminæ separating. Surface cleft whole length in two places. Symbol.]

In memory of Harriet Daughter of Mr Samuel & Mrs Hannah Jackson who died Sept. 17, 1793 aged 10 months & 3d   (piece gone)

Babes thither caught from Womb and Breast
Claim Right to sing above the Rest
Because they found the happy shore
They never saw nor sought before.

No. 786.

[Mottled marble. On granite base. Inclosed in granite curbing with No. 787. Good condition.]

ELLIS BARNES Died in Whatcom, Washington Territory, Aug. 29, 1858, Aged 31 y'rs.

An affectionate son & brother.

No. 787.

[Similar to 786.]

WILLIAM BREWSTER BARNES Died Dec. 14, 1870 Aged 59 y'rs 10 m's.

An affectionate Husband & Father.

No. 788.

[Blue slate. Weatherworn. Skull at top; under this, crossbones and symbol.]

In memory of Mrs Joanah Holmes who departed this life Decr 17th 1773 in the 76th year of her age.

[NOTE. Young trees, growing close to stone, conceal part of the inscription.]

No. 789.

[Low, blue slate. Laminæ separating. Moss-grown. Symbol.]

In Memory of Jonathan son of Captain Elkanah Bartlett & Mrs Sarah his wife who died Sept ye 17th 1781 aged 15 months.

No. 790.

[White marble on granite base. Good condition.]

WILLIAM E. BARNES, died Aug. 27, 1870, Æ. 34 y'rs 8 mo's 15 days.

God calls our loved ones, but we lose not wholly,
What He hath given:
They live on earth in thought and deed as truly
As in his heaven.

No. 791.

[White marble on marble plinth, granite base.]

MARTHA L. Wife of David Turner, died Nov. 6, 1839, Aged 29 yrs.

116 BURIAL HILL :

No. 792.
[Similar to 791.]
DAVID TURNER died May 14, 1869. Aged 66 yrs. 4 mos.
"When Christ. who is our life, shall appear then shall ye also appear with him in glory."

No. 793.
[Blue slate. Good condition. Symbol.]
To the memory of Mrs Rebekah Bartlett wife of Mr Elkanah Bartlett who died July 17th 1797 in the 28th year of her age Also Rebekah their Daughter who in her 11th month died June 9th 1797

No. 794.
[Low, blue slate. Moss-grown, but sound. Symbol.]
In Memory of Southworth son of Mr Job & Mrs Rebecca Rider who died Octr 15 1793 aged 6 years and 3 months.

No. 795.
[Blue slate. Good condition. Urn.]
In memory of ANN L. BOUTELL, who died Dec. 5, 1835, aged 16 yrs. Also ELLEN G. BOUTELL, who died Sept. 3, 1823, Aged 6 yrs. Also Nath. G. Boutell who died at Lexington Sept. 26, 1816, Aged 1 year and 3 mon.

No. 796.
[Low, blue slate. Part of surface scaled off. Moss-grown. Inclined. Symbol]
Rebecca Fuller deceased Dece   25 1772 Aged 1 year 4 months and 13 days Daughter of Mr John Fuller and Rebecca his Wife.

No. 797.
[Blue slate. 3 1-2 feet high. Pyramidal shape. Urn between roses.]
To the memory of Mrs Rebeckah Bartlett Consort of Mr. John Bartlett who died Decbr 18th 1804, in the 26th year of her age.

    That female virtue wich adorn'd thy bloom
    Friendship recalls and weeps upon thy tomb
    Their sad remembrance drops a silent tear
    And chaste affection stands a mourner their.

No. 798.
[Blue slate. Upper moiety broken off and gone.]
mem   Rebeckah B   daughter   Mr John Bartlett   Mrs Rebeckah his   who died Sepr 27, aged 3 years & 2 months & 17 days

    'Tis God who lifts our comforts high
    Or sinks them in the grave,
    He gives, and, blessed be his name,
    He takes but what he gave.

No. 799.

[White marble on granite. Good condition. Three links of chain at top.]

JOSEPH B. WHITING died July 2, 1877, aged 36 y'rs. 4 mo's.

No. 800.

[White marble in granite socket. Good condition.]

DANIEL DEACON died March 13, 1842, Aged 51 y'rs. POLLY T. His widow Died Sept. 28, 1875, Aged 82 y'rs. SUSAN A. their dau. Died May 22, 1836, Aged 3 y'rs.

No. 801.

[Low, Goodwin stone. Moss-grown. Slightly marred at top. Two symbols.]

In memory of Josiah son to Mr. John Cobb and Sarah his wife who died Sepr ye 10 AD. 1744 in ye 6th year of his age   Likewise a Daughter died not named aged 11 days.

No. 802.

[A Goodwin stone. Two and a half feet high. Moss-grown. Letters cut uncommonly large. Symbol.]

Here lies interr'd the Body of Mr. JOHN COBB who departed this life July ye 16th AD. 1750 in the 41 Year of his Age.

No. 803.

[A Goodwin stone. Moss-covered. Cleft at top parallel to surface. Symbol.]

Here lies interr'd ye Body of Mr JOHN COBB who departed this life August the 7th AD. 1769 in the 27th year of his Age.

No. 804.

[Blue slate. Good condition. Symbol.]

To the memory of Mrs Sarah Delano wife of Capt Nathan Delano who died Sept 21st 1781 in the 69th year of her age.

No. 805.

[Blue slate. Slightly injured on surface. Symbol.]

To the memory of Mrs Mary Cobb who died Augst 6, 1799 in the 58th year of her age

No. 806.

[Blue slate. Good condition. Urn under festoons.]

To the memory of Mrs Sarah Cobb who died in Jany 1805 aged 59 years

No. 807.

[Blue slate. Good condition. Four feet in height. Urn between rose-twigs.]

Erected to perpetuate the memory of two Sons of Thomas & Sarah Wethrell Who Died in the West Indies

William Wethrell Deed at St Thomas March 23d 1803
Aged 22 years. Isaac Wethrell Deed at Martinico January 23d 1803 Aged 19 years.

> By foreign hands thy dying eyes were clos'd
> By foreign hands thy decent limbs compos'd
> By foreign hands thy humble graves adornd
> By Strangers honourd and by Strangers mourned

No. 808.

[Blue slate. Good condition. Weeping willow and urn.]

In remembrance of Miss HARRIOT WETHRELL who resigned this Life May 7 1815 aged 23 years

> "Calm be thy rest
> Soft as the slumbers of a saint forgiven
> And mild as opening gleams of promised heaven."

No. 809.

[Blue slate. Pyramidal. Good condition. Urn under festoons.]

To the memory of Mrss Eliz'h Wethrell who departed
this life January 5 1814 in the 59 year of her age

No. 810.

[This and the following Nos. to 814 inclusive, are inclosed in iron
fence. The name "Wethrell" and date "1857" are cast on the gate
of entrance. No. 810 is in good condition.]

THOMAS WETHRELL Born Dec. 4th 1742, Died
Dec. 10th 1809.

No. 811.

[Good condition.]

SARAH WETHRELL wife of Thomas Wethrell, Born Aug.
6 1753, Died Oct. 30th 1794. LUCIA, their Daugh.
Deceased Oct. 27th 1790, Aged 1 year

No. 812.

[On marble block based on granite. Good condition.]

Rev. Isaac Wethrell Son of Thomas and Nancy Shaw
WETHRELL Born in Plymouth October 24 1806 Died
in Boston November 30 1881.

Requiescat in pace.

No. 813.

[Set in stone socket. Inclined backward. (This monument is to
the widow of Joseph Bartlett, a native of Plymoutn; H. U. 1782,
afterward attorney-at-law in Portsmouth, N. H., and in Boston,
Mass.)]

ANNA M. BARTLETT, Born January 31. 1771.
Died November 20, 1864.

Asleep in Jesus.

No. 814.

[Good condition.]

ANNA Wethrell wife of Thomas Wethrell. Born Feb. 20th 1747 Died Sept. 12th 1778. WILLIAM their Son Deceased Sept 6, 1770. Aged 1 year

No. 815.

[Low, white marble. Good condition. Rosebud and leaves at top.]

BETSEY, Dau. of Lemuel & Mehitable Raymond Died March 18, 1850 Aged 3 weeks.

No. 816.

[Low, blue slate. Moss-grown. Piece broken off lower left corner. Symbol.]

In Memory of Mr JOSEPH RIDER Jun who departed this Life May ye 13th ʃ779, in the 65th year of his age.

No. 817.

[Blue slate. Surface lamina mostly separated and gone. Symbol.]

buried   Rider   Decd 29th   17   In
5t y

No. 818.

[Purple slate. Solid. On stone socket with brimstone cement. Good condition.]

FATHER. MERRICK RYDER. Died June 8, 1858, Aged 68 y'rs. 9 mo's.

No. 819.

[Similar to 818.]

MOTHER. Lucy Delano, Wife of Merrick Ryder, Died April 28, 1865, Aged 70 y'rs. 9 mo's.

No. 820.

[Blue slate. Fair condition, save moss-grown and inclined. Symbol.]

In Memory of Miss Bathsheba Holmes Daughter of Mr Elnathan Holmes & Mrs Bathsheba his wife who died Sept ʃʃth ʃ784 aged ʃ6 years ʃʃ months & 4 days.

No. 821.

[Blue slate. Good condition, save a threatening seam near the ground. Urn with rosebud on each side.]

In memory of Mr ABNER HOLMES who died May 26th 1803 aged Twenty five years Also in memory of Mrs MARY HOLMES relict of Mr ABNER HOLMES who died april 17th 1804, aged 24 years and of their infant Mary who died July 21th 1803 aged 4 months.

What is this World we saw this youthful pair
Belov'd and happy every prospect fair
Now in the grave but kindred cease your sighs
To them twas but the path to Christ above the skies.

No. 822.

[Blue slate. Good condition. Urn.]

To the memory of Mr Benjamin Bartlett who Died Decr 24th 1801, aged 64 years Likewise his late Consort Jamima Bartlett who died February 15th 1808 aged 66 years.

No. 823.

[Blue slate. Sound. Symbol]

To the memory of Mary Brewster Holmes Daughter to Elnathan Holmes & Deborah his wife who died Sep 21 1794 aged 2 months also thare son who died Sepr 17 1795 aged 5 hours.

The Babe that's caught from womb and breast
Claim right to sing above the rest
Because they found the happy shore
They neither saw nor sought before.

No. 824.

[White marble. Weathering rough. Moss-grown.]

SARAH, widow of Capt. America Brewster died Dec. 22, 1850, aged 75 y'rs.

No: 825.

[White marble. Moss-grown. First four words ornamented.]

Died 17th Nov. 1847, Capt. America Brewster, aged 74 yrs.

No. 826.

In Memory of MRS. LUCY widow of Mr. Thomas Burgess, who departed this life July 5th 1843, aged 58 yrs.

No. 827.

[Fine, blue slate. Good condition. Weeping willow and urn.]

Erected to the memory of Mrs. SARAH LANMON who departed this life Sep 18 1827 in the 74 year of her age

Cold in the dust her perish'd heart may lie
But that which warm'd it once, will never die.

No. 828.

[Blue slate. Moss-grown. Fair condition.]

Sacred to the memory of Capt. Richard Holmes who died October 22, 1820, in the 76 year of his age.

God, my Redeemer, lives,
And often from the skies
Looks down, and watches all my dust
Till He shall bid it rise.

No. 829.

[Blue slate. Sound, but moss-grown. Urn.]

In memory of Mrs Abigal Holmes Consort of Capt Richard Holmes who died April 8th 1807 in the 53 year of her age

No. 830.
[White marble. On granite base. Five feet in height. At top, figure of a chain—six broken links—with legend "Parted below, United above."]

SARAH HOLMES, died April 1, 1868, aged 86 years.

No. 831.
[Blue slate. Inclined. Sound. Urn.]

In memory of Henry Holmes Son of Mr Nathaniel Holmes and Mary his wife who died Decr 8 1795 aged 2 years 8 months & 8 days.

No. 832.
[Blue slate. Shape, pyramidal. Four and one-half feet high. Covered with moss. Weeping willow and urn.]

Erected to the memory of Miss Ruth Crandon daughter of Benjamin & Sukey Crandon, who departed this life October 10, A. D. 1830 in the 36 year of her age.

No. 833.
[Blue slate. Sound. Weeping willow and urn.]

Erected to the memory of Miss Mary B. Crandon Daughter of Mr. Benjamin Crandon. & Mrs. Sukey his wife, who departed this life September 6, 1819. in the 15th year of her age

No. 834.
[Low, blue slate. Good condition. Symbol.]

To the memory of Jane Crandon Daughter of Mr Benjamin Crandon & Mrs Sukey his wife died Novm 2J J800 Aged 8 months & 9 days

No. 835.
[Fine, blue slate. Pyramidal. Good condition. Weeping willow.]

Erected to the memory of Mrs. Nancy B. Jackson widow of Mr Cornelius S. Jackson, and daughter of Mr. Benjamin Crandon, who died Novr 2, 1819 aged 27 years & six months. Also to the memory of Mr. Cornelius S. Jackson. who died at Gaudalope August 31 AD. 1815 aged 33 years.

No. 836.
[Blue slate. Good condition. Weeping willow and urn.]

Erected to the memory of Miss Sarah Crandon Daughter of Mr. Benjamin Crandon, and Mrs. Sukey his wife, who Departed this Life March 24, AD. 1820, in the 23 year of her age.

No. 837.
[Blue slate. Flaming urn. Good condition.]

In memory of SUKEY CRANDON, wife of Benjamin Crandon who died July 16, 1835 in her 67 y.r.

I I

No. 838.

[Blue slate. Good condition, save being inclined. Flaming urn.]

In memory of Benj. Crandon Esq., who died Sept. 28, 1841, in his 78th year He was app'd Inspector of the Customs of Duxbury, under the administration of General Washington. and held the office of Dep. Collector and Inspector of Plymouth, until April 20, 1841, having held the office under every President of the United States.

No. 839.

[Blue slate. Good condition. Two urns, connected by an arch having the legend "Daughter and Mother."]

In Memory of MEHITABLE P. LYNCH, who died June 5, 1839, in the 29 y.r of her age. Also MEHITABLE P. SMITH, who died April 22, 1826, aged 44 y.rs

No. 840.

[Blue slate. Good condition. Symbol.]

To the memory of Mr David Bates who died July 11, 1802, in the 66 year of his age.

No. 841.

[Blue slate. Sound, but moss-grown. Weeping willow and urn.]

In memory of Mrs. Thankful Bates wife of Mr. David Bates who died November 11, 1815 in the 77 year of her age.

No. 842.

[Blue slate. Sound. Weeping willow and urn.]

In memory of Mrs. Deborah Gammons wife of Mr. Benjamin Gammons who died August 1st 1824 aged 72 years

Make Christ your friend who never dies
All other friends are vanities
Make him your life your all
Prepare for death that Solemn call.

No. 843 a.

[Blue slate, broken across; upper moiety gone. What remains of the inscription is as follows:]

Also in memory of Fanny H. Gardner daughter of Mr Harwood & Mrs Mehetabel Gardner who died Octr 6, 1803, aged 1 year, 5 months & 17 days

No. 843 b.

[Loose piece of purplish blue slate, evidently the upper portion of a stone which must have been broken across. All that is visible of the inscription is as follows:]

To the memory of Jerusha Bartlett wife of John Bartlett

No. 844.

[White marble. Four and a half feet high. Fair condition.]

Erected by Ezra Finney & wife to the memory of DEA. JOHN BISHOP, who died March 26. 1830: Also his wife ABIGAIL BISHOP, who died March 24. 1830. both buried in one grave. he was Deacon of the Church 34 years & lived together over 60 years.

No. 845 a.

[Low, blue slate. Sound, but moss-grown. Symbol.]

To the memory of Henry Bishop son of Dea. John Bishop & Abigail his wife who died April 14, 1797 in the 3d year of his age.

> Tis God who lifts our comforts high
> Or sinks them in the grave,
> He gives, and blessed be his name,
> He takes but what he gave.

No. 845 b.

[Dark blue slate. Good condition. Symbol.]

In memory of Capt John Bishop Junr who departed this life July 27 AD 1802 in Dominica in the 24th year of his age. Also in memory of George Bishop who departed this life August 1st 1802 in Dominica in the Fifteenth year of his Age.

> Short is the date of Sublunary Joys
> The evening lowers soon as the sunbeams rise,
> Short is the uncertain life of helpless man
> His days how justly liken'd to a span.

No. 845 c.

[Blue slate. 'Good condition, save moss-grown. Symbol.]

Here lies buried 4 Ch'n of Capt John Bishop & Mrs Abigail his wife Viz 1st Mary died Sept 24th 1772 aged J year & JJ months 2d Abigail died Jany 7th 1774 aged 7 days. 3d Mary died January 15th 1774 aged 15 days. 4th John died Sept 25th 1778 aged JJ months.

No. 846.

[Blue slate. Good condition. Weeping willow and urn.]

In memory of WILLIAM BISHOP who died Oct.r 13 1822 : Aged 30 yr.s.

> "His was the radiance of the risen day."

No. 847.

[White marble, on granite. Good condition.]

Sarah T. Daughter of William & C. B. BISHOP Died April 2, 1852 Aged 3 mo's.

No. 848.

[White marble, on granite base. Good condition.]

KATIE B. Daughter of William & C. B. BISHOP Died April 2, 1876, Aged 15 y'rs. 10 mo's.

No. 849.

[White marble, on granite. Good condition.]

CATHERINE B. Wife of WILLIAM BISHOP Died July 16, 1884, Aged 57 y'rs 3 mo's.

No. 850 a.

[Low, white marble. Weathering rough. Inclined. Urn.]

Sacred to the memory of MARY S. HOLMES who died May 12, 1828 aged 2 years Daughter of Truman & Jennette Holmes.

No. 850 b.

[Low, blue slate, of good quality. A large portion broken off, and gone, from left hand corner. Symbol.]

Enoch Randall   ed Septr 25th 1791 in the 33 Year of his Age. & is here Inter'd

No more to foreign climes the bark he steers
No more his safe return his kindred cheers
Snatch'd in his prime of life's best joys possest
'Tis God's command whose name be ever blest.

No. 851.

[Handsome veined marble, set in freestone block, with brimstone which has crumbled. Is inclined, and liable to fall.]

In Memoriam Father Mother & Family. WILLIAM ROBBINS, died Aug. 17, 1844, in his 86th y'r. LOIS ROBBINS His wife Died May 28, 1832 in her 69th y'r.

——— —

Also their children, Theophilus, Lois, Thomas C. William Nathaniel, Rufus, Alexander, Julia Ann & Edmund.

No. 852.

[Blue slate. Good condition. Weeping willow and urn.]

Sacred to the memory of Mr. Joseph Johnson, who died Sept. 3, 1828, aged 68 years. Also Capt. Joseph Johnson Jr. who died Mar. 16, 1820, aged 24 years.

No. 853.

[Blue slate. Good condition. Weeping willow and urn.]

Mrs. Betsey Johnson. wife of Mr. Joseph Johnson. who departed this life Jan. 15, 1833, aged 63 years.

No. 854.

[Blue slate. Good condition. Urn.]

To the memory of Mr Jeremiah Holmes Junr who died October 17 1799 in the 43d year of his age Also In memory of Mrs Nancy his wife who died at orrington in the County of Hancock April 3, 1797.

No. 855.

[Blue slate. Four feet and a half in height. Seams across surface. Moss-grown. Weeping willow between two urns.]

In memory of Peter Holmes. who died at Port-au-Prince Sept. 15, 1794, aged 38 years Also Mary Holmes. Consort of Peter who died Sept. 2, 1829, Aged 73 years.

No. 856 a.

[Blue slate. Set in freestone socket with brimstone for cement. The brimstone has crumbled; the monument is inclined, and liable to fall.]

PHEBE, wife of Capt Thomas Farmer. Aged 40 y'rs.

No. 856 b.

[Blue slate. Condition good. Urn between bouquets.]

Anna May Wethrell Daughter of Thomas Wethrell Jur and Nancy his wife died Octor 12, 1802 Aged 15 Months and 10 days.

No. 856 c.

[Low, blue slate. Good condition. Symbol.]

John May Wethrell Son of Thomas Wethrell & Mrs Nancy his wife decd Octor 28th 1800 aged 8 mouths & 23 days

No. 857.

[Blue slate. Badly shattered. Symbol.]

In memory of Mrs Rebecah Wethrell wife of Mr Thomas Wethrel decd 1755 Aged

No. 858.

[Low, blue slate. Broken.]

el son Thom Wethrel & Elisabeth his wife died April ye 4th 1742 Aged 10 mon & 19 days

No. 859.

[Thick, blue slate. Laminæ separating. Moss-grown. Symbol.]

Here lyes interd ye body of Mr Thomas Wethrell who died April ye   1747 in ye 63d year of his age

No. 860.

[Low, blue slate. Laminæ separating. Symbol.]

Hannah daur to Thomas Wethrell Junr & Elisabeth his wife died July ye 28th 1740 Aged 14 mon & one day

No. 861.

[Low, blue slate. Laminæ separating. Symbol.]

Lemuel Son to Mr Thomas & Mrs Rebekah Witherly his wife decd octor ye 13th 1738 in ye 9th year of his age

No. 862.

[Similar to 861.]

Hannah dautr to Mr Thomas & Mrs Rebeckah Witherly his wife decd June ye 10th 1736 Aged   year & 10 mouths

No. 863.

[Low, blue slate. Marred. Symbol.]

Here lyes   body of Joshua Wethrell decd Sepbr in ye year 1727 aged about 45 years

No. 864.

[Low, blue slate. Fair condition, save moss-covered. Symbol.]

To the memory of Mrs Elisabeth Nelson wife of Capt Saml Nicols Nelson who died Octr 26th 1793 Aged 67 years

No. 865.

[Blue slate. Good condition. Pyramidal. Symbol.]

To the memory of Priscilla Harlow Daughter of Mr Seth Harlow and Mrs Priscilla his wife who died June 22sd 1804 aged 2 months & 12 days

No. 866.

[Fine, blue slate. Three and a half feet high. Urn under festoons.]

To the memory of NANCY WETHRELL Consort of Thomas Wethrell who departed this life April 23 1811 in the 31 year of her age.

No. 867.

[White marble. Rough. Moss-grown.]

William Thomas died Nov. 30, 1830, Æt. 5 months 5 days Thomas died Jan. 25, 1844 Æt. 17 days Hiram died March 7, 1845 Æt, 2 y'rs 3 mo Children of Ths and Maria P. Tribble.

So fades these lovely blooming flowers.

No. 868.

[White marble. Rough. Bad condition. Urn.]

Maria Thomas daughter of THOMAS and MARIA P. TRIBBLE. died Nov. 23, 1838 Æt. 17 y.rs 16 days.

Calm be the spot where her form now reposeth
May the friends who once loved her revisit her grave
And feel though the cold sod her ashes encloseth
She lives in the presence of him who can save.

[NOTE. The above epitaph can be most easily read in the forenoon at an hour when the sun's rays fall nearly parallel with the surface of the stone.]

No. 869.

[White marble. Not in good condition. Urn.]

In memory of MARIA P. wife of THOMAS TRIBBLE who died July 16, 1848 Æt. 44 y'rs 5 mos, & 16 days

No. 870.

[White marble, in marble block. The whole inclined backward; otherwise in good condition.]

Henry F. Eddy Co E. 29 Mass. Reg't Died Jan. 20, 1864 Aged 23 y'rs 2 m's

No. 871.

[White marble, mottled. Set in freestone base. Good condition.]

FATHER & MOTHER. WILLIAM C. GREEN, Died Oct 18, 1846. Aged 40 y'rs MARCIA C. his wife Died March 9, 1873, Aged 78 y'rs 6 mo's.

Why do we mourn departed friends
Or shake at death's alarms?
'Tis but the voice that Jesus sends
To call them to his arms

No. 872.

[Blue slate. Four feet high. Good condition. Weeping willow and urn.]

In Memory of JOSEPH HOLMES who died July 4, 1848, Æ. 60 yrs. 3 mo. & 20 days

Calm be the spot where his form now repose,
May the friends who so lov'd him revisit the grave,
And feel though the cold sod his ashes enclose,
He lives in the presence of him who can save.

No. 873 a.

[Blue slate. Fair condition. Weeping willow and urn.]

In memory of Mr. NATHANIEL HOLMES who died August 2, 1825, aged Seventy eight years.

His spirit gone and took its flight,
To dwell in uncreated light,
His body rest beneath the sod
Till call'd by his creator God.

No. 873 b.

[White marble. Good condition.]

ADONIRAM J. HOLMES Co. E. 32 Regt. Mass. Vols. Died Nov. 15, 1883, Aged 68 yrs. 3 mos. 6 days.

No. 874.

[White marble. Fair condition. Urn.]

PATIENCE C. HOLMES, Daug. of Nathan and Ruth Holmes, died April 1, 1845, in her 24 y'r

"Shed not for her the bitter tear
Nor give the heart to vain regret
'Tis but the casket that lies here
The gem that fill'd it sparkles yet."

No. 875.

[Blue slate. Good condition. Weeping willow and urn.]

In memory of MRS. RUTH HOLMES, wife of Mr. Nathan Holmes, who died Nov, 15, 1839, in the 63d. yr of her age.

Thrice happy souls who're gone before
To that inheritance divine!
They labor, sorrow, sigh no more,
But bright in endless glory shine.

No. 876.

[Blue slate. Good condition. Urn.]

In memory of Mr. NATHAN HOLMES who died Nov. 3, 1838 ; in the 63d. yr. of his age.

> "Now he resides where Jesus is,
> Above this dusky sphere,
> His soul was ripen'd for that bliss,
> While yet he sojourn'd here."

No. 877.

[Veined marble, set in a marble block. Good condition.]

JOSEPH HOLMES Co. F. 32 Regt. Mass. Vols. Died Mar. 7, 1883 Aged 59 y'rs. 4 ms. 7 days.

No. 878.

[White marble. Weathering rough. Urn and wreaths.]

In Memory of two children of Cha's & Mary R. Whitten, JOSEPH W. died Jan. 3, 1839 Æ. 10 mo. EDWARD W. died April 6, 1849. Æ. 5 y'rs 6 mo. 4 ds.

No. 879.

[White marble. Set in freestone. Brimstone cement crumbled. Stone inclined.]

ELISHA C. WHITTEN, Died March 4, 1864, Aged 23 y'rs 2 mo's 14 days.

> Blessed are the dead which die in the Lord.

No. 880.

[Blue slate. Sound and compact. Urn.]

Erected in memory of Thomas Dike Son of Capt Anthony Dike and Molley his wife who died in Martinico July 26 1802 in the 18th year of his age.

No. 881.

[Thick, blue slate. Two feet high. Moss-covered. Weeping willow and urn.]

In memory of Cap ANTHONY DIKE who died March 14, 1810 in the 60 year of his age

No. 882.

[Fine, blue slate. Good condition.]

MARY DYKE, widow of Capt. Anthony Dyke, died June 28, 1819, in the 63d year of her age

> I know that my Redeemer lives.

Erected by her dau. Mary Jones.

No. 883.

[Blue slate. Four feet high. Good condition, save moss-grown. Picture at top,—vessel floating, keel uppermost ; above this a winged figure with flowing robe, and wings spread as if flying; the figure holding a trumpet to its mouth. Festoons above the figure.]

Erected to the memory of RICHARD HOLMES, 2d son of William & Hannah Holmes, who was drowned in the

Pacific Ocean near the port of Lima on the first of June 1828 aged twenty two years.

As brothers we adopt these lines in testimony of respect for those many virtues that adorned thy bloom.

> The sad remembrance drops a silent tear
> Knows thy worth when thou wast here.

No. 884.

[A fine, compact, handsome slate. Height 3 1-2 feet. Good condition.]

In memory of NATHANIEL CLARK, who died April 28, 1840, aged 75 years. Also ABIGAIL CLARK wife of the above, died Nov. 18, 1817, aged 54 years.

No. 885.

[Blue slate. Good condition. Symbol.]

To the memory of Anna Rider Daughter of Capt Samuel Rider and Mrs Anna his wife who died Octr 5th 1798 aged 1 year 9 months & 14 days

> Why do we mourn departing friends
> Or shake at death's alarms
> 'Tis but the voice that Jesus sends
> To call them to his arms.

No. 886.

[Light blue slate. Badly seamed. Symbol.]

In Memory of Mrs NANCY DUNHAM wife of Capt GEORGE DUNHAM who died April 5th 1789 in ye 41st year of her age. Also in Memory of George their son who died Sepr 3d 1773 aged 1 year & 3 months.

No. 887.

[Blue slate. (This and the three next are squared at the top.) Good condition. Weeping willow and urn.]

Erected in memory of CHARLES ALLEN GRATON, son of Alwin M. & Mary D. GRATON who died Oct. 10, 1843, Æt. 19 years 6 mo.

No. 888.

[Blue slate. Good condition.]

Miss Esther P. Holmes, died June 3, 1830, Aged 21 yrs. Also Esther P. Holmes died March 20, 1808, Aged 2 yrs.

No. 889.

[Blue slate. Good condition. Weeping willow and urn.]

Erected In memory of ALWIN M. GRATON, who was lost at Sea June 4, 1825, Æt. 30 years. Also MARY D. GRATON, who died January 5. 1840 Æt. 41 years.

No. 890.
[Blue slate. Good condition.]
JOSEPH HOLMES, died Dec.r 9, 1825. Aged 48 yrs.
Also MARTHA, his wife died April 3, 1830 Aged 53 yrs.

No. 891.
[Blue slate. Pyramidal. Festoons.]
In memory of William S. Holmes son of Mr Joseph
Holmes and Mrs Martha his wife' who Died Oct. 31st 1802
aged 1 year and 4 months.

No. 892.
[Blue slate (facing No. 891). Some moss; otherwise in good condition. Symbol.]
In memory of Mr RICHARD HOLMES who Died June 5th
1787 in ye 44th year of his Age. Also In Memory of
Mrs MERCY HOLMES his wife who died May 20th 1779 in
the 45th year of her Age.

No. 893.
[Low, blue slate. Seamed. Moss-grown. Symbol.]
In memory of Mrs Lydia Holmes wife of Mr G   rs
um Holmes who Decd Nour ye 20th 1760 In ye 47th
year of her age.

No. 894.
[Blue slate. Pyramidal. Good condition. Festoons. Urn.]
To the memory of Richard Holmes son of Mr William
Holmes & Mrs Hannah his wife who died October 15,
1802 aged 12 years 11 months & 12 days
> The loveliest flower in nature's garden placed,
> Permitted just to bloom, and plucked in haste
> Angles behold him rise for joys to come
> And called by god's command their brother home.

No. 895.
[Blue slate. Good condition. Weeping willow and urn.]
To the memory of Mrs Mary Holmes wife of William
Holmes 3d and daughter of Capt Eliphalett Holbrook and
Mary his wife who Departed this life October 26th 1810
aged twenty years and nine months.
> Blessed are they that monru
> For they shall be comforted.

No. 896.
[Blue slate. Good condition. Weeping willow and urn.]
In memory of William R. Holmes. Son of William
Holmes 3d & Mrs Bathsheba his wife who died October
20. 1817 aged one year 6 months
> Our days are as the grass,
> Or like the morning flower,
> If one sharp blast sweep o'er the field,
> It withers in an hour.

No. 897.

[Blue slate. This and 898, standing side by side, each 5 feet high, are noticeable in a row of five very tall gravestones. Good condition. Weeping willow and urn.]

BATHSHEBA JAMES widow of Capt William Holmes 3d Mariner and daughter to Capt Joseph Doten Do. she was kill'd instantaneously in a thunder storm by the Electrich fluid of lightning on the 6th of July 1830, aged 35 years and 26 days.

She was an affectionate wife; a dutiful Daughter, a happy mother, a kind and sincere friend. Alas sweet Blossom short was the period that thy enlivening virtues contributed to the Happiness of those connections; But oh, how long have they to mourn the loss of so much worth and Excellence.

> Farewell dear Wife untill that day more blest
> When if deserving I with thee shall rest,
> With thee shall rise with thee shall live above
> In worlds of endless bliss and boundless love.

No. 898.

[Blue slate. Good condition. Weeping willow and urn.]

CAPT. WILLIAM HOLMES who died in Valparaiso May 10, 1831, aged 40 years.

> He that giveth to the poor lendeth to the Lord.
> Rest generous mortal, rest thy toils are ore
> Thy spirits landed on that peaceful shore
> Where are not troubles or distress or pain
> But peace and happyness infinitely reign.

No. 899.

[White marble in freestone socket. Four feet in height. Cement gone; stone inclined, and liable to fall.]

HANNAH BURT wffe of Laban Burt, Died April 21, 1832, Aged 43 y'rs 9 mo's. LABAN BURT, Died Nov. 13, 1842, Aged 60 y'rs 2 m's. 7 da's. SUSAN L. BARNES. Died Oct. 6, 1836, aged 21 y'rs 6 mo's.

"For if we believe that Jesus died and rose again, even so them also which sleep in Jesus will God bring with him."

No. 900.

[Low, blue slate, (facing No. 898). Inclined. Appears to have been partly buried in preparing the ground for other monuments. Somewhat moss-grown. Laminæ separating, but in fair condition for a stone which has stood more than a century. Symbol.]

In memory of 2 children sons of Mr Richard Holmes & Mrs Abigail his wife, 1st Reuben born June 8th 1782 died Aug.st 24th 1783 2d Reub born Sepr 18th died 26th 1785.

No. 901.

[Blue slate. Five and one-fourth feet high, Good condition. Mausoleum.]

CAPT. WILLIAM HOLMES died Jan,y 13, 1833, aged 65 years HANNAH, widow of William Holmes, died Feb. 22, 1854. Æ. 87 y'rs. Also Miss POLLY HOLMES, died April 2, 1849, Æ. 60 y'rs.

No. 902.

[White marble. Weathering rough. Flaming urn, under festoons.]

BATHSHEBA, the affectionate wife of Ansel H. Harlow and dau'tr of Capt Wm Holmes 3d she died Aug,st 11, 1833 ; aged 20 yr,s.

"Behold I shew you a mystery: we shall not all sleep, but we shall all be changed. In a moment, in the twinkling of an eye, at the last trump; for the trumpet shall sound, and the dead shall be raised incorruptible, and we shall be changed."

ST. PAUL.

No. 903.

[White marble. In stone socket, with brimstone,—a substance which, it is said, expands with cold, and contracts with heat. Good condition.]

ANSEL H. HARLOW Born Dec. 1. 1804, Died May 21, 1882.

No. 904.

[Blue slate. Fair condition. Symbol.]

Here lyes buried the body of Mr Thomas Morton son to Mr Thomas Morton & Mrs Martha his wife who decd July ye 10th 1731 in ye 31st year of his age.

No. 905.

[Blue slate. Similar to 904.]

In Memory of Mr Lemuel Morton who departed this Life Jany ye 26th j779 in ye 75th year of his age

No. 906.

[Blue slate. Surface cracked and moss-grown. Symbol.]

In Memory of Mrs MARY MORTON wife of Mr. NATHANIEL MORTON who decd March 7th j78j in the 63d year of her Age.

No. 907.

[Blue slate. Somewhat seamed. Fair condition. Symbol.]

Here lyes buried the Body of Mrs SARAH MORTON wife of Mr LEMUEL MORTON who departed this Life April 17th 1785 in the 23d year of her Age.

In Her United all that's Fair and good
Short was her Race, yet Virtue's Path she trod.

No. 908.

[Low, blue slate. Moss-grown. Otherwise in fair condition. Symbol.]

In Memory of Sarah Daughter of Mr Lemuel Morton & Mrs Sarah his wife who was born April 3d 1785 and dec'd the same day.

No. 909.

[White marble in stone socket. Roughened.]

Margaret H. wife of Samuel N. Diman, Died Dec. 8, 1849, Aged 32 yrs. and 6 Mon.

> Rest, sleeping dust, In silence rest,
> In the cold grave that Jesus blest,
> In faith and hope we lay thee there,
> Safe in our Heavenly Father's care.

No. 910.

[White marble. Weathering rough.]

In memory of Mrs. POLLY DIMAN, Consort of the late Dea. Josiah Diman, died Nov. 15, 1847, aged 71 years

> So Jesus Slept:—God's dying Son
> Pass'd thro' the grave and bless'd the bed:
> Rest here, blest saint, till from his throne
> The morning break and pierce the shade.

No. 911.

[White marble in marble block. Good condition. In wooden paling, under small elm tree.]

NATHANIEL DOTY died Dec. 9, 1871, Aged 63 y'rs 2 mo's JOANNA, His wife died Sept 5, 1885, Aged 59 y'rs 10 mo's.

No. 912.

[Low, blue slate. Top broken off, and gone.]

CRYMBLE Dautr   Quintin & Elizabeth Crymble his wife deed April ye 14th 1724 in ye 5th month of her age.

No. 913.

[Low, blue slate. Top marred.]

HOLMS CRYMBLE son to QUINTIN And ELIZABETH CRYMBLE his wife deed March ye 20th 1724 in ye 4th year of his age

No. 914.

[Blue slate. Laminæ separating. Moss-grown.]

Here lyes ye body of Mrs Phebe Holmes wife to Mr Ebenezer Holmes who deed April ye 16th 1734 in ye 62d year of her age

No. 915.

[First of four new and beautiful white marbles, set in pairs on marble blocks, resting on granite sub-base. Iron stains on marble block. (probably from dowels). At top, surrounded by ornamental carving, the letter "H."]

DAVID C. HOLMES Died Dec. 21, 1870, aged 69 years.

No. 916.

[White marble. Good condition.]

LOUISA SAVERY wife of DAVID C. HOLMES, Died Sept 4, 1855, aged 45 yrs. 6 mo.

No. 917.
[White marble. Good condition.]

LOUISA, Dau. of David C. and Louisa S. HOLMES
Died Apr, 13, 1852 Aged 17 yrs. 3 mo.

No. 918.
[White marble. The marble block on which the monument rests is broken in the midst; otherwise in good condition.]

CEPHAS A. Son of David C. & Louisa S. HOLMES
Died Feb. 11, 1849 Aged 9 years.

No. 919.
[Blue slate. Three and one-fourth feet high. About one-third of this stone is broken off, but remains standing in place, and shows several seams. Flaming urn.]

To the memory of MR. LEMUEL COBB who died Jan.y
4th, 1841, in the 66th yr of his age.

That manly virtue that adorned thy bloom,
Friendship recalls and weeps upon thy tomb,
The sad remembrance drops a silent tear,
While chaste affection stands a mourner here.

No. 920.
[Low, blue slate. Weatherworn and somewhat marred.]

Gershem son to Garshem & Lydia Holmes his wife
Died Augst ye 22d 1732 Aged 10 mo & 2 days

No. 921.
[Blue slate. A double stone. i. e., two symbols and two inscriptions side by side on same monument. Weatherworn. Moss-grown.]

(On the left;)
Here lyes ye body of Richard Holmes who decd Nov.br
ye 12th 1733 in the 15th year of his age.

(On the right:)
Here lyes ye body of Nathll Holmes who decd Novbr
ye 14th 1733 in the 32d year of his age.

No. 922.
[Blue slate. Similar to preceding.]

(On the left:)
Here lyes ye body of Elener Holmes Who decd Decbr
ye 12th 1733 in ye 24th year of her age

(On the right:)
Here lyes ye body of Joshua Holmes who decd Decbr
ye 13th 1733 in ye 29th year of his age

No. 923.
[Blue slate. Cleft downward through surface. Inclined forward. Two heads (or symbols) one above the other; apparently encased in helmets.]

Here lyes ye body of Mary Kempton wife to Thom
Kempton she Died Sepbr ye 13th 1742 in ye 30th year of
her age

No. 924.
[Blue slate. Good condition. Symbol.]

Here lyes buried the body of Mr Isaac Doten Died April ye 13th 1725 in ye 46th year of his age

No. 925.
[Low, blue slate, between two inclosed lots. Good condition. Symbol.]

Here lyes buried the body of Mrs Martha Doten wife to Mr Isaac Doten died Septr 9th 1745 in ye 63d year of her age.

No. 926.
[White marble. Cemented in granite. Good condition.]

ELIJAH RICKARD Died July 22, 1864, Aged 80 years

"Let me die the death of the righteous, and may my last end be like his."

LUCY RICKARD, died April 3, 1863, Aged 70 y'rs.

"Precious in the sight of the Lord is the death of his saints."

No. 927.
[White marble, on granite. Good condition.]

Husband. FREEMAN W. RICKARD died Jan. 21, 1882, Aged 67 y'rs 9 mos 10 ds.

No. 928.
[White marble, on granite. Good condition.]

(On reverse:)

WIFE (a hand pointing upward).

(On obverse:)

Adeline W. Wife of Freeman W. Rickard, Died Jan. 18, 1875, Aged 49 y'rs 18 d's.

She has gone to heaven before us
But she turns and waves her hand
Pointing to the glories o'er us
In that happy spirit land.

No. 929.
[Low, white marble. Good condition.]

(On upper service:)

Georgie

(On obverse:)

Son of F. W. & A. W. Rickard. Died Sept. 22, 1864, Aged 6 mo's 11 d's.

No. 930.
[White marble. Good condition. Enclosed with three similar monuments (to No. 933) in wooden paling on granite foundation.]

(On upper surface of block, the word:)

Husband

(On obverse:)
JOHN W. PERRY Died Feb, 9, 1884, Aged 45 years 5 mos.

(On reverse, sword on open book, and the legend:)
K. of P.

No. 931.

[White marble, on granite. Good condition.]

(On upper surface:)
TENIA.

(On obverse:)
ALBERTENIA L. Dau. of L. W. & E. A. Whitten, Died Dec. 24, 1866, Aged 12 y'rs 8 mo's 18 days

(On reverse, a bouquet, and the legend:)
Gone home loved one But we shall meet again.

No. 932.

[White marble. Good condition.]

(On upper surface:)
Wife.

(On obverse:)
EMELINE A. wife of LEWIS H. WHITTEN Died Jan. 13, 1887, Aged 54 y'rs 4 mo's 15 days.

(On reverse:)
No sin, no grief, no pain,
Safe in my happy home.

No. 933.

[White marble. Discolored. Seam across obverse surface.]

(On upper surface:)
HUSBAND.

(On obverse:)
Lewis H. Whitten Died Nov. 24, 1874, Aged 43 y'rs 7 mo's.
Waiting on the other Shore.

(On reverse:)
Hand pointing upward, and three links of chain.

No. 934.

[White marble on granite. Good condition. This No. and 935 and 936 are inclosed in wooden paling.]

Father & Mother CAPT LEWIS FINNEY. Lost at Sea Sept. 1818, Aged 39 y'rs ELIZABETH, His widow Died Dec. 2, 1867. Aged 80 y'rs 3 mo's.

No. 935.

[Veined white marble, on marble plinth. Granite base. The whole mass inclined at an angle about 40°]

KATE C Wife of Harrison Finney Died Jan. 1, 1855, Aged 30 y'rs. Harrison K. their Son Died Apr. 22, 1863, Aged 2 y'rs 2 mo's.

No. 936.

[White marble, on marble plinth, granite base. Good condition.]

HARRISON FINNEY Died July 27, 1878, Aged 64 y'rs 4 mo's 11 days.

No. 937.

[Blue slate. Sound. Inclined. Weeping willow and urn. Is inclosed with 938 in granite posts and iron chains.]

In memory of ADALINE, Daug. of Mrs BETSEY E. and Capt. Robert Hutchinson died June 28th AD. 1833, aged 10 months. GEORGE W. their son Died Feb. 27th AD. 1835, aged 5 years, 6 months. Also their two infants.

> Here in the low and grassy bed
> Brothers and sisters dear are laid
> Cold death has nipp'd them in the bud
> And they are gone to rest with God.

No. 938.

[White marble, on granite base. Good condition.]

CAPT. ROBERT HUTCHINSON Died Dec. 27, 1868, Aged 80 y'rs. DEBORAH, His Wife June 30, 1821, Aged 28 y'rs.

> Even so, Father, for so it seemed good in thy Sight.

No. 939.

[This and the Nos. to 943 inclusive are inclosed with iron rails in granite posts. No. 939 is white marble, four feet in height. Good condition.]

Father & Mother OLIVER KEMPTON, died Sept. 30th 1803, on the Banks of Quereau, in his 36th. yr. SALLY, his Widow died Feb. 18th. 1855, Aged 84 years.

> There is rest in Heaven.

No. 940.

[Blue slate. Good condition. Urn.]

In Memory of SALLY KEMPTON Died Dec. 20, 1812, in the 13. y.r of her age Daughter of Oliver & Sally Kempton.

> Here sleep dear daughter all alone
> With aching hearts we leave thee
> To thee our sorrows are not known
> Nor can our absence grieve thee

No. 941.

[White marble. In freestone socket. Good condition.]

ELIAS E. COX, son of Elias & Eliza Cox, died April 8, 1866, Aged 27 y'rs 6 mo's. 28 days.

> So near perfection in his early day,
> Why should we weep to see him snatched away
> To see him reach at once the immortal prize
> And rise triumphant to his native skies?

12

No. 942 a.

[Veined white marble, on marble plinth. Granite base.]

ELIZA O. wife of ELIAS COX, Died Feb. 24, 1884, Aged 81 y'rs 4 mo's 11 days

No. 942 b.

[White marble on granite base. Good condition.]

ELIAS COX Died Jan. 20, 1878, Aged 79 y'rs 11 mo's.

No. 943.

[White marble. Set in granite socket. Discolored, and somewhat moss-grown.]

WILLIAM, Son of Ichabod & Mary Morey, Died Oct. 13, 1863, Aged 27 y'rs 1 mo. 18 days.

> The pains of death are past,
> Labor and sorrow cease,
> And his life's warfare closed at last,
> His soul now rests in peace.

No. 944.

[White marble. Four and one-fourth feet in height. Weathering rough. Inscription not very distinct.]

MARY ANN, wife of Mendal Pierce, Died June 2, 1844, in her 25th. yr.   Also their dau'tr ANN ELIZABETH, died Jan, 22, 1844, aged 5 mo. 15 ds.

> Behold the righteous marching home,
> And all the angels bid them come,
> While Christ the judge their joy proclaims
> Here, come my Saints I know their names.

No. 945.

[Low, blue slate. Weatherworn and seamed. Symbol.]

Here lies buried Mrs Elisabeth Hill wife to Mr Andrew Hill who decd Febry ye 3d 1767 in the 22d year of her age

No. 946.

[White marble. Fair condition.]

HULDY, wife of ALBY WOOD, died March 3, 1841, aged 48 years.

No. 947.

[Low, white marble. Rough.]

NATHANIEL E. son of Alby & Huldy WOOD, died Jan. 19, 1858. aged 2 mo's.

No. 948.

[Blue slate. Laminæ separating. Surface seamed. Symbol.]

Memento Mori. In Memory of Mrs Eunice wife of Mr Ebenezer Robbins: who Died June ye 4th, 1781, in the 40th Year of her Age.

In Memory of Ebenezer their son who died in Captivity in the 21st Year of his Age.

Also In Memory of 4 infant Children viz. Consider, Levi, Joanna, & Levi.

No. 949.

[Blue slate. Weatherworn. Scarcely legible. Symbol.]

In memory of Mr Ephraim Cobb who departed this life Sepr ye 6th 1775, Aged

No. 950.

[Purplish blue slate. Sound.]

To the memory of Mrs MARGARET COBB widow of the late Mr. EPHRAIM COBB who died Febry 26, 1796 aged 85 years. Also to the memory of their son Capt Ephraim Cobb who died in Jamaica, 1771 aged 27 years.

No. 951.

[Blue slate. Pyramidal. Four feet in height. Urn under festoons. Small piece broken out of side. Some moss. Appears solid and compact, with the exception named.]

To the memory of Mr John Churchill who whas lost at Sea, In the year 1779 aged 34 years. Also to the memory of Mrs Olive Churchill died June 28th 1780 aged 29 years. Relict of Mr. John Churchill. Here lies interred The body of Mr John Churchill Died October 28th 1800 in the 21st year of his age Only Son to the above Parents.

> Hark! the Archangel's trumpet rends the skies
> From Earth and Ocean see the Dead arise
> The Parents, Son, and Daughter meet again
> Where perfect love shall banish fear and pain.

No. 952.

[Blue slate. Pyramidal outline. Good condition. Urn. Festooned.]

To the memory of Lemuel Cobb Robbins son of Capt Ansel Robbins and Hannah his wife who died Oct 2sd 1801 aged 1 year & 10 days

> We have no Reason for to mourn
> For gods will must be don
> He lent him for a little space
> Then sudden Called him home

No. 953.

[Blue slate. Three and one-half feet high. Good condition. Weeping willow and urn.]

Erected to the memory of Mr CROSBE LUCE died August 21, 1829, aged 44 years Consort of Mrs Betsey Luce.

> Our life is ever on the wing,
>   And death is ever nigh;
> The moment when our lives begin,
>   We all begin to die.

No. 954.

[White marble. Discolored.]

CROSBY LUCE, died Aug. 21, 1829 Æ. 44 years.
Also Betsey, his widow died Sept. 10, 1854, Æ. 65 years
& 5 mo's.

No. 955.

[Blue slate. Good condition. Weeping willow and urn.]

To the memory of ISAAC COAL Son of Mr. Isaac
Coal and Mrs. Sarah his wife who died Aug. 28, 1825 in
the 17 year of his age

> Friends and Physicians could not save
> His mortal body from the grave
> Nor can the grave confine him here
> When CHRIST shall call him to appear

No. 956.

[White marble. Four feet in height. Moss-grown.]

In memory of SALLY HALL, who died Oct. 8th. 1854.
aged 63 yrs. Also NATHAN T. HALL, who died Feb. 12th.
1854, Aged 25 years

No. 957.

[Purplish blue slate. Good condition. Symbol.]

In memory of Mr SETH LUCE Died May 6th 1802, in
the 58th year of his age

No. 958.

[White marble, on broken marble plinth. Granite base.]

SUSAN WESTON, Died Feb. 27, 1869, Aged 55 y'rs
7 mo's 14 days

> "The memory of the just is blessed."

No. 959.

[Blue slate. Three and one-half feet high. Good condition.]

Mr. LEWIS WESTON died Jan. 22d. 1825, aged 47 years
Mrs. BETSEY, his wife. died Oct. 28th. 1851, aged 73
y'rs. Also Four Children Viz. HARRIET, died Jan.
10th, 1825, in her 9th. yr. LEWIS, died Jan. 25th 1838,
in his 16th. yr. LEWIS died Sept 21st 1800, aged 17
Months. LEWIS, died May 8th. 1802, aged 2
Months.

No. 960.

[Low, blue slate. Good condition. Symbol.]

To the memory of 2 Children of Mr Lewis & Mrs Elizabeth Weston ɪst a son Lewis died Sept 21st 1800 aged 1
year 7 months and 20 days. 2d a son Lewis died May
3d 1802 aged 1 month and 23 days

No. 961.

[Blue slate. (In wooden inclosure with No. 962.) Thick. Pyramidal top. Good condition. Urn between rose-twigs.]

Here lies buried the body of Elizabeth Symmes Daughter of Mr Lazarus Symmes and Polly his wife who died July 21st 1804 aged 1 year 6 months & 9 days.

No. 962.

[White marble. Discolored.]

Our Father and Mother have gone to rest. LAZARUS SYMMES, Died Dec. 25, 1851 Aged 70 yrs. Also his wife MARY, Died Dec. 4, 1863 Aged 79 years

I am the resurrection and the life, he that believeth on me though he were dead yet shall he live.

No. 963.

[White marble, rounded top. Four feet in height. Inclosed in wooden paling.]

CHARLOTTE T. Wife of Asa Kendrick, died July 14, 1862; aged 52 years 6 mos. REUBEN R. KENDRICK died Mar 18, 1862; aged 24 years. MARY B. Wife of Mr Reuben R. Kendrick died May 2, 1862; aged 22 years. ELIZABETH F. daughter of Asa & Charlotte T. Kendrick died Jan. 19, 1858, aged 17 years 9 mos.

No. 964.

[This and the following Nos. to 969 inclusive, are white marble in wooden paling. All in good condition.]

Ambrose E. son of William & Betsey NICKERSON, Died Feb. 27, 1849 Aged 4 y'rs & 4 mos.

No. 965.

[Rose, surrounded by wreath.]

BETSEY, Wife of WILLIAM NICKERSON, died Mar. 19, 1855; Æ. 36 years & 8 mo's.

———

CHARLES H. their son died Mar. 4, 1853, Æ. 4 y'rs 6 mo's & 17 days.

A bitter cup the angel gave
To her, a mother and a wife,
She drank; death was not in the wave.
To her it was eternal life.

Beyond the dark and swelling flood
She vanished from our yearning sight,
The radiant gate of heaven was closed,
And welcomed home the child of light.

No. 966.

[Rose in wreath.]

MARY B. wife of William Nickerson, died Nov. 18, 1840, aged 37 years. MARIA H. died Oct. 3. 1826; Æ. 1 day.

WARREN M.	MARIA A.
died Mar. 8, 1830, Æ. 2	died June 21, 1822, Æ. 2
days.	mo's 22 days.

Children of William & Mary Nickerson.

No. 967.

WM. T. NICKERSON, Son of William & Mary Nickerson, Died Jan. 11, 1867. Aged 29 y'rs 9 mo's. 22 days.

No. 968.

JOAN BRADFORD Wife of Wm. Nickerson. Died Oct. 13, 1869, Aged 61 y'rs. 1 mo. & 11 days.

And those dear eyes have shone through tears,
But never looked unkind:
For shatter'd hopes and troubled years,
Still closer seemed to bind
Thy pure and trusting heart to mine,
Not for thyself didst thou repine,
But all thy husband's grief was thine,
My beautiful, my wife.

No. 969.

WILLIAM NICKERSON. Died January 15, 1884. Aged 79 y'rs 11 mo. 11 days.

At Rest.

No. 970.

[Low, blue slate. Good condition. Symbol.]

Here lyes buried the Body of Mr LEMUEL COBB, died Octr 22, 1743 in the 38th year of his age.

No. 971.

[Blue slate. Good condition. Urn.]

In memory of Mrs Mary Doten who died March 10 1809 aged 90 years

No. 972.

[Thick, blue slate. Moss-grown. Urn, with roses on either side. Part of this "anaglyph" on an inch thick lamina broken off.]

In memory of Mr Jabez Doten who Died April 6, 1805 in the 50th year of his age Also in memory of Four infant Daughters of Mr Jabez Doten and Mrs Hannah his wife

No. 973.

[Blue slate. Several seams across face.]

In memory of Mrs Hannah Doten Relict of Mr Jabez Doten who Died Septr 11th 1808 in the 49 year of her age

No. 974.

[Low, blue slate. Good condition. Symbol.]

In Memory of Martha Torrey, Daughter of Mr. James & Mrs. Martha Doten who died Novr 26 1792 aged JJ months & 6 days

No. 975.

[Thick, blue slate. Good condition. Urn.]

In memory of Mr Isaac Doten who died March 6 1809 in the 74 year of his age

No. 976.

[Blue slate. Pyramidal. Good condition. Urn, with cherub on each side.]

To the memory of Mrs POLLY BARTLETT Consort of Mr DAVID BARTLETT who died July 22 1803 in the 25th year of her age also in memory of David son of Mr David & Mrs Polly Bartlett who died Decr 30th 1803 aged 1 year 2 months & 14 days

> Death like an overflowing stream
> Sweeps us away our life's a dream,
> An empty tale a morning flower
> Cut down and wither'd in an hour

No. 977.

[Blue slate. Good condition. Two symbols.]

In memory of 2 Sons of Mr John Doten & Mrs Sally his wife John Died July 18. 1793 aged three months and nine days William Died Aug 25th 1794 aged two years one month & 16 days.

> Our days were few on earth
> We could no longer stay
> The Blessed JESUS doth appear
> To bear our souls away.

No. 978.

[White marble, cemented in marble. Good condition.]

THOMAS H. GIBBS Co. A. 3 N. Y. Regt. Died Apr. 29. 1863 Aged 17 y'rs 8 m's.

No. 979.

[White marble. On granite base. Good condition.]

CAPT. ANSELM RICKARD Died at Martinico, Oct. 6, 1801, Aged 34 y'rs.

MARGARET. his wife Died Nov. 21, 1852, Aged 81 y'rs.

No. 980.

[Similar to 979. Inclined.]

ANSELM RICKARD. Died Nov. 20, 1869. Aged 71 y'rs.

CYNTHIA, his wife Died March 6, 1867, Aged 72 y'rs.

No. 981.

[Low, blue slate. Shattered and seamed; a mere ruin.]

ory of   son of Capt A   os Rider &
Mehitable his W   who d   4th 1777 Aged J year

5 mon   5 days Also In Memor   os their 2d son
who died   88 Aged 3 months & JJ days.

No. 982.

[White marble. Set in freestone. Rough. Moss-grown. Inclined.]

Mrs. BETSEY, wife of David Bradford, died Nov. 26, 1843 : aged 46 yrs. 4 mo. Also 5 Children DESIRE H. died July 28, 1825, aged 19 mo. ANDREW J. died June 10, 1833, aged 18 mo. LYDIA H. died Aug. 9, 1834, aged 8 mo. LYDIA H. died Sept. 27, 1837. aged 2 yrs. 2 mo. DAVID L. died Aug. 31, 1838, aged 17 yrs. 4 mo.

No. 983.

[White marble in freestone. Good condition.]

CAPT. DAVID BRADFORD Born April 28, 1796 ; Died July 22, 1860.

No. 984.

[Purplish blue slate. Good condition, but some moss upon it. Urn between roses.]

In memory of Mrs POLLY DOTEN Consort of Mr THOMAS DOTEN who died February 24th 1803 in the 25th year of her age Also their Son an infant who Died February 9 aged 23 days

> Amidst the bloom of life
> The fondest joys decay
> And here in silence sleeps
> Till the grate rising day.

No. 985.

[Low, marble block. Good condition.]

(On upper surface:)

ALBERT B.

(On obverse:)

Son of James & Eleanor Kendrick.

> Called from earth to bloom in Heaven.

(On reverse:)

Died May 26, 1874, Aged 1 y'r 6 mo's 28 d's.

No. 986.

[White marble in freestone. Good condition.]

JAMES KENDRICK Died May 18, 1872 Aged 51 y'rs 10 mo's, 18 days HATTIE B ; Died Feb. 22, 1864, Aged 3 days. Dau. of James & Elenore Kendrick

> Rest Kind Husband and Father rest,
> Until the trump of God shall sound,
> Then thou shall be raised to glory,
> immortality and eternal life.
> To dwell with God, and thy loved of earth
> to part no more.

No. 987.

[White marble. Granite base. Good condition.]

DEBORAH wife of JAMES KENDRICK died June 11, 1856. Aged 27 years.

When Christ who is our life shall appear, then shall ye also appear with him in glory.

No. 988.

[White marble. Good condition.]

SALLY K. wife of James Kendrick Died Dec. 15, 1848, aged 27 years Also an Infant Daughter.

Rest, Kind mother and companion, rest.
Thy cares are all o'er
O may we meet in heaven above
And there to part no more

No. 989.

[White marble. Disintegrating.]

MARY E., Daughter of James & Deborah Kendrick died May 29, 1856, Æ. 2 y'rs 10 mo's & 13 days

No. 990.

[Blue slate. Good condition. Weeping willow and urn.]

Sacred to the memory of MRS. MARY LANMAN Widow of Mr. Peter Lanman, who died Jan. 5, 1838, aged 73 y.rs.

No. 991.

[Blue slate. Good condition. Weeping willow and urn.]

Sacred to the memory of Mr. Peter Lanman. who departed this life Sept. 14, 1825, in the 66 year of his age

My Saviour shall my life restore
And raise me from my dark abode,
My flesh and soul shall part no more
But dwell forever near my GOD,

No. 992.

[Blue slate Good condition. Symbol.]

In Memory of MR. SAMUEL LANMAN who died Jany 10, 1794 in the 73 year of his age

In thy fair book of life divine
My God inscribe my name
There let it fill some humble place
Beneath the slaughter'd Lamb.

No. 993.

[White marble. On granite base. This monument has a small cleft at lower part, where in contact with marble plinth; otherwise in good condition.]

JESSE H. TURNER, Died July 14, 1869, aged 53 yrs.

No. 994.

[White marble. On marble plinth. Granite base. Fair condition.]

(On obverse:)

CAPT JESSE TURNER   ELIZABETH H. his wife.

13

(On reverse:)

CAPT JESSE TURNER. Lost at sea on passage from Plymouth to West India, Dec, 5, 1830, aged 48 y'rs. ELIZABETH H. his wife Died Mar. 18, 1834, Aged 45 y'rs

No. 995.

[Blue slate. Good condition. Flaming urn.]

Erected to the memory of MRS. LYDIA RIDER, widow of Mr. William Rider died March 2, 1838, in the 80 year of her age.

> I now confide in Christ alone,
> No other guide nor Lord I own
> Rejoice my soul rejoice and sing,
> He's both thy Saviour and thy King.

No. 996.

[Blue slate. Seams run diagonally across face. Weeping willow and urn.]

To the memory of MR. WILLIAM RIDER who was born June 17, 1750, and died May 5, 1816.

> Our life is ever on the wing,
> And death is ever nigh
> The moment when our lives begin
> We all begin to die.

No. 997.

[Blue slate. Moss-grown. Weatherworn. Symbol.]

In memory of John Rider who deed March ye 11th 1756 Aged 47 years wanting 4 days

No. 998.

[Blue slate. Moss-grown. Defaced. Symbol.]

In Memory of Mrs MARY RIDER widow of Mr JOHN RIDER who deed August 24th 1785 aged 60 years 10 months & 25 days

No. 999.

[Low, blue slate. Marred at top; otherwise in good condition.]

In memory of Abigail Thomas Dunham Daughter of Mr William & Mrs Elizabeth Dunham his wife who died July 2, 1801 aged 9 years

No. 1000.

[White marble. Removed from broken socket, and placed in the ground.]

WILLIAM DUNHAM Born Oct. 13, 1764, Died Oct. 8. 1833. Aged 69 y'rs.

> Our life is ever on the wing,
> And death is ever nigh;
> The moment that our lives begin,
> We all begin to die.

No. 1001.

[White marble. Removed from broken socket, and set in the ground.]

ELIZABETH widow of William Dunham, Born Mar. 20 1770; Died July 20, 1854, Æ. 84 y'rs & 4 mo's.
When the Christian's race is run
Though long she slumbers in the ground
Her virtues like the setting sun
Shall shed a heavenly lustre round

No. 1002.

[Blue slate. Good condition, but moss-grown. Symbol.]

Here lies buried ye Body of Mr WILLIAM RICKARD who departed this Life August 20, 1766 Aged 62 years Also his Infant Son Buried October 18th 1764.

No. 1003.

[Low, blue slate. Moss-grown. Face of symbol scaled off, at a seam which extends down the face of the stone.]

In Memory of Henry son of Mr Barnabus Otis & Mrs Polly his wife who died July ye 22d J783 aged J0 Months & 8 Days

No. 1004.

[Blue slate. Weatherworn. Seamed. Read with difficulty. Symbol.]

Here lyes ye body of Abigail Rider who decd Nov
ye   1725 in ye 26 year of her age

No. 1005.

[Purple slate. Moss-covered. Symbol.]

Here lies Buried ye Body of Mrs Hannah Jackson widdow of Mr Jeremiah Jackson who Deced June 29th 1763 in ye 84 year of her age.

No. 1006.

[Purplish slate. Marred and moss-grown. Symbol.]

Here lyes ye ody of Mr Samuel Ryder who decd July ye 1715 About ye 85th year of his age.

No. 1007.

[Low, wide, purplish slate. Laminæ separating. Symbol.]

Here lyes ye body of Mr John Ward Decd March ye 15th 1719-20 in ye 53d year of his age

No. 1008.

[Purple slate. Laminæ separating. Part of superficial lamina missing.]

Here l   Body of Mr Joseph Bartlett deceased F brury ye 13, 1711 in ye 73d year of his age
lo here their bodys near togather lay
till ye bright morn of ye Resurrection day

No. 1009.

[White marble. Weathering rough.]

William T. son of Harvey & Olive L. Raymond died
Nov. 12, 1852, aged 2 yrs & 4 mo.

> Parents and Friends
> Weep not for me,
> Nor ov'r this Body mourn
> Soon soon you'll meet with me again
> When Christ shall call you home.

No. 1010.

[White marble, on marble plinth. Granite base. A beautiful stone.
Good condition.]

HARVEY H. RAYMOND Born Sept. 19, 1809 Died
March 18, 1854.

No. 1011.

[Blue slate. Four and a half feet high. Good condition. Weeping
willow and urn.]

this stone is erected to the memory of Mrs Fear Bartlett Late Consort of Capt Isaac Bartlett who died April
18, 1811 in the 32 year of her age

> More worth and virtue seldom warm'd a breast,
> Than hers who here lies, undisturb'd at rest
> A tender mother and a faithful wife,
> Exemplary in every walk of life,
> He infant children feel the chastening rod
> Her husband bows submissive—her spirit ascends to God.

No. 1012.

[Blue slate.—purplish. Good condition. Weeping willow and urn.]

In memory of Rebecca Bartlett Daughter of Isaac and
Rebecca Bartlett who died November 14, 1817 aged 4
years & 3 months.

> Behold a sweet and lovely Child
> Which once so fair serene and mild
> has bid the world adieu
> To save the darling child from woe
> And guard her from all harms
> From all the griefs you feel below
> I call'd her to my arms.

No. 1013.

[Blue slate. Good condition. Two figures of weeping willow and
urn.]

In memory of two children of Isaac & Rebecca Bartlett An infant Son born June 6, and died June 9, 1822;
CALEB born April 21; 1824, and died July 21, 1826.

> How sweetly sleeps the smiling flowers,
> Born but to blossom and decay,
> O GOD! how solemn was the hour
> When their blest spirits fled away.
>
> May angels watch around their bed,
> And JESUS his kind mercy show
> Till God shall bid their bodies rise
> And bloom where lasting lillies grow.

No. 1014.

[Blue slate. Good condition. Weeping willow and urn. Wreaths around the inscription.]

Sacred to the Memory of EPHRAIM BARTLETT; who was born Feb,y 19, 1809 died Dec,r 3, 1832.

There is a calm for those who weep,
A rest for weary pilgrims found.
And while the mouldering ashes sleep
Low in the ground
The soul of origin divine
God's glorious Image freed from clay
In Heaven's eternal sphere shall shine
A star of day.

No. 1015.

[Low, blue slate. Good condition, but moss-grown. Weeping willow and urn. Symbol.]

In memory of Jane Leonard Daughter of Oliver and Rebeca Weston died July 12, 1825 aged 2 years 6 months

O may thy spirit wait
The first at heaven's gate
To meet and welcome Me.

No. 1016.

[Blue slate. Good condition. Weeping willow and urn.]

Erected to the memory of Mrs. Abigail Leonard wife of Mr William Leonard who died Jany 4, 1821, in the 48 year of her age.

Raised from the dead we live anew
And justified by Grace
We shall appear in, glory too
And see our father's face.

No. 1017.

[Blue slate. Seam across face. Fair condition. Weeping willow and urn.]

In memory of Mrs Susanna Leonard Wife of Mr William Leonard who died Decr 14th 1808 in the 45th year of her age. Their infant Ephraim Bartlett Leonard died Janny 31st 1809 aged 7 months and 14 Days.

No. 1018.

[Purplish blue slate. Good condition. Urn.]

To The memory of Mrs Rebekah Leonard wife of Mr William Leonard who died Oct 2th 1801 in the 32 year of her age.

No. 1019.

[Blue slate. Seamed. Fair condition. Symbol.]

To the memory of Mr EPHRAIM BARTLETT who was drowned on the Grand Bank Sept 9th 1800 in the 34th year of his age

The voice of this alarming scene
May every heart obey
Nor be the heavenly warning vain
Which calls to watch and pray.

No. 1020.

[Low, wide, blue slate. Good condition, Symbol.]

Here lyes ye body of John Drew aged 79 years Died July the 27th 1721.

No. 1021.

[Blue slate. Shattered and ruined.]

John   Aged   Deces   25th

[NOTE. In Kingman's excellent work, "Epitaphs from Burial Hill," the inscription on No. 1021—probably copied by Wm. S. Russell, Esq., about the year 1858,—is given as follows:

Here lyes buried ye body of JOHN RICKARD Aged about 55 years Decsd March ye 25th 1712.]

No. 1022.

[Blue slate. Somewhat marred. Symbol.]

Here lyes buried ye body of Mary Rickard Aged 55 years Decesd August ye 28th 1712.

No. 1023.

[Blue slate. Weatherworn, seamed, and moss-grown. Symbol.]

In memory of Mrs JEMIMA TAYLOR wife of Capt JACOB TAYLOR who decd March 14th 1783 In ye 52d year of her Age   Also In Memory of Mr JACOB TAY-LOR her Son who was Drowned Nov. 26th 1783 in ye 21st year of his Age.

No. 1024.

[Blue slate. Right wing of symbol broken off; otherwise in good condition.]

To the memory of Capt JACOB TAYLOR who died May 2, 1788 aged 59 years.

> Through life he brav'd her foe
> if great or small,
> And march'd out foremost at his
> Country's call.

No. 1025.

[Low, blue slate. Much injured.]

re   es ye Body of   les Curtis who   d Novbr ye 19th 1729 in the 18th year of his age.

No. 1026.

[Blue slate. Laminæ separating. Seams opened. Pieces gone. Enough of the border left to show that it was a handsome piece of sculpture. Only beginning and ending of lines remain.]

Her   of   Dogg   to M   ZAR Dog-get   decd Decbr   7th 1731 in ye 38th year of her age.

[NOTE. No. 1026 is the grave of Elizabeth Doggett, wife of Ebenezar Doggett, as appears by Kingman's work, and was probably copied by Wm. S. Russell, Esq., in the year 1858.]

No. 1027.

[Blue slate. Laminæ open. Surface seamed and cleft. Symbol.]

Here lies Buried Mr Lothrop Rickard who died March ye 6th, 1759 Aged 27 years.

No. 1028.

[Light blue slate. Laminæ separating somewhat, but condition fair. Symbol.]

In Memory of Mrs SARAH BARTLETT wife of Dea'n JOSEPH BARTLETT who died Decr 23d 1785 in the 80th year of her age

No. 1029.

[Blue slate. Broken. Cannot endure much longer. Symbol.]

In Memory of Dea'n JOSEPH BARTLETT who died May 30 J783 in the 80 year of his age.

No. 1030.

[Blue slate. Fair condition. Skull and crossbones.]

Here lies Interr'd the Body of Mr JOHN BARTLETT who departed this life February the 6th A. D. 1773 Æ. 77 years.

No. 1031.

[Blue slate. Five and a half feet high. Good condition. Mausoleum.]

Erected to the memory of CAPT. FINNEY LEACH, who departed this life Novr 5th 1839, in the 65 year of his age.

————

Forever, O Lord, thy word is settled in Heaven

————

Tread lightly o'er this sacred ground,
A resting place for mortal man,
Free from all care which earth abounds
Stop! view your bed of earthly clay,
And think how soon your race is run,
Prepare yourself without delay,
For soon must be your setting sun.

No. 1032.

[Blue slate. Moss-grown; otherwise in good condition. Weeping willow and urn.]

Erected in memory of ROBERT BARTLETT LEACH Son of Capt. Finney & Mrs. Mercy Leach who departed this life Sept 12th 1830, aged 21 years Also Four Children of the same VIZ Marcia, died Oct. 25th 1813, aged 6 months Rebecca B. died May 4th 1818, aged 10 weeks Louisa died Oct. 17th 1818 aged 1 year & 11 mo. George. Edwards died Dec, 22d 1820, aged 6 yrs. and 1 month.

No. 1033.

[White marble. Moss-grown. Inclined forward.]

EPHRAIM WHITING Died in Jamacia W. I. 1803 : aged 28 Y'rs. Also ELIZABETH, widow of the late Ephraim Whiting Died Sept. 27, 1855 : Aged 80 years.

May their souls meet in heaven.

No. 1034.

[Purplish blue slate. Sound and compact. Symbol.]

Here lyes buried the body of Mrs SARAH BARTLETT wife to Mr Robert Bartlett who died Febry ye 8th 1744–5 in the 74th year of her age

No. 1035.

[Low, blue slate. Inclined to right. Fair condition. Symbol.]

James Bartlet aged 22 years Died Janry ye 13th 1723

No. 1036.

[Blue slate. Good condition. Urn under festoons.]

To the memory of David Leach son of Capt Finney Leach and Mrs Mercy his wife who died Aug 9th 1803 aged 2 months & 8 days.

Where shall i go where shall i flee
But to my loveing Saviours breast
There within his arms to be
And safe beneath his wing to rest.

No. 1037.

[Blue slate. Pyramidal. Narrow. Good condition. Urn between rose twigs.]

In memory of Marcia Leach Daughter of Capt Finney Leach and Mercy his wife born Febuy 10th,–1805 died Octr 6th 1806.

God in his lovely word hath said
Childre'n were for his Kingdom made
Then may we all to God submit
Who calls them hom as he sees fit.

No. 1038.

[Blue slate. Curiously sculptured. Inscription in a heart-shaped space. Symbol under hour-glass.]

Here Lyes buried ye body of Mrs. Hannah Bartlet wife to Mr Joseph Bartlett deces'd March ye 12th 1710 in the 72 year of her age.

[NOTE BY THE EDITOR. The foregoing Nos. are west of the pathway leading north from the Cushman monument. No. 1039 is at the extreme north of the easterly division of the Hill.]

No. 1039.

[White marble on marble plinth. Granite base. Good condition.]

ZEPHANIAH BRADFORD died Sept. 1, 1868, Aged 69 y'rs. 1 mo. 17 days.

No. 1040.

[Similar to preceding.]

SALLY H. wife of Zephaniah Bradford died Oct. 24, 1879, Aged 81 y'rs 1 mo. 23 days.

No. 1041.

[This No. and the two following are inclosed with wooden palings. 1041 and 1042 are beautiful white marble, resting on the same granite base. Good condition.]

CATHARINE B. wife of SETH MORTON died July 8, 1883, Aged 77 years 1 mo.

No. 1042.

SETH MORTON Died Jan. 6, 1884, Aged 86 years 1 mo.

No. 1043.

Marble obelisk, on marble plinth, with freestone base. Fair condition. Chain with legend "Parted below, United above."]

LUCIA W. wife of William H. MORTON, died May 4, 1859, aged 25 years & 4 mos.

"Oh! why should we in anguish weep."
"She is not lost, but gone before."

No. 1044.

[White marble, set in freestone socket. Fair condition. Rose twig.

MARY D. Dau. of William & Jane STEPHENS, died July 24, 1866, Æ. 21 y'rs. 8 mo's.

Cold is that form once filled with youthful bloom
It sleeps, alas! within the lonely tomb
Commingling with the dust it wears away,
Companion only for its fellow clay
But that ethereal spark of "heavenly flame,"
Too strong to live within its earthly frame,
Has winged its flight, we trust to realms above,
Forever to enjoy a Saviour's love.

No. 1045.

[White marble, set in freestone. Good condition, save being inclined. Rose breaking from stem.]

EMMA E. Dau. of William & Jane STEPHENS, Died Sept. 11, 1875 ; Æ. 21 y'rs. 7 mo's. 20 days.

The memory of thy lovliness
Shall round our every pathway smile
Like moonlight when the sun has set,
A sweet and tender radiance yet.

No. 1046.

[White marble, set in freestone. Good condition. Chain with broken links, and the words "Parted below, United above."]

Capt. WM. STEPHENS Died at Matanzas, Oct. 15, 1857 : Æ. 46 yrs. 9 mos. & 20 days.

AUGUSTA FRANCES, daughter of Wm. & Jane Stephens died Aug. 4, 1854: Æ. 3 yrs. 6 mos. & 17 days.

> Though distant from us thou wast called,
> Beneath a tropic sun,
> To hear thy Master call for thee
> Yet, Lord, Thy will be done.
> We mourn as those who have a hope
> For death to thee was gain:
> In habitations with the blest
> Thou wilt forever reign.

No. 1047.

[White marble, in granite socket. Good condition.]

CAPT. JOSEPH W. COLLINGWOOD Co. H. 18th Reg. Mass. Vols. wounded at the battle of Fredericksburg, Va. Dec. 13, 1862 Died Dec. 24, 1862, Aged 41 years

> He who gives his life for his country gives his own but for a higher life.

No. 1048.

[Similar to No. 1047.]

REBECCA W. widow of CAPT. JOSEPH W. COLLINGWOOD, Died Oct. 29, 1886, Aged 70 y'rs 11 mo's.4 days.

> "Her children shall rise up and call her blessed."

No. 1049.

[A broken slab of white marble.]

Lieut. JOHN B. COLLINGWOOD, died Jan.

No. 1050.

[White marble, set in freestone with brimstone for cement. Cement crumbled away, and base broken.]

MARTHA T. Died Feb. 18, 1872, Aged 19 y'rs 3 mo's NELLIE F. Died Jan. 21, 1873, Aged 11 y'rs 5 mo's. WILLIE B. Died Sep. 18. 1860. Aged 4 y'rs 2 mo's. WILLIE L. Died Aug. 10, 1855, Aged 11 mo's. Children of Thomas & M. A. Collingwood.

> Dear Children gone to rest,
> On Canaan happy shore;
> And we hope to meet again
> Where parting will be no more.

No. 1051.

[White marble, in freestone socket. Good condition.]

CORPORAL THOMAS COLLINGWOOD, Co. E, 29 Reg. Mass. Vols. Died at Crab Orchard. Ky. Aug. 31, 1863, Aged 32 y'rs 9 mo's. 21 days.

> Why do we mourn departing friends
> Or shake at death's alarms
> 'Tis but the voice that Jesus sends
> To call them to his arms.

No. 1052.

[White marble. Loose in freestone socket, and liable to fall.]

MOTHER.   MARY W. wife of Edward L. Doten, Died
July 30, 1857, Aged 27 y'rs 6 mo's.

"Blessed are they that mourn for they shall be comforted."

No. 1053.

[Blue slate. Four feet by three. Good condition.]

BATHSHEBA TRIBBEL, wife of JOHN TRIBBEL,
died July 24th. 1815 ; in the 30th year of her age.

ALBERT TRIBBEL, died March 30th, 1817 ; in the
10th year of his age.

MARCIA TRIBBEL died February 1st, 1818 ; in the
4th year of her age.

GUSTAVUS TRIBBEL, died July 5th 1821 ; aged 9
years & 2 mon.

LAVANTIA TRIBBEL, died March 9th, 1824 ; aged
2 years & 9 mon.

CHRISTIANA D. TRIBBEL, Died December 2d,
1821 ; aged 19 years.

No. 1054.

[White marble, in stone socket. The whole mass inclined.]

WINSLOW M. TRIBBLE died Jan 5, 1860 ; Æ. 49
years & 1 mo.

Also three of his Children ;

MARSTON W. died Dec. 2, 1858 ; Æ. 25 years & 2
mos. HORACE G. died Nov. 7, 1859 ; Æ. 21 years &
4 mos. CHRISTIANA D. died Sept. 22, 1837 ; Æ. 1
year & 25 days. ———

Eternal upward progression is the destiny of all in Spirit life.

No. 1055.

[White marble. Carving at top, representing a scroll, a book, and
square and compasses.]

John B. Atwood Died May 12, 1864 Aged 60 y'rs.

No. 1056.

[Blue slate. Good condition. Weeping willow and urn; star on
either side.]

In memory of Capt WILLIAM BARNES, who died
Novr 22, 1826, in the 60th year of his age.

The year rolls round and steals away,
The breath which first it gave;
Whate'er we do whate'er we be
We're marching to the grave.

No. 1057.

[Blue slate. Star on each side of urn.]

In memory of Mrs SALLY, Consort of Capt. William
Barnes who died April 19, 1836, Aged 59 y.rs.

Fled from the raging storms of time,
And wafted to a smoother clime.

No. 1058.

[Blue slate. Good condition. Weeping willow.]

In memory of WILLIAM H. JEWETT, who died March 21, 1841, in the 26 year of his age.

No. 1059.

[Blue slate. Five feet by three. Handsome, compact. Weeping willow and three urns.]

Erected to the memory of RICHARD FISHER aged 31: of SALEM, JOHN JACOBS aged 28: and WILLIAM WRIGHT aged 21; of NEW YORK who were drowned by the oversetting of a boat in Plymouth Harbour Augt 9. 1826.

> O time is a stream flowing rapidly onward,
> As life is advancing we rush without fear,
> On temptation's rough sea, and pleasure's bland wave,
> Till we sink in its current, and reach the dark grave.

No. 1060.

[White marble. Set in freestone. Fair condition. Inclosed in wooden paling.]

JAMES BARTLETT, Died June 17, 1867, Aged 64 y'rs. 1 mo.

No. 1061.

[Gray marble. Good condition.]

DAVID N. son of David & Mary Ann Craig died May 24 1857, in his 8th year.

> Suffer little children to come unto me, and forbid them not; for of such is the Kingdom of Heaven.

No. 1062.

[White marble. (Near a large square block of hammered granite apparently intended for base of a monument.) Set in freestone. Good condition.]

Erected to the memory of JOSHUA SAWYER, who died Sept. 10, 1854, Aged 33 years.

> To this lone spot I love to stray
> Where sleeps the dust of that dear one
> Who fled so soon from earth away
> Ere yet his life was scarce begun
>
> O lovely spot! O husband dear!
> I almost envy thee thy bliss
> O gladly would I leave earth's care
> For such a resting place as this.

No. 1063.

[Blue slate. Seam across, at upper third of stone. Urn.]

In memory of Mr. Lewis Lumber who departed this life' July 27th 1802 in Dominico in the 24th year of his age

Also in memory of Elizabeth Lumber who died Sept 13th 1802 in the 16th year of her age.
Sleep silent dust till the Archangels sound
Bid soul and Body both unite again
And call thee forth from underneath the ground
To meet thy God with him to live & reign.

No. 1064.

[Blue slate. Good condition. Urn.]

To the Memory of Mr Moses Breck who departed this life May 1st 1807 in the 40th year of his age.
Strangers & friends while you gaze on my urn
Remember death will call you in your turn
Therefore prepare to meet your God on high
When he rides glorious through the upper sky

No. 1065.

[Blue slate. Good condition. Festoons.]

To the memory of Sarah Tyler Breck daughter of Mr Moses Breck & Mrs Mary his wife who departed this life Octr 7th 1801 aged 1 & 8 months
they die in Jesus and are blest
How kind their slumbers are
from suffering and from sin released
And freed from every snare

No. 1066.

[Thick, blue slate. Four and a half feet high. Good condition. Flaming urn on mausoleum.]

In memory of Mrs. Sarah. widow of John Warland of Cambridge who died Feb. 9, 1845, aged 84 yrs.

No. 1067.

[Blue slate. Good condition. Two symbols.]

In memory of Lemuel Brown who died Octr 13th 1801 aged 1 year 7 months Also in memory of Sarah Palmer Brown who died Octr 5 1802 aged 1 year 2 months Children of Mr Lemuel Brown and Mrs Sarah his wife

No. 1068.

[Blue slate. Good condition. One of three monuments standing side by side, each 4 1-2 by 2 feet. No 1068 has figure of mausoleum.]

In memory of SARAH, wife of Lemuel Brown who died June 5th 1821 aged 46 years.

SARAH PALMER, died June 30, 1807 aged 2 years & 7 months ANNE RICE, died June 29, 1809, aged 11 years. Children of Lemuel & Sarah Brown.

No. 1069.

[Similar to 1068.]

In memory of Lemuel Brown who died Nov. 19th 1845 aged 73 years.
The dead how sacred.
Young.

No. 1070.

[Blue slate. Good condition.]

In memory of Mrs. ANN BROWN, widow of Mr. LEMUEL BROWN, Born 14 March 1783, Died 28th Jany 1847.

No. 1071.

[Fine, mottled marble. Marble plinth on granite base. Good condition. Wreath of leaves.]

ELIZA H. CLARK Dau. of the late Capt. John & Mary Roberts Clark Died Dec, 23, 1882 Aged 78 yrs. 1 mo. & 10 d'ys.

"I am the Resurrection and the Life."

No. 1072.

[Blue slate. Four and 3-4 by 2 3-4 feet. Good condition. Flaming urn, with columns on sides.]

Erected to the memory of CAPT. JOHN CLARK who died May 30, 1841 aged 74 years.

Hark! the sad sound, that spirit bright has fled,
That once loved form lies numbered with the dead
He was a tender husband, father, dear,
Come, all who knew him drop a social tear.

No. 1073.

[Similar to preceding.]

ERECTED to the memory of MRS. MARY, widow of Capt. John Clark, who died June 6, 1855, aged 85 y'rs & 8 mo.

"It is well."—2d Kings, 4th 26.

Thy wish is granted thou art free from ev'ry earthly pain,
We miss thee but it would be wrong to wish thee back again.
But we shall meet thee, blessed thought, where partings never come,
While ending ages rolling all, will find us all at home.

No. 1074.

[Blue slate. Good condition. Weeping willow and urn.]

Mrs. Sarah R, Barstow, wife of Mr. Ichabod W, Barstow and Daughter of Mr. John & Mrs. Mary Clark, who died August 15th 1832, aged 36 years.

Sweet spirit dear, a sad farewell,
Till we shall meet again.
The place where happy souls do dwell,
Is free from toil and pain.

Great were her suffrings mighty GOD
We heard her groan and die.
But Jesus Christ's most precious blood
Was shed on Calvary.

No. 1075.
[Blue slate. Good condition. Weeping willow and urn.]
This stone is Erected to the memory of Robert Roberts who died at the island of St. Domingo Aprl 12, 1775 in the 32d year of his age. Also in memory of Sarah Roberts widow of the Above who died March 1, 1826 aged 78 years. Also their Daughter Sarah who died March 4, 1775 aged 2 years & 6 months.

> Till Christ shall come to rouse the slumbering dead
> Farewell, pale lifeless clay a long farewell.

No. 1076.
[Blue slate. Pyramidal. Good condition. Weeping willow and urn.]
In memory of Sylvanus H. Roberts Son of Cap Robert Roberts & Eliza his wife who departed this life January 15 1815 aged 5 years & 6 months

No. 1077.
[White marble. Disintegrating. Urn]
Sacred to the memory of Mrs. Eliza Davis Consort of Mr. Joseph Davis & Daughter of Joshua & Elizabeth Colby of Newbury port who died Novr 8. 1824 aged 30 years.

No. 1078.
[Wide, blue slate. Two semicircular spaces at top, each with weeping willow and urn.]
In memory of Capt Thomas Mathews who was born in South Shields England Feby 17th 1725 died June 1807 Aged 82 years Also in memory of Mrs Desire Mathews his wife who died September 15, 1807 aged 75 years.

No. 1079.
[Low, white marble. Scarcely legible.]
LYDIA ANN Dau. of Joshua & Lydia Standish died July 1. 1843 aged 3 yrs & 6 mo.

No. 1080.
[White marble. Discolored.]
Our Mother LYDIA STANDISH, died Dec. 27. 1864, Aged 44 y'rs. 4 m's. 14 days.

No. 1081.
[Blue slate. Height, 4 feet. Good condition. Weeping willow and urn.]
HENRY McCARTER, died in Martinique W. I. Jan. 7th, 1822, aged 34 yr.s. NANCY McCARTER, wife of the above died Jan. 1st. 1827, aged 34 yr.s & 3 mo.

> A living faith the soul sustains
>   When death appears in dread array,
> It triumphs o'er our mortal pains,
>   It points on high to endless day
> There happy ransomed spirits dwell,
> The triumphs of the cross to tell.

No. 1082.

[Low, blue slate. Good condition. Pyramidal shape. Symbol.]

To the memory of Hannah Huesten daughter of Mr William & Mrs Mary Huesten who died Novr 16th 1802 aged 2 years 2 months & 15 days.

But comfort from a better source doth come
For GOD in mercy calls his children home.

No. 1083.

[Blue slate. Some seams on face. Piece, about 8 by 3 inches, broken out and standing apart,—which piece contains part of each line of the epitaph. Weeping willow and urn.]

In memory of NATHANIEL HUESTEN. who died Oct. 23. 1831. in the 45 year of his age.

Where ere thy steps are bent,
Death hovers by thy side,
Thou knowest not what an hour
May to thy fate betide.

No. 1084.

[White marble. Freestone socket. Fair condition.]

NANCY HOLMES, wife of Nathaniel Huesten Born June 30, 1791, Died Sept. 4, 1866.

"Blessed are the pure in heart, for they shall see God."

No. 1085.

[Blue slate. Seams across face. Weeping willow and urn.]

In memory of Mrs. Mary Huesten. wife of Mr. William Huesten who died May 30th 1832 in the 74 year of her age.

My soul my body I will trust
With him who numbers every dust;
My Saviour faithfully will Keep
His own—their death is but a sleep.

No. 1086.

[Blue slate. Good condition. Urn.]

In Memory of MR. WILLIAM HUESTEN. who died Dec. 25, 1834 Aged 79 years.

Fled from the rageing storms of time,
And wafted to a smoother clime.

No. 1087.

[Blue slate. Good condition. Symbol.]

In memory of Elizabeth Husten Coventon daughter of Mr Thomas Coventon & Mrs Elizabeth his wife who died Sepr 12th 1799 aged 1 year & 3 months & 14 days

The infant smiles in lisping speech
And in the grave in silence sleeps

No. 1088.

[White marble. In freestone socket. Good condition.]

GEORGE RAYMOND Died May 23, 1868 Aged 85 y'rs. 10 mo's.

No. 1089.

[White marble. In freestone socket. Fair condition.]

PRISCILLA, wife of George Raymond, died Apr. 6, 1866, Aged 81 y'rs. 6 mo's.

"Jesus saith, because I live, ye shall live also."

No. 1090.

[White marble. Weathering rough. Weeping willow and urn.]

In memory of PHEBE SOULE, wife of J. RUSSELL DIKE, who died May 16, 1843, Æ. 24 y'rs. Also their son, RUSSELL R. Æ. 3 mo. 11 days.

No. 1091.

[White marble. Set in marble block. Good condition.]

JAMES JORDAN Drowned in Smelt Pond June 25, 1837, Aged 27 y'rs
Buried on the day he was to have been Married.

No. 1092.

[White marble. Set in marble block. Good condition.]

CHARLES, Son of Geo. & Priscilla Raymond Died March 19, 1822, Aged 16 y'rs.

No. 1093.

[Blue slate. Good condition. Weeping willow and urn.]

In memory of MISS. DRUSILLA GOULD late of Franklin, (Mass.) who died May 31, 1833, aged 64 years.

No. 1094.

[White marble. In freestone socket. Fair condition, but inclined.]

THOMAS W. HAYDEN, of Co. E, 29 Mass. Vol's. Died at Crab Orchard, Ky. Sept. 4, 1863, Aged 33 years & 2 mo's.

———

A precious sacrifice for freedom.

No. 1095.

[White marble. Set in freestone. Weathering rough. Within wooden paling. Figure of lamb.]

Sweetly fell asleep in Jesus, Feb. 17, 1858, Elisabeth Abby, only dau. of Otis & Elisabeth B. Wright. Aged 11 y'rs 11 mo. 2 ds.

> The once loved form now cold in death
> Each mournful thought employs
> And nature weeps her comforts fled
> And withered all her joys.
>
> Hope looks beyond the bounds of time,
> When what we now deplore
> Shall rise in full immortal prime
> And bloom to fade no more.

14

No. 1096.

[A marble block set in freestone, inscribed:]

LITTLE LIZZIE.

[This and the following Nos. to 1101 inclusive are marble, mostly in good condition, and are inclosed in wooden paling.]

No. 1097.

OUR FATHER

WILLIAM BARNES, DIED Apr. 31, 1865, Aged 70 y'rs 4 mo.

How sweet and ever green thy memory.

No. 1098.

OUR MOTHER

PHEBE J. BARNES DIED April 20. 1857, Aged 58 y'rs 2 mo.

Holy thoughts cluster about thy name.

No. 1099.

Anna Elisabeth, wife of Wm. M. Barnes, Dau. of Capt. Gideon Holbrook Died Oct. 25, 1881, Aged 59 y'rs. 7 mo. 4 ds.

No. 1100.

[Handsomely sculptured. Figure of three buds.]

Dearly loved one! Jesus called thee home To adorn a brighter sphere. ANNIE FRANCES BARNES, Died June 4, 1860, aged 8 ys. 9 mo. 15 ds.

No. 1101 a.

[Sculptured lamb on summit of marble block which is set in freestone socket. The block is inscribed:]

LITTLE WILLIE Willie H. Barnes Died Aug. 18, 1850, Æ. 10 mo. 11 ds.

No. 1101 b.

[A handsome granite block, in same inclosure as the above. On upper surface the name "WILL" in relief.]

WILLIAM T. BARNES 1868–1889.

No. 1102.

[A wooden slab, not lettered. Has decayed and fallen. Inclosed in wooden paling.]

No. 1103.

[Beautiful mottled marble on marble plinth. Granite base.]

(On obverse:)

SAMUEL SAMPSON Feb. 22, 1818, Dec. 27, 1887.

(On reverse:)

FATHER.

No. 1104.

[Similar to foregoing No.]

(On obverse:)

ALICE BRADFORD Daughter of Samuel & Rebecca SAMPSON Nov. 2, 1844, Dec. 26, 1885.

(On reverse:)

ALICE.

No. 1105.

[White marble. Discolored and roughened.]

In this town June 7, 1850 Mary Allerton dau. of Samuel & Rebecca Sampson Æ. 3 y'rs. 10 mo.

No. 1106.

[White marble, cemented in freestone socket. Four and a half feet high. Weathering rough. Basket of flowers sculptured at top.]

JERUSHA T. Wife of CAPT. ALBERT HOLMES, died Jan. 30, 1864; Æ. 37 years 5 mos. 25 days.

CARRIE CLIFTON, died April 9, 1861; Æ. 3 years 10 mos. 16 days.

CHARLES EDWARD, died March 31, 1857; Æ. 2 years, 8 mos.

ALBERT HENRY, died April 7, 1845; Æ. 4 mos. 25 days.

Children of Albert & Jerusha T. Holmes.

We mourn, but not without hope.

No. 1107.

[This and the following Nos. to 1112 inclusive are inclosed in a wooden paling. No. 1107 is white marble set in granite. Fair condition.]

ICHABOD SHAW, Died March 20. 1873, Aged 69 y'rs. MARY SAMPSON, Wife of Ichabod Shaw Died May 18, 1851, Aged 47 y'rs.

MARY ELIZABETH, Died June 23, 1858, Aged 27 y'rs. REBECCA BARTLETT, Died April 16, 1859, Aged 25 y'rs. Daughters of Ichabod & Mary S. Shaw.

No. 1108.

[White marble. Weathering rough.]

SOUTHWORTH SHAW, Born July 28, 1775, Died January 18, 1847: aged 71 years, 5 mos 21 days

No. 1109.

[White marble. Similar to 1108.]

MARIA SHAW, wife of Southworth Shaw, Born March 20, 1778, Died October 5, 1850, aged 72 years, 6 mos. 15 days.

No. 1110.

[Blue slate. Good condition. Mausoleum.]

In memory of Esther Shaw. Widow of the late Ichabod Shaw, who died Nov. 1, 1840, in the 78 yr. of her age.

No. 1111.

[Blue slate. Good condition. Mausoleum.]

In memory of ICHABOD SHAW, who was born November 14, 1769, and died July 26, 1837.

No. 1112.

[Blue slate. Fair condition, save being moss-grown. Elaborate carving at top,—a tomb, tree and urn beside it, and over these a cherub or symbol.]

To the memory of Mrs BETSY SHAW, wife of Mr. ICHABOD SHAW who died Decr 6, 1795 aged 20 years Also her infant daughter Betsy Holmes by her side, aged 7 months & 15 days

No. 1113.

[Marble slab, placed horizontally on columns. The earlier inscriptions at top rapidly fading out. The slab is broken across the middle, and the pieces are held together by iron plates and rivets.]

Mrs. LYDIA CUSHING GOODWIN. Died Decr 15, 1815, aged 53 years. WILLIAM GOODWIN, Jr. died at Havana, Decr 15, 1821, aged 38 years. WILLIAM GOODWIN, died July 17th 1825, aged 69 years. SIMEON S. GOODWIN died July 27, 1847 aged 65 years. ISAAC GOODWIN, died at Worcester, Sept. 10, 1832, aged 46 years. JOHN A. GOODWIN died at Lowell, Sept. 21, 1884, aged 60 years.

HIC NON CORPUS SED ILLI LOCUS CARISSIMUS

No. 1114.

[Blue slate, 3 1-2 feet high. Face of stone carved to represent large urn shaded by a willow. On this urn is the inscription, the base containing the epitaph.]

Died Captain Simeon Samson June 22, 1789 Aged fifty-three years.

O ye whose cheek the tear of pity stains
Draw near with pious reverence and attend
Here lie the loving Husbands dear remains
The tender Father and the courteous Friend
The dauntless heart yet touched by human woe
A Friend to man to vice alone a Foe

No. 1115.

[Blue slate. Rough, weatherworn, and seamed. Symbol.]

Here lyes buried 5 children of Capt. Simeo   Samson & Mrs Deborah his   Viz ɪst Simeon born May 6th ɪ76 dec d March 22d ɪ766 Simeon born Dec. 8th ɪ766 died

Dec r ɪ0th ɪ766 3d A Son still born   ep t ɪ5th ɪ770 4th
Mary born June 3d ɪ775 died Oct r ɪst ɪ777 5th Martha
Washington born Sep r 4th ɪ779 dec'd Sep r 25th ɪ780

No. 1116.

[Purplish blue slate. Good condition. Urn.]

In memory of Elizabeth Diman who departed this life
April 14, 1807 in the 47 year of her age.

Blessed are the dead
That die in the Lord.

No. 1117.

[This and the two following Nos. are of like height and form; are
on marble plinth and granite base; inclosed with wooden fence. No.
1117 is in fair condition. Foul anchor, well carved, at top.]

ISAAC DAVIE Died Oct. 29, 1864, Aged 73 years 8
mo's.

Which hope we have as an anchor of the soul, both sure and stead-
fast, and which entereth into that within the vail.

No. 1118.

[Good condition. Sheaf of wheat.]

Rhoda C. Davie, Died Oct. 11, 1881, Aged 86 years 1
mo's.

Rest for the toiling hand,
Rest for the anxious brow
Rest for the weary wayworn feet,
Rest from all labor now.

No. 1119.

[Good condition. Hands clasped under the words "I love thee."]

Mary B. C. wife of James Morton died Sept. 12, 1883,
Aged 66 years 11 mo's.

I lean o'er thee my Best Beloved
My heart on thy heart lay
I lean o'er thee and do weep
For the time to come for us to meet.

No. 1120.

[Blue slate, 2 1-2 feet high. Surface of upper half, and right portion
of lower, scaled off, and have disappeared.]

Novr   Aged ɪɪ years &
Not youth, nor parts nor frie   could save
The unsuspecting victim from
Like a fair flower that fades in earl
In life's bright morn he met his early to
Tho harsh the stroke and most severe the ro
Cease mourner cease—it was a stroke from God.

(On the footstone are the words:)

Isaac Samson ɪ782

No. 1121.

[White marble; on freestone.]

In memory of GEORGE COOPER who died April 29,
1864; Æ. 66 years 8 mos.

No. 1122.
[Similar to No. 1121.]
In memory of MARY C. wife of GEORGE COOPER,
died Nov. 3, 1867 Æ. 70 years 10 mos.

No. 1123.
[White marble (next concrete walk). Inclined forward at an angle
of about 40 degrees.]
In memory of GEORGE W. COOPER who died Oct.
17, 1837, Æ. 5 years 5 mos. 16 days.

No. 1124.
[Blue slate. Pyramidal. Good condition. Urn, with symbol on
either side.]
Abigail Leach died Decr 24th 1795 aged 10 years Ebenezer Leach Died Jan 31st 1796 aged 13 years Children
of Mr Caleb & Mrs Abigail Leach And here lie buried.

No. 1125.
[This and following, to No. 1129 are inclosed with iron rails set in
hammered granite posts. No. 1125 is white marble, in the usual
weatherworn and discolored condition of that material.]
WILLIAM BARTLETT Died July 30, 1863 ; aged 77
years

No. 1126.
[Blue slate. Good condition. Weeping willow and urn.]
Sacred to the memory of Rebecca Bartlett wife of Joseph
Bartlett Esq. who died March 5, 1821 aged 55 years
This woman was full of good works
And alms deeds which She did.

No. 1127.
[Blue slate. Good condition.]
In memory of Capt. Joseph Bartlett Born June 16,
1762 Died March 4, 1835. Also to his five sons JOHN,
JOSEPH, SAMUEL, BENJAMIN, and AUGUSTUS.

No. 1128.
[Blue slate. Fair condition]
LUCY D. BARTLETT, widow of Capt Joseph Bart-
lett, died July 30, 1853, Aged 75 y'rs.

No. 1129.
[Blue slate. Good condition. Mausoleum.]
Susan Bartlett, died Feb. 18, 1847, aged 52 yrs.

No. 1130.
[Blue slate. Good condition, but inclined. Weeping willow and
urn.]
In memory of Rufus Churchill who Died April 14,
1828 ; in the 57 year of his age,   Also his Child who died
Sepr 12, 1799 aged 5 months and 11 days.

No. 1131.

[White marble; set in granite. Good condition.]

EUNICE, wife of Rufus Churchill Died March 25, 1875, Aged 97 y'rs 11 mo's

No. 1132.

[Beautiful, variegated marble. Marble plinth. Granite base.]

SETH McLAUTHLIN 1812-1869 PRISCILLA his wife 1813-1886

No. 1133.

[White marble. Four feet in height. This and the Nos. to 1138 inclusive, in iron rails with granite posts. No. 1133, weathering rough. Inclined.]

Father & Mother: JOHN PERRY, died Aug. 19th 1831, in his 64th yr. RHODA PERRY, died July 10th 1855 in her 83d. y'r.

Why do we mourn departing friends
Or shake at death's alarms?
'Tis but the voice that Jesus sends
To call them to his arms.

No. 1134.

[Blue slate. Good condition. Weeping willow and urn.]

This stone is erected to consecrate the memory of Miss Mary B. Perry daughter of Mr. John Perry and Mrs. Rhoda his wife who was born October 28, 1793 deceased October 30, 1814 aged 21 years & 2 days.

Come view the scene
'Twill fill thee with surprise
Behold the loveliest form in nature dies.

No. 1135.

[White marble. Good condition.]

SARAH, wife of Lewis Perry, & Dau. of David & Sally Drew, Died Jan. 10, 1869, Aged 65 y'rs. 9 mo's.

Yet, ah—and let me lightly tread—
She sleeps beneath this stone
That would have soothed my dying bed,
And wept for me when gone.

No. 1136.

[White marble. Good condition.]

Lewis Perry, Died Oct. 11, 1876, Aged 78 y'rs 7 mo's.

Jesus can make a dying bed
Feel soft as downy pillows are,
While on his breast I lean my head,
And breathe my life out sweetly there.

No. 1137.

[White marble. Good condition.]

RUTH, wife of JOHN PERRY, Born Feb. 24, 1811, Died June 18, 1874.

Safe in the arms of Jesus.

No. 1138.

[White marble. Weathering rough.]

`* JOHN PERRY, died Jan. 6, 1846, aged 49 yrs. Also two children of John & Ruth Perry. Viz LEWIS, died Feb. 1, 1843, aged 2 y'rs & 2 Mon. LEWIS, died Feb. 17, 1846, aged 3 y'rs & 4 Mon.

> The graves of all the Saints he bless'd
> And soften'd ev'ry bed
> Where should the dying members rest,
> But with their dying Head.

No. 1139.

[White marble. Rough. Discolored. Inclined about 45°. Weeping willow and urn.]

In memory of Solomon Sampson who died April 3. 1851 Æ. 28 y'rs.

> Dearest Husband thou hast left me
> Here thy loss I deeply feel
> But 'tis God that hath bereft me,
> He can all my sorrows heal.

No. 1140.

[White marble, in freestone, with brimstone for cement. Fair condition. Rose twig.]

GEORGE F. Son of Francis H. & Sarah J. P. Robbins, died Apr. 20, 1865, aged 1 year 8 mo. & 21 days. also an infant daughter.

No. 1141.

[White marble. Pyramidal form. Cemented at base. (Near concrete walk.)]

JOHN E. died Sept. 7, 1854, Æt. 10 mo's 12 dys.

JOHN E. died Aug. 23, 1855, Æt. 4 weeks.
Children of Ellis T. & Jane Lanman.

No. 1142.

[White marble. Fair condition.]

GEORGE LEBARON RAYMOND died Jan. 24, 1860 Æ. 27 years

No. 1143.

[Similar to 1142.]

GEORGE RAYMOND Jr. drowned at Billington Sea Jan. 12, 1850, aged 45 years

No. 1144.

[White marble. Fair condition.]

LYDIA widow of George Raymond Jr. Died Aug. 13th 1855. Aged 47 y'rs 6 Mo.

No. 1145.

[Low, white marble. Fair condition.]

MARGARET HODGE and Benjamin Gleason. Children of George & Lydia A. Raymond April 1849.

No. 1146.

[White marble, on granite base. Good condition. This and No. 1147 are inclosed with wooden fence.]

Ruby F. wife of Samuel R. Dickson, Died Aug. 25, 1880, Aged 68 yrs.

> We shall miss her, but not us alone,
> Others have lost a friend;
> Ever ready in time of need
> A helping hand to lend.

No. 1147.

[White marble. In marble socket. Good condition.]

SAMUEL R. Son of S. R. & R. F. DICKSON, Died Jan. 13, 1856 Aged 22 yrs, 8 mos. 19 days

No. 1148.

[White marble, on marble plinth. Freestone base. Good condition. Foul anchor.]

MY HUSBAND CAPT. ALBERT HOLMES Died June 4, 1870, Aged 48 years

> Life's uncertain, death is sure
> Sin's the wound, and Christ the cure.

No. 1149.

[White marble. Set in freestone. Somewhat moss-grown.]

MRS. LYDIA KEYES, Died Nov. 18, 1861, Aged 89 y'rs. MISS LYDIA KEYES, Died June 30, 1873 Aged 75 y'rs.

No. 1150.

[This and No. 1151 are inclosed with wooden paling. No. 1150 is white marble in freestone. Inclined. Discolored.]

WILLIAM H. RICHMOND Died January 14, 1864; aged 49 years 7 mos.

> Just as I am, without one plea,
> But that thy blood was shed for me,
> And that thou bid'st me come to thee,
> O, Lamb of God, I come.

No. 1151.

[White marble. Set in granite. Good condition.]

ELLEN wife of WILLIAM H. RICHMOND Died Dec. 21, 1865. Aged 43 y'rs.

WILLIAM H. their Son Died July 24, 1872, Aged 27 y'rs 3 mo's, 6 days.

15

No. 1152.

[This No. and No. 1153 are alike, and are inclosed with wooden paling. No. 1152 on marble plinth, granite base. Is cracked in two places at base, where dowels are inserted. The fence interferes with the convenient reading of other inscriptions.]

ANTOINETTE, wife of Franklin B. Holmes, Died Sept. 25, 1868, Aged 39 y'rs 2 mo's.

Waiting on the other shore.

No. 1153.

[Good condition.]

FRANKLIN B. HOLMES, Died Oct. 23, 1880, Aged 55 y'rs 9 mo. & 22 d'ys.

No. 1154.

[Blue slate. Good condition. Scroll above symbol,]

Here lies Inter'd the body of Mr SAMUEL MARSON who departed this life Aug. 23, A. D. 1769.

No. 1155.

[Blue slate. Good condition.]

In memory of Elizabeth Savery, wife of Lemuel Savery who died August 1, 1831, Aged 71 years.

Remember me as you pass by,
As you are now so once was I;
As I am now so you must be,
Prepare for death to follow me.

No. 1156.

[Blue slate. Cleft perpendicularly, its whole length, near centre. Weeping willow and urn.]

To the memory of Mrs Joanna White wife of Captain Gideon White who died September 23 1810 in the 95th year of her age

No. 1157.

[Blue slate. Weatherworn. Bad condition. Part of surface scaled off.]

In em   Mr GIDEO   HITE who departed this life March J6th J779 Aged 62 years Also In Memory of Capt CORNELIUS WHITE his son who Foundered at Sea Sepr ye 22 1779 Aged 35 years

No. 1158.

[White marble. Four and a half feet high. Fair condition.]

This stone is erected, by her surviving connexions, to perpetuate the memory of HANNAH WHITE, daughter of Gideon and Joanna White, who died January 3, 1841, aged 93 years

Her long pilgrimage on earth was ennobled by the practice of the duties of Christianity, cheered by its hopes, and sustained by its faith.

No. 1159.

[Low, blue slate. Laminæ separating. Moss-grown. Symbol.]

In Memory of Elizabeth Daughter to Mr Gideon White and Mrs Joanna his wife born April ye ɟst ɟ75ɟ & died Decemr ye 26th ɟ7

(The last two figs. are marred).

No. 1160.

[Blue slate. Weatherworn. Broken. Defaced. Symbol.]

memory o   Experience Dau   ter to Gid on White & Joanna his wife who Decd May ye 5th 1756 Aged 9 years 11 days

No. 1161.

[Low, blue slate. Moss-covered. Broken at top. Symbol.]

Thomas Son of Capt Gideon & Mrs Johanna White died April ye 10th 1759 aged 10 months & 10 days.

No. 1162.

[White marble. Almost ruined.]

Erected in memory of two Children of Zabdiel Sampson Esq & Mrs Ruth his wife : viz. Algernon Sidney who died July 15, 1815 ; aged 6 years and 5 months and Milton who died at New Bedford July 19, 1806 aged 9 months

No. 1163.

[White marble. Four and a half feet in height. Discolored. Covered with a minute vegetable growth. Weeping willow and urn.]

In this sacred spot are deposited the remains of MRS. RUTH SAMPSON, relict of Hon. Zabdiel Sampson born April 10, 1784, died Feb. 16, 1837

No. 1164.

[Similar to preceding.]

In this sacred spot are deposited the remains of HON. ZABDIEL SAMPSON Faithful and assiduous in public trust ; amiable and exemplary in private life the tears of friendship and affection embalm his memory Born August 22, 1781 ; Died July 19, 1828.

No. 1165.

[White marble. Weathering rough. Urn, with flame from top.]

Sacred to the memory of Miss CAROLINE SAMPSON dau. of Mr. George & Mrs. Hannah Sampson who died Feb. 5, 1824, aged 22 years, 1 mo. & 26 days

Hers was the mildness of the rising morn.

No. 1166.

[Pyramidal. Blue slate. Good condition. Festoons. This and the following to No. 1172 b. inclusive are inclosed.]

In memory of Esther Cooper daughter of Mr John Cooper and Mrs Jerusha his wife who died Sept. 9th 1803 aged 2 years & 2 months

The infant smiles in lisping speach
And in the grave in silence sleeps.

No. 1167.

[Blue slate. Good condition. Weeping willow and tomb.]

In memory of Mrs. Lucy, wife of Capt. Joseph Cooper, who died Oct. 13, 1842, aged 70 years

No. 1168.

[Similar to preceding.]

In memory of Capt. Joseph Cooper, who died Nov. 25, 1851, aged 82 years

No. 1169.

[Beautiful white marble. Good condition. On marble plinth. Granite base.]

MARY B. COOPER died Dec. 3, 1887 aged 77 y'rs 8 mo's.

No. 1170.

[Low, blue slate. Good condition, save a small fracture at right hand corner. Symbol.]

In memory of George Cooper son of Mr Joseph Cooper & Lucy his wife who died Novr 7 1796 aged 2 years & 22 days

No. 1171.

[Blue slate. Good condition. Weeping willow and urn.]

In memory of Lucy Taylor Cooper Daughter of Capt Joseph Cooper and Mrs Lucy his wife who died Septer 19th 1803 aged one year 5 months

An emblem in this glass we see
Of what we all must quickley be,
The infant has resigned its breath
Sleeps in the icy arms of death.

No. 1172 a.

[White marble. Moss-grown. Rough.]

EMELINE P. wife of William B. Cooper died Aug. 9, 1835, aged 20 years and 8 mon.

A partner's withered hope is here
Here friendship gives a faithful tear.

No. 1172 b.

[Beautiful veined marble, on granite base.]

Lucy T. Cooper died Nov. 25, 1889, aged 83 y'rs 11 mo's.

· No. 1173.

[Blue slate. Good condition, but moss-grown. Weeping willow and urn.]

Erected in memory of Capt JOHN VIRGIN who died at Sea, in his passage from St. Ubes to Boston, Octr 23. 1822, in the 32 year of his age

Death but entombs the body
Life the soul.

No. 1174.

[White marble, on marble plinth and base.]

ABIGAIL, widow of Capt. John Virgin whose earth life closed, Feb. 13, 1880, Aged 87 y'rs 7 mo's. 16 days
Blessed are the pure in heart.

No. 1175.

[Blue slate. Good condition. Bust of man, in relief.]

This Stone is erected to the memory of Capt JOHN VIRGIN who died Oct. 3, 1814 aged forty seven.
Protected by thy Saviour friend
Whom wind & seas obey
Here peaceful rest till time shall end
Then rise to endless day.

No. 1176.

[Blue slate. Good condition. In place of the symbol, the letters
"P. W."]

This Stone is erected to the memory of MRS. PRISCILLA WESTON who died May 30, 1853 aged eighty six years Her first husband was Capt. John Virgin.

No. 1177.

[Purplish blue slate. Good condition. Two symbols.]

In memory of William Henry Virgin Son of Capt John Virgin and Mrs Priscilla his wife, who died Decr 9th 1796 aged 5 days Also In memory of William Henry Virgin Son of Capt John Virgin and Mrs Priscilla his wife who died Sepr 13th 1798 aged 9 months & 4 days.
Unblemisht innocence what beauty
Husht to rest, shrouded from ills
Which riper years infest.

No. 1178.

[Blue slate. Seamed. Moss-grown. Weeping willow and urn.]

To perpetuate the memory of Mrs Sally Robbins consort of Mr. William R. Robbins of North Carolina who was Born September 5, 1777 and deceased May the 27 1808 aged 31 years
So fades the lovely blooming flower
Such and so withering are our early Joys.

No. 1179.

[Blue slate. Good condition. Two symbols.]

In memory of Thomas Tribbel Son of Mr Joseph Tribbel and Mrs Mary his wife who died Novr 18th 1795 aged 11 months Also In memory of Mary Tribbel daughter of Mr Joseph Tribbel and Mrs Mary his wife who died Octr 18th 1799 aged 1 year & 14 days

No. 1180.

[Blue slate. Pyramidal. Good condition. Urn between roses.]

To the memory of John Dickson son of Mr John & Mrs Phebe Dickson who died Octr 7th 1802 aged 1 year 1 month & 9 days

In early days away from us he flys
No more his pleasing actions charmes our eyes
Gone but not lost I see him from afare
That sublime part like a bright morning star
A happy change from earth to sure above
Now takes his dwelling in the realms of love.

No. 1181.

[White marble. Fair condition.]

FATHER. JOHN DICKSON, Died July 13, 1821 Aged 46.

No. 1182.

[Similar to preceding.]

MOTHER. Phebe Dickson, Died February 26, 1858, Aged 81.

No. 1183.

[Low, blue slate. Inclosed. Good condition. Urn.]

Sacred to the memory of Samuel Dickson son of Mr Samuel Dickson & Mary his wife who Died Sepr 10th 1807 aged one year 5 months & 22 days

No. 1184.

[Blue slate. Good condition. Weeping willow and urn.]

In Memory of BENJAMIN DEXTER, Son of Benjamin & Mary Bullard, Died Jan,y 20, 1830 : Aged 2 years & 5 months.

Let parents with thankfulness own
The encouragement Jesus hath give'n ;
Be delighted to hear him declare
Of such is the kingdom of Heaven.

No. 1185.

[Blue slate. Good condition. Weeping willow and urn. Columns sculptured in low relief on sides.]

MARY wife of Benjamin Bullard, died Mar. 9, 1835 ; Aged 31 years.

Why do we mourn departing friends
Or shake at death's alarm,
Tis but the voice that Jesus sends
To call them to his armes.

No. 1186.

[White marble. Four feet high. Rough. Discolored.]

In memory of CAPT. ANDREW BARTLETT who died May 6, 1832, aged 67 yrs. & 5 mo. Also. ELIZABETH widow of the above, who died July 9, 1844, aged **73 yrs. & 4 mo.**

> When we at death must part
> How keen how deep the pain;
> But we shall still be joined in heart,
> And hope to meet again.

No. 1187.

[Blue slate. Laminæ separating. Fair condition. Symbol.]

In Memory of Mrs ABIGAIL DOTEN wife of Mr WM DOTEN who died July 5, 1783, Aged 25 years

No. 1188.

[Blue slate. Good condition, but moss-grown. Symbol.]

In Memory of Mr SAMUEL COLE who dec'd July 30th 1786 Aged 30 years

No. 1189.

[Blue slate. Good condition, but moss-grown. Weeping willow and urn.]

In memory of Mrs Abigail Sylvester who died June 20, 1820 aged 88 years wife of Abner Sylvester

No. 1190.

[Blue slate. Good condition. Three and three-fourths feet high. Pyramidal. Festoons. Curtains looped up.]

A. D. 1781, March 4, died WILLIAM WATSON Jun, Aged 24 Years : June 24, died BENJAMIN WATSON in the 21st Year of his Age : Only Sons of William Watson Esqr. and Elizabeth his Wife, And Here lie Interred
(On each of the lower corners is sculptured an urn, the left having the initials "B. W." the right "W. W.")

No. 1191.

[Blue slate. Pyramidal. Purplish color—which seems to indicate great durability. Festoons; curtains and tassels.] .

Here lies interred the remains of Mrs ELIZABETH WATSON wife of WILLIAM WATSON Esqr who departed this life Septr 2d 1798 in the 66th year of her age

No. 1192.

[Blue slate. Similar to No. 1191.]

In memory of HON. WILLIAM WATSON, faithful in public trust, in every relation exemplary, this stone is erected, with grateful recollections of his kindness and worth, by his surviving children.

Born May 6, A D 1730, O. S. Died April 27, A D 1815

No. 1193.

[Blue slate. Five feet by 2 3-4. Some moss on surface. Urn.]

JOSEPH TRIBBLE, Jr. died March 13, AD. 1828. Æt. 55 years. MARY, widow of JOSEPH TRIBBLE

176   BURIAL HILL:

Jr. died Feb. 10, AD. 1833. Æt. 58 y,rs.   Also their two
sons WM. died at Port au Prince AD. 1827, Æt. 23 y,rs.
ROBERT F. died at Savannah AD. 1832, Æt. 21 y,rs.

No. 1194.

[Low, blue slate,—purplish. Fresh as if cut yesterday. Symbol.]
In Memory of Sarah Daughter of Mr Joseph Tribell Jur
& Mrs Sarah his wife who died Octr 8 1774 aged 1 year

No. 1195.

[Blue slate. Removed from freestone socket, and set in the earth.
Weeping willow and urn.]
JOSEPH TRIBBLE, Jr. died Jan. 9, 1828, aged 75
years.   SARAH, widow of Joseph Tribble Jr. died Dec.
8, 1848, aged 98 years

No. 1196.

[Blue slate. Good condition. Symbol.]
To the memory of Mr William Goddard who died at
sea & was buried at Marthas Vineyard July 10th 1709
aged 26 years   Here lies buried William son of the above
William Goddard & Sarah his wife who died Sepr 22 1798
aged 1 year & 9 months.

Why do we mourn departing friends
Or shake at death's alarms?
'Tis but the voice that Jesus sends
To call them to his arms.

No. 1197.

[Blue slate. Good condition. Weeping willow and urn.]
In memory of Mr RUFUS GODDARD who departed this
life August 26, 1805 in the 29th year of his age

No. 1198.

[Blue slate. Good condition. Weeping willow and urn.]
In memory of Mary Goddard, widow of Benjamin
Goddard, who died April 23, 1822, aged 77 years.

No. 1199.

[Blue slate. Good condition; but somewhat moss-grown. Urn.]
In memory of Mr. Samuel Battles who died July 31
1812 in the 78 year of his age

No. 1200.

[Purplish blue slate. Pyramidal. Weeping willow and urn.]
In memory of William Battles son of Mr Samuel &
Mrs Deborah Battles who died Decemr 12th 1802 aged 2
months & 18 days

No. 1201.

[Blue slate. Good condition, save being inclined. Urn.]
In memory of Hariot Bartlett daughter of Mr Stephen
Bartlett & Mrs Polly his wife who died Sept 18th 1802
aged 2 years

No. 1202.

[Blue slate. Good condition. Mausoleum.]

In memory of WILLIAM TRIBBLE, who was born Jan 2, 1783, died June 14, 1832.

No. 1203.

[Blue slate. Good condition. Mausoleum.]

BETSEY, widow of William Tribble, born Sept. 8, 1789, died April 24, 1846. FRANCIS., their son died Feb. 14, 1830 aged 5 mos.

No. 1204.

[White marble. Weathering rough. Inclined. Weeping willow and urn.]

OUR MOTHER. PELLA, wife of George Perkins, Born Feb. 5, 1782, Died Febr. 2, 1826, WILLIAM, Born June 19, 1810, Died Sept. 4, 1811, HANNAH, Born March 2, 1816, Died Sept. 16, 1825. Children of George & Pella Perkins.

No. 1205.

[Blue slate. Purplish. Urn.]

GEORGE PERKINS, died Feb. 6, 1834, in the 54th y.r of his age.

> Receive, O earth, his faded form,
> In thy cold bosom let it lie;
> Safe let it rest from every storm—
> Soon must it rise no more to die.

No. 1206.

[Blue slate. Good condition. Urn.]

To the memory of Capt Thomas Doten who died Febry 28th 1794 in the 49th year of his age.

No. 1207.

[Blue slate. Moss-covered. Symbol.]

In Memory of Mrs Jerusha Doten wife of Capt Thomas Doten who departed this Life Apriel ye 24th 1777 in ye 31st year of her age

No. 1208.

[Blue slate. Good condition. Urn under festoons.]

In memory of Miss Patience C. Turner, Daughter of Capt Lothrop Turner and Mrs Susan his wife who died Nov. 10, 1816, aged 15 years and 9 months

> The pale consumption sure but lingering power,
> Nip'd at an early date the tender flower;
> She mark'd its near approach without a sigh,
> Mildly resigned alike to live or die.

No. 1209.

[Low, blue slate. Good condition. Urn.]

To the memory of Eleazar S. Turner, son of Capt Lothrop and Mrs Susanna Turner who died Novr 9th 1800 aged 1 year & 39 days

No. 1210.

[Blue slate, sound and compact. Symbol.]

In Memory of Mrs ELIZABETH TURNER wife of Mr LOTHROP TURNER who died August 16th 1789, in ye 24 year of her age

No. 1211.

[Blue slate. 4 feet in height. Good condition. Urn.]

In Memory of SUSANNAH TURNER, wife of Lothrop Turner, who departed this life May 15, 1837, aged 70 y.rs.

No. 1212.

[Similar to preceding.]

In memory of LOTHROP TURNER, who departed this life June 16, 1835 aged 73 years.

No. 1213.

[Wide, blue slate, 3 by 2 1-2 feet. Good condition. Ornamentally carved with portrait of a woman.]

Here lies Interr'd the Body of Mrs PATIENCE WATSON, the wife of Mr ELKANAH WATSON. She departed this life April 20, 1767 In the Thirty fourth Year of her Age.

No. 1214.

[Blue slate. Good condition, but inclined. Willow.]

This Stone is placed here to the memory of Mr ELKANAH WATSON who died Sept r 7 1804, aged 73 years Also Charles L. Watson his son who Died 16 of the same month aged 11 years.

No. 1215.

[Blue slate. Fair condition. Some moss. Fig. of sun on the horizon.]

Beneath this Sod lies buried all that was mortal of Miss Lucia Watson. (The youngest daughter of Mr Elkanah & Mrs Patience Watson) who at the age of 26 years without one reluctant Sigh calmly resign'd her Spirit to the Creator who gave it: firmly perswaded that in his Infinite Benevolence She should enjoy an endless & a happy Immortality. She was born November 11, 1765 Died March 20, 1792.

No. 1216.

[Blue slate. Good condition.]

In memory of WILLIAM TAYLOR, aged 47 Born in London April 25, 1804, Died in Boston June 27. 1851

No. 1217.

[Low, blue slate. Fair condition, but somewhat seamed.]

In Memory of Mrs KETURAH HOVEY wife of Cap t SAMUEL HOVEY who died Feb y 14, 1790 in ye 37 year of her age Also In Memory of Rachel, their Daughter who died Oct r J4 J790 aged 8 months & 5 days.

No. 1218.

[White marble. Good condition. On marble plinth. Granite base.]

EDWARD W. WATSON Born on Clark's Island, Dec. 17, 1797, Died Aug. 8, 1876.

No. 1219.

[White marble. Rough. Defaced.]

EUNICE, Relict of the late John Watson, Born Feb. 5, 1759, Died Sept 14, 1838. ELIZA ANN, Dau. of the above, Born March 28, 1799, Died Sept. 14, 1847.

No. 1220.

[Blue slate. Good condition. Flaming urn.]

In Memory of JOHN WATSON Esq. Born Aug,st 26, 1748, Died Feb,y 1, 1826. Also his Wife Mrs. Lucia Watson, dau,tr of Benjamin Marston Esq. of Salem, Born Feb,y 15, 1748, Died Oct,r 15, 1793.

No. 1221.

[Blue slate. 4 1-2 feet high. Good condition. Panel.]

In memory of EXPERIENCE, widow of Beza Hayward Esq. who died March 4th. 1851, aged 88 years & 8 Months.

No. 1222.

[Similar to preceding.]

In memory of BEZA HAYWARD. Esq. who died June 4th A D. 1830, aged 78 years

No. 1223.

[Blue slate. Good condition. Weeping willow and urn.]

In memory of Mr BEZA HAYWARD Jr. Son of Beza Hayward Esq who was drowned in Plymouth Harbour Feb y 5, 1814 : in the 22 year of his age.

No. 1224.

[White marble. Rough. Discolored.]

ELIZABETH ANN HAYWARD dau. of Nathan & Joanna Hayward, died Feb. 3, 1840, aged 35 years.

No. 1225.

[Similar to 1224.]

CHARLES FIELD Born Jan. 14, 1804 Died Aug. 22, 1838.

No. 1226.

[Purplish blue slate. Good condition. Urn under festoons.]

To the memory of Edward W. Hayward Son of Dr Nathan Hayward & Joanna his wife who was born the 18th & died the 19th August, 1808.

No. 1227.

[Blue slate. Good condition. Urn between rosebuds.]

To the memory of G. W. and J. A. Hayward twin Children of Dr. N. Hayward and Joanna his wife who were born & died 17th November 1803

No. 1228.

[Low, blue slate. Good condition. Festoons.]

To the memory of Penelope P. Hayward Daughter of Dr Nathan Hayward and Joanna his wife who was born the 21th and died the 22th March 1801

No. 1229.

[Blue slate. Good condition. Urn under festoons.]

To the memory of Mary W. Hayward Daughter of Dr. Nathan Hayward and Joanna his wife who was born the 16th and died the 20th October 1797.

No. 1230.

[Blue slate. Four feet in height. Weeping willow and urn.]

Erected in memory of WILLIAM ATWOOD, Consort of Temperance Atwood who was drowned at Sea March 11, 1821 ; aged 42 years   Also three children WILLIAM ATWOOD Jr. died October 1, 1807 ; aged one year. ISAAC R. ATWOOD died March 24, 1814 ; aged four years.   HENRY R. ATWOOD died May 30, 1828 ; aged sixteen years.

No. 1231.

[Low, white marble. Good condition.]

(On obverse:)
CHARLES T. Son of Charles S. & Hannah C. SWAN died Oct. 21, 1868, aged 11 mo's 15 days.
(On reverse:)
Charlie.
"Of such is the Kingdom of Heaven."

No. 1232.

[White marble in freestone socket. Discolored.]

NANCY K. wife of Lewis Palmer ; died Dec. 11, 1870, aged 52 y'rs 11 mos. & 6 ds.
Weep not.
Sweet was her life—exceeding sweet
To deeds of kindness given ;
A rounded life—by love complete
And bearing her to heaven

No. 1233.

[Blue slate. Inclined. Moss-covered. Symbol.]

Here lies buried Patience daugh tr to Mr David Turner & Mrs Deborah his wife who died Decmbr ye 9th 1773 Aged 4 Months & 27 days

No. 1234.

[Low, blue slate. Laminæ separating. Face cleft. Symbol.]

In memory of Patience Coleman Turner daugh tr to Mr David Turner & Mrs Deborah his wife dec d Octo br ye 1775 Aged 10 Months & 4 days

No. 1235.

[Blue slate. Good condition. Festoons.]

To the memory of Charles L. Hayward Son of Beza Hayward Esq and Experience his wife who was born January 21, 1802 & died August 17 1811.

No. 1236.

[Reddish brown stone. Fair condition. Thick, heavy block, orna·
mentally carved like Gothic arch.]

WILLIAM S. RUSSELL, Born Jan. 11, 1782, Died Feb. 22, 1863.

No. 1237.

[Blue slate. Good condition. Symbol.]

In memory of Mr ELISHA DUNHAM who died Nov r 14th 1803 in the 58 year of his age

No. 1238.

[Blue slate. Cleft. Laminæ separating. Surface partly scaled off.
Portion of symbol remains.]

In memory of Mr David Turner who died Octo br ye 4th 1775 in ye 45 ye a r of his Age

No. 1239.

[Blue slate. Somewhat weatherworn. Symbol.]

In memory of Mr David Turner who dec d Jan ry ye 18th 1769 in ye 76th year of his age

No. 1240.

[Blue slate. Laminæ separating. Symbol.]

Here lies buried ye body of that virtuous woman Mrs Rebecca Turner wife of Mr David Turner who died Jan ry ye 25   1766 Aged 54 years 10 Months

No. 1241.

[Blue slate. Fair condition. Symbol.]

Here lies buried the body of that virtuous woman Mrs Ruth Turner wife to Mr Dauid Turner & Daugh tr to Mr Nathaniel Jackson. She was a member of the ıst Church of Christ in Plymouth she dec d March ye 28th ɪ755 Aged 55 years & 5 Months.

No. 1242.

[Blue slate. Good condition. Symbol.]

In memory of Meroa Turner Daughter of Mr David Turner and Mrs Lydia his wife who died July 10 1806 Aged 5 months

No. 1243.

[Low, blue slate. Good condition. Symbol.]

In Memory of Lydia Prince Daughter of Mr. David &
Mrs Lydia Turner who died Jan y 19 1735 aged 9 months
& 12 days

No. 1244.

[Blue slate. Sound and compact. Symbol.]

To the memory of David Turner son of Mr David
Turner & Mrs Lydia his wife who died Sep r 30 1798
aged 1 year 9 months & 20 days

    And must thy children die so soon.

No. 1245.

[Blue slate. Fair condition, but marred slightly. Symbol.]

In memory of David Turner son of Mr David Turner
& Mrs Lydia his wife who died Sep r 20th 1802 aged 1
year & 9 months & 3 days

No. 1246.

[Blue slate. Moss-covered. Somewhat marred.]

In Memory of Seth Foster who died Octo ye 18th 1756
In ye 4th year of his age & of Lemuel Foster died March
ye 16th 1757 aged one Week Both Children of Thomas
Foster Esqr & Mary his wife.

No. 1247.

[Low, blue slate. Weatherworn. Moss-grown. Difficult to read.]

In memory of HANNAH FOSTER daughter to Mr
Thomas Foster Jun r & Mercy his wife who deces d April
25 1748 aged 7 months & 6 days

No. 1248.

[Blue slate. Older than preceding which is close by it, both facing
west; while that is moss-grown and scarcely legible, this is clean,
compact, and as easily read as on the day it was put in place. Symbol.]

Here Lyes the Body of SAMUEL FOSTER son of Mr
Samuel Foster & Margaret his wife Aged 18 years 1 m o
& 7 d s who died Sept ye 27th 1744

No. 1249.

Low, blue slate. Part of surface scaled off. Symbol.]

In Memory of Thomas Forster Prin   son of Mr
Jam   Prince & Mrs Eun   ce his wife who died Sep r
17th 1783   Aged   year   & 4 months

No. 1250.

[Blue slate. Fair condition, but somewhat marred and moss-grown.
The rounded portion of the stone at top is occupied by a carving in
relief of a skull and crossbones,—part of skull scaled off.]

In memory of THOMAS FOSTER Esq r who departed
this life Jan y ye 24th 1777 in ye 74th Year of his Age

No. 1251.

[Blue slate. Left corner broken off, but not injuring inscription. Surface seamed. Symbol.]

In memory of Mr JOB FOSTER who departed this life Jan y ye 22d J777 in ye 22d Year of his Age

No. 1252.

[Purple slate. Good condition.]

REBEKAH, Relict of Noah Gale, Died Aug. 10. 1840, Æt. 86. NOAH GALE, Lost in a Storm on Block Island Nov. 1806, Æt. 49.

Rest in peace.

No. 1253.

[Blue slate. Four and a fourth feet high. Good condition. Weeping willow and urn. Wreath around the inscription.]

Erected In memory of ELIZABETH GALE wife of Daniel Gale and daughter of Edward Winslow of Duxbury Died Sep. 6, 1817: aged 19 years

As in adam all die so in
CHRIST shall all be made alive.

No. 1254.

[A Goodwin stone. Moss-grown. Symbol.]

To perpetuate the memory of Mrs Mary Bacon Consort of the Rev Mr Jacob Bacon who departed this life much Lamented Nov r 17th 1772 in ye 55th year of her Age: is this stone here set up & thus marked with her name

No. 1255.

[Low, blue slate. Laminæ separating. Moss-grown. Symbol.]

Thomas Son of the Rev d Mr Jacob Bacon & Mary his wife Born Feb y 15th 1753 & Died August 6th 1753 N. S.

No. 1256.

[Low, blue slate. Good condition. Symbol.]

In memory of Betsy Daughter of Mr Samuel & Mrs Betsy Brooks who died April 19, 1794 aged 5 years & 6 months

No. 1257.

[Blue slate. Good condition, but inclined. Symbol.]

To Perpetuate the memory of Charles Henry Bacon Son of David Bacon and Mrs Abigail his wife who died September 6, 1802 in the Sixth year of his age

In early life prepared for Death
Heaven call'd and I resign'd my Breath
Weep not dear friends your tears dismiss
Nor wish me from the Realms of Bliss.

No. 1258.

[Low, blue slate. Fair condition, save moss-grown. Symbol.]

In Memory of Henry Sampson Son of Mr. David Bacon
& Mrs Abigail his wife who died Jan y 2ɹ ɹ787 aged ɹ4
days

No. 1259.

[Blue slate. Fair condition, but moss-grown. Weeping willow
and urn.]

To Perpetuate the memory of Mrs Abigail Bacon wife
of David Bacon Esq who died July 19, 1829 in the 75
year of her age

No. 1260.

[Blue slate. Three and one-half feet high. Good condition. Weeping willow and urn.]

In memory of Cap. Nathaniel Sylvester. who died
March 18, 1830, aged 61 years. Also his wife Elsey
Sylvester who died January 29, 1830, aged 57 years.
Prepare to meet thy GOD
This only can prepare the heart
For death's surprising hour

No. 1261.

[Low, white marble. Rough. Disintegrating.]

WILLIAM ALFRED, son of William & Mary B. Sylvester died March 9, 1837 aged 22 days

No. 1262.

[Low, white marble. Rough. Urn.]

Mary Harlow, Daughter of W & M. B. Sylvester, died
October 31, 1835 aged 3 months

No. 1263.

[Purple slate. Good condition.]

In memory of MISS MARY FAUNCE died Feb. 1, 1844,
aged 61 yrs.

No. 1264.

[Fine, blue slate. Good condition.]

In memory of Mrs. LUCRETIA BURR WATSON, widow of
Benjamin M. Watson, Born at Fairfield, Conn., Nov. 21,
1781, Died at Plymouth, Aug. 29, 1864.

No. 1265.

[Fine, blue slate. Good condition Urn.]

In memory of BENJAMIN M. WATSON Esq. Born
Nov. 15, 1774, Died Nov. 12, 1835.

No. 1266.

[Blue slate. Good condition. Flaming urn.]

In Memory of LUCRETIA ANN Born April 12, 1806.
Died Aug,st 10, 1807. ELIZABETH MILLER, Born

Sept,r 18, 1810. Died Feb,y 28, 1811. BENJAMIN MARSTON Born April 16, 1816. Died March 26, 1817. Children of B. M. & L. J. Watson

No. 1267.

[Blue slate. Good condition. Flaming urn.]

In Memory of JONATHAN STURGES Born April 8, 1822, Died Jan,y 20, 1823. Mrs. LUCRETIA WATSON; wife of Rev. H. B. Goodwin, of Concord, Born Feb,y 15, 1808. Died Nov,r 11, 1831. Children of B. M., & L. B. Watson.

No. 1268.

[White marble. Taken from stone socket, and set in the ground.]

LUCRETIA, wife of Capt. Otis Rogers, Died Jan. 10, 1869. Aged 40 y'rs 29 d's.

In memory of thy name, dear one (The remainder of the epitaph is covered by the original socket.)

No. 1269.

[White marble. Discolored. Set in freestone socket.]

LIZZIE G. DIMAN, Died May 7, 1863 Aged 25 y'rs 1 mo. 1 day HATTIE A. DIMAN, Died Feb. 8, 1864, Aged 21 y'rs 9 mo's, 5 days, MIRIAM G. DIMAN, Died Apr. 9, 1865, Aged 18 y'rs 5 mo's. 9 days

A sleep in Jesus.

No. 1270.

[White marble. In freestone socket. Discolored.]

MARIA S. DIMAN Died Jan. 15, 1875, Aged 38 y'rs 8 mo's 23 days

Asleep in Jesus! blessed sleep
From which none ever wake to weep.

No. 1271.

[White marble. Discolored. Marble plinth. Freestone base.]

Father and Mother.

No. 1272.

[White marble. Moss-grown. Rough.]

Mary Holmes, dau. of William B. and Mary Ann Cox, died Dec. 23, 1819, aged 7 mo. & 9 ds.

No. 1273.

[White marble, in white marble plinth. Good condition.]

EDWARD SOUTHWORTH Died Feb. 7 1863, Aged 93 yrs 5 mos 20 days. RUTH D. his wife Died May 8 1879, Aged 101 yrs. 10 mos. 13 days

No. 1274.

[Low, blue slate. Fair condition. Symbol.]

Mary Dautr to mr James & mrs Faith Shurtliff His wife died May 1, 1742 in ye 13th month of her age

16

No. 1275.

[Blue slate. Bad condition. Much of face split off and gone. Remains of symbol.]

lyes ye   of Mr   Shurtliff   Mr James
She Decd   h ye 28th   43 in   27th year
her age

No. 1276.

[Blue slate. Fair condition, but somewhat seamed. Symbol.]

In memory of *Miss Thankful* Shurtleff, who died July 10, 1807, aged 57 years.

No. 1277.

[Blue slate. Good condition. Symbol.]

Here lyes Buried the Body of Mrs LOIS FOSTER the wife of Mr Thomas Foster who died September ye 21st 1743 with one child buried in her arm and five more by her side. Viz. Elisha John Gershom Gershom & Hannah

No. 1278.

[Low, white marble. This and the next three Nos. are inclosed with iron rustic fence. Good condition.]

Lemuel F. son of L. T. & Lydia Robbins died May 18th 1841 3 years & 3 months

No. 1279.

[White marble.]

In Memory of Sarah B. dau. of L. T. & Lydia Robbins, who died March 19, 1849 Æ. 6 years.

No. 1280.

[Low block of white marble.]

(On upper surface:)
Sarah B.
(On obverse:)
Born Feb. 22, 1850, Died Dec. 15, 1864.

No. 1281.

[Tall granite obelisk.]

(On west side, midway:)
1872.
(On plinth:)

ROBBINS.

No. 1282.

[Very low, blue slate. Good condition. Symbol.]

Samuel Burn ye son of Michell & Eliz th Burn died May 8th 1741 aged 7 months

No. 1283.

[Blue slate. Moss-covered. Somewhat defaced. Symbol.]

Here lyes buried   body of Mr SAMUEL JACKSON He departed this life Novbr   2d 1745 in ye 55th year of his age

No. 1284.

[White marble, once in stone socket. It is now set in the ground, which probably hides part of the inscription.].

OLIVE W. GRIFFIN, died   21 1858.

No. 1285.

[White marble. Top ornamentally carved. Weathering rough. Inclined.]

Sacred to the memory of CHARLES ROBBINS Master Mariner who died at St. Pierre Martinique Jan. 22, 1803, aged about 34 years.   Also to MARY his wife who died Sept. 23, 1854, aged 84 years

No. 1286.

[Blue slate. Four and one-half feet in height. Good condition. Urn.]

LUCIA R. dau. of Nathan B. & Lucia W. Robbins, died Sept 7, 1845, in the 22 yr. of her age

No. 1287.

[Blue slate. Four and one-half feet in height. Seamed across, above the epitaph. Weeping willow and urn.]

To the memory of LUCIA W. ROBBINS, Consort of NATHAN B. ROBBINS, who died Jan. 19, 1826 ; aged 28 years

Thus from thy kindred early torn
And to thy grave untimely borne,
Vanish'd forever from my view
Thou partner of my youth adieu.

Still with my first idea's twin'd,
Thine image oft will meet my mind.
And while remembrance brings thee near,
Affection sad will drop a tear.

As in adam all die even so in Christ
Shall all be made alive.

No. 1288.

[Blue slate. Good condition. Weeping willow and urn.]

In memory of Lucia Robbins Daughter of Nathan B. Robbins & Lucia his wife died October 1, 1821 aged 1 year 9 months and 1 day

So fades the lovely blooming flower,
Frail, smiling solace of an hour;
So our transient comforts fly,
Pleasure only blooms to die.

No. 1289.

[Blue slate. Good condition. Weeping willow and urn.]

In memory of Capt Nathan Bacon who died at Sea April 10, 1786, aged 50 years   Also Mrs Mary Bacon his wife who departed this life January 17, 1825 aged 84 years.

No. 1290.

[White marble. Weathering rough.]

LUCY B. wife of WILLIAM MANTER, died Dec. 3, 1856, Æ. 48 y'rs & 5 mo's.

No. 1291.

[White marble. Weathering rough. Inclined.]

WILLIAM F. MANTER, died Oct. 30, 1846, aged 19 y'rs & 6 mo's.

WINSLOW MANTER, died Dec. 7, 1835, aged 7 years

LUCY E. MANTER, died October 25, 1837: aged 6 y'rs & 10 mo's.

LUCY M. MANTER, died Sept. 7, 1842: aged 13 mo's.

Children of Wm. & Lucy B. Manter.

No. 1292.

[White marble. In freestone socket. Discolored.]

George E. Wadsworth, of Co. E. 29th Mass. Reg. died at Crab Orchard, Ky. Aug. 31, 1863, aged 35 yrs. 8 mos.

"So calm, so constant was his rectitude
That, by his loss alone, we know his worth,
And feel how true a man has walked with us on earth.

No. 1293.

[White marble. Similar to preceding.]

In Memory of CHARLES WADSWORTH, of Co. B. 39th Mass. Reg. who died a Prisoner of war at Salisbury, N. C. Nov. 10, 1864, Aged 31 yrs 4 mos.

Who shall offer youth and beauty
On a Nation's shrine
With a loftier sense of duty
Or truer heart than thine.

No. 1294.

[White marble. Wreath of flowers above the inscription. Over wreath the words:]

Christ is our victory, even here.

SUSAN E. WADSWORTH, Died July 7, 1868, aged 38 y'rs

No. 1295.

[Wooden slab. Painted letters, somewhat worn away.]

MARY   ETTER died Feb 11th 1869. Aged 1 years 6 mos.

No. 1296.

[Wooden cross. Painted letters, fading out. The inscription appears to be as follows:]

Caroline, Infant child of Conrad & Magdaline Shade Died July 29 1869

No. 1297.

[Blue slate. Laminæ separating. Symbol.]

Here lyes ye body of Cap tt William Shurtlef who dec d Feb ry the 4th 1729-30 in the 72d year of his age

No. 1298.

[Blue slate. Good condition. Symbol.]

In memory of *Miss Lydia Shurtleff*, who died Oct. 31, 1809, aged 67 years.

No. 1299.

[Blue slate. Defaced. Shaky. Symbol.]

In Memory of CAPT JABEZ SHURTLEFF who decd Janu ry ye 22 ᴊ76ᴊ in ye 77th year of his Age.

No. 1300.

[Blue slate. Weathering rough. Face of stone scaling off.]

Elisha   on to Thomas & Lois Foster his wife decd Nov br ye 19th 1730 aged   months & 7 days.

No. 1301.

[Blue slate. A curiously wrought stone, splitting, seamed, and moss-grown. Design at top, a skeleton whose right elbow rests upon a tomb, the right hand grasping a scythe. Upon the tomb is an hourglass, and on this are crossbones. At left of skeleton a flaming urn, at base of which is a rose tree bearing buds and flowers. Near the tomb is a skull leaning against a dead shrub. An iron hood, placed so as not to conceal the sculpture, would prolong the life of this monument.]

Here lyes buried the body of Mr NATH   JACKSON who died July ye 4th 1743 in the 79th year of his age.

No. 1302.

[Blue slate. Weatherworn. Defaced. Splitting to pieces. Mossgrown. Symbol.]

Here lyes ye body of mrs RUTH JACKSON wife to Mr Nath Jackson who decd March ye 29th 1742 in ye 79th year of her age

No. 1303.

[White marble. In a broken stone socket. Three and three-fourths feet high. The marble part in fair condition.]

FATHER & MOTHER. Sacred to the memory of CAPT. GEORGE BACON, who was drowned at Sea, on a voyage from Hamburg, to New York, Sept. 6, 1826, Æ. 53 y'rs. ELIZABETH, his widow died Jan. 6, 1859, Æ, 5 months

"There is rest in Heaven.

No. 1304.

[Granite block on granite base. Polished surface.]

MARY T. BACON Died Nov. 12, 1860, Aged 50 yrs. 10 mos.

No. 1305.

[Blue slate. Fair condition. Inclined. Symbol.]

Here lyes ye body of Samuel West who decd Aug
ye 22d 1731 in ye 20th year of his age.

No. 1306:

[White marble. Three and three-fourths feet high. Freestone socket
with brimstone cement. Good condition—for white marble.]

In memory of SETH W. EDDY a member of Co. H.
58th Reg. Mass. Vols. who died Aug. 13, 1864, aged 27
years and 8 days.   WILLIE O. Son of Seth W. & Frances M. Eddy, died Mar. 5, 1859 : aged 4 mos.

Bloom brightly sweet roses
Bloom brightly above,
The mound that encloses
The form that we love.

No. 1307.

[White marble. In marble socket. Good condition. Inclosed in
wooden paling.]

LEVONZO D. BARNES Co. B, 3 Mass. Regt.   Died
Aug. 30, 1878, Aged 62 y'rs 1 mo.

No. 1308.

[White marble. In freestone socket. Good condition.]

VALENTINE DITMAR died Oct. 14, 1865, aged 39
y'rs. 5 m's 24 days.

No. 1309.

[White marble block, in marble plinth, on granite base. Good condition.]

HIRA BATES Died Jan. 13, 1870, Aged 50 y'rs 6
mo's 29 days. ·

(On base:)

BATES.

No. 1310.

[This and the next are similar white marble blocks, set in same
granite base. Good condition. This No. is inscribed on obverse:]

MOTHER.   UNITED ABOVE.

(On reverse:)

MARTHA HOLMES, Died Oct. 17, 1871, Aged 90
y'rs 3 mo's 12 days.

No. 1311.

(On obverse:)

FATHER.   PARTED BELOW.

(On reverse:)

ANSEL HOLMES Died April 2, 1868, aged 90 y'rs
11 mo's, 21 days.

No. 1312.

[Granite block. Granite base. Good condition. Face polished.]

ANSEL HOLMES Dec. 6, 1802, March 3, 1841.
MIRIAM C. his wife May 7, 1810, Feb. 27, 1887.

No. 1313.

[Low, white marble. Good condition.]

Massena Francis. Son of Ansil & Miriam C. Holmes. died Feb. 19, 1834, aged 17 mon.

> Ere sin could blight or sorrow fade
> Death kindly came with friendly care
> The opening bud to heaven conveyed
> And bade it Bloom forever there.

No. 1314.

[Blue slate. Good condition. Weeping willow and urn.]

In memory of Miss Charlott Barnes who died Feb. 22, 1833, in the 60th year of her age

> I call that legacy my own
> Which Jesus did bequeath
> 'Twas purchased with a dying grown
> And ratified in death.

No. 1315.

[Blue slate. Weeping willow and urn. Seam across urn. Otherwise in good condition.]

In memory of Capt. Corbin Barnes who was Drowned off the Gurnet May 28, 1807, aged 75 years, and his Grandson Stephen Harlow in the 11th year of his age Also Mrs Mary Barnes who died May 9th 1824 in the 83 year of her age widow of the above

> The withering age and Blooming youth
> Must yield to death; we feel this truth.

No. 1316.

[Low, blue slate. Good condition, save part of symbol has scaled off.]

In memory of Corban Son of Capt Corban Barnes & Mrs Mary his wife who died July 21st J777   Aged J year 2 Months & J5 days.

No. 1317.

[Blue slate. Fair condition, but moss-grown. Symbol.]

In memory of Mrs. Rebekah Barns ye Wife to Mr Corban Barns   She dec d Nou ye 3d J762 in the 26th Year of her Age

No. 1318.

[Blue slate. Fair condition, but moss-grown. Symbol.]

Here lyes the Boody of Mrs Joanna Atwood ye wife to Mr John Atwood who decd Octo ye 29th J762·in the 46th year of her age

No. 1319.

[Blue slate. Fair condition, but seamed near right edge. Weeping willow and urn.]

In memory of Capt RICHARD COOPER who departed this life September 10, 1819, aged 80 years.

No. 1320.

[Blue slate. Good condition. Weeping willow and urn.]

In memory of Mrs HANNAH COOPER wife of Capt Richard Cooper who departed this life September 23, 1826, aged 82 years.

No. 1321.

[White marble block. Three and a half feet high. On marble plinth. Freestone base. A handsome monument. Clefts on the reverse.]

Rev. Aurin Bugbee born Sept. 12, 1808 died April 14, 1859

No. 1322.

[Blue slate. Shivered, seamed, broken, defaced. Part of symbol remaining.]

Here lyes bur   body of Mart   Waite who depart this life Nov br ye 28th 1735.

No. 1323.

[Blue slate. Fair condition. Symbol.]

In memory of Mrs MARY·ALLEN Relict of Mr Ezra Allen who decd Jan. 20th 1785 Æ. 63.

No. 1324.

[Blue slate. Seamed. Moss-grown. Symbol.]

In Memory of Mr EZRA ALLEN who departed this life Nov r ye 22d ɪ779 Aged 6ɪ years.

No. 1325.

[Blue slate. Weatherworn. Moss-covered. Symbol.]

Here lye ye bodys of Peleg & Marey Durphey His Wife
He   decd Nov. ye │ She   decd Octr ye
6th   ɪ730   in │   23d   ɪ730   in
ye   34th year of his age │ ye   33d   year of her age
Peleg their son decd Novbr ye   ɪ2th   ɪ730 aged 4 year

No. 1326.

[Blue slate. Good condition, save a seam in upper part of stone. Symbol. This and the following 6 Nos. are inclosed in a granite curbing.]

To the memory of Jane Bartlett Daughter of Capt James & Mrs Mary Bartlett who died Dec r 24th 1802, aged 2 years & 7 months

My times of sorrow & of joy
Great God are in thy hand
My choicest comeforts come from thee
And go at thy command.

No. 1327.
[Blue slate. Good condition.]
JAMES BARTLETT, Born Aug. 7, 1760, Died Dec. 22, 1840.

No. 1328.
[Blue slate. .Good condition.]
MARY BARTLETT, widow of JAMES BARTLETT, Born May 19, 1759, Died April 9, 1852.

No. 1329.
[White marble, in freestone socket. Fair condition.]
MARY T. BARTLETT, Daughter of James & Mary Bartlett, Born Jan. 11, 1784, Died Feb. 16, 1864.

No. 1330.
[Similar to preceding.]
REBECCA BARTLETT Daughter of James & Mary Bartlett, Born Aug. 3, 1798, Died Aug. 2, 1869.

No. 1331.
[White marble block. Marble plinth. Granite base. Good condition.]
MERCY B. LOVELL, wife of Leander Lovell, Born April 22, 1796, Died Nov. 6, 1872.

No. 1332.
[Similar to preceding.]
LEANDER LOVELL, Born March 9, 1799, Died Oct. 1, 1879.

No. 1333.
[Blue slate. Sound and compact. Weeping willow and urn.]
In memory of George T. Bacon 3d Son of George Bacon and Elizebeth his wife who died Octo r 11, 1819 aged 2 years & 7 months Also Leverett T. Bacon who died July 1, 1823 aged 6 weeks and 3 days.

No. 1334.
[Low, blue slate. Good condition. Festoons.]
In memory of George Taylor Bacon son of George Bacon and Mrs Betsy his wife who died Sept the 8th 1802, aged 18 months 8 days

No. 1335.
[Blue slate. Good condition. Two semicircles at top, each carved with weeping willow and urn.]
This Stone is Erected to the memory of two Sons of Capt George Bacon and Elizebeth his wife viz George T Bacon 2sd who departed this life Jan. 11, 1816 in the 12

17

year of his age   Also Nathan Bacon who departed this
life Nov r 7, 1815 aged 13 months.

We have Buried three Blooming Flowers
Which were nipt in unexpected hours.

No. 1336.

[Blue slate. Good condition. Weeping willow and urn.]

Erected in remembrance of Colo John B. Bates, who
died March 6, 1831, aged 47 years   Also to Abby Washburn daughter of John B. & Mary Bates who died Oct 3d,
1841, aged 1 year & 5 months.

No. 1337.

[Blue slate. Good condition. Tree represented on left of surface,
its leaves drooping over the inscription. This and the following seven
Nos. are inclosed in iron fence. They are similar to each other in
form and style. Pyramidal.]

SILVANUS T. Son of James & Sarah Bartlett was
born Feb. 2, 1820, & died April 14, 1822.

No. 1338.

JAMES T. son of James & Sarah Bartlett was born
Oct. 29, 1818, & died Dec. 14, 1818.

No. 1339.

James Thomas Bartlett Son of James Bartlett Jun &
Sarah his wife was born May 1, 1814, and died 31 August
following.

No. 1340.

Jane Samson Bartlett daughter of James Bartlett Ju &
Sarah his wife was born July 11, 1809, & died April 25,
1811.

No. 1341.

Silvanus Taylor Bartlett Son of James Bartlett Jun and
Sarah his wife died August 7th, 1808, aged 7 m. & 29
days

No. 1342.

MARY A. dau. of James & Sarah Bartlett was born
Dec. 19, 1825, & died Jan. 13, 1829.

No. 1343.

REBECCA T dau. of James & Sarah Bartlett was born
Dec. 31, 1828 & died Oct. 23, 1833.

No. 1344.

CHARLES T. son of James & Sarah Bartlett, was born
Dec. 14, 1824, & died Aug. 2, 1825.

No. 1345.

[White marble. Weathering rough. Taken from a broken socket, and placed in the ground.]

In memory of HANNAH wife of Ephraim Bradford who died Apr. 17, 1817 ; aged 32 years. Their daughter ELEANOR MORTON, died Sept. 11 1807, aged 13 mos.

No. 1346.

[Blue slate. Good condition. Mausoleum.]

BENJAMIN F. son of Benjamin & Alice Dunham died March 2, 1832, aged 14 days.

No. 1347.

[White marble, in stone socket. Fair condition. Is within a wooden paling.]

GEORGE S. 2ND. Lost at Sea Dec. 15, 1868, Aged 19 y'rs 3 mo's. MARY H. Died Nov, 22, 1868, Aged 24 y'rs 18 d's. Children of Stevens & Helena C. Ellis.

No. 1348.

[White marble. Removed from socket and set in the ground. Dis colored.]

CLARISA A. wife of George F. Green, died Aug. 7. 1861 ; aged 25 years 4 mos.

No. 1349.

[White marble block. Mottled. New and handsome. On marble base.]

(On upper surface:)

FATHER.

(On obverse:)

Paulding.

(Five marble blocks near 1349, are severally inscribed:)

Claribel   Herbert S.

Allie B.   Sylvanus S.

Frances A.

No. 1350.

[Blue slate. Seamed across face. Weeping willow and urn.]

In memory of Mrs. Susan Bartlett wife of Mr. Nathaniel Bartlett who died July 26 1818 in the 24 year of her age.

Peace all our angry passions then
Let each rebellious Sigh
Be Silent at his Sovering will
And every murmur die.

No. 1351.

[Blue slate. Fair condition, save moss-grown. Symbol.]

Here lies ye Body of Miss Abigail Hedge Daughter of Mr Barnabas Hedge & Mrs Mercy his Wife who deed Decmbr ye 9th 1763 aged 26 years.

[Blue slate. Good condition. Urn.]

Sacred to the memory of Mr SAMUEL COLE who departed this life March 18th 1811 in the Eightieth year of his Age

No. 1353.

[Blue slate. Broken and moss-covered. Symbol.]

Here lyes ye Body of JAMES COLE who decd Novbr ye 28th 172 in the 22d year of his age ·

No. 1354.

[Blue slate. Laminæ separating. Moss-grown. Symbol.]

Here lyes ye Body of mrs Dorothy Carver wife to Mr Josiah Carver decd Janry ye 20th 1730—1 Aged 28 years 11 mon tt 17 days & near her 5 of their chln as may be seen on the footstone.

No. 1355.

[The footstone has an appearance similar to the headstone No. 1354. It is broken and badly seamed. Inclined. Symbol.]

hildren of Mr Josiah Carver (the 1st born) Joseph

	y	0	A
	y	m	d
deed July 6th 1722 Agd	0	0	7
A Daughr decd April 29th 1723 Agd	0	0	1
Dorothy decd Jany 2d 1730—1 Agd		7	13
James decd Jany 15 1730—1 Agd	1	8	0
A daur decd Jany 17 1730—1 Agd		0	0

No. 1356.

[Dark blue slate. Good condition. Two rosettes.]

To the memory of Capt EDWARD TAYLOR who was drowned in attempting to go ashore from his vessel Novr 25th 1798 & whose remains were found July 10th 1799 & here interred aged 33 years.

> The wide Atlantic past—his raptured sight
> Beholds his wish'd for home, his best delight,
> Adverse the tide—in boat the surge he braves
> And meets his fate beneath o'erwhelming waves,
> Thus fell the husband kind, the parent dear,
> The loving brother, and the friend sincere.

No. 1357.

[White marble slab, on freestone supports. Fair condition.]

JOHN RUSSELL died Oct. 11, 1800; Æt. 42. CHARLES, son of John & Mary Russell; died Nov. 2,

1791 ; Æt. 1. NANCY, daughter of John & Mary Russell, died Aug. 10, 1797, Æt. 2. MARY, relict of John Russell, died Oct. 18, 1826, Æt. 65.

No. 1358.

[Granite bowlder.]

THOMAS RUSSELL Born Sept. 26, 1825, Died Feb. 9, 1887.

No. 1359.

[Blue slate. Three and a half feet high. Good condition. Weeping willow and urn.]

In memory of Dean Josiah Diman who died August 22d 1829 in the 63d year of his age.

No. 1360.

[Beautiful white marble. On granite base. Sheaf of wheat.]

SALLY BRADFORD. Daughter of Nathaniel & Rebecca Bradford, Died April 19, 1882, Aged 99 y'rs 3 mos. 11 days.

She was the last of the sixth generation in direct descent from the Pilgrim Governor William Bradford.

No. 1361.

[Low, blue slate. Weatherworn. Symbol.]

Here lyes ye Body of Mr Jonathan Barnes Aged About 73 years Died Augst ye 20th 1714

No. 1362.

[Low, blue slate. Laminæ separating. Moss-grown. Symbol.]

Here lyes ye Body of   Elizabeth Barns wife to Mr Jonathan Barns who decd   ecbr ye 15th 1731 in 8th year of her age

No. 1363.

[Purplish blue slate. Good condition. Symbol.]

In Memory of Capt BARNABAS HEDGE who Departed this Life January the 18th 1762 Aged 36 Years & 22D.

No. 1364.

[Blue slate. Good condition. Symbol.]

To the Memory of Mrs MERCY HEDGE Relict of Capt BARNABAS HEDGE who died December 25, AD. 1791 aged 83 years.

No. 1365.

[Blue slate. Cleft. Moss-grown. Symbol.]

Here lyes ye Body of Sarah Cole wife to Ephraim Cole Dyed Oct. ye 26th 1730 Aged about 32 years   Their Son Ephraim aged 12 years decd   1730 Sarah their Daur aged 7 years decd 1739

(On badly broken footstone:)

Sarah Cole & 5 children 3 of them decd in infancy.

No. 1366.

[Blue slate. Sound. Moss-grown. Symbol.]

Here lyes ye Body of Mr Samuel Cole Decd Aug. ye 18th 1731 in the 23d year of his age.

No. 1367.

[Low, blue slate. Cleft. Inclined.]

Experience Dau to Deacon John Atwood & Experience his wife Decd June ye 12th 1732.

No. 1368.

[Blue slate. Weatherworn. Defaced. Symbol.]

Peleg son to Mr Peleg & Mrs Mary Durfy his wife decd Decbr ye 7th 1721 in ye 3d year of his age.

No. 1369.

[Blue slate. Wider than high. Weatherworn. Defaced. Symbol.]

Here lyes ye Body of Mr Ephraim Cole who decd May ye 15th 1731 in ye 71st year of his age.

No. 1370.

[Blue slate. Weatherworn. Moss-covered. Symbol.]

Here lyes ye Body of Elizabeth Phillips who decd Jan ry ye 5th 17–6—7 in ye 0th year of her age.

No. 1371.

[Similar to preceding.]

Here lyes ye Body of. mrs Mary OSMENT who decd Augst ye 17th 17 0 in ye 72d year of her age.

No. 1372.

[Blue slate. Good condition. Symbol.]

To the memory of BATHSHEBA RICKARD widow of Capt John Rickard who died Dec. 9th 1798 in the 72d year of her age.

No. 1373.

[Blue slate. Moss-covered. Symbol.]

In memory of Mrs Hannah Dier Widow of Mr John Dier who died Decr 27 J776 in the 79 year of her age.

No. 1374.

[Blue slate. Moss-grown. Symbol.]

Here Lyes buried Cap t JOHN DYAR who died October 18 1741 in the 70th year of his age.

No. 1375.

[Blue slate. Fair condition, but moss-grown. Symbol.]

Here lyes ye Body of mrs Hannah Dyer wife to Capt John Dyer who decd Decbr ye 23d 1733 in the 68th year of her age.

No. 1376.

[White marble. Imitation of scroll. Fair condition.]

Twins. Albert B. & Betsey J. Harlow. Æ. 5 months.

No. 1377.

[Blue slate. Good condition.]

REBECCA CHURCHILL. died Sept. 15, 1872 ; aged 84 y'rs 11 mo's.

Not slothful in business, fervent in spirit, serving the Lord.
Romans XII. 11.

No. 1378.

[Blue slate. Good condition. Mausoleum.]

In Memory of Mrs, Sarah Churchill Consort of Mr. Isaac Churchill, who died Dec. 28, 1825, in the 69 year of her age.

No. 1379.

[Blue slate. Good condition. Weeping willow and urn.]

In memory of Mr Isaac Churchill & Son was lost at Sea Octor 1797 Mr Isaac Churchill aged 40 years Isaac Churchill Junr aged 16 years Also in memory of William Churchill who died Augu t 10, 1817 aged 21 years

No. 1380.

[White marble. Marble plinth. Granite base. Good condition.]

US SIX. William K. Son of William & Barbara Hemmerly, Died in Boston, Feb. 8, 1880, Aged 23 yrs. 4 mos. 11 days.

No. 1381.

[Wooden slab.]

Geo D. Hemmerly Died Sept. 7, 186   Aged 2 yrs, 10 months.

No. 1382.

[Wood. Paint washed off,—leaving letters in relief.]

Wm. Hemmerly Died   Aged

No. 1383.

[White marble. Marble plinth. Granite base. Four and a half feet in height. Fair condition, save patches of yellow moss. Broken chain, with motto:]

Parted below. United above.

MARY BROWN died Aug. 16, 1860: aged 71 years, 6 mos. & 23 days.

No. 1384.

[Blue slate. Four feet high. Cracked diagonally across face. Mossgrown. Symbol above an urn.]

In memory of Mr. ROBERT BROWN who departed this life April 13 1810 in the 69 year of his age Also in memory of Robert Son of ROBERT BROWN and Mary his wife died at the City of Washington October 14 1806.

No. 1385.

[Blue slate. Firm and solid, but moss-grown and inclined. Symbol above urn.]

In memory of Mrs MARY BROWN wife of ROBERT BROWN who departed this life March 4 1810 in the 58 year of her age Also in memory of two Children of ROBERT BROWN & Mary his wife William died august 9 1785 aged 2 years Margret died april 28 1792 aged 1 year

No. 1386.

[White marble. Weathering rough. Moss-grown.]

NABBY, widow of WILLIAM BROWN Esq. Died Feb. 8, 1858 : in the 74th year of her age.

No. 1387.

[Similar to preceding.]

WILLIAM BROWN Esq. died May 9, 1845, in the 61st y'r of his age. Also three children Viz. LYDIA, died Sept. 28, 1809, aged 9 weeks. WILLIAM died Sept. 14, 1813, aged 3 y'rs & 2 Mon. ABIGAL ALLEN, died Sept. 28, 1813 aged 1 y'r & 5 Mon.

No. 1388.

[White marble. Weathering rough. Moss-covered.]

BARNABAS A. BROWN, died Jan. 6, 1846, in the 27 y'r of his age.

No. 1389.

[White marble. Fair condition.]

LYDIA ALLEN BROWN, died Aug. 15, 1825, Aged 11 yrs & 6 Mon.

No. 1390.

[White marble. Fair condition.]

LYDIA ALLEN BROWN. died Aug. 20, 1832 Aged 6 yrs.

No. 1391.

[Blue slate. Fair condition, but moss-grown. Bust of woman, holding rose with leaves.]

In Memory of Mary Brown Daughter to Robert Brown & Mary his wife who Expir'd on Sepr 27th AD. J782. Aged 5 years J Month & 14 Days.

Sleep silent Dust till Christ our Lord
The Omnipotent will speak the word
Then Soul & Body both will arise
To endless joys above the Skies.

No. 1392.

[Blue slate. Laminæ separating. Moss-grown. Symbol.]

In Memory of ROBERT BROWN Esqr who Departed this Life January 21st AD. 1775 in the 93d year of his Age

No. 1393.

[Dark blue slate. Solid, except a cleft at right hand corner. Symbol with a smiling face.]

Here lyes Buried the Body of Madam PRISCILLA BROWN the wife of ROBERT BROWN ESQR who Died September the 7th 1744 in the 44th Year of her Age, with three Children Buried by her Side ROBERT MARTHA & MARGRET.

No. 1394.

[Low, blue slate. Cleft. Defaced. Nearly ruined. Faint remains of symbol. Inscription in capital letters.]

Robe   on   to   Rober   own Es   Priscilla his wife died June ye 19th J732 Aged 10 years.

No. 1395.

[Blue slate. Moss-grown. Flaming urn.]

SALLY, the wife of Daniel Churchill died Nov. 3, 1836, in the 60 yr of her age.

No. 1396.

[Blue slate. Good condition. Weeping willow and urn.]

Sacred to the memory of DANIEL CHURCHILL who departed this life March 2, 1855 aged 83 years

No. 1397.

[Low, blue slate. Moss-grown. Symbol.]

In memory of Mrs Deborah Howland wife of Mr Caleb Howland who departed this Life Septr 8th 1784 in ye 48th year of her Age

No. 1398.

[Blue slate. Fair condition, but seamed. Urn and foliage.]

In memory of Thomas S. Saunders Son of John and Betsey Saunders Died Decr 22, 1826, aged 2 years.

No. 1399.

[Purplish blue slate. Good condition, but inclined. Weeping willow and urn.]

In memory of Joann Perkins Daughter of Stephen Perkins & Joann his wife who died Sepr 10, 1825 Aged one year and 1 month

No. 1400.

[White marble, roughened. Inclined. This and the next in wooden paling.]

In memory of LEWIS HARLOW, who died Oct. 10, 1806, in the 35th yr. of his age. HANNAH widow of the above died Aug. 3, 1848, aged 72 years

Even as the Father willed
The path of life was trod;
Rest, for ye have fulfilled
The mission of your GOD.

Earth to its native earth
And dust to dust be given
But the pure spirit's birth
Hath made it heir of Heaven

No. 1401.

[White marble. Discolored. Disintegrating.]

ELIZABETH F. died Sept. 4, 1845, aged 23 yrs.
LEWIS O. was lost at Sea Oct. 3, 1811, aged 17 yrs.
BARNABAS L. died June 5, 1838, aged 3 yrs. & 5 mon.
Also 4 Infants, children of Lewis & Betsey Harlow

No. 1402.

[Blue slate. Sound. Inclined.]

In memory of Elkanah Churchell son of Ephraim
Churchell and Sally his wife who died Apr l 13th 1808
aged 2 months and 7 days

No. 1403.

[Blue slate, 3 and 3-4 feet high. Sound. Inclined. Weeping willow
and urn. This and the three following are inclosed in a wooden
paling.]

Sacred to the Memory of GEORGE MORTON Son of James
& Betsey Morton who died Sept. 14, 1839, Aged 18
years

Father, thou art gone above thy
Precious soul has flown,
where tears are wiped from every
eye, and sorrows are unknown;
And when the Lord shall summon
us, whom thou has left to mourn
May we, untainted by the world,
Meet at our Father's throne.

No. 1404.

[Blue slate. Good condition. Weeping willow and urn.]

In memory of Rebekah Morton Daughter of James &
Betsey Morton who died June 17, 1824 aged 4 months
and 21 days.

For of such is the kingdom of heaven.

No. 1405.

[White marble, in stone socket. Fair condition. Carved to represent pointed Gothic arch.]

OUR MOTHER, BETSEY MORTON died June 11, 1861:
aged 64 years

Dear mother you have soared away,
To dwell in everlasting day,
Up to the shining courts above,
To enjoy your Saviour and your GOD.

No. 1406.

[Blue slate. Four and 1-4 feet in height. Moss-grown. Weeping willow and urn.]

Sacred to the memory of Mr. JAMES MORTON, who died Dec. 5, 1834, aged 33 y,rs Also of Abraham C. son of James & Betsey Morton. who died Nov. 25, 1825 Aged 7 yr,s. And of four deceased infant children.

Above life's scenes faith lifts her eye
To brighter prospects given
Where rays divine disperse the gloom ;
Beyond the confines of the tomb
Appears the dawn of heaven.

No. 1407.

[Low, blue slate. Fair condition. Symbol.]

In Memory of Mrs Ruth Marshall wife of Mr Bartlett Marshall who died July 24 J79J Aged 37 years

No. 1408.

[Blue slate. Good condition. Urn.]

In memory of *Mr Bartlett Marshal* aged 45. Also of Samuel Marshal aged 16, both lost at Sea in 1799, Also of *Bartlett Marshal* Jnr aged 19, who died in Charleston, S. C. of a Malignant Fever, 1799, Also of *Hannah Marshal*, who died Sep tr 26th 1806. Aged 21 years. She only is here interred.

Their sudden change and shorten'd date
Bid Youth & Age prepare;
Their lifeless clay describes our fate
And shows how frail we are.

No. 1409.

[Blue slate. Seamed and moss-grown. Weeping willow and urn.]

This stone is erected to the memory of Mr Samuel Sherman, who died Novem 8, 1818, in the 67 year of his age

Hail glorious morn, auspicious day!
When Christ shall wake the sleeping clay;
When mouldering dust shall rise and find
Salvation free for all mankind.

No. 1410.

[White marble, 4 and 1-2 ft. high. In stone socket. Good condition.]

ELIZABETH J. wife of William A. Perkins, died March 5, 1857, aged 35 years. PRISCILLA, died July 30, 1851, aged 16 years. PELLA M. died March 25, 1853, aged 28 years. Daughters of Joseph & Eliza Holmes.

No. 1411.

[Blue slate. Good condition. This and the six next following are inclosed in handsome granite curbing.]

Erected to the Memory of ELIAS COX. Who died June 8, 1843, in the 71 y'r of his age.

No. 1412.

Erected to the Memory of Patience Cox, widow of the late Elias Cox, who died July 14, 1853, in the 81 y'r of her age.

No. 1413.

In memory of Cap t Zephaniah Holmes who died Sepr 13, 1813, in the 47 year of his age. Also their children Rufus Holmes died August 5, 1799. Nancy Holmes died October 13, 1802, aged 2 years and 22 days.

No. 1414.

In memory of Mrs Bethiah, relict of the late Capt. Zepheniah Holmes, who died Oct. 25, 1847, in her 69 y'r.

No. 1415.

Erected to the memory of Mr. John C, Holmes who departed this life May 17, 1826 ; aged 28 years.

> Lean not on earth; 'twill pierce thee to the heart,
> A broken reed at best, but oft a spear,
> On its sharp point peace bleeds and hope expires.

No. 1416.

NANCY HOLMES wife of JAMES COX. Born Feb. 17, 1803. Died Sept. 13, 1880.

No. 1417.

JAMES COX Born July 23, 1803, Died April 22, 1887.

No. 1418.

LUISE daughter of Valentine & Caroline Zahn died May 31, 1860 Æ. 2 yrs. & 3 mos.

No. 1419.

Magdalena   ner

No. 1420.

In Memory of David son of Mr Joseph Croswell & Mrs Lucy his wife who died Sepr 29th 1783 aged 1 year 2 months & 8 days.

No. 1421.

[Low, blue slate. Laminæ separating. Moss-grown. Partly defaced. Symbol.]

In Memory of Rebecca Daughter   Mr Joseph Croswell   Mrs Lucy his wife who died Feb y ye 3d ɪ780-ɪ
Aged 8 Months & 5 Days.

No. 1422.

[Blue slate. Good condition.]

To the Memory of JOSEPH Son of Mr JOSEPH CROSWELL
& LUCY his wife who died Decr 8th ɪ775 Aged 2 Years &
ɪ Month & ɪɪ Days.

No. 1423.

[Low, purplish blue slate. Good condition. Symbol.]

In Memory of ABIGAIL RUSSELL Daughter of Mr JOHN
RUSSELL & MERCY his wife Aged ɪ8 Months Died Oct.
23d ɪ766.

No. 1424.

[Stump of blue slate. All that remains is:]

wi   ed   Sep 7, ɪ7   18 months.

No. 1425.

[Blue slate. Good condition. Weeping willow and urn.]

In memory of Dea n Josiah Diman who died August 22d
1829, in the 63 year of his age

> They die in Jesus and are blest,
> How kind their slumbers are
> From suff'rings and from sin releas'd,
> And freed from ev'ry snare

No. 1426.

[Blue slate. Good condition. Weeping willow and urn.]

In memory of Sophia Diman wife of Dea n Josiah
Diman who died August 7, 1814, in the 36 year of her age

> Far from this world of toil and strife
> They're present with the LORD
> The labors of their mortal life
> End in a large reward.

No. 1427.

[Blue slate. Seamed. Symbol.]

To the memory of Mrs Susanna Diman wife of Mr
Josiah Diman who died Octr 24th 1798 in the 33d year of
her age also in memory of their son Josiah who died Sepr
16th 1798 aged 7 days

No. 1428.

[Blue slate. Good condition. Flaming urn.]

In memory of MR. NATHANIEL BRADFORD who died
Nov. 24, 1837, in the 90th year of his age Also REBECCA,

his wife died June 15, 1838, in the 85th year of her age
ELIZABETH, their dau. died Oct, 1800 aged 6 yrs NA-
THANIEL their son died in New York June 11, 1830, aged
55 yrs.

No. 1429.

[White marble. Fair condition. Inclined. Four feet in height.]

JOHN H. BRADFORD Born July 14, 1780. Died
Dec. 7, 1863.

No. 1430.

[Blue slate. Good condition. Symbol.]

In Memory of Mrs MARY BRADFORD wife of Mr LEMUEL
BRADFORD who died Decr 2J J790 in ye 36th year of her age.

No. 1431.

[Low, purplish blue slate. Symbol.]

Here lies buried the body of Mr NATHANIEL BRADFORD
died March 27th.1751, in the 36 year of his age.

No. 1432.

[Purple slate. Has two arcs of circle at top. Protected by iron hood.
Symbol.]

Here lyes interred ye body of Mr Joseph Bradford son
to the late Honourable William Bradford Esqr Governour
of Plymouth Colony who departed this life July the 10th
1715 in the 85th year of his age.

[A wooden slab beside this stone reads: "The Grave of Joseph
Bradford Died July 10, 1715."]

No. 1433.

[Blue slate. Four and a half feet in height. Seam extending from
top to ground. Flaming urn.]

In memory of CAPT. LEMUEL BRADFORD who died
May 22, 1828: Aged 77 years Also LYDIA, wife of the
above died June 6, 1838: aged 77 years.

No. 1434.

[Blue slate. Badly cleft, diagonally. Symbol.]

Here lyes ye body of Mrs ELIZABETh BARNS wife
to Jonathan Barns who decd Decbr ye 15 1731

No. 1435.

[White marble. Marble plinth. Freestone base. Fair condition.]

In memory of Lydia Bradford, born Jan. 25, 1795,
Died Apr. 14, 1868. Also of Cornelius Bradford, who
died at New Orleans, Aug. 16, 1824: Æ. 31 years.

No. 1436.

[Blue slate. Good condition. Four and one-half feet by two and one-
half feet. Flaming urn.]

SACRED to the memory of LUCIA wife of Thomas
Somes of Boston and dau,tr of the late Capt James Rus-

sell, who died Mar. 22, 1835 : aged 47 yr,s. Also, in memory of JAMES RUSSELL, son of the late Capt James Russell, who was lost at sea, May 12, 1819 ; aged 29 y,rs.

No. 1437.

[Purplish blue slate. Good condition. Weeping willow and urn.]

In Memory of *Capt James Russell* who died Sepr 28 1792 aged 32 years And also *Mr Thomas Russell* supposed to be lost at Sea in a severe Snow storm Decr 4 & 5 1786 aged 24 years both sons of the late Mr John & Mrs Mercy Russell.

No. 1438.

[Light blue slate. Good condition. Iron hood. Symbol.]

In Memory of Bradford Son to Mr Caleb Stetson & Mrs Abigail his Wife who Died Sepr ye 5th 1758 aged 1 year 3 Months & 15 days.

No. 1439.

[Blue slate. Good condition. Iron hood.]

Here lies the body of ye honorable Major William Bradford, who expired Feb. ye 20th 1703-4, aged 79 y'rs.

> He lived long but still was doing good
> & in his countres service lost much blood;
> After a life well spent he's now at rest,
> His very name and memory is blest.

[NOTE. The original inscription & epitaph on this stone were in capitals; but the face of the stone disintegrated and scaled off, wherefore the surface was smoothed, and the legend recut in "lower case" letters. "Here lyes ye" was changed to "Here lies the"; the "u" in "honourable" was omitted, and the short "&" beginning the second line of the epitaph was replaced by "And"; Bradford's age formerly seemed to read "70 y'rs " but "79"—the correct age—appears in the newly cut inscription.—B. D.]

No. 1440.
[Blue slate. Fair condition. Symbol.]

Here lyes the body of Mrs HANNAH COOPER ye wife to Mr JOHN COOPER who decd March ye 14th 1765 aged 59 years 4 Months & 18 days.

No. 1441.
[Blue slate. Weatherworn. Seamed. Partially defaced. Symbol.]

Here lyes the body of Mr JOHN COOPER who died Decemb r the 6th 1760 aged 62 years 11 months & 14 days.

No. 1442.
[Blue slate. Moss-grown. Weatherworn. Symbol.]

Here lyes ye body of Mrs HANNAH COOPER wife to Mr Richard Cooper dec d Decbr ye 16th 1718 in ye 57th year of her age.

No. 1443.
[Blue slate. Moss-covered. Weatherworn. Symbol.]

Here lyes ye body of Mr RICHARD COOPER who decd March ye 29th 1724 in ye 85th year of his age.

No. 1444.
[Low, blue slate Moss-covered, but otherwise in fair condition. Symbol.]

HANNAH daughter to Deacon John Atwood & Sarah his wife dec d July ye 14th 1753 Aged about 4 years.

No. 1445.
[Blue slate. Broken. Defaced. Moss-covered. Cleft. Ruined. Part of symbol.]

In Memo   Mrs Exper   Atwood wif   to Deacon Joh Atwood   She decd April ye 14th 1762 in ye 58th year of her age.

No. 1446.
[Blue slate. Moss-grown. Defaced. Cleft. Broken symbol.]

ere lyes Buried   body of Mrs Sarah Atwood wife to Deacon John   decd Jan r   ye 22d 1725 in ye 37th year of her age.

No. 1447.
[Purplish blue slate. Nearly covered with moss. Symbol surrounded with blossoms.]

The memory of the Just is Blessed.

Here lyes the Body of Mr JOHN ATWOOD who Died on the 6th of August AD 1754 Ætatis 70 Years He was a Man of Piety & Religion Adorned with every Christian

grace & Virtue & therefore well qualified for ye office of
a *Deacon* which he discharged in ye first *Church* of Christ
in this *Town* for about 40 Years with Honesty & upright-
ness and in the Course of his Life adorned the Doctrine
of His Saviour by a well ordered Conversation.

No. 1448.

[Low, blue slate. Laminæ separating. Moss-grown. Defaced.
Symbol.]

Experience Dau r to Deacon John   Mrs Sarah
Atwood his wife decd July ye 7th 1730 in ye 6th year of
her age.

No. 1449.

[Blue slate. Cleft whole length at about one-third of width from
left edge.]

In Memory of Mrs HANNAH LEWIS wife of Mr NATHA-
NIEL LEWIS who died May 29, 1790, in ye 38 year of her
age.

No. 1450.

[Blue slate. Broken diagonally across. Upper moiety gone. Moss-
covered.]

ody of Mrs   la   Drew   e of Mr
    Lemuel   rew who decd Oct. ye   2d J757
Aged 25 years 5 months & 2 days Buried with 2 small
ch'n by her side.

No. 1451.

[Blue slate. Moss-covered. Cleft diagonally across from right upper
corner to below left centre. Symbol.]

In Memory of James Drew who died May 5th 1788 in
ye 60 year of his age.

No. 1452.

[White marble. Very rough. Disintegrating rapidly. Moss-grown.]

In memory of LUCY wife of George Bramhall &
daughter of Tho's. & Ruth Morton who died July 21,
1810, aged 32 years & 10 mo. Also LUCY M. daughter
of George & Lucy Bramhall; Died Feb. 6, 1824 aged 20
years & 5 mo.

No. 1453.

[Blue slate. Fair condition, but moss-grown. Symbol.]

Here lies Buried Mrs. RUTH DOTY the wife of Coll o
THOMAS DOTY who Departed this Life October 11th 1757
in ye   year of her age

(The year of her age was never cut on the stone.)

18

No. 1454.

[Blue slate. Moss-grown. Defaced. Broken. Symbol.]

Here lyes ye body of Mary Curtis wife to Eb e nezer Curtis : Died   March ye 17th 1717 in ye 131st year of her age.

(NOTE. If there is any error in regard to the age of Mrs. Curtis, I do not know how it can be rectified. The figures "131" are distinctly cut on the slate.)

No. 1455.

[Blue slate. Fair condition. Some moss. Inclined forward. Symbol.]

Died Sept. J0th J796   ANDREW CROSWELL *Esq.* Aged 59 years & JJ days.

No. 1456.

[Blue slate. Fair condition. Symbol.]

Here lyes buried the Body of Mrs MARY CROS ELL wife of Mr ANDREW CROSWELL who departed this Life August 30th 1773 in ye 29th year of her Age.

No. 1457.

[Low, blue slate. Laminæ separating. Cleft from top to bottom. Symbol.]

Here lies buried Sarah daughter of Mr Andrew & Mrs Sarah Croswell who decd Sep br 28th J782 Æt. J year & 4 days.

No. 1458.

[Very low broken remains of a blue slate monument. Remnant of symbol.]

Here lies   Rebekah   to Mr Andrew Croswell & Mrs Mary his wife who decd Feb ry ye 2d 1767 Aged 5 days.

No. 1459.

[Blue slate. Fair condition, but somewhat marred. Symbol.]

Here lies buried Andrew son of Mr Andrew & Mrs Sarah Croswell who decd Sepr 23d J777 Æt. 13 Months & 17 days.

No. 1460.

[Blue slate. Badly seamed. Somewhat marred.]

In Memory of Mr Silas Morton who died Oct o ye 30 th 178   In the 55th Year of his age.

No. 1461.

[Blue slate. Cleft. Somewhat defaced. Symbol.]

Here lyes ye body of Mrs Mary Morton wife to Mr Timothy Morton who died March ye 22d 1735 in ye 47th year of her age.

No. 1462.

[Blue slate. Weatherworn. Symbol.]

Eliza th   dau r to mr Timothy & Mrs Mary Morton his wife decd May ye 3d 1734 Aged 1 year & 4 Mo & 14 days.

No. 1463.

[Blue slate. Seamed, and badly broken.]

ere lyes   body of John Morton he died March ye 21st 1740 in ye 24th year of his age.

No. 1464.

[Purplish blue slate. Good condition. Symbol.]

Here lyes ye body of Mr John Churchell deceased June ye 13th 1723 in ye 66th year of his age.

No. 1465.

]Purplish blue slate. Good condition. Symbol.]

Here lyes ye body of Mrs Hannah Churchell wife to Mr John Churchell decd April ye 22d J723 in the 61st year of her age.

-No. 1466.

[Low, blue slate. Laminæ separating. Face cleft and moss-grown. Symbol.]

John Son to Mr John & Mrs Bethiah Churchill his wife dyed Sepr ye 28th 1725 Aged 1 year 11 months.

No. 1467.

[Bradford obelisk. More than 8 feet in height. White marble on granite base.]

(On south side:)

H I William Bradford of Austerfield Yorkshire England. Was the son of William and Alice Bradford He was Governor of Plymouth Colony from 1621 to 1633 1635 1637 1639 to 1643 1645 to 1657

(On north side a Hebrew sentence, said to signify:) Jehovah is our help.

(Then follows:)

Under this stone rest the ashes of Will   m Bradford a zealous Puritan & sincere Christian Gov. of Ply. Col. from 1621 to 1657, (the year he died) aged 69, except 5 yrs. which he declined.

No. 1468.

[Low, blue slate. Cleft in centre, its entire length. Appears to be a footstone, but there is no corresponding headstone.]

Mrs Elizabeth Tillson Cap t Edmund Tillson.

No. 1469.

[Blue slate. Cracked from summit to base. Moss-covered. Symbol.]

Here lyes ye body of Hannah Drew wife to Lemuel Drew who decd Octr ye 25th 1731 in ye 36th year of her age.

No. 1470.

[Blue slate. Fair condition, but some seams on surface. Symbol, a winged skull with crossbones resting upon it.]

Here lyes buried the Body of Mr JOHN BARNES Dec d May the 15 1744 in the 76th year of his age.

No. 1471.

[Blue slate. Inscription in capitals. Piece broken from right upper corner. Symbol.]

Here lyes buried the body of Mrs Sarah Samson wife to Mr Jonathan Samson died Augt ye 21st 1748, in the 22d year of her age.

No. 1472.

[Blue slate. Laminæ separating. Face seamed. Cleft. Part of symbol remaining.]

Here lies Buried Mr John Barnes who decd decm br ye JJth J745 in ye 52d year of his age.

No. 1473.

[Low, blue slate. Moss-covered. Weatherworn. Symbol.]

In Memory of William son to Mr James Drew & Mrs Mary his wife born Decmbr ye 29th 1755 Decd Sept 25th 1757

No. 1474.

[Very low, dark blue slate. Good condition. Symbol.]

In Memory of Elizabeth Daughter of Mr James Drew & Mrs Mary his wife died July 24th 1772 aged 2 years 10 months & 12 days.

No. 1475.

[Blue slate. Fair condition. Some moss. Symbol.]

In memory of Mrs MARY DREW widow of Mr JAMES DREW who died Augt 29th 1802 Aged 72 years

No. 1476.

[Blue slate. One-third of face scaled off. Moss-grown.]

Here   Mrs Sarah Bar   who decd March ye 21st 1762 In the 63d year of her age

No. 1477.

[Blue slate. Fair condition, but moss-grown. Symbol.]

Here lies buried Mrs Sarah Barn s ye wife of Mr Seth Ba r ns who decd March ye 19th 1770 in the 67th year of her age

No. 1478.

[A Goodwin stone. Appears to be a footstone, but has no corresponding headstone. Symbol.]

JAMES CURTIS J767.

No. 1479.

[Blue slate. Cleft its whole length, into two nearly equal parts. Moss-covered. Symbol.]

Here lyes buried ye body of Mrs Mary Barnes wife to Mr John Barnes Decd Febry ye 20th 1726—7 in the 55th year of her age.

No. 1480.

[Low, purplish blue slate. Top broken off. Seamed. Symbol.]

Elizabeth daur to Richard & Mary Waite Aged 13 mo. & 20 Ds Dec d Sepr ye 16 1730.

No. 1481.

[Very thick, light blue slate. Laminæ separating. Symbol under festoons.]

Here lyes the remains of JOHN WATSON Esqr who deceased Sep r the 9. 1731 in tne 53d year of his age.

No. 1482.

[Blue slate. Inscription in capitals. Fair condition. Somewhat moss-grown. Symbol.]

Here lyes ye body of mrs Rebeckah Morton wife to Mr Eleazar Morton who decd Novbr ye 6th 1730 in ye 66th year of her age

No. 1483.

[Blue slate. Good condition. Urn.]

Here lies inter'd the Body of Coll Thomas Lothrops who departed this life January 23 1794 aged 54.

No. 1484.

[Blue slate. Good condition. Urn.]

Sacred to the memory of ISAAC LOTHROP Esq. who departed this Life the 25 of July 1808 in the 75 year of his age.

No. 1485.

[White marble, in granite socket. Fair condition.]

OUR MOTHER POLLY S. wife of Thomas Diman, died Aug. 22, 1847, Aged 42 y'rs 5 mo's. Their children POLLY S. Died Oct. 11, 1835, Aged 2 mo's. MARY H. Died Nov. 30, 1838, Aged 9 mo's.

No. 1486.

[Very low, blue slate. Laminæ separating. Moss-grown. Symbol.]

Here lies buried Elizabeth Daughter to Mr Benjamin Barns & Mrs Elizabeth his wife who died April ye 21st 1764 aged one year & 6 Months.

No. 1487.

[Blue slate. Defaced. Split. Going to pieces. Symbol.]

Here lies the   dy of Mr Jonathan Barnes who decd Oct br ye 2d 1748 aged 45 years.

No. 1488.

[Blue slate. Like preceding, dropping to fragments.]

Here lies the Body of Mrs Phebe Barnes widow of Mr
Jonathan Barnes who decd May ye 23d 1753 aged 49
years.

No. 1489.

[Low, blue siate. Seamed. Moss-covered. Symbol.]

Elisab th Daur to Fraun   Courties Jur & Elisabeth
his wife decd Jan ry ye 26th   1740—1 Aged 17 mon &
26 days.

No. 1490.

[Blue slate. Two and a half feet wide by 2 feet high. Moss-grown.
Symbol.]

Here lyes ye body of Mr John Churchill who decd
Feb ry ye 25th day 1729—30 in the 39th year of his age.

No. 1491.

[Blue slate. Solid.* Moss-covered. Inclined. Symbol.]

In Memory of Mr. Mathew Lemote who decd Ocbr ye
27th 1762 Aged 51 years & 20 days.

No. 1492.

[Blue slate. Laminæ separating. Moss-covered. Symbol.]

In Memory of Mrs. Mercy Lemote wife to Mr Matthew
Lemote She decd Augst ye 8th 1758 in ye 34 year of her
age.

No. 1493.

[Low, blue slate. Laminæ separating. Moss-covered. Symbol.]

Here lyes ye body of Daniel son to ye Revd Mr Nathanael Leonard & Priscilla his wife decd Janry 18th 1733
—4 aged 9 days.

No. 1494.

[Low, blue slate. Fair condition, but mossy. Symbol.]

Here lyes ye body of Mary Dau'r to ye Rev d Mr Nathanael Leonard & Priscilla his wife decd Sepr 26 1729
aged 2 months.

No. 1495.

[Blue slate. Weatherworn. Moss-grown. Symbol.]

Here lyes buried ye body of Anna Dautr to ye Rev d
Nathaniel Leonard Born Nov br ye 23d 1725 Dec d Febry
ye 12th 1725—6.

No. 1496.

[Blue slate. Good condition. Skull and crossbones. Skull about
8 inches from upper incisors to apex ; crossbones about 16 inches in
length.]

Here lies interr'd the body of Mr Melatiah Lothrop who
Departed this Life Jul 6th 1771 Aged 70 Years.

No. 1497.

[Blue slate. Good condition. Urn.]

Here lies buried the Remains of Doctor Nathaniel Lothrop who died October 10, 1828 aged 92.

No. 1498.

[Blue slate. Good condition. Weeping willow and urn.]

Mrs ELLEN LOTHROP Consort to NATHL LO-THROP and only Daughter of the late Revd Mr NOAH HOBART of Fairfield was born October 26, 1741 and died June 1st 1780. This Stone an unavailing Tribute of affliction is Erected by her Husband To her Memory.

To name her Virtues ill befits my grief
What once was Bliss can now give no relief.
A Husband mourns—the rest let friendship tell
Friends knew her worth a Husband knew it well

No. 1499.

[Blue slate. Nearly covered with moss. Urn.]

Here lies buried the Remains of *Mrs Lucy Lothrop* Consort to *Doctor Nathaniel Lothrop* who died April 17 1826, in the 72 year of her age.

No. 1500.

[Blue slate. Seamed and broken. At top crossbones between two hour-glasses; under the crossbones, the cherub or symbol.]

Here lyes buried the body of Mrs Hannah Lothrop wife to Mr Jsaac Lothrop Junr decd Decr ye 11th 1730 in the 22d year of her age.

No. 1501.

[Low, blue slate. Good condition. Symbol.]

Freeman Lothrop son to Mr Jsaac & Mrs Hannah Lothrop aged 4 weeks & 5 d. decd Jan ry ye 19th 1739.

No. 1502.

[Blue slate. Moss-covered. Symbol.]

Here lyes ye body of Daniel Johnson Junr son to Danl Johnson Esqr & Betty his wife who died March ye 27th 1743 in the 17th year of his age & in ye 5th month of his apprenticeship with Robert Brown Esqr.

No. 1503.

[Low, blue slate. Fair condition. Symbol.]

GEORGE WATSON son to Mr George & Mrs Abigail Watson who departed this life Feb ry ye 26th 1749 aged 27 days.

No. 1504.

[Dark blue slate. Good condition. A beautiful stone. Crossbones and two symbols.]

Here lies interr'd the Body of Mrs ABIGAIL WATSON wife of GEORGE WATSON ESQR and Daughter to the Honble

RICHARD SALTONSTALL ESQR who departed this Life March ye 15th 1750 Æ. 22. also their son still-born March 11th 1750

No. 1505.

[Blue slate. Good condition. Symbol.]

Here lies the Body of GEORGE WATSON son of GEORGE WATSON ESQR & ELIZABETH his wife died August 10th 1757 aged 16 Days.

No. 1506.

[Low, blue slate. Fair condition. Symbol.]

In memory of ELIZABETH WATSON Dau r of GEORGE WATSON ESQR & ELIZ TH his wife Died Septbr 14th 1764 Aged 15 Days.

No. 1507.

[Dark blue slate. Handsomely wrought. Two symbols (one broken). Festoons on each side of the inscription. At the lower corner of each festoon an hour-glass, spade, and pickaxe or mattock. On this kind of slate I have not found any moss.]

Here lies Interr'd the Body of Mrs ELIZABETH WATSON the wife of GEORGE WATSON ESQR & Daughter to the Honble PETER OLIVER ESQ R who. Departed this Life February ye J9th J767 Aged 32 years.

No. 1508.

[Blue slate. Good condition, but moss-grown. Portrait in old style wig and ruffles.]

Here lies buried the Body of JOHN WATSON ESQR who departed this Life Jany 3d 1753 in the 37th year of his Age.

No. 1509.

[Blue slate. Good condition. Crossbones above two symbols.]

Here lies Interr'd the Body of Mrs ELIZABETH WATSON the wife of JOHN WATSON ESQR who departed this Life September ye 14th 1750 Æ. 28.

No. 1510.

[Blue slate. Fair condition. Inclined. Symbol.]

Here lies the Body of DANIEL WATSON Son of JOHN WATSON ESQR & ELIZABETH his wife Died June 29th 1756 Aged 6 years 9 months & 13 Days.

No. 1511.

[Dark blue slate. Good condition. Symbol.]

To the Memory of Mrs ELISABETH CLARKE who died September 27th J77J Æt. 26.

Though this pale Corpse is in the Grave confin'd
She leaves a Pattern for her Sex behind.
The Sun of Virtue never can decay
It shines in Time, & gives eternal Day.

No. 1512.

[Dark blue slate. Good condition. Very handsomely wrought. Weeping willow and urn. Initials "G. W." on the urn.]

In memory of GEORGE WATSON Esqr who died the 3d of December 1800 in the 83d Year of his Age.

No folly wasted his paternal Store,
No guilt no sordid av'rice made it more.
With honest fame and sober plenty crown'd,
He liv'd and spread his cheering influence 'round.

Pure was his walk, and peaceful was his end—
We bless'd his rev'rend length of Days
And hail'd him in the public ways
With veneration and with praise,

Our Father and our Friend.

No. 1513.

[Blue slate. Good condition. Weeping willow and urn.]

Here lies interred the Body of MADAM PHEBE WATSON, Relict of GEORGE WATSON, ESQ. died October 28, 1825 : aged 83 years, Her first Husband was JOHN SCOTT ESQ.

No. 1514.

[This and the following Nos. to 1517 inclusive are inclosed with iron rails in granite posts. No. 1514 is white marble on marble plinth; granite base. Good condition.]

GEORGE H. DREW Born Oct. 21, 1808, Died Nov. 23, 1881 Aged 73 years, 1 mo. & 2 dys.

No. 1515.

[Blue slate. Four and a half feet high. Good condition, Weeping willow and urn.]

Erected to the memory of five children of Capt Atwood Drew & Mrs. Lydia Drew his wife, viz. Lydia died August 25, 1804 aged one year 10 months. Eliza A. Drew died Sepr 5, 1805 aged one year & 4 months.. Lydia W. Drew died Apr. 11, 1806 aged 7 months. William R. Drew died Octr 9, 1815 aged 10 months. Eliza Drew died Octr 17, 1817 aged one year 6 months.

It is not the will of your father which is in heaven,
That one of these little ones should perish.

Christ.

No. 1516.

[Blue slate. Four and a half feet in height. Figure of a tomb with initials "A. D."]

Erected to the memory of Capt Atwood Drew, who departed this life May 10, 1823 aged 43 years.

Mourners forbear, the ways of heaven are just,
Afflicted mortals should believe and trust
By a wise hand the universe is sway'd,
Which justly limits every life it made.

19

No. 1517.

[White marble in form of Gothic arch. Set in granite socket. Good condition.]

Lydia Drew widow of CAPT. ATWOOD DREW Born Jan. 7, 1782 ; Died Jan. 3, 1861.

We mourn for her: we still do weep:
No more we'll see her here;
In Jesus she doth sweetly sleep;
Why shed for her a tear?

No. 1518.

[Blue slate. Good condition. Mausoleum.]

In memory of Mr. JAMES MORTON. who died Octr 19, 1832, aged 58 years.

No. 1519.

[Blue slate. Good condition. Symbol.]

In Memory of Mrs MARY MORTON wife of Mr THOMAS MORTON who died Augt 28, 1780 in ye 52 year of her age.

No. 1520.

[Blue slate. Pyramidal. Inscribed in oval, over which is figure of a willow.]

Adry Anna, dau. of William & Mary Churchill, died May 15: 1837 Aged 5 yr.s 3 mo.s & 11 ds. Also a female Infant died Dec.r 12, 1834 aged 19 days.

No. 1521.

[White marble. Four feet in height. Moss-grown.]

In memory of HANNAH BARTLETT, who died April 20th 1855, Aged 65 years.

Faithful in life.

No. 1522.

[White marble, in freestone socket. Good condition.]

JOHN L. MORTON, died July 22, 1857 ; Æ. 68 years & 9 mos. SALLY his wife died Oct. 6, 1810 : aged 20 years.

No more can we their forms behold,
Which now in death lie lifeless—cold
But may we meet when life is o'er,
And dwell at last on Canaan's shore.

JOHN B. MORTON, died Mar. 6, 1811, aged 1 year & 3 mos.

No. 1523.

[Similar to preceding.]

LILLY R. MORTON, wife of John L. Morton, died May 17, 1865 : Æ. 74 years.

Dear as thou wert, and justly dear;
We will not weep for thee:
One thought shall check the starting tear,
It is that thou art free.

No. 1524.

[Blue slate. Good condition, but moss-grown. Urn.]

This monument is erected in memory of Mr. James Bartlett Junr who died in the Island of Dominico Feb. 4th 1808 in the 23 year of his age.

The time was once my youthful friends •
I liv'd & bloom'd like thee
The time will come, 'tis hasting on
When you shall fade like me.

No. 1525.

[Blue slate. Good condition. Weeping willow.]

MARY, widow of George Morton, died Sept. 4, 1844, aged 88 years. Also HANNAH WITHERELL, died Jan. 18, 1834. aged 94 yr.s.

No. 1526.

[Blue slate. Good condition. Weeping willow and urn.]

This Stone is Erected to the memory of Mr. George Morton, who departed this Life November 30, 1818, in the 60 year of his age.

No. 1527.

[White marble. In stone socket. Fair condition.]

Polly Morton, died November 4, 1858, Aged 73 years.

Dearest sister, we will meet thee
In that land where all is blest;
There where sorrows never enter
We will dwell forever blest.

No. 1528.

[White marble. In stone socket. Inclined.]

REBECCA, wife of JACOB TINKHAM, Died Oct. 17, 1859, Æt. 76.

"Blessed are the dead that die in the Lord."

No. 1529.

[Blue slate. Laminæ separating. Surface seamed. Symbol.]

In Memory of Mrs Asenath Churchill wife of Mr Thaddeus Churchill who died May 4, 1788 in ye 38 year of her age.

No. 1530.

[Blue slate. Good condition. This and the Nos. following to 1538 inclusive, are inclosed in iron railing.]

In memory of MRS. MARY THACHER, who died March 3, 1838, aged 81 years.

No. 1531.

[White marble. Fair condition.]

ELIZA ANN, and ELIZABETH THACHER, children of William and Susan T. Bartlett.

No. 1532.

[White marble. Fair condition.]

SUSAN THACHER. wife of William Bartlett, died
August 25, 1862, Æ. 68 years.

No. 1533.

[White marble. Fair condition, but somewhat moss-grown.]

In Memory of JAMES THACHER, M. D.

a surgeon
in the army during the war of the Revolution : afterwards,
for many years, a practising physician, in the county of
Plymouth : the author of several historical and scientific
works ; esteemed of all men for piety and benevolence,
public spirit and private kindness. Born February 14,
1754, Died May 26, 1844. Also of SUSAN THACHER
for 57 years his pious and faithful wife, who died May
17, 1842, Aged 86 years.

No. 1534.

[Blue slate. Good condition. Two symbols.]

This Stone is Erected to the Memory of Hersey Thacher
who died 17th April 1793 Aged 1 year And 4 months And
Catharine Thacher died 10. Febry 1800 Aged 3 years.
Children of Dr James And Mrs Susanna Thacher.

Early, Bright, Transient, Sweet. As
Morning Dew They Sparkled
Were Exhaled And Went To Heaven.

No. 1535.

[Blue slate. Good condition. Two symbols.]

In Memory of Sukey Thacher who died Decr 8, ₁790,
aged 2 years & 8 months. and of James Thacher who
died Decr 12, ₁790, aged 2 days. Children of Dr James
Thacher & Mrs Susannah his wife. Both of whose remains are here deposited.

Sleep on my babes and take your quiet rest,
'Twas God who called you when he thought it best.

No. 1536.

[White marble. Weathering rough.]

In Memory of Susan Louisa, youngest daughter of
Daniel B. Elliott Esq deceased, of Waynesboro,
Georgia. She died January 16, 1811, Aged 10 months ;
Leaving a Widowed mother, who is consoled for the loss
of a lovely Child by the assurance that of such is the
Kingdom of Heaven.

No. 1537.

[White marble. Fair condition.]

Betsey Hayward wife of Michael Hodge, Died Feb. 27,
1871, Aged 84 y'rs 8 mo's.

No. 1538.

[White marble. Weathering rough.]

Michael Hodge, A. M. graduate of Harvard College, formerly of Newburyport Counsellor at Law, died July 6, 1816, Aged 36 years

Genius and sensibility science, virtue and benevolence adorned his life.
The tears of friendship and love embalm his memory.

No. 1539.

[Blue slate. Good condition. Weeping willow and urn.]

Died Mr John Churchill October 14, 1814 aged 39 years

Death burst the revolving
Cloud and all was well.

No. 1540.

[Blue slate. Good condition. Urn.]

MRS. NANCY CHURCHILL widow of Mr. John Churchill died June 11, 1838, in her 54th year.

Also their son JOHN, died May 15, 1806, aged 11 mon.

Yet again we hope to meet thee
When the stay of life is fled
Then in heaven with joy to greet thee,
Where no farewell tear is shed.

No. 1541.

[Blue slate. Good condition. Weeping willow and urn.]

To the memory of Mrs Bethiah Churchill wife of Mr Ansell Churchill who died Dec r 6th 1806 in the 61st year of her age.

No. 1542.

[Blue slate. 3 1-2 feet in height. Pyramidal. Good condition. Weeping willow and urn.]

Erected to the memory of Miss NANCY CHURCHILL dau. of Mr. John Churchill and Mrs. Nancy his wife who died Aug. 22, 1822, aged 14 years.

When spotless innocence resigns her breath
And beauty's faded in the armes of death
When youth's consigned to mingle with the dead
How pungent are the tears survivors shed.

No. 1543.

[White marble. Removed from socket, and placed in ground. Good condition.]

BETSEY HOBART, died Aug. 29, 1870, aged 78 y'rs. and formerly wife of JOSHUA PERKINS; who Died Feb. 9, 1820, aged 34 y'rs. And their children BETSEY M. Died Nov. 16, 1837, aged 26 y'rs. JAMES A. Died Nov. 22, 1840, aged 26 y'rs. CHARLES T. died June 8, 1842, aged 24 y'rs.

Gone before.

No. 1544.

[Blue slate. Fair condition. Weeping willow and urn.]

In memory of Capt NATHL MORTON who died September 21, 1823, aged 39 years.

> Why do we mourn departing friends,
> Or shake at death's alarms?
> 'Tis but the voice that Jesus sends,
> To call them to his arms.

No. 1545.

[Blue slate. Good condition. Urn.]

SARAH, relict of Thomas Morton, died May 22, 1841, aged 81 yrs & 9 mo.

> My Saviour summons me away,
> A brighter world to see,
> Although a while behind you stay,
> Weep not, weep not for me.

No. 1546.

[Blue slate. Good condition. Urn.]

In Memory of Mr. THOMAS MORTON, who died Oct. 15, 1833, in the 77 year of his age Also his son THOMAS. who died at sea on a passage from Savannah to Philadelphia July 14, 1815 aged 18 years.

No. 1547.

[Blue slate. Good condition. Urn.]

In memory of three dau. of Samuel & Sally Cole, Viz. JANE R. died Sept. 27, 1827, aged 18 mo. DEBORAH B. died April 30, 1837, aged 18 years. CAROLINE E. died Sept. 13, 1842, aged 20 years.

> May we not meet in Heaven above
> With love that has no trembling fears
> In that dear home far far above
> This land of tears.

No. 1548.

[Blue slate. Nearly 5 feet in height. Good condition. Urn.]

In memory of SALLY. widow of the late Samuel Cole, died Oct 23d, 1855, in her 73d year.

For I know that my Redeemer liveth, and that he shall stand at the latter day upon the earth.
> JOB 19-25.

No. 1549.

[Blue slate. Good condition. Urn.]

In memory of SAMUEL COLE, who died April 1st. 1843, aged 62 years.

No. 1550.

[Wooden slab.]

CATHERINE REIDLE, Died Aug 17th, 1868 aged 6 months.

No. 1551.

[Wooden slab.]

MARY REIDLE Died Feb. 14th 1868 aged 33 years.

No. 1552.

[Blue slate. Good condition. Urn.]

In memory of Cynthia Bartlett, widow of John Bartlett 3d, who died Sept. 11th, 1843, aged 47 years.

She died in hope, she died in faith
A life of suffering o'er,
She smiling met the shafts of death,
And lives to die no more.

No. 1553.

[Blue slate. Good condition. Weeping willow and urn.]

Died of a lingering Distressing Sickness Mr John Bartlett Feb. 16, 1825 in the 29 year of his age.

Oh Death! lover and friend
Hast thou put far from
His bere a ved Consort and her
Acquaintance into darkness.

No. 1554.

[Blue slate. Four feet in height. Good condition. Weeping willow and urn. This and the next No. are inclosed in wooden paling.]

SALLY wife of Nathaniel Harlow. died Dec.r 7, 1819, aged 44 yrs. Also three children viz SALLY, died Sept. 26, 1817 aged 17 yrs. SALLY, died April 12, 1818 aged 7 Mon. CALEB BOWTEL, died June 7, 1820, aged 9 Mon.

Their flesh shall slumber in the ground
Till the last trumpet's joyful sound
Then burst the chains with sweet surprise,
And in the Saviour's image rise.

No. 1555.

[White marble. Discolored. Rough. Rose twig.]

CATHARINE Daug. of Nathaniel & Betsey Harlow, died Nov.r 30th 1841, aged 11 years 2 Mon. & 28 days.

No. 1556.

[Blue slate. Fair condition, Symbol.]

In Memory of Lemuel Stephens Robbins Son of Mr. Joseph Robbins & Mrs Elizabeth his wife who died April 1st 1786 aged 3 years 2 months & 7 days.

No. 1557.

[Blue slate. Good condition. Urn.]

This Stone is Erected to the memory of Mrs REBEKAH FINNEY Consort of Mr JOSIAH FINNEY the Eldest Daughter of Maj r BENJ. WARREN who died June 4th 1805, in the 37th year of her age. Also to the memory of their son Josiah who was Born May 22, 1805 Died May 28, 1805.

No. 1558.

ELKANAH CHURCHILL, died Oct. 7, 1845, in his 37 year.

Look here, my friends, and read your doom,
For you are hast'ning to the tomb.

No. 1559.

LYDIA A. dau. of Elkanah & Lydia CHURCHILL, died Dec. 17, 1852; aged 15 y'rs. & 3 mo's.

Her youthful hopes were like the morning flower
Cut down at noon and withered in an hour;
But hopes more fair and bright, than youth or health can give
Rise in immortal bloom beyond the grave.

No. 1560.

FATHER. DAVID DREW, Born May 3, 1777; Died April 16, 1825.

No. 1561.

MOTHER. SALLY DREW, Born May 7, 1782; Died May 19, 1864.

No. 1562.

CHILDREN. LUCINDA, died July 29, 1807; aged 4 months. SOLOMON, died April 6, 1813; aged 9 months. SOLOMON A. died Feb. 15, 1821; aged 8 months.

No. 1563.

Erected to the memory of MR. NATHAN REED, who died January 12, 1842 in the 78 yr of his age.

No. 1564.

REBECCA, wife of NATHAN REED, Died March 2d 1859, Aged 81 y'rs. & 9 mo's.

The memory of the just is blessed.

No. 1565.

FATHER & MOTHER. JOHN BARTLETT Died June 12, 1870, Aged 71 y'rs.

CAROLINE, His wife Died May 31, 1846, Aged 46 years.

Gone home.

No. 1566.

[Blue slate. Good condition. Weeping willow and urn.]

In memory of Capt Josiah Cotton, who died March 7, 1829, aged 76 years. Also in memory of Sarah D. Cotton, died Oct. 14, 1820 aged 19 years.

No. 1567.

[Blue slate. Good condition. Flaming urn.]

In memory of MRS. LYDIA COTTON widow of Capt. Josiah Cotton, died Jan. 28th. 1843, aged 63 years.

No. 1568.

[Blue slate. Good condition. Weeping willow and urn.]

In memory of Mr. John Otis, who departed this life March 27, 1817, in the 74 year of his age. Also in memory of his Oldest Child Mrs. Temperance Cotton, Consort of Capt Josiah Cotton, who departed this life december 24th 1816, in the 49 year of her age.

They sleep in Death
But will arise in Glory.

No. 1569.

[Low, blue slate. Good condition, save moss-grown. Symbol.]

In Memory of HANNAH OTIS wife of Mr JOHN OTIS, who died March 28, 1793 in the 47 year of her age.

No. 1570.

[Low, purplish slate. Inscription scaling off. Symbol.]

Here lyes buried the Body of Mr Stephen Churchell died Septr 5, 1751 in the 36 year of his Age.

No. 1571.

[Blue slate. Good condition, save moss-covered. Symbol.]

To the memory of Mrs HANNAH HOWES wife of Mr JEREMIAH HOWES Relict widow of Mr STEPHEN CHURCHILL who died June ye 15th A. D. 1793 in the 75th year of her age.

No. 1572.

[Blue slate. Laminæ separating. Moss-grown. Symbol.]

To the memory of   lenor Churchill Daughter of Capt Stephen Churchil And Lucy his Wife Who died Oct. 3d 1792 in the 10th year of her age   .

No. 1573.

[Blue slate. Fair condition. Symbol.]

In Memory of John Bartlett Son of Mr John & Mrs Dorothy Bartlett who died Jany 15 1793 aged 17 years.

Those eyes which once so sparkl'd with delight
Are e'en now clos'd in Deaths eternal night.

No. 1574.

[Low, blue slate. Laminæ separating. Symbol.]

In memory of John Lewis son of Mr John Bartlett & Mrs Dorothy his wife who died April ye ɹt 1776 Aged 2 years and 27 days

No. 1575.

[A Goodwin stone. Moss-covered. Inclined. Badly weatherworn, but at top can be discerned a half length figure of a human being.]

Here lies buried y body of Lewis ye Son of John Bartlett & Dorothy his Wife who departed this life January ye 9th ɹ772 Aged ɹ Year 9 months & 20 Days

No. 1576.

[Blue slate. Surface scaling off. Symbol.]

In Memory of Mr JOHN BARTLETT who died April 26 1790 in ye 53 year of his age.

Here lies the man who nev r   friends denie
Nor never gave them grief but   hen he died

No. 1577.

[Blue slate. Weatherworn. Moss-covered. Seamed and cleft. Vase of flowers.]

In memory of Miss Dolly Bartlett Daugtr of Mr John & Mrs Dorothy Bartlett who died Sepr ɹɹ ɹ796 in her 25 year.

This virtuous soul whose dust is laid
In the drear mansions of the dead
Shall rise and leave its native ground
At the last trumpet's solemn sound.

No. 1578.

[Blue slate. Surface cleft at top. Seam on the right. Weeping willow over a tomb.]

To the memory of Mrs DOROTHY BARTLETT widow of Mr John Bartlett & Daughter to DEACON JOSIAH CARVER who died Mar, 11, 1805 aged 69 years

Alas and has She gone and has She fled
Gone to the Silent mansions of the dead,
She is gone we trust to join the joys on high
With Saints and angles o'er the starry sky

No. 1579.

[This and the three following Nos. are white marble set in freestone, are inclosed in handsome iron fence, and are in good condition.]

In memory of DR. JOHN GODDARD surgeon of the U. S. frigate Boston dec d in Gibraltar bay June 15, 1802 aged 32 years. Also of his wife GRACE HAYMAN deed Feb. 8, 1851 aged 80 years. And of ABIGAIL OTIS deed Feb. 11, 1853 in her 70th year.

No. 1580.

ABRAHAM JACKSON Born Nov. 29, 1791, Died February 6, 1859 : Æ. 67 years.

No. 1581.

HARRIET OTIS Wife of Abraham Jackson died Jan. 21, 1872 ; Æ. 74.

No. 1582.

HORACE JACKSON Died in Norfolk, Va. Sept. 9. 1855 ; Æ. 27 years & 5 mo's.

No. 1583.

[Blue slate. Fair condition, save seams on surface. Symbol.]

To the memory of Mrs ELIZABETH FINNEY wife of Mr THOMAS FINNEY who died March 3d J795 in the 53 year of her age.

No. 1584.

[Blue slate. Moss-grown. Cleft from near summit to base.]

To the memory of Mr THOMAS FINNEY who died Janry 5. AD. 1791 in the 53d year of his age.

No. 1585.

[Low, blue slate. Defaced. Inclined. Symbol.]

In memory of Nancy Daughter of Mr Josiah & Mrs Rebecca Finney who died Augt 13 1792 aged   month

No. 1586.

[Blue slate. Four feet by 2 1-2. Good condition. Urn, with weeping willow on each side.]

Erected In memory of CAPT RUFUS ROBBINS, who died at New Orleans July 4, 1826 aged 45 years. Also in memory of Mrs. MARGARET ROBBINS his wife who died Jan. 14, 1827 aged 43 years.

No. 1587.

[Blue slate. Fair condition. Weeping willow and urn.]

To the memory of Mr Lemuel Robbins who departed this life July 28, 1822, in the 64 year of his age. Also in memory of Mrs Mary Robbins his wife who departed this life March 5, 1821 in 62 year of her age.

Ye living men, the tomb survey!
Where you must shortly dwell,
Hark ! how the awful summons sounds
In ev'ry funeral knell.

No. 1588.

[White marble. In granite socket. Good condition.]

FATHER. CHANDLER ROBBINS Born Jan. 1793, Died Oct. 1857.

"The memory of the just is as a shining light."

No. 1589.

[White marble. Discolored. This and the next No, are inclosed in wooden palings.]

SAMUEL A. son of Antonio & Sarah C. Frank Born May 4, 1849, Died Jan. 12 1863.

He was our best loved one,
Kindly and gentle ever,
Death early claimed his own,
We can forget thee never.

No. 1590.

[Wooden slab.]

ANTOINE FRANK Died Feb. 19th AD. 1875 Aged 67 years.

No. 1591.

[White marble. In freestone socket. Inclosed in wooden paling.]

HENRYETTA MILLER Born in Germany, July 22, 1807, Died June 13, 1869.

No. 1592.

[Blue slate. Pyramidal. Cleft through urn at top.]

In memory of Mrs JERUSHA TRASK who Died Augt 20, 1807 in the 68 year of her Age

Sins promis'd joys are turned to pain
And i am drownd in Grief
But my dear Lord returns again
He flies to my relief

Siezing my soul with sweet surprise
He draws with loving hands
Divine Compassion in his eyes
And pardon in his hands

No. 1593.

[Blue slate. Fair condition. Urn between roses.]

To the memory of Mr JOSEPH TRASK who died Feb. 26 1802 aged 67 years. Also in memory of 3 Sons of Mr Joseph & Mrs Jerusha Trask viz Joseph & Thomas died at sea aged 23 years William aged 15 years.

God my redeemer lives and often from
The skies looks down and watches all my dust
Till he shall bid it rise

No. 1594.

[Blue slate. Pyramidal. Good condition. Urn.]

To the memory of Mrs ELIZABETH KEMPTON wife of Mr JOHN KEMPTON who died May 23th 1801 aged 82 years. Also in memory of 6 children of Mr John & Mrs Elizabeth Kempton viz John & Saml died June 2th 1737 aged 1 month Nathaniel died June 9th 1756 aged 13 years Priscilla died Augst 15, 1760 aged 4 years Sarah died Feb. 23th 1770 aged 13 years Samuel died at sea Augst 1777 aged 22 years.

> Beneath this monument lies Zion dust
> Which in the resurrection of the just
> Shall rise in union to the head
> And sit in Glory that shall never fade.

No. 1595.

[Blue slate. Badly seamed about midway across face, and supporting a luxuriant growth of mosses. Urn.]

This Stone is Erected To the memory of Mr JOHN KEMPTON who died April 18, 1806 in the 90 year of his age.

> I ask them whence their victory came
> They with united breath
> Ascribe their conquest to the Lamb
> Their triumph to his death.

No. 1596.

[Purplish blue slate. Good condition. Weeping willow and urn.]

In memory of ABIGAIL W. KEMPTON Consort of ZACHEUS KEMPTON who died Novemr 26, 1820 aged 25 years and 6 months.

> GOD my Redeemer lives,
> And often from the skies
> Looks down and watches all my dust
> Till he shall bid it rise.

No. 1597.

[Blue slate. Good condition. Weeping willow and urn.]

In memory of Mrs SARAH KEMPTON wife of Mr ZACHEUS KEMPTON who died January 31, 1824, Sixty-one years and eight months.

> Why do we mourn, why do we weep?
> For a departed friend
> For she has left a world of woe
> And gone to a just friend.

No. 1598.

[Blue slate. Good condition. Weeping willow and urn.]

In memory of Four Children of Mr Zacheus Kempton & Sarah his wife viz Sally aged 36 years Charles aged 21 years Woodard aged 17 years Robinson aged 2 years They died between 1802 & 1820.

> Stop traveller and shed a tear
> Uppon the sod of children dear.

No. 1599.

[Blue slate. Fair condition. Urn.]

In memory of Mrs Polly Ripley Consort of Mr Levi Ripley who died March 8 1807 in the 34 year of her age Also their child Levi died March 3. 1807 aged one year

> Here peaceful rest till Christ shall come
> To call the from beneath the ground
> His powerful voice shall rouse the Tomb
> With sweet Salvation in the sound

No. 1600.

[White marble, in granite socket. Good condition save discoloration.]

LOVICA T. MCGLATHLIN Born Sept. 28, 1780, Died Aug. 28, 1865.

> We shall meet beyond the River.

No. 1601.

[Blue slate. Good condition. Weeping willow and urn.]

In memory of Consider Bradford Son of James Bradford who died December 25, 1826; aged 11 mo. & 17 days.

> Short was thy day, sweet babe, but this will give
> A longer space of heavenly life to live.

No. 1602.

[White marble. Weathering rough.]

ELEANOR, wife of James Bradford, died July 29, 1840, aged 43 years WILLIAM, their son died Oct. 24, 1836, aged 9 yrs.

> But thou, O Heaven, keep, keep what thou hast taken,
> And with our treasure keep our hearts on high.
> The spirit weak, and yet by pain unshaken
> The faith, the love, the lofty constancy—
> Guide us where those are with our blessed flown,
> They were of thee, and thou hast claimed thine own.

No. 1603.

[Similar to preceding.]

JAMES BRADFORD, died March 1, 1836, aged 49 yrs. Sarah their Dau. died Oct. 19, 1832, aged 2 yrs. & 7 Mon.

> Earth, guard what here we lay in holy trust,
> That which hath left our home a darkened place,
> Wanting the form, the smile, was veiled in dust,
> The light departed with our fathers face;
> Yet from thy bonds undying hope springs free;
> We have but lent our father unto thee.

No. 1604.

[White marble. Rough. Difficult to read. Rose tree.]

ELIJAH J. WESTON died Jan. 14, 1864. Aged 30 years 6 mos.

> I trust my blood was spilled for thee
> Who shed thy precious blood for me
> Here lies a husband and a father
> Who was kind and gentle ever
> Death early claimed thee
> We shall forget thee never.

Also our gentle child, JOHNNY C. Son of Elijah J. & Susan Weston, died Aug. 12, 1863; Æ 1 year 8 mos 5 days.

> They were dearly loved on earth by us all
> I trust now they are loved in Heaven.

No. 1605.

[White marble. Some words scarcely legible.]

To the memory of Lois Diman the   Daughtr of Mr David Diman & Mrs Lois his wife who died Oct. 18. 1801 in the 18th year of her age.

(Epitaph, four lines of poetry, of which the last line only is legible, as follows:)

Which pity must demand.

No. 1606.

[Low, blue slate. Good condition. Symbol.]

In Memory of David son of Mr David Diman & Mrs Lois his wife who died Augt 4 J788 aged 3 years J month & 26 days.

No. 1607.

[Low, blue slate. Good condition. Symbol.]

In Memory of David son of Mr David Diman & Mrs Lois his wife who died Oct. 9, 1784 Aged 2 years & 5 days.

No. 1608.

[Blue slate. Cleft downward near centre. Symbol.]

Here lies buried Mrs Elisabeth Diman ye wife of Mr Daniel Diman who decd July ye JJ J768 In ye 78th year of her age.

No. 1609.

[Blue slate. Two and a half feet high. Weatherworn. Part of surface scaled off. Symbol, nearly gone.]

In memory of Capt Josiah Morton who Decd May ye J9th J76J in ye 74th year of his age.

No. 1610.

[Blue slate. Fair condition. Symbol.]

In Memory of Mrs Elezebeth Morton widow of Capt Josiah Morton who decd MARCH ye 2Jst J763 In ye 7Jst year of her age.

No. 1611.

[Blue slate. Laminæ separating. Face of stone scaling off.]

n Memory of   ANNA DIMAN wife of DANIEL DIMAN who departed this Life April 4th J786 in ye 60th year of her Age.

No. 1612.

[Purplish blue slate. Good condition. Symbol.]

In Memory of Mrs MARY DIMAN wife of Mr DANIEL DIMAN who died Feby J5 1792 in ye 55 year of her age.

No. 1613.

[Similar to preceding.]

To the memory of Mr DANIEL DIMAN who died Decr 16th 1797 aged 69 years and 10 months

But the salvation of the Righteous is of the
Lord he is their strength in time of trouble.

No. 1614.

[Blue slate. Good condition.]

LOIS DIMAN wife of David Diman died Dec. 16, 1831 in the 75 year of her age.

Look down and view
The hollow gaping tomb;
This gloomy prison waits for you
Whene'er the summons come.

No. 1615.

[Blue slate. Defaced. Laminæ separating. Symbol.]

Here lyes ye body of Deacon George Morton who decd Augst ye 2d 1727 in ye 80th year of his age

No. 1616.

[Similar to preceding No.]

Here lyes ye body of Thomas Morton who decd March ye 8th 1738 in ye 43th year of his age.

No. 1617.

[Blue slate. Nearly ruined.]

ere Mrs Jo   wife of   Morton who   June
ye   1728 in ye 93d year of her age

No. 1618.

[Blue slate. Weatherworn. Moss-grown.]

Here lyes ye body of Ephraim Morton who decd Feb ry ye 18th 1731–2 in ye 84th year of his age

No. 1619.

[Blue slate. Seamed. Scarred. Cleft. Symbol.]

Here lyes ye body of mr John Morton who decd Feby ye 4th 1738–9 in ye 59th year of his age

No. 1620.

[Similar to preceding No.]

Here lyes ye body of Mrs Reliance Morton wife to Mr John Morton who decd Decbr ye 4th 1735 in ye 55th year of her age

No. 1621.

[Low, purplish slate. Bad condition. Inclined. Symbol.]

Here lyes ye Body of Elisha Morton decd Octbr ye 23d 1727 in the 13th year of his age

No. 1622.

[Blue slate. Four and a half feet in height. Good condition. Two
mausoleums.]

PHINEAS PIERCE died Aug.st 10th 1841 aged 37
years Also Rebecca Jane Daughter of Phineas & Dorcas
M. Pierce died Sept.r 8th 1833, aged 4 years

No. 1623.

[Blue slate. Part of face scaled off. Symbol.]

In memory of Mrs REBECCA MORTON wife of Mr
NATHANIE MORTON who departed this life May ye
15th 17 in ye 41st year of her Age

No. 1624.

[Blue slate. Laminæ separating. Cleft. Symbol.]

Here lyes ye Body of Mr NATHANIEL MORTON who
deed Novbr ye 7th 1731 in ye 25th year of his age

No. 1625.

[Blue slate. Good condition. Figure of man standing behind a
tomb (?) on the top of which are two pairs of crossbones.]

In memory of Mr NATHL MORTON ye 3d who departed this life Novbr ye 20th 1776 in ye 23d year of his
Age

No. 1626.

[Blue slate. Compact. Good condition. Female figure at top,
curiously drawn.]

In memory of *Mrs Joanna Morton* widow of the late
Nathaniel Morton deceased who died November 14th 1818
in the 86th year of her age

No. 1627.

[Blue slate. Good condition. Some moss. Symbol.]

To the memory of Mrs Moriah Mendil who died Novr
22th 1801 and 80 years wife of Mr Jabez Mendil.

No. 1628.

[White marble. Two feet high. Rough. Moss-grown. Inclined.]

HELEN AUGUSTA, Daug.tr of Ann and William
Drew 2d died Jany 24, 1836, Aged 4 yrs & 4 mo.

> Transplanted from the woes to come
> To heaven's immortal bower
> Through all eternity to bloom
> A sweet and fadeless flower

No. 1629.

[Blue slate. Good condition. Urn.]

In memory of Mrs Elisabeth Stephens widow of the late
Eleazer Stephens Deceasd who died April 30, 1806 in the
71 year of her age.

> My flesh shall slumber in the ground,
> Till the last trumpet's joyfull sound;
> Then burst the chains with sweet surprise,
> And in my Saviour's image rise.

20

No. 1630.

[Blue slate. Laminæ separating. Surface cleft. Symbol]

In Memory of Mr ELEAZER STEPHENS who departed this Life Sepr 5th J785 in the 63d year of his Age.

No. 1631.

[Low, blue slate. Bad condition. Symbol.]

In Memory of Mrs Sarah Stephens ye wife of Mr Eleazer Stephens who decd Octo ye 28th 1763 in ye 43d year of her age

No. 1632.

· [Blue slate. Moss-covered. Symbol.]

Here lies buried Mrs Susanna Stephens wife to Mr Eleazer Stephens who decd Decemr ye 30th J766 in ye 37th year of her Age.

No. 1633.

[Blue slate. Good condition. Symbol.]

In memory of Mrs Hannah Stephens Daughter of the late Mr Eleazer Stephens and Mrs Elizabeth his wife who Died Augst 28th 1801 in the 25th year of her Age.

No. 1634.

[Blue slate. Good condition. Symbol.]

Here lies buried the Body of Mrs SARAH CHURCHILL the wife of Mr JOHN CHURCHILL who died March 31st 1752 in the 22d Year of her Age.

(Crossbones under the inscription.)

No. 1635.

[Purplish blue slate. Good condition. Two urns.]

In memory of two Children of Samuel M. & Harriet B. Whitten, viz. SAMUEL died Dec 24th 1844 in his 4th yr HARRIET B. died Aug. 15th 1838, aged 3 weeks.

Twise deaths keen shafts have smitten here
Spoiling what nature holds most dear
Fond parents faint not GOD reproves
And chastens all whom most he loves.

No. 1636.

[Low, blue slate. Split. Defaced. Ruined.]

Math   Mr Ma   mote & Mrs Marcy   is wife born June ye 25th 1738 decd Sepr   1739

No. 1637.

[Low, blue slate. Moss-grown. Seam across face. Symbol.]

In memory of Abigail Daughtr to Mr Mathew Lemote & Mrs Marcy his wife Born June ye 6th 1733 Decd Octo ye 25th 1734.

No. 1638.

[Low, blue slate. Moss-grown. Face of stone partially scaled off.
Part of figure at top remains.]

In Memory of Mathew son to   Mathew Le   te &
Mrs Marey his wife Born Novr ye 30th 17 2 decd Jany
ye 22d 1733.

No. 1639.

[Low, blue slate. Moss-grown. Cleft. Defaced.]

In Memory of Mathew son to Mr Mathew Lemote &
Mrs Marey his wife Born Augst ye 18th J730   July
ye 15th J733.

No. 1640.

[Low, blue slate. Corner at right, broken off. Symbol.]

Nathaniel L.   Churchell Aged 21 years Died March
ye 24th 1714.

No. 1641.

[Low, marble block. Good condition. On upper surface the word:]

FATHER.

(On obverse:)

WILLIAM STEPHENS.

No. 1642.

[Similar to preceding. On upper surface the word:]

MOTHER.

(On obverse:)

NANCY wife of Wm Stephens.

No. 1643.

[Blue slate. Moss-grown. Two semi-circular roundings at top, each
with symbol and crossbones.]

In memory of Mr Ephraim Churchell who decd Decemr
ye 14th 1749 in the 4Jst year of his age In memory of
Mrs Priscilla ye wife of Mr Ephraim Churcll who decd
Decemr ye JJth J749 Aged 41 years.

No. 1644.

[Low, blue slate. Defaced. Moss-covered. Much inclined. Symbol.]

In memory of Ephraim son to Mr Zacheus Churchill &
Mrs Mary his wife who decd Novr ye 7th J76J Aged J
year & 2 months.

No. 1645.

[This and the next two Nos. are inclosed in wooden paling. They
are of white marble. Fair condition.[

IN MEMORY OF CAPT ROBERT COWEN who died
Mar. 30, 1863 ; Æ. 62 years & 10 mos

No. 1646.

[Similar to preceding. Marble plinth. Freestone base.]

IN MEMORY OF *Ann T. Cowen*, who died May 16, 1865
Æ. 57 years 11 mos. & 9 days.

No. 1647.

[White marble in freestone socket.]

MARY ANN died July 3, 1834, aged 3 yrs & 4 mo.
ROBERT, died May 5, 1833, aged 3 mo. & 24 days.
Children of Robert & Ann Cowen.

> Let little children come to me,
> Our blessed Saviour said;
> And to his arms on wings of love,
> Their spotless souls have fled.

No. 1648.

[Blue slate. Laminæ separating. Face of stone cleft in twain.
Symbol.]

Here lyes ye body of John Faunce who decd Novbr ye
28th 1734 in ye 26 year of his age.

No. 1649.

[Blue slate. Laminæ separating. Defaced. Seamed. Symbol.]

Here Lyes   body of Nath   Faunce who decd Augst
ye 29th 1732   Aged 26 years.

No. 1650.

[Blue slate. Face of stone scaling off. Symbol.]

In memory of *Zepheniah Morton* who decd Octo ye 19th
1760 In ye 46th year of his age.

No. 1651.

[Blue slate. Laminæ separating. Part of design at top broken off.
Symbol remains.]

In Memory of Mr NATHANAEL MORTON who departed
this life August ye 15th 1781 in ye 50th year of his Age.

No. 1652.

[Purplish slate. Good condition. Half length figure of female, with
a flower on each side.]

To the Memory of Miss ELIZABETH MORTON who departed this Life May ye 21st 1790 in ye 20th year of her
age.

No. 1653.

[Marked by wooden slab on which are these words and figures:
"The Grave of Elder Thos. Faunce Died Feb. 27, 1745." The stone
is a handsome purplish slate, nearly three feet high. Uninjured.
Figure of a skeleton seated on an hour-glass; left hand of skeleton
holding a scythe. Wings are attached to the hour-glass. Above the
figure is a drawing of a scallop shell.]

Here lyes buried the Body of Mr THOMAS FAUNCE ruling ELDER of the first Church of CHRIST in *Plymouth* deceased Febry 27th An: Dom. 1745-6 in the 99th year of
his Age

> The Fathers where are they?
> Blessed are the dead who die in the Lord.

No. 1654.

[Blue slate. Broken. Moss-grown Much of the monument gone.
Two feet high, one foot wide. Symbol.]

Lyes ye bod   Ephraim Kem   on who   cd
Decbr ye   th 1720   ye 18th year of his age.

No. 1655.

[White marble. Rough. Not now set in earth, but leaning against
No. 1656.]

In memory of JOHN C. son of Stephen D. & Lydia
W. Drew, Died Sep. 10, 1850, Æ. 11 Months.

No. 1656.

[Low, white marble. Fair condition. Endangered by larger stone
leaning against it.]

In memory of Leman L. son of Stephen D. & Lydia
Williams Drew Died Jan. 24, 1853 Æ 6 Months.

No. 1657.

[White marble. Weathering rough. Weeping willow and urn, on
design resembling a brick wall.]

IN MEMORY OF LYDIA W. Wife of Stephen D. Drew,
who died Aug. 28, 1852 Æ. 41 y'rs 5 mo.

My hour has come, I lay me down,
With the dark grave in view;
And hoping for a heavenly crown,
I bid the world adieu.

No. 1658.

[Blue slate. Cleft in various directions. Laminæ separating.
Moss-grown. Symbol.]

In Memory of Mr EPHRAIM CHURCHILL, who deed
Septr ye 21st 1754 in ye 72nd year of His Age.

No. 1659.

[Blue slate, moss-covered. Fair condition for so old a monument.
Face scaling off. Symbol.]

In memory of Mrs Hannah Churchill wife of Mr Eleazer Churchill who died Septr ye 19th 1757 in ye 67th year
of her age.

No. 1660.

[Purplish blue slate. Good condition, but moss-covered.]

Here lyes ye body of Mr Eleazar Churchell Deed March
ye 25th 1716 in ye 64th year of his age

No. 1661.

[Low, purplish blue slate. Good condition, but inclined. Symbol.]

Here lyes ye body of Mrs Mary Churchell wife to Mr
Eleazar Churchell aged 60 deces'd Decr ye 11th 1715.

No. 1662.

[Low, blue slate. Fair condition. Symbol.]

In Memory of Mr Edward Stephens who decd July ye 30th 1756 in the 77th year of his age.

No. 1663.

[Blue slate. Moss-covered. Right corner of surface scaled off, taking ends of lines. Symbol.]

Here lyes   body of M   Stephen wife   Stephens decd Jany ye 25th 1723-4 in ye 35th year of her age.

No. 1664.

[Blue slate. Moss-covered. Seamed and defaced. Symbol,]

In Memory of Mr EDWARD STEPHENS who died April 9, 1788 in ye 66th year of his age.

No. 1665.

[Blue slate. Four feet in height. Has some moss. Urn, with flowers on each side thereof.]

In memory of Mr ELKANAH CHURCHILL who was drowned at Sea October 17, 1804 in the 27th year of his age Also in memory of Mrs EUNICE his wife who died Nov. 1st 1803 in the 24th year of her age

Not blooming health nor beauty pleasing charmes
Can shield or save them from the Tyrants arms
God in his Unerring wisdom had designed a watery Grave to be my
    Tomb.

No. 1666.

[Low, blue slate. Moss-covered. Squared at top. Ornamented border.]

Zacheus son to Mr Stephen & Mrs Experience Churchill his wife decd Sepr ye 12th 1733 Aged 13 years 10 Mo & 19 days.

No. 1667.

[White marble, in granite socket. Good condition.]

BETSEY, widow of William Ellis, Died Oct. 19, 1868, aged 93 y'rs 3 mo's. WILLIAM Their Son Drowned Sept. 24, 1837, Aged 22 years.

No. 1668.

[Blue slate. Pyramidal. Good condition, save that a small piece has been broken from left hand corner at top. Festoons.]

In memory of Mrs Abigail Faunce wife of Capt Barnabas Faunce died July 15th 1805 in the 32d year of her age.

No. 1669.

[Blue slate. Pyramidal. Good condition. Festoons.]

In memory of Mrs Sarah Faunce wife of Capt Barnabas Faunce died July the 15th 1803 in the 35th year of her age

No. 1670.

[Blue slate. Good condition. Pyramidal in form. Urn.]

In memory of Mrs ZILPAH FAUNCE, Consort of Capt Barnabas Faunce died Sept. 17, 1837, in the 75 year of her age.

No. 1671.

[Purple slate. Good condition.]

Elizabeth Faunce widow of the late Capt. Barnabas Faunce, died Apr. 23, 1859 ; Æ. 85 years.

Blessed are they who die in the Lord.

No. 1672.

[Blue slate. Four and one-fourth feet in height. Good condition. Mausoleum.]

Erected In memory of BATHSHEBA, widow of the late Capt. Bartlett Sears, who departed this life Sept. 25th, 1852, aged 74 years.

No. 1673.

[Blue slate. Four and a half feet in height. Good condition. At top an eye, radiating; under which are square and compasses. Column on each side of square and compasses, with ball on summit of each column.]

Erected In memory of CAPT BARTLETT SEARS, who departed this life August 2, 1821, aged 45 years.

That once loved form now cold and dead,
Each mournful thought employs;
And nature mourns her comforts fled,
And withered all her joys.

No. 1674.

[Low, blue slate. Laminæ separating. Cleft across face. Symbol.]

Here lyes buried 4 Children of Mr Jesse Churchell & Mrs Abigal his wife Viz 1th Jesse born Novr 10th 1772 Aged 2 days 2d Abigal Worcester   rn June 25th 1778 Aged 2 Months   2 days 3d Abigal born March 23d 1782 dec'd July 24th 1783 4th David born July 30, 1784 died Jany 11 1788.

No. 1675.

[Blue slate. Good condition. Urn under drapery.]

To The memory of Miss Hannah Churchill Daughter of Cap Jesse Churchill and Mrs Abigail his wife who died Nov. 6, 1811 In the 23 year of her age

All you that do behold my stone
Consider how soon I was gone,
Death does not always warning give,
Therefore be cautious how you live,
Prepare in time, no time delay,
I in my youth was call'd away.

No. 1676.

[White marble in granite socket. Good condition.]

FATHER & MOTHER. CAPT. SETH MORTON, Died April 12, 1844, Aged 69 y'rs 8 mo's, MERCY, His wife Died April 10, 1872, aged 96 y'rs.

No. 1677.

[Blue slate. Good condition. Urn.]

Sacred to the memory of *JAMES MORTON* who died Jan. 18, 1838 aged 31 y'rs.

> Tis but at most a short farewell,
> We bid to those we fondly love,
> Soon death will summons us to dwell,
> With them in brighter spheres above.

No. 1678.

[Blue slate. Four and one-half feet in height. A seam extends diagonally across the centre of the stone. Two urns.]

Erected to the memory of WILLIAM MORTON, who died Nov. 2, 1834 in the 32d. year of his age And to HENRY MORTON who died March 3, 1840, in the 25th. year of his age.

> To weep for those with heart sincere,
> And in their graves to drop the tear,
> Revives their memory—calls from the tomb
> Their life, their love, their early doom
> Yet while we weep, we can rejoice
> In those who make of heaven their choice.

No. 1679.

[Blue slate. Good condition. Urn.]

In memory of Mrs Mercy Morton wife of Mr Seth Morton who Died Aug. 24, 1806 in the 72 year of her age.

> My flesh shall slumber in the ground,
> Till the last trumpet's joyful sound,
> Then burst the chains with sweet surprise,
> And in my Saviour's image rise.

No. 1680.

[Low, blue slate. Defaced. One wing of symbol remains.]

In memory of Mr SETH MORTON who died April J7 J789 in the 54 year of his age.

No. 1681.

[White marble in freestone socket. Much inclined. Cement gone. Rough.]

OUR FATHER WHO ART IN HEAVEN. ANTIPAS BRIGHAM Died Aug. 6, 1832 Aged 33 years.

Mercy Sampson his widow Aged 92 years.

No. 1682.

[Blue slate. Moss-grown. Weeping willow and urn.]

To the memory of Mercy M. Brigham, Dau. of Antipas Brigham and Mercy his wife Died June 15, 1827, aged 9 mo. and 5 days.

> Sleep, lovely babe thy toils are o'er
> The choisest comforts of her parents
> That GOD of love has called her home
> Why do we weep, why do we mourn.

No. 1683.

[White marble obelisk, on marble plinth. Granite base. Eight feet in height. Good condition.]

JOHN BATTLES born Feb. 26, 1778, died Sept. 20, 1855, ELIZABETH his wife died Sept. 29, 1800, Aged 23 yrs. 5 mo's. LYDIA wife of John Battles, died April 20, 1865, Aged 86 y'rs 3 mo's.

(On plinth:)

BATTLES.

No. 1684.

[Blue slate. Compact and sound. Symbol.]

Here lies the Body of Mrs Elizabeth Battles the wife of Mr John Battles who died Sepr the 29th 1800 aged 23 years And 5 months.

[A marble slab set in front of this stone, prevents reading the epitaph.]

No. 1685.

[Blue slate. Defaced in part. Moss-grown. Seamed. Inclined. Symbol.]

Here lyes ye Body of Mrs Rebekah Drew wife to Mr Nicholas Drew who decd Novbr 1729 in ye   of her age.

No. 1686.

[Similar to preceding.]

Here lyes ye Body of Mrs Lydia Drew wife to Mr Nicholas Drew decd   173

No. 1687 a.

[White marble. Rough. Disintegrating.]

HEMAN CHURCHILL died Mar 22, 1840, in his 69 yr. Also Jane his widow died April 2, 1848, in her 73 yr.

> Why do we mourn departing friends
> Or shake at death's alarm?
> 'Tis but the voice that Jesus sends,
> To call us to his arms.

No. 1687 b.

[Fine white marble block.]

Mary A. Churchill Died Jan. 22, 1889 Aged 72 years

No. 1688.

Erected To the memory of LEMUEL B. CHURCHILL,
who died Dec 30, 1833 aged 23 yrs. 2 mo's & 17 days
Son of Heman & Jane Churchill Also six children viz
HEMAN died Oct. 1, 1802, Aged 3 years & 11 mos.
JANE died June 11, 1808, Aged 7 years & 3 mos. HE- ·
MAN, died April 26, 1808, Aged 2 years & 3 mos.
JANE H died April 26 1812, Aged 2 years 3 mos. & 25
days.

Two sons in their Infancy.

> "Sweet is the thought, the promise sweet
> Thai friends long sever'd friends shall meet
> That kindred souls on earth disjoin'd
> Shall meet from earthly dross refined
> Their mortal cares and sorrows o'er
> Shall mingle hearts to part no more.

No. 1689.

[Purplish blue slate. Four and 3-4 feet high. Good condition.]

In memory of Deacon Solomon Churchill, who died at
Perry, Ohio, April 10, 1835, aged 73 years: And of
Elizabeth his wife (whose remains rest here) deceased
Oct. 20, 1811 aged 45 years.

No. 1690.

[Blue slate. Fair condition, but moss-grown. Weeping willow and
urn.]

In memory of Mr Thomas Bartlett who departed this
life Sep. 17, 1808 in the 67 year of his age.

No. 1691.

[Blue slate. Good condition. Weeping willow and urn.]

In memory of Mrs. Elisabeth Bartlett wife of Thomas
Bartlett who departed this life Sep. 20, 1779 in the 59 year
of her age.

No. 1692.

[Blue slate. Broken. Part of symbol remains.]

To the memory of Mrs Mary Hill wife of Mr Jonathan
Hill who died Novbr 14th 1795 in the 42d year of her age.

No. 1693.

[Purplish blue slate. Seamed at top centre a few inches downward.
Festoons.]

CAPT. ELEAZAR MORTON Died June 5, 1823, Æ.
69 y'rs JEMIMA his wife died Feb'y 26, 1823, Æ. 60
y'rs Also eight children Lazarus S. was lost at Sea Dec.
1800 Æ. 22 y'rs Eleazar Jr. William, Zephaniah, Amasa,
Jemima, Jerusha, Jane.

No. 1694.
[White marble. Set in granite. Whole mass falling backward.]
JACOB T. MORTON Died May 4, 1871, Aged 88 y'rs.
LYDIA, His wife Died May 15, 1838, Aged 53 y'rs.

No. 1695.
[White marble. Four feet in height. Rough and moss-grown.]
Erected in memory of PHEBE FINNEY wife of Capt.
Ephraim Finney died Sept. 26, 1847, aged 64 yrs & 7 mo.

No. 1696.
[Blue slate. Good condition. Weeping willow and urn.]
This Stone is erected to the memory of twin children of
Ephraim Finney and Phebe his wife who were born Octr
27, 1822, Elizabeth died March 10, 1823, Ezra died Sep-
tember 14, 1823.
> My friends behold what death has done
> Taken these babes when they were young
> Prepare to live prepare to die
> Prepare for long Eternity.

No. 1697.
[Low, white marble. Ornamental design at top.]
Caroline E. Bartlett Daughter of John & Eliza Bartlett,
died Aug. 4, 1830, aged 4 months.
> The Babe shall live and bloom again.

No. 1698.
[White marble block. On marble plinth. Granite base. Good con-
dition but inclined. Rose.]
(On upper surface:)
Alice.
(On obverse:)
Alice A. Neal, Dau. of Samuel and Alice A. Brown,
Died April 7, 1859, Aged 29 yrs. 7 mos. 2 ds.

No. 1699.
[Blue slate. Good condition. Flaming urn.]
ABIA, widow of Capt. William Pearson died April 21,
1847, aged 84 years.

No. 1700.
[Blue slate. Good condition. Three pointed domes.]
To the memory of CAPT. WILLIAM PEARSON who died
Nov. 25, 1831, aged 72 years.
> A true Patriot & A Hero of the Revolution.

No. 1701.
[Blue slate. Fair condition, but moss-grown. Symbol.]
In Memory of Stephen son of Mr William Pearson &
Mrs Mercy his wife who died Sepr ye 10th 1781 in ye 2d
year of his Age.

No. 1702.

[Blue slate. Four feet in height. Good condition. Weeping willow and urn.]

In memory of Mr THOMAS FISH who Died September 29th 1806 in the 25th year of his Age.

No. 1703.

[Blue slate. Good condition. Weeping willow and urn.]

 This monument is erected to the memory of Cap. Jeremiah Holbrook who departed this life April 18, 1815 aged 31 years Also in memory of Lucy Holbrook daughter of Jeremiah Holbrook and Bethiah his wife died June 7 1814 aged 10 months.

No. 1704.

[Blue slate. Good condition.]

BETHIAH widow of Jeremiah Holbrook, died May 26, 1835 : Aged 48 yrs. Also two infant Children.

No. 1705.

[Low, blue slate. Fair condition. Symbol.]

In Memory of Mrs Sarah Churchill wife of Mr. Samuel Churchill who died June 26 1791 in ye 40 year of her age. Also in memory of their son who was born June 5th 1786 died the same day.

No. 1706.

[Blue slate. Good condition. Urn.]

In memory of *Mr Samuel Churchill* who died Dec. 15, 1810, aged 57 years

He was a good neighbour a kind Husband a tender Parent

No. 1707.

[Blue slate. Good condition. Urn.]

ELIZABETH widow of Samuel Churchill died July 7th, 1839, in the 83d year of her age.

No. 1708.

[White marble. Discolored. Inclined.]

ELISABETH wife of Edward Burt died Nov. 13, 1852, Æ. 54 yrs & 2 mos.

No. 1709.

[Similar to preceding.]

EDWARD BURT died July 6, 1861, Æ. 66 yrs & 10 mos. THOMAS B. son of Edward & Elisebeth Burt died at Harwood Hospital Washington D. C. Oct. 31, 1862 ; Æ. 23 yrs & 9 mos. A Member of Co. E, 29 Reg. Mass. Vols.

No. 1710.

[Blue slate. Good condition. Urn.]

In Memory of Mrs Eunice, widow of Elijah Dunham, died Oct. 31, 1831 in the 78 yr of her age.

No. 1711.

[Blue slate. Good condition. Weeping willow and urn. Upon the urn are the initials E. D.]

In memory of Mr Elijah Dunham who died Augt 11th 1827. aged 74 years

My flesh while buried in the dust
Jesus shall be thy care
These withering limbs with thee I trust
To raise them strong and fair.

No. 1712.

[Blue slate. Fair condition. Two urns.]

In memory of two children of Abraham & Patience Dunham Abraham died May 10 1818 aged 2 years & 5 months. Elizabeth C. Dunham died May 11 1818 aged 4 years & 24 days.

No. 1713.

[White marble, in freestone socket. Fair condition.]

Father and Mother ABRAHAM T. DUNHAM died Aug 28, 1847, Aged 60 y'rs Patience, his widow Died Sept 23, 1870, Aged 73 y'rs 9 mo's.

No. 1714.

[White marble on granite base. Fair condition.]

FATHER & MOTHER. ISAAC TRIBBLE, Born July 31, 1789, Died Feb. 16. 1865. LOIS TRIBBLE, Born Dec. 14, 1788, Died Mar. 31, 1860.

No. 1715.

[White marble. In stone socket. Figure of obelisk at top.]

In memory of Gideon H. Son of Isaac & Lois Tribble, Born March 3, 1813 Died Dec. 19, 1855, aged 42 y'rs 9 mo's & 16 days.

No. 1716.

[Blue slate. Good condition. Inscription in urn-shaped space.]

In memory of Augustus, Son of Isaac & Lois Tribble Born July 5, 1816, Died Dec. 20, 1820.

No. 1717.

[Blue slate. Pyramidal. Good condition. Weeping willow and urn.]

To the memory of Miss Sally Holbrook Daughter of Capt Gideon Holbrook and Mrs Sally his wife who Died August 29, 1809 in the 18th year of her age.

No. 1718.

[Blue slate. Good condition. Inscribed in figure of urn raised on the stone.]

In memory of Isaac, son of Isaac & Lois Tribble, Born July 26, 1830, Died April 12, 1836.

No. 1719.

[White marble in granite socket. Fair condition.]

CHARITY S. wife of Stephen D. Drew. Died Jan. 25, 1868, Aged 44 y'rs.

No. 1720.

[White marble. Fair condition.]

LEWIS W. PERRY, died Oct. 30, 1851, in his 28th y'r Also LEWIS F. son of Lewis W. & Charity, S. Perry died Mar. 29, 1852, aged 7 Mon.

No. 1721.

[Blue slate. Good condition.]

In memory of MOSES HOYT, died Jan. 23d 1851, aged 71 y'rs. Also two Son's viz. MOSES, died in Peru, Ill. Oct. 3d, 1838, in his 30th yr. OTIS died Jan. 19th, 1851, in his 28th yr.

No. 1722.

[White marble. Granite socket. Fair condition.]

BETSEY, Widow of Moses Hoyt, Died Jan. 3, 1879 ; Aged 88 y'rs 4 mo's. CROSBY their son Died Sept. 23, 1857, Aged 42 y'rs.

No. 1723.

[Blue slate. About 4 feet by 2 1-2. A fracture extends across and through it, from upper left to lower right hand corner, dividing the stone into two nearly equal parts.]

In Memory of CAPT. EZRA FINNEY who was Lost at Sea in the winter of 1780, aged 37 yrs. Also Mrs. HANNAH, his wife who died June 17, 1811, aged 64 yrs.

No. 1724.

[White marble. Fair condition.]

Abigail, widow of Henry Hollis, died Sept. 27, 1859, aged 63 y'rs.

" Whosoever liveth and believeth in Me shall never die."
John 11-26.

No. 1725.

[White marble. Fair condition.]

Erected to the memory of HENRY HOLLIS, who died Mar. 9, 1838, aged 45 y'rs.

No. 1726.

[Purplish blue slate. Good condition. Weeping willow and urn.]

In memory of Elizabeth Owen Daughter of Henry and Abigail Hollis, died January 30, 1825, aged 3 years & 5 months

> Alas her tuneful warbling breath
> Is hushed forever, hushed in death
> And that still heart within the bier
> Can feel not e'en a parent's tear.

No. 1727.

[White marble. Fair condition.]

To the memory of THos. LEONARD, lost at sea, on a voyage from Martinique to Plymouth, Jan. 19, 1803, aged 32 yr's. Also his wife SALLY, who died Dec. 22, 1834, aged 67 yr's.

No. 1728.

[Blue slate. Three and a half by 3 feet. Fair condition, but shows seams.]

This Stone is erected to the memory of CAPT. ELIPHALET HOLBROOK who died Febry 7 1815 Aged 70 years.

> What is the life of man, with all his cares,
> Tis like a shade which quickly disappears,
> But if that taper GOD allows to men ;
> Continue burning threescore years and ten
> Yet when 'tis spent and death puts out its light
> 'Tis like a tale thats told a watch by night.

No. 1729.

[Purplish blue slate. Good condition. Weeping willow and tomb.]

In Memory of NANCY, wife of Benjamin Holmes 2d died August 29th, 1839, in the 27th y'r of her age.

No. 1730.

[White marble. Has left its stone socket, and been set in the ground.]

CATHERINE, wife of James T. Paulding, died May 7, 1872, aged 46 y'rs 6 mo's.

No. 1731.

[Similar to preceding No.]

OUR MOTHER. MARY A. wife of Joshua Pratt, Died Mar. 25, 1869. Aged 55 y'rs 5 m'os. Also three infant Children.

> It hath heard the angel welcome
> Met the friends who've passed before
> Robed itself in light and beauty
> On the radiant spirit shore
>
> There it lives to watch and guide us
> On our path to shed a light
> Walk an angel form beside us
> Through the shadows of the night.

No. 1732.

[Purplish blue slate. Good condition.]

Our Father. JOSHUA PRATT, died March 17, 1869, aged 87 y'rs 5 mo's. Also his wife ELENER BOYSE, Died May 1829, Aged 45 y'rs.

God calls our loved ones but we lose not wholly
what he has given
They live on earth in thought and deed as truly
as in heaven.

No. 1733.

[White marble. Rough. Discolored.]

BETSEY M. wife of Lloyd Keith of Bridgewater, and dau. of Israel Hoyt of Plymouth, Died June 7, 1847, in the 22d yr of her age

God lent us the flower and now doth reclaim
The exotic in radiant bloom
In love from our Father the reaper Death came
And exhaled the spirits perfume

The casket is all that is left us below
The gem that it bore lives above
While mem'ry its incense around us doth throw
As we guard this dear spot with our love.

No. 1734.

[Similar to preceding No.]

Sacred to the memory of ISRAEL HOYT, who died May 6, 1842, Aged 53 y'rs Also BETSEY M dau. of Israel & Ruth Hoyt died June 6, 1824, aged 3 yr's.

No. 1735.

[White marble. Rough. Discolored.]

SACRED to the memory of RUTH, widow of Israel Hoyt, died Aug. 10, 1859, Aged 60 yr's.

No. 1736.

[Blue slate. At top a device of some unknown structure.]

Erected In memory of SARAH, wife of Joseph R. Peckham, who died June 29, 1834, in her 34 yr.

No. 1737.

[Grayish stone.]

EUNICE STURTEVANT died May 10, 1843 ; aged 15 years. SAMUEL DREW was lost at sea Feb. 1, 1857 ; aged 18 years. Children of Perkins & Elizabeth Raymond.

That gentle one has passed away
No more to roam with us below ;
And gone to realms of brighter day,
Where storms of woe shall cease to flow
Where'er our eyes do chance to fall,
We find some relic left behind

That will her feeble form recall
And bring her peaceful voice to mind
Then we'll not wish her back again,
But think she's happy now on high
No more to strive with earthly pain
No more to weep and groan and die
And as we ne'er can meet below
Our only wish & prayer shall be
That when far hence we're called to go,
We may in heaven her spirit see.

No. 1738.

[Grayish stone.]

NAOMI, died Dec. 7, 1837 aged 9 mo. & 18 ds.
HORACE, died March 4, 1841 aged 6 Mo. & 9 ds. Children of Edward & Julia Seymour.

No. 1739.

[Blue slate. Four by 2 1-2 feet. Good condition. Weeping willow
and urn.]

Erected to the memory of ELEANOR HOWARD consort of the late JOHN HOWARD, who died Oct. 12, 1826 ; aged 75 years. Also to the memory of CAPT JOHN HOWARD who was lost at Sea March 1788 : aged 43 years.

No. 1740.

[Blue slate. Fair condition, but moss-grown. Weeping willow and
urn.]

In memory of John W. Howard Son of Capt. James Howard & Mrs. Hannah his wife born March 20, 1815 died April 2. 1815

He glanc'd into the world to see
A sample of our misery.

No. 1741.

[Blue slate. Good condition. Weeping willow and urn.]

In memory of Capt. *James Howard* who departed this Life at St. Martin's West Indies June the 15 1818, aged 41 years

Life what a fleeting hour it is
How swift our moments fly
Here today we draw our breath,
But soon we groan and die.

No. 1742.

[Blue slate. Four by 2 1-2 feet. Good condition. Urn.]

In Memory of *James H. Howard*, who returned to his friends from Eastport, Me. June 2 after an absence of several years on account of feeble health, died Aug. 7, 1832 ; aged 24 yr,s & 9 mo,s.

His mind was tranquil and serene,
No terrors in his looks were seen,
His saviour's smiles dispelled the gloom
And smoothed the passage to the tomb

No. 1743.

[Blue slate. Good condition. Weeping willow and urn.]

Erected in memory of Mr. SETH RIDER, who died Janu 21, 1826 ; in the 82 year of his age. Also in memory of Mrs HANNAH RIDER, his wife who died Sept 26, 1814 ; in the 60 year of her age

> Our age to seventy years is set,
> How short the term, how frail the state!
> And if to eighty we arrive,
> We rather sigh and groan than live.

No. 1744.

[Handsome white marble, in white marble socket.]

BETSEY ROBBINS, Died March 22, 1839, Aged 51 years. SALLIE CURTIS, Died Sept. 10, 1839. Aged 11 years JESSE ROBBINS. Died June 3, 1855, Aged 74 years.

No. 1745.

[Blue slate. Fair condition.]

DORCAS, wife of Ephraim Morton, died June 12, 1838 ; in the 54th yr. of her age. Also their dau. tr Dorcas died Oct,r 16, 1806 aged 3 yr.s.

(Stone set so deep that the months and days could not be easily ascertained.)

No. 1746.

[White marble. Cemented in freestone socket. Good condition.]

JOHN S. PAINE, Died Sept. 29, 1878 ; aged 89 y'rs 7 mo's 24 days. SUSAN B. Dau of John S. & Susan W. Paine, Died Oct. 19. 1835 : Aged 4 mo's.

No. 1747.

[Blue slate. Good condition. Weeping willow and urn.]

In memory of Deborah Paine wife of John S. Paine, Died October 10, 1818 ; aged 27 years. Daughter of John S. & Deborah Paine died March 2, 1818 aged 6 months.

No. 1748.

[White marble. Granite socket. Brimstone for cement. Good condition.]

SUSAN W. PAINE Born Aug. 8, 1804, Died Dec. 16, 1882, Aged 78 y'rs, 4 ms. 8 days.

No. 1749.

[Blue slate. Good condition, save seam across surface. Weeping willow and urn.]

In memory of Mrs. MARY ROBERTSON wife of Capt DAVID ROBERTSON and Daughter of Capt DAVID

CORNISH and MERCY, his wife who died Augt 12th 1825 ; in the 26 year of her age
> Her happy spirit sighed
> To leave these wastes of woe
> To join the Ransom,d Church above
> And full fruition know.

No. 1750.
[White marble, Discolored.]

HANNAH ELLIS, wife of Joseph W. Burgess, died Aug. 11, 1850, in her 34th yr. also 4 Infant Children.
> Mourn not for her ye who below
> Beneath the afflictive stroke are bending,
> For your loved one has gone to know
> A bliss above which has no ending.

No. 1751.
[Blue slate. Moss-grown. Willow.]

In Memory of ELISHA LAPHAM, died March 8, 1837 ; aged 19 yrs. 6 mo. ELIZA ANN, died Nov. 17, 1824 : Aged 10 mo. ELIZA ANN, died Nov. 20, 1823 : aged 1 year 2 mo. Children of Elisha & Mary Lapham.

No. 1752.
[Low, white marble. Discolored. Difficult to read.]

Jerome W. died May 6, 1853. Aged 6 y'rs & 6 mo. Mary E. died Sept. 22d 1846 Aged 1 y,r & 10 mo. Children of William & Lydia C. Purington.
> These buds were pluck
> ed before half blown,
> Because thare maker
> Call'd them home.

No. 1753.
[Marble obelisk, marble plinth, granite base. About 7 ft. high.]
(On South side:)

FREDERIC HOLMES, Lieut. 38 Mass. Vol. Infantry, aged 28 years. was killed June 14, 1863, while leading his men to the assault on the enemy's works at Port Hudson, La.
(On East side;)
His memory shall not be less green, nor his heroic virtues less honored that his body lies amid the ruins of the Rebellion he gave his life to destroy.

No. 1754.
[White marble obelisk, about 7 1-2 feet high. Marble plinth, granite base. Protected by iron inclosure. Good condition. On summit figure of large book.]
(On East side:)

Dea. JOSIAH ROBBINS died Jan. 30, 1859 : Aged 72 years 10 mo.

(On South side:)
MRS. EXPERIENCE wife of Dea. Josiah Robbins, born Sept. 22, 1789, died Feb. 11, 1807.

PELLA MORTON ROBBINS born Feb. 3, 1807, died March 3, 1811.

Mrs. ANN G. wife of Dea. Josiah Robbins, died Sept. 6, 1817, Aged 29 years.

JOSIAH ADAMS died August 24, 1816, Æ 7 m's.

ANN G. CUSHMAN died Sept. 19, 1817, Aged 6 weeks.

(On West side:)
PELLA M. ROBBINS born March 29, 1815, died June 4, 1889.

(On North side:)
Mrs. REBECCA JACKSON, wife of Dea. Josiah Robbins, died Oct. 19, 1850, Aged 61 years & 26 days.

REBECCA J. ROBBINS born Nov 5, 1819, died Jan. 31, 1820.

ANN CUSHMAN born Jan. 16, 1825, died July 11, 1825.

No. 1755.

[Low, white marble. Marble plinth. Freestone socket. Discolored. This and the following Nos. to 1762 inclusive are inclosed in wooden paling.]

SARAH FRENCH, only daughter of John B. & Sarah A. E. Russell, died Jan. 13, 1863, aged 3 years 7 mos. 26 days.

She has gone to heaven before us
But she turns and waves her hand
Pointing to the glories o'er us,
In that happy Spirit land

No. 1756.

[White marble, in broken socket. Fair condition. Crucifix.]

ELIZABETH B. only daughter of Bridgham & Betsey F. RUSSELL, died May 7, 1856, aged 27 y'rs & 3 mos.

May her dear memory serve to make
Our faith in goodness strong.

No. 1757.

[White marble, in stone socket. Fair condition.]

BETSEY FARRIS RUSSELL wife of Bridgham Russell, Died March 3, 1866, Aged 72 years.

A devoted wife, a fond mother, a kind and sympathizing friend to all in distress or affliction.

No. 1758.

[White marble, in freestone socket. Discolored. Moss-grown.]

BRIDGHAM RUSSELL died March 29th, 1840; aged 47 years

The many excelences of his character in public and private life—endeared him to an extensive acquaintance, who will long cherish his virtuous memory Blest thought; he is not lost But gone before us.

No. 1759.

[Blue slate. Good condition. Weeping willow and urn.]

Departed this life May 24, 1833; in the 74th yr of her age Mrs. REBECCA RUSSELL Relict of Jonathan Russell, late of Barnstable. .

No. 1760.

[Purplish blue slate. Good condition. Festoons.]

In remembrance of Miss BETSEY RUSSELL, who resigned this life Novr 3d 1820, aged 30 years.

No. 1761.

[Blue slate. Good condition.]

In Remembrance of Miss MERCY RUSSELL, who resigned this life March 2, 1837, aged 50 years.

No. 1762.

.[White marble. Marble plinth, granite base. Good condition.]

REBECCA RUSSELL Died Aug. 26, 1876, aged 76 y'rs 1 mo. 13 days.

No. 1763.

[Low, white marble, much discolored. Inclined. In wooden paling. Stone loose and movable. Rose twig, with bud broken off.]

GEORGE AUGUSTUS, son of Simon R. & Jane E. Burgess, died July 31, 1851 Æ. 9 y'rs 3 mo.

No. 1764.

[A structure divided into six tombs. The year of its erection, 1833, appears plainly in the centre of the front. Over the doors of four of these tombs are inscribed severally the words:]

"Town," "Finney," "Barnes," "Stephens."

No. 1765.

[White marble. Granite base. Good condition.]

BETSEY HOLMES Died Sept. 5, 1874, Aged 86 years.

Died in Faith.

No. 1766.

[Blue slate. Firm and compact.]

ABIGAIL ROGERS died Oct. 7, 1838, aged 86 yrs Consort of SAMUEL ROGERS, who died at sea July 1795 aged 42 yrs.

[Low, blue slate. Weatherworn. Somewhat defaced. Symbol.]

To the memory of Deborah Daughter of Mr William Harlow & Mrs Sarah his wife who died Dec. 23d 1775.

No. 1768.

[White marble. In stone socket. Fair condition.]

GEORGE E. CHASE, died 1824 ; Æ. 15 years Wm CHASE died 1830 ; Æ. 23 years SAMUEL R. CHASE died Aug. 21, 1849 ; Æ. 20 years & 5 mos. HENRY CHASE died July 1860 ; Æ. 43 years. Sons of John & Abigail Chase.

No. 1769.

[White marble. Set in stone block. Fair condition.]

JOHN CHASE Died Dec. 15, 1855: Æ. 74 years ABIGAIL, his wife Died Sept. 17, 1872 : aged 89 yrs 4 mo's.

No. 1770.

[Handsome blue slate. Good condition. Symbol.]

Here lyes buried the Body of DEACON JOHN FOSTER who departed this life Dec. ye 24th 1741 in ye 76th year of his age.

No. 1771.

[Similar to preceding.]

Here lyes buried the Body of Mrs HANNAH FOSTER the wife of DEACON JOHN FOSTER Died April ye 30th 1747, in the 77th year of her age.

No. 1772.

[Low, blue slate. Weatherworn. Moss-grown. Symbol.]

Here lyes ye body of GERSHEM FOSTER who decd July ye 11th 1733 in ye 25th year of his age.

No. 1773.

[Low, blue slate. Surface above inscription scaled off.]

Here lyes ye Body of Mr JOHN FOSTER Jur who dyed April ye 26th 1723 and aged 22 years.

No. 1774.

[Blue slate. Pyramidal. Four and a half feet in height. Good condition. Flaming urn.]

In memory of ELLIS HOLMES died Oct. 18, 1854, in his 88th yr.

No. 1775.

[Similar to preceding.]

GRACE, wife of Ellis Holmes, died March 30, 1839, aged 71 years. Also POLLY their Dau. died Sept. 7, 1813, aged 22 mon.

No. 1776.

[White marble. Marble plinth. Freestone base. Good condition.]

SOPHIA B. wife of Pelham Whiting, Died Sept. 4, 1866, Aged 41 years.

No. 1777.

[Blue slate. Top broken off, and gone. Several seams across the stone, in a direction parallel to the break.]

The memory of Mr Benjamin Morton died April 9, 1816 aged 53 years Their son Joseph Morton died August 24, 1795 aged 1 year and 5 months.

No. 1778.

[Blue slate. Good condition. Festoons.]

To the memory of Mrs REBEKAH HOLMES Consort of Capt ICHABOD HOLMES who died July 25th 1803 in the 75th year of her age.

No. 1779.

[Blue slate. Fair condition, but seamed on the left, above the name. Weeping willow and urn.]

In memory of CAPT ICHABOD HOLMES who was Born February 17, 1725 died April 10, 1817 aged 92 years.

No. 1780.

[Blue slate. Sound and compact. Figure of vessel at sea, upper spars gone; angel above, blowing a trumpet.]

In memory of Capt Chandler Holmes Jr who died October 4, 1831, aged 27 years.

He spoke the meaning of his heart
Nor slandered with his tongue
Would scarce believe an ill report
Nor do his neighbor wrong.

No. 1781.

[Blue slate. Good condition. Three symbols.]

To the memory of 3 Children of Ichabod Holmes & Rebekah his wife 1st a son Ichabod died August 26, 1784 aged 11 days 2d a daughter Rebekah died Novr 13, 1786 aged 2 months & 14 days 3d a son Ichabod Died Janry 13 1799 aged 17 months.

Fresh in the morn the summer rose
Hangs withered ere the noon
We scarce enjoy the balmy gift
But mourn the pleasure gone.

No. 1782.

[White marble in freestone socket. Weathering rough. This and the next two Nos. are inclosed in granite curbing.]

CAPT WILLIAM SHERMAN, died at sea, Jan. 9, 1796 : aged 32 years Elizabeth Sherman, his wife died Oct. 9, 1849 : aged 83 years, 10 months.

God calls our loved ones but we
lose not wholly
What he hath given
They live on earth in thought and
deed, as truly
As in His Heaven.

No. 1783.

[Beautiful, mottled marble. Marble plinth. Granite base.]

ELIZABETH. wife of Isaac Sampson, Born June 19,
1795 : Died February 22, 1881.

No. 1784.

[Blue slate. Four and one-half feet high. Good condition save
a seam just below the urn.]

In memory of ISAAC SAMPSON : who died May 7,
1832 ; aged 42 yrs. Also ISAAC, son of Isaac & Elizabeth Sampson died Dec, r, 11, 1833 ; Aged 3 yrs & 8
mo.s.

"How vain is all beneath the skies,
How transient every earthly bliss,
How slender all the fondest ties
That binds us to a world like this.

"Then let the hope of joys to come
Dispel our cares and chase our fears,
If God be ours we're travelling home
Though passing through a vale of tears."

No. 1785.

[Blue slate. Good condition. Mausoleum.]

Erected to the memory of William Barnes, who died
Dec. 29th 1831, aged 66 years.

"Immortality o'ersweeps
All pains, all tears, all time, all fears—
and peals
Like the eternal thunders of the deep,
Into my ears this truth, Thou liv'st
forever."

No. 1786.

[Blue slate. Good condition. Urn.]

Erected in memory of MERCY, widow of William
Barnes, who died April 21, 1849, in the 79 y.r of her age.

No. 1787.

[Low, blue slate. Fair condition. Symbol.]

Here lyes buried the Body of Mr WILLIAM BARNES
who died March ye 31st 1751 in the 81st Year of his Age.

No. 1788.

[Blue slate. Four and one-fourth feet high. Good condition.
Weeping willow and urn.]

Erected August 22, 1824 In memory of Joseph Barnes
who died in Cape Francois January 25, 1795 Aged 58

years Hannah Barnes Widow of the above died November 12, 1815 Aged 76 years Hannah Harlow wife of Zacheus Harlow & Daughter of the above died December 26, 1807 aged 47 years Also Nathaniel Barnes who died in Martinico July 9, 1794 aged 23 years.

No. 1789.
[White marble. Rough.]

SILVANUS ROGERS Born Nov. 24, 1798 Died April 20, 1860 Æ. 62 yrs & 7 mos. JANE ROGERS his wife Born Jan. 2, 1800 Died Sept. 15, 1861, Æ. 61 y'rs & 8 mos. Also their daughter Jane F. Born Jan. 4, 1824 Died Sept. 12, 1825 Æ. 1 year 8 mos.

"There is rest in Heaven."

No. 1790.
[Low, blue slate. Fair condition, but inclined. Symbol.]

In Memory of Mrs Polly Holmes wife of Joseph Holmes who died July 3, 1794 aged 26 years.

Death is a debt to nature due
Which I have paid & so must you.

No. 1791.
[Purple slate. Moss-covered, but in fairly good condition yet. Symbol.]

Here lyes ye body of Mrs Sarah Barnes Aged about 32 years decd April ye JJth J7J8.

No. 1792.
[Blue slate. Good condition.]

BETSEY, Daughter of John & Lucy Burbank, died Aug. 18th, 1839, aged 10 years & 1 mo.

Her mother's hopes of earthly joys are flown;
Oh! who can tell her grief so reft and lone!
Her lovely daughter, late her sole delight,
For whom she lived no more can bless her sight.

No. 1793.
[Blue slate. Good condition.]

AMY ALLEN, Daughter of John & Lucy Burbank, died June 6th, 1838 ; aged 2 years.

As the sweet flower that scents the morn,
But withers in the rising day
Thus lovely was the infant's dawn
Thus swiftly fled its life away.

No. 1794.
[Blue slate. Good condition.]

In memory of MR. JOHN BURBANK JR. who died Nov. 30th, 1835, aged 40 years.

Behold I die, but GOD shall be with you.

22

No. 1795.

[Blue slate. Four and three-fourths feet high. Good condition. Flaming urn.]

Erected to the memory of JOHN BURBANK, who died Sept. 26th, 1825, in the 56 th y.r of his age. *Also* LYDIA, widow of the above who died March 20th, 1842, Aged 70 years.

No. 1796.

[Blue slate. Broken; about 1-5 of the stone being separated from the larger portion by a cleft. Urn.]

In memory of Mrs HANNAH BURBANK the wife of Mr. NEHEMIAH BURBANK who departed this life Aug. 7, 1811 in the 32 year of her age. Also their infant Daniel Torrey who died January 21, 1805 aged two months.

Peace peace no murmur tis the will of GOD
That GOD who orders all things for the best.

No. 1797.

[Blue slate. Seamed. Urn.]

This Stone is erected to the memory of Mr Nehemiah Burbank who died February 8, 1814 in the 37 year of his age.

'Tis GOD who lifts our comforts high
Or sink them in the grave.
He gave, and (blessed be his name)
He takes but what he gave.

No. 1798.

[Blue slate. Good condition. Flaming urn.]

ERECTED to the memory of Miss. POLLY BURBANK who died Aug. 23d 1842, aged 70 years.

No. 1799.

[Blue slate. Fair condition. Symbol.]

To the memory of Mr EZRA BURBANK who died Feby 25th 1800 aged 62 years.

No. 1800.

[Low, blue slate. Moss-covered, but sound. Symbol.]

In memory of Mr BENJAMIN BARNES son of Mr William Barnes He decd Aprl ye 12th 1760 in the 43 year of his age

No. 1801.

[Blue slate. Compact and sound. Symbol.]

Mr TIMOTHY BURBANK died Octbr 13th 1793 Ætatis 90 Mrs MERCY his wife died Janry 27th 1771, Ætatis 63 and here lie interred

No. 1802.

[Blue slate. Fair condition. Curious figure of Time, standing still, scythe in right hand, hour-glass in left.]

Here lies the Body of Bathsheba Drew wife to Mr Nicolas Drew who departed this life June ye 8th AD 1767 Aged 55 Years & 3 Months

No. 1803.

[Blue slate. Good condition. Flaming urn, with flowers on each side.]

To Perpetuate the memory of Mr SAMUEL BARNES who died September 25th 1803 in the 25th year of his age

No. 1804.

[This and the three following numbers are white marble, each with marble plinth on granite base; all in good condition, and protected by a granite curbing.]

LUCY, Wife of Ivory Harlow, died Oct, 18, 1872, Aged 88 y'rs 10 mo's.

(On reverse:)

MOTHER.

No. 1805.

IVORY HARLOW, died Nov. 2, 1813, in the 30th year of his age.

(On reverse:)

FATHER.

No. 1806.

Benjamin Goddard, Born March 3, 1813, Died Oct. 15, 1875. ANN E. Goddard, Born Sept. 1, *1841*, Died Aug. 3, 1842.

Beloved ones rest in peace.

(On reverse:)

HUSBAND.

No. 1807.

LUCY, Wife of Benjamin Goddard, Born Jan. 10, 1814, Died July 24, 1877,

Gone home to enjoy the promised rest.

(On reverse:)

WIFE.

No. 1808.

[Low, blue slate. Laminæ separating. Defaced. Part of symbol remains.]

In Memory of Abner Son to Mr Ebenezer Rider & Mrs Sarah his wife born June ye 20th 1760 Decd Augst ye 19th 1765

No. 1809.

[Blue slate. Fair condition, but moss-grown. Symbol.]

To the memory of Mr Nathaniel Doten, who died March 12th 1801 aged 60 years

No. 1810.

[Purplish blue slate. Good condition. Urn.]

MERCY DOTEN widow of Nathaniel Doten, died Oct. 11th, 1824, aged 86 years; Also three Children of Prince & Susan Doten. viz Samuel died April 3, 1825 aged 11 days. Sylvanus H died Oct. 12, 1825, aged 2 y'rs & 2 mon. A Dau. died July 13th, 1826, aged 3 hours.

No. 1811.

[Blue slate. Good condition. At top sculptured mausoleum and obelisk.]

MARY wife of Nathaniel Doten, died Sept. 23, 1834, in the 59 y.r of her age.

Thus fell the wife most kind
The partner dear
The tender parent,
And the friend sincere.

No. 1812.

[White marble in freestone socket. Fair condition.]

NANCY E. Wife of John A. Morse, Died July 9, 1876, Aged 65 y'rs. 22 days.

No. 1813.

[Blue slate. Good condition. Urn.]

Erected to the memory of PHEBE C. wife of Thomas Bartlett who died Jan 25, 1841 aged 29 years.

No. 1814.

[White marble in freestone socket. Fair condition.]

PRINCE DOTEN died Nov 11, 1870, Aged 89 years.
He has gone to the land of the blest.

No. 1815.

[White marble. Similar to preceding.]

SUSAN, Wife of Prince Doten, died Jan. 25, 1874, aged 86 y'rs.

No. 1816.

[Blue slate. Pyramidal. Good condition. Urn.]

In memory of Henry Caswell son of Daniel Caswell and Caroline his wife who died June 26, 1803, aged 4 years.

No. 1817.

[Beautiful mottled marble on plinth of same. Granite base.]

JOHN R. DAVIS Died Dec. 28, 1885, Aged 73 y'rs 10 m's 10 days.
He died in hope of a glorious resurrection.

No. 1818.

[White marble on marble plinth. Granite base. Good condition.]

WINSLOW M. Died Aug. 3, 1853, Aged 10 mo's.
ANN E. Died May 26, 1854, Aged 10 y'rs 11 mo's.
Children of John & Betsey B. Davis.

No. 1819.

[This and the following six numbers are inclosed in iron fence. White marble. Discolored.]

SARAH DAVIE, daughter of Capt. Ichabod & Joanna Davie, died Sept. 12, 1827, Æ. 29 y'rs

> While o'er these dear remains affection weeps
> A voice proclaims she is not dead but sleeps
> Jesus again descending from the skies
> Shall break her slumbers, saying maid arise.
> Then gently lead her to her father's feet
> Then shall command to give her angels meat
> Ascend in hope we wait the promised hour
> Tho' sown in weakness it is raised in power.

No. 1820.

[White marble. Fair condition.]

JOANNA DAVIE, Wife of Capt. Ichabod DAVIE, died Nov. 2, 1803, in the 31st year of her age.

No. 1821.

[White marble. It fell from socket, and is now set in the ground.]

In memory of ICHABOD DAVIE, Born Nov. 11, 1771, Died April 4, 1848,

> Affection to thy cherished memory rears
> This stone—a tribute poor to worth like thine
> But Faith alone can check her flowing tears,
> And point to realms of peace and joy divine
> Where thy pure spirit dwells which earth could not enshrine
> Blessed are the dead—who rest in humble hope.

No. 1822.

[White marble. In same condition as the preceding.]

In memory of NANCY DAVIE, Born Oct. 30, 1785, Died Oct. 10, 1867.

No. 1823.

[Low, blue slate. Laminæ separating. Top broken. Symbol half scaled off.]

In memory of DEBORAH ye Daughter of Mr Thomas & Mrs Sarah Davie who decd May ye 4th 1759 aged 2 years 11 months & 26 Days.

No. 1824.

[White marble. Fair condition.]

ELIZABETH DAVIE, Daut. of Capt. Ichabod & Joanna Davie, died Aug. 15, 1826: Æ. 25 y'rs.

Farewell, but not a long Farewell,
In Heaven may I appear:
The triumphs of my faith to tell,
In thy transported ear.
And sing with thee the eternal strain,
Worthy the lamb that once was slain.

No. 1825.
[White marble. Fair condition.]

JOANNA DAVIE daut. of Capt. Ichabod & Joanna
Davie, died Dec. 31, 1827: Æ. 28 y'rs.
Her rest is sweet in earth's cold arms,
She mingles dust with dust;
On Jesus breast she leans her head
In firm unshaken trust,
Quickley shall burst the bolted tomb
And rise in full unfading bloom.

No. 1826.
[Blue slate. Four and 1-4 by three and 1-4 feet. Good condition.]

BETSEY THOMAS BARNES, Consort of Isaac
Barnes Jr who died May 14, 1830, aged 33 years. Also
their Children WINSLOW died Oct. 10, 1825. aged one
year 6 mo. & 15 days. BETSEY WINSLOW died Dec.
21, 1825 aged 10 days. WINSLOW died Sept. 6, 1828
aged 13 mon.

No. 1827.
[Purplish blue slate. Good condition.]

In memory of MARY, Consort of Lewis Churchill,
died July 19, 1843, aged 32 yrs. Also two Children
STEPHEN aged 1 y'r STEPHEN aged 3 Mo.

No. 1828.
[White marble. Good condition.]

MARY, wife of Abner Pierce, Died Aug. 25, 1858,
aged 33 years. Also an infant daughter.

No. 1829.
[Purple slate. Good condition. Urn.]

EBENEZER P. died April 6, 1845, aged 4 yrs. 9 mo.
JOHN, died Nov. 9, 1843, aged 4 mo. 9 ds. Children of
Benj. & Martha Bates.

No. 1830.
[Purplish blue slate. Four ft. by 3. Good condition.]

SALLY, wife of Robert Dunham, died Oct,r 29, 1831:
aged 56 years. ROBERT DUNHAM died Jan,y 13,
1833: aged 54 years.

No. 1831.
[Blue slate. Broken. Defaced. Seamed. Symbol.]

NATHL son   Nathl Foster & Mercy his wife died
Deebr ye 11th 1739 aged 4 months & 2 days

No. 1832.

[Purplish blue slate. Fair condition. Symbol.]

The Remains of Mrs Mercy Foster wife to Mr Nathl Foster who died Decemr ye 24th 1746 in the 33d year of Her Age daughtr to the Revd Mr. *Peter Thatcher* late of Midleh decd April the 22d 1744, The Remains of SUSANAH daugtr to Mr NATHL & Mrs MERCY FOSTER died Janry ye 20th 1746.

No. 1833.

[Blue slate. Pyramidal. Good condition. Urn.]

In memory of Ichabod Shaw Holmes son of Capt. Chandler Holmes & Mrs Phebe his wife who died Novr 1st 1802 Aged 1 year 4 months

The tender Parants have Scarce time to wipe
Their weeping eys loe heaven cauls and the other dies

Also in memory of Chandler Holmes ther son who died Novr 6th 1802 Aged 4 years 10 months

They were Lovly and Pleasant in ther Lives
And in ther Death were not Devided

No. 1834.

[Blue slate. Good condition. Urn.]

In memory of Miss. ESTHER HOLMES who died Jan. 6, 1842, aged 32 yrs.

No. 1835.

[White marble. Marble plinth, granite base. Good condition.]

MEHITABLE HOLMES Born March 2, 1811 Died May 9, 1876.

Safe in the arms of Jesus.

No. 1836.

[Blue slate. Fair condition. Urn.]

In Memory of MRS PHEBE, Consort of Chandler Holmes, who died July 26, 1836, aged 65 y,rs.

Blessed are the dead who die in the Lord.

No. 1837.

[Purple slate. Good condition. Flaming urn.]

In memory of Capt. CHANDLER HOLMES who died Jan. 14, 1844, in the 72 year of his age.

No. 1838.

[White marble. Weathering rough.]

Miss. SUSAN W. HOLMES, Died April 29, 1850 aged 43 years.

No. 1839.

[Blue slate. Good condition. Two symbols.]

To the memory of Two Children of Capt Eleazer Holmes & Mrs Betsy his wife 1th a son Samuel A who died Sept 29th 1802 aged 9 months & 10 days. 2d a daughter Eliza who died June 25th 1803, aged 3 years & 3 months & 19 days.

> Fresh in the morn the summer rose
> Hangs wither'd ere its noon
> We scarce enjoy the balmy gift
> But mourn the pleasure gone.

No. 1840.
[Blue slate. Bad seam across the middle of urn.]

To the memory of CAPT ELEAZER HOLMES this monument is Erected.   Obit December 22, 1804 aged 47 years.

No. 1841.
[Blue slate. Good condition. Symbol.]

To the memory of Mrs POLLY HOLMES wife of Capt Eleazar Holmes and daughter of Capt CORBAN BARNES and Mary his wife who died Sepr 16, 1795 Ætatis 28 and her Infant Daughter Jenny by her side who died Dec 5 Ætatis 1 year.

No. 1842.
[Blue slate. Moss-covered. Symbol.]

To the memory of Mr ELEZER HOLMES who died Febry 21 1798 Ætatis 84

> Thro' a long life in devious paths I trod
> And liv'd alas forgetful of my God
> But Oh the triumphs of redeeming Power
> A sinner ransomed at the Eleventh hour
> Repairs to Christ the Lord his Righteousness
> And dies proclaiming free and sovereign Grace

No. 1843.
[Blue slate. Weatherworn. Moss-grown. Symbol.]

In Memory of Mrs ESTHER HOLMES wife   Mr ELEAZER HOLMES who died Augst 26 1759 in ye 39 year of her age.

No. 1844.
[Blue slate. Surface seamed. Moss-grown.]

In Memory of Mrs MARCY FOBES widow of Mr JOSHUA FOBES who died Novbr 19th 1774 in the 78th year of her age.

-        ## No. 1845.
[Blue slate. Laminæ separating. Moss-grown. Symbol.]

Here lyes ye body of Hannah Holmes who died May ye 10th 1735 in ye 23d year of her age

No. 1846.
[Low, blue slate. Good condition. Urn.]

In memory of Lucy Sturtevant Daughter of Mr Silvanus Sturtevant and Mrs Hannah his wife who died July 4th 1812 in the 17 year of her age

Relations and my Parents dear
Mourn not for me I'm Sleeping here
My debt is paid now Death is free
Therefore prepare to follow me

No. 1847.

[Blue slate. Good condition. Weeping willow and urn.]

In memory of Mrs Thankfull Sturtevant Daughter of Mr Silvanus Sturtevant And Mrs Hannah his wife who died April 24th 1811 in the 18th year of her age

The time was once my youthfull friends
I lived and bloomed like the
The time will come 'tis hastening on
When you must fade like me.

No. 1848.

[Blue slate. Good condition. Weeping willow and urn.]

In memory of Mr Joseph Sturtevant who died July 6th 1819, in the 28th year of his age

Farewell my wife and children dear
I leave you for a while
For God has call'd and I must go
And leave you all behind

No. 1849.

[White marble, in freestone socket. Good condition.]

MERCY STURTEVANT Died Nov. 12, 1872, Aged 78 y'rs 5 mo's. 15 days. Mercy A. Her dau. Died July 19, 1839, Aged 23 y'rs 3 mo's.

No. 1850.

[White marble. Rough.]

Joseph Sturtevant died Nov. 3, 1849, aged 35 y'rs & 3 Mon. Also three Children of Joseph & Marcia Sturtevant, viz. JOSHUA P. died Aug. 23, 1842, aged 5 Mon. & 21 days. JAMES T. died Jan. 14, 1845, aged 1 year & 7 Mon. MARCIA ANN, died Sept. 15, 1846, aged 1 year & 18 days.

Then shall the dust return to the earth as it was, and the spirit shall return unto GOD who gave it.

No. 1851.

[Blue slate. On each side of the inscription a figure of a column supporting a globe.]

CHARLES R. son of R. & E. Flemmons, who died In Taunton, Feb. 5, 1836, aged 3 yr's 10 mon. & 18 days.

When from our eyes such loveliness is torn
'Tis not for them but for our Selves we mourn

No. 1852.

[Blue slate. Pyramidal. Good condition. Urn under festoons.]

In memory of Mr Ichabod Holmes Jur who deceast March 29th 1802 in the 44th year of his age

23

No. 1853.

[Very low, blue slate. Moss-covered. Inclined. Symbol.]

Here lies buried Barnabe Son to Mr Benjamin Morton
& Mrs Hannah his wife who decd Novbr ye 7th ɟ7 4 Aged
ɟ0 days

No. 1854.

[Low, blue slate. Moss-covered. Symbol.]

In Memory of Abigail daughter to Mr Benjamin Morton born Febry ɟ8th ɟ76ɟ died Augst ye 20th ɟ762

No. 1855.

[Small, blue slate. Like the two preceding, nearly buried in the
ground. Of this, only 5 inches are above the surface. Stone marred.
Symbol.]

Memory of Barnaba   n to Mr Benjamin Morton
born Janry ye 28th 1759 decd Augst ye 28th 1765

No. 1856.

[Low, blue slate. Marred. Symbol.]

In Memory of hannah Daughter to Mr Benjamin Morton born Octo Augst ye 15th 1755 decd Octo ye 16th 1756

NOTE.—The stone-cutter having finished the word "born," allowed
his eye to fall on "Octo," which he inserted faintly before noticing
that he had skipped to the date of decease. He suffered the "Octo"
to remain, and followed it with "Augst."

No. 1857.

[Low, blue slate. Fair condition. Symbol.]

Here lyes   body of Giles Rickard Aged 30 (50?)
years died January ye 1709   14

NOTE.—Whether Mr. Rickard were 30 or 50 years of age cannot be
determined from the stone, as the first figure has the distinguishing
characteristics of both 3 and 5.

No. 1858.

[Blue slate. Good condition. Weeping willow and urn.]

In memory of DEBORAH, wife of Benjamin Thomas,
died Janu 5, 1828, aged 36 years. Also their son Josiah.
died Jan. 13, 1828, aged 1 year. & 3 months.

No. 1859.

[Blue slate. Good condition. Weeping willow and urn.]

In memory of Mr Thomas Davie who died at Sea March
5, 1771 aged 27 years   Also in memory of Mrs Jane
Davie who died Jany 25, 1824, aged 75 years widow of
the above

Blessed are the dead that die in the Lord.

No. 1860.

[Blue slate. Good condition. Symbol.]

To the memory of Mr Thomas Davee who died April
6th 1797 aged 26 years

No. 1861.

[White marble. Four and one-fourth feet in height. Fair condition.]

MARIA, died Feb. 12, 1844, aged 15 y'rs & 8 mo's.

> She bid farewell to all below
> To dwell among the just,
> And thus resigned her youthful form
> To slumber in the dust.
>
> To parents, brothers, sisters dear,
> She speaks in tones of love,
> I shall meet you all again
> In realms of bliss above,
>
> When every tear is wiped away
> From all our weeping eyes,
> When the last trumpets joyful sound
> Shall echo through the skies.

JOHN died Jan. 10, 1819, aged 1 yr & 11 mo's. JACOB, died May 16, 1823, aged 1 y'r & 8 mo's. JACOB, died Aug. 16, 1825, aged 1 y'r & 1 mo. Children of John & Lydia Nickerson.

No. 1862.

[White marble. Removed from broken socket, and set in the ground.]

JOHN NICKERSON, Jr. Died May 31, 1858, Aged 39 years 9 mo's.

> When a few short years have fleeted
> When our work on earth is done,
> May our circle all unbroken,
> Find with thee in Heaven our home.

No. 1863.

[White marble. Removed from freestone socket, and set in the ground. Spotted. Discolored.]

JULIA ANN, died Sept. 4, 1842; Æ. 3 yrs & 7 mos. NATHANIEL T. died June 25, 1853; Æ. 19 mos. ALMIRA W. died Mar 6, 1855; Æ. 11 weeks, LAURA W. died Mar. 7, 1858; Æ. 19 mos. LAURA A. died Oct. 13, 1860: Æ. 8 mos. Children of James & Almira Sears.

No. 1864.

[Blue slate. Good condition. Flaming urn under festoons.]

To the memory of 5 Children of Mr Wm. Barnes & Mrs Mercy his wife viz. Eleanor, died March 28th 1791 aged 8 days, 2d Mercy, died August 12th 1801 aged 3 months & 14 days, 3d Nathaniel died Septr 15th 1802 aged 3 months & 9 days, 4th Calvin Carver died Octr 19th 1802 aged 4 years & 2 months, 5th Calvin Carver died April 22d 1805 aged 1 year & 7 months and 7 days.

> In early days, away from us they fly
> No more their pleasing actions charmes our eyes,
> A happy change from earth to sure above.
> Now take their dwelling in the realmes of love.

No. 1865.

[Purplish blue slate. Good condition. Urn with festoons.]

Died July 27, ɿ798 Mrs Betsy Holmes wife of Capt. Lewis Holmes Aged 27 Year Also 3 Children by her side Rebecca Diman died ɿ796 Aged ɿ year & ɿ Month Esther ɿ798 Aged 5 Months Phebe Lewis ɿ799 Aged ɿɿ Months

No. 1866.

[Purplish blue slate. Good condition. Symbol.]

Died at Demerara December 3ɿst ɿ798 Capt Lewis Holmes Aged 32 Years

Their cold remains though distant lands divide
To burst the bars of death the SAVIOUR died,
The eye of faith their union sees again
Where scenes of love and bliss immortal reign.

No. 1867.

[Blue slate. Fair condition. Symbol.]

To the memory of Willard Sears son of Mr Willard Sears & Mrs Mary his wife who died May 22 1796 aged 20 years

No. 1868.

[Blue slate. Broken. Seamed. Defaced. Part of symbol remains.]

In memory of Mrs Hannah Holmes ye widdow of Mr Elezer Holmes Born March ye 15th 16 2 Decd April ye 7th 1758 Aged 66 years

No. 1869.

[Blue slate. Good condition. Symbol.]

Here lies buried the Body of Mr Eleazer Holmes who died Augst 21st 1754 Aged 65 years 10 Months & 5 days

No. 1870.

[Blue slate. Pyramidal. Four feet high. Good condition. Human face under festoons.]

In memory of Capt Robert Davie who Deceased Decm the 17th 1800 In the 32 year of his age   Also In memory of Elizabeth Davie Daughter to Capt Robert & Mrs Jerusha Davie who Died Aug. the 30th 1800 Aged 11 months and 4 Days

Distressing scene to see in life fair prime
A Husband parent languish out of time
Consoling thorght our saviour is the door
To worlds of bliss where parting is now more

No. 1871.

[Low, blue slate. Moss-grown. Weatherworn. Symbol.]

Here lyes ye body of Mrs Marcy Holmes wife to Mr Nathll Holmes who decd Febry ye 11th 1731-2 in ye 81st year of her age

No. 1872.

[Blue slate. Weatherworn. Moss-grown. Seamed. Symbol,]

Here lyes ye body of Mr Nathaniel Holmes who Decd July ye 26th 1727 in ye 84th year of his age

No. 1873.

[Low, blue slate. Fair condition. Symbol.]

Abigail Deleno Dautr to Mr Nathan & Mrs Bathsheba Deleno Aged 1 year 6 Mo & 4 Ds Died May ye 10th 1747

No. 1874.

[Blue slate. Cleft. Seamed. Bad condition.]

In Memory of Mrs Bathsheba Deleno the wife of Capt Nathan Deleno who decd April ye 21st 1755 Aged 51 years & 5 months

No. 1875.

[White marble. Rough. Moss-grown.]

HARRIET N. Daughter of Eleazer & Polly Sears, Died Dec. 29th, 1841, Aged 19 years

From the grave so dark & drear
Thoughts of comfort rise;
Our darling Sister is not here
She lives beyond the skies.

No. 1876.

[Blue slate. Fair condition. Weeping willow and urn.]

MISS MARY ANN SEARS died April 17, 1836, in the 29 year of her age HIRAM R, died April 28, 1815, aged 19 mon. Children of Eleazer & Polly Sears.

Farewell, a short farewell
Till we shall meet again above
In the sweet groves where pleasures dwell
And trees of life bear fruits of love.

No. 1877.

[White marble. Four and one-fourth feet high. Rough. Moss-grown.]

EUNICE B. Daughter of Eleazer & Polly Sears, Died Sept. 14, 1852, aged 27 years.

Rest sleeping dust in silence rest
In the cold grave that Jesus blest,
In faith and hope we lay the there
Safe in our Heavenly Father's care!
O may we heed thy warning given,
Prepare to die and go to Heaven.

No. 1878.

[Blue slate. Fair condition. Symbol.]

In Memory of Mrs Rebecah Sears who died April 14, 1789 in the 52d year of her age

No. 1879.

[Blue slate. Good condition. Weeping willow and urn.]

In memory of Mr Willard Sears who died January 5, 1826 : in the 78 year of his age

What is the life of man with all its cares
Tis like a shade which quickly disappears.

No. 1880.

[Blue slate. Moss-grown. Defaced. Symbol.]

Here lyes ye Body of Marcy Cob wife to Ebenzer Cob decd March ye 2d 1725-6 in ye 53d year of her age.

No. 1881.

[Blue slate. Weatherworn. Symbol.]

Here lyes ye body of John Cob who decd Augst ye 22d 1731 in ye 23d year of his age

No. 1882.

[Blue slate. Worn and moss-grown. Symbol.]

Here lies ye Body of Mr Ebenezer Cobb who decd July 29th 1752 In ye 71st year of his age

No. 1883.

[Low, blue slate. Piece broken from left hand corner at top. Symbol.]

A T H A N Son   o John &   arcy Holmes   is wife decd   ecbr ye 23d 1726 in

No. 1884.

[Blue slate. Good condition. Weeping willow and urn.]

This Stone is Consecrated to the memory of Mrs ELIZA CARVER Consort of Capt JOSIAH CARVER who died Novr 22, 1815, in the 43 year of her age

Mourn not my friends, nought but my dust lies here
To be in Glory calls not for a tear
Prepare for death, and then we all shall meet
In realms of Bliss, fruition all complete.

No. 1885.

[Blue slate. Pyramidal. Good condition. Symbol.]

To the memory of Mrs Joanna Holmes Daughter of the late Mr Ephraim Holmes and Mrs Lucy his wife who died August 12th AD 1801 in the 22 year of her age

That Female Virtue which adornd thy bloom
Friendship recalls and weeps upon thy tomb
There sad remembrance drops a silent tear
And chaste affection stands a mourner there.

No. 1886.

[Blue slate. Good condition. Symbol.]

In memory of Mrs Sarah Davee Daughter of Mr Robart Davee & Mrs Elizabeth his wife who died Nov 13th 1796 in the 30th year of her age

No. 1887.

[Blue slate. Good condition. Symbol.]

To the memory of Mr Robart Davee who died July 4th 1795 in the 54th year of his age.

(NOTE —The date, 1795, is plainly cut on the stone.)

No. 1888.

[Blue slate. Weatherworn. Seamed. Symbol.]

In Memory of Capt James Doten who departed this life July 25th 1786 in the 58th Year of his Age.

No. 1889.

[Blue slate. Fair condition; but moss-grown. Urn.]

To the memory of Mrs Ruth Churchill wife of Capt Benjamin Churchill who died Augst 22d 1798 aged 73 years

No. 1890.

[Blue slate. Pyramidal outline. Good condition. Festoons.]

Died March J4th J790 Stephen Son of Capt Nathaniel Carver & Joanna His wife Aged 49 days And their daughter Mary died Sept 24th J798 aged J year & 8 months

No. 1891.

[Purplish blue slate. Good condition, but inclined. Urn.]

In memory of Mrs Sally Torrey Consort of Mr Joshua Torrey who Died Decr. 7th 1806 in the 44th year of her age

No. 1892.

[Low, blue slate. Good condition. Symbol.]

In Memory of Mr. James Doten who Died June 6th, 1794, in the 32 year of his age.

Death is a debt to nature due
Which I have paid and so must you

No. 1893.

[Low, blue slate. Moss-grown. Inclined 45 degrees. Symbol.]

Here lies Buryed the body of Joseph Doten Son of Mr Joseph Doten & Mrs Elizabeth his wife Who Departed this life Febry 11th 1802 aged 2 years 7 months & 8 days.

No. 1894.

[This and the four following it are white marble, inclosed in iron fence. Good condition.]

JERUSHA T. TALBOT, wife of SAMUEL TALBOT, Died Sept 8, 1856 ; Æ. 54 years

Peace to thy soul; no more shall earth
Thy spirit pure oppress:
No more shall sorrow waste thy frame
For thou hast gone to rest.

NANCY E. their daughter died April 22, 1838 : aged 19 mo's.

No. 1895.

JERUSHA TALBOT, wife of SAMUEL TALBOT, died Nov. 22, 1829 ; Æ. 31 years.

> When spirits from this cumbering clay
> Ascend to heavens bright shore,
> Our hoping hearts in triumph say
> "Not lost, but gone before."

Jerusha, their daughter died Sept. 22, 1837 : Æ. 9 years & 4 mo's.

No. 1896.

[On marble plinth. Granite base.]

SAMUEL TALBOT died Sept. 28, 1883, Aged 88 yrs. 2 mos. 14 days.

No. 1897.

ROBERT D. TALBOT, Born May 13, 1834, Died Dec. 2, 1857.

> His was an early summons to the tomb
> But though so brief, his life was not in vain—
> God does not call his children hence too soon—
> For such, "to live is Christ, to die is gain."

No. 1898.

GEORGE W. TALBOT, Born December 29, 1838 ; Died Nov. 1, 1859.

> A good boy.

No. 1899.

[Low, white marble. Discolored.]

HARRIET FRANCES, dau. of Robert & Fanny Davie died Aug. 4, 1836, aged 7 yrs. 6 mo.

No. 1900.

[Fine, white marble in granite socket.]

FANNY EDDY widow of Capt. ROBERT DAVIE Born Aug. 11, 1804, Died Oct. 16, 1885.

No. 1901.

[Blue slate. Good condition. Weeping willow and urn.]

In memory of Cap. ROBERT DAVIE, who died July 19, 1829, aged 32 years.

> 'Tis God that lifts our comforts high
> Or sinks them in the Grave:
> He Gives and blessed be his name,
> He takes but what he Gave.

No. 1902.

[White marble, in freestone socket. Fair condition, but inclined.]

In memory of Mrs REBECCA HARLOW. Relict of Capt. Ezra Harlow, Born Jan. 5, 1795, Died Dec. 18, 1852.

> "There is rest in Heaven."

No. 1903.

[Blue slate. Four and 1-3 ft. high. Good condition save moss-grown. Weeping willow.]

He that wounds can heal.

Sacred to the memory of CAPT. EZRA HARLOW, who died suddenly Oct. 27th 1840, aged 68 yrs.

Our loss is his gain, though the body lies mouldering beneath the sod, the Spirit has gone to God, there to receive the reward of all his labours of love. he lived a life of self denial that he might releive the distress'd, though dead he lives forevermore O glorious hope, O bles'd abode, I shall be near and like my God, O the depth of the riches both of the wisdom and knowledge of God! how unsearchable are his judgments; and his ways past finding out!

I leave the world without a tear,
　Save for the friends I hold so dear,
To heal her sorrow, Lord, descend,
　And to the friendless prove a friend.

The sick, the pris'ner, poor and blind,
　And all the sons of grief,
In him a benefactor found
　He loved to give relief.

Tis love that makes religion sweet
　Tis love that makes us rise
With willing minds and ardent feet
　To yonder happy skies.

No. 1904.

[Blue slate. A cleft divides the stone—cutting off the right-hand third part. Urn.]

In memory of Mrs LYDIA HARLOW Consort of CAPT EZRA HARLOW who Died July 9th 1805 in the 30th year of her age

No. 1905.

[Blue slate. Good condition. Weeping willow and urn.]

In memory of Theodore S. Carver Son of Capt Josiah Carver & Abbigail his wife who died Septr 5 1823 aged Three years one month & twenty seven days

Suffer little children to come unto me and forbid them not.

No. 1906.

[Low, blue slate. Moss-covered. Whole inscription in capitals. Symbol.]

In Memory of Zacheus Curtis Son to Mr Zacheus Curtis and Lydia his wife who died Sept ye 12th 1744 aged JJ months & 9 days.

No. 1907.

[Blue slate. Fair condition. Figure of man standing behind what appears to be a tomb.]

In Memory of Mr Nathaniel Curtis who was Drowned at Marshfield March ye 8th 1778 Aged 2J years JJ months and J2 days.

No. 1908.

[Blue slate. Fair condition, but seamed. Tree bending over a tomb; a cherub flying above.]

To the memory of Mrs SARAH T. ROBBINS Consort of Mr JESSE ROBBINS who died Novr 6th 1802 in the 24th year of her age

> Here lies intomb'd within this house of clay
> The mortal part of an engageing wife
> Whose virtue shone amid the blaze of day
> Whose kind affection ended with her life
> Till Gabriel's trumpets animating sound
> Bid soul and body meet and reunite
> Here rest in silence in the vaulted ground
> Then meet th y God with rapture and delight

No. 1909.

[White marble. Rough. Weatherworn and moss-grown.]

In memory of MR SAMUEL ELLIS who died April 2, 1842, aged 49 years

No. 1910.

[White marble. Roughened by exposure.]

LYDIA ELLIS wife of Samuel Ellis, Died Sept 8, 1865, Aged 71 yrs.

No. 1911.

[White marble. Roughened.]

REBECCA ELLIS Died Jan. 11, 1854, Aged 50 years & 9 Months. NATHANIEL ELLIS, Lost at Sea Dec. 6, 1812, aged 21 years & 11 Months.

No. 1912.

[Blue slate. Four and one-half feet high. Good condition. Two urns.]

In memory of CAPT. NATHANIEL ELLIS, who died July 30th, 1816, in his 59th yr. Also of his Widow JANE ELLIS, who died June 1st. 1851, in her 87th yr.

No. 1913.

[Low, blue slate. Good condition. Symbol.]

Died Novr J3, 1795 Jenne Ellis Daughter of Mr Nathaniel Ellis & Mrs Jenne his wife in the 10th year of her age

No. 1914.

[Blue slate. Laminæ separating. Seamed. Inclined. Symbol.]

In Memory of Mrs LYDIA REED wife of Mr Nathan Reed who died Octr J2, J793 in ye 32 year of her age.

No. 1915.

[Blue slate. Good condition. Weeping willow and urn.]

In memory of MRS. DEBORAH PATY Relict of the late CAPT JOHN PATY who died Feby 7, 1826 ; aged 67 years.

> Bless'd hour when virtuous friends shall meet,
> Shall meet to part no more,
> And with celestial welcome greet,
> On an immortal shore.

No. 1916.

[Blue slate. Seamed in various directions.]

In memory of Capt John Paty who died January 17, 1821 in the 62 year of his age.

> See smiling patience smooth his brow
> See bending angels downward bow
> To cheer his way on high,
> While eager for the blest abode
> He joins with them to praise the GOD,
> Who taught him how to die.

No. 1917.

[Low, blue slate. Fair condition, but moss-grown. Two symbols.]

To the memory of two children of Mr John Paty & Deborah his wife viz Silvia died Octr ye 22d aged 3 years 6 months & 26 Days Meriah Died Aug. ye 11 AD 1793 aged J year—s & 26 Days.

No. 1918.

[White marble. Four feet high. In stone socket, but erect. Fair condition save roughened.]

OUR MOTHER. REBECCA, widow of William Rogers Jr. died June 19, 1861 ; Æ. 70 years & 2 mos.

No. 1919.

[White marble. Inclined. Rough. Moss-grown.]

WILLIAM ROGERS Jr. died Dec. 23d, 1822, aged 34 yr's. JOHN ROGERS, died Dec. 1st, 1825, Aged 27 yr's. ICHABOD ROGERS, died March 18th, 1854, Aged 50 yr's & 10 Mon.

No. 1920.

[White marble. Like preceding.]

ELIZABETH, wife of William Rogers, died June 14th, 1827, Aged 58 y'rs.

No. 1921.

[White marble. Like preceding but quite erect.]

WILLIAM ROGERS, died June 16, 1844, Aged 77 y'rs & 6 Mon.

No. 1922.

[White marble. Removed from freestone socket, and set in the ground.]

NANCY B Dau. of Elizabeth & William Rogers, Died Feb. 3, 1876 Aged 69 y'rs 7 mo's 4 days.

No. 1923.

[Low, blue slate. Good condition, save at corner marred. Symbol.]

Died October th 1798 John Rogers son of Mr Wm Rogers & Mrs Elizebeth his Wife Aged 2 year & 1 week

No. 1924.

[Low, blue slate. Moss-covered. Symbol.]

To the memory of Polly Rogers Daughter of Mr William Rogers & Mrs Elisabeth his wife who died Sepr 5th 1793 aged 1 year & 10 months

No. 1925.

[White marble. Three and one-half feet high. Fair condition. Freestone base. Hand pointing upwards with words, "Joined above, Separated below."]

WILLIAM H. ROGERS DIED July 12, 1859, aged 23 yrs. 5 mos. Only son of A. B. & Eliza Rogers.

No. 1926.

[Blue slate. Good condition. Weeping willow.]

LYDIA H. dau. of America & Eliza Rogers died Jan. 17th. 1840, aged 2 yrs. & 1 mo.

> Cease thy regrets fond parents cease,
> Thy infant dwells in joy and peace,
> Tis free from care, grief and pain;
> To her thy los is perfect gain.

No. 1927.

[Blue slate. Fair condition, but moss-covered. Flaming urn.]

In memory of THOMAS BURGESS who died June 11, 1839, in the 51 year of his age.

No. 1928.

[Low, blue slate. Good condition, but inclined. Symbol.]

In memory of Eunice Daughter of Mr Ebenezer Howard & Mrs Bethiah his wife, who died July 30. 1793 aged 3 years 1 month & 7 days.

No. 1929.

[Blue slate. Pyramidal. Good condition. Weeping willow and urn.]

In memory of Sylvia Cooper Daughter of Joseph Cooper Jun & Sylvia his wife who died Octobr 7. 1815 aged one year & 2 months.

> Though our fond hopes & schemes are crush'd
> And with the laid beneath the dust,
> Yet still we would not dare complain;
> Our los is thy eternal gain.

No. 1930.

[Blue slate. Fair condition, but moss-grown.]

Erected in memory of Mrs Sylvia Cooper wife of Capt Joseph Cooper Jur who died September 29, 1820, in the 25 year of her age.

> That once loved form now cold and dead
> Each mournful thought employs,
> And nature weeps her comforts dead
> And withered all her joys.

No. 1931.

[White marble. Removed from freestone socket, and set in the ground.]

FATHER WILSON CHURCHILL, Died April 21. 1865 aged 85 y'rs 2 mo's.

No. 1932.

[White marble. Removed from freestone socket, and set in the ground.]

MOTHER SUSAN, Wife of Wilson Churchill, Died Jan. 31, 1848, Aged 54 y'rs 4 mo's.

No. 1933.

[Blue slate. Fair condition. Weeping willow and urn.]

To the memory of Mrs Ruth Churchill wife of Mr Wilson Churchill who died September 26, 1812 in the 33 year of her age.

Remember me as you pass by
As you are now so once was I
As I am now so you must be
Therefore prepare to follow me

No. 1934.

[Blue slate. Good condition. Urn with flower on each side.]

To the memory of CAPT JOSEPH DOTEN who died at Guadaloupe February 4th 1803 in the 33 year of his age

Time on its wing conveys us home,
To the mouldring ground whence we come:
Prepare to meet the solemn call,
When the last trumpet calls us all.

No. 1935.

[Blue slate. Four and one-fourth feet high. Good condition, but inclined. Urn.]

Erected to the memory of CAPT THOMAS PATY who died Nov. 26, 1846, aged 73 years Also his Grandson Tho's P. Harlow who was lost at sea Sept. 1848, Æ. 25 years.

Blessed are the dead who die in the Lord.

No. 1936.

[Similar to preceding.]

Erected to the memory of JERUSHA PATY, widow of the late Thomas Paty, who died Dec. 29, 1854 aged 81 years.

The love that seeks another's good
In her did warmly burn,—
Oh, let us imitate that love
Nor ask for her return.

No. 1937.

[Blue slate. Pyramidal. Good condition. Two symbols.]

In memory of Thomas Paty son of Mr Thomas Paty and Mrs Jerusha his wife who departed this life Oct 7th 1802 aged 2 years 10 months and 20 days.

And must thy childrin Dye so soon.

No. 1938.

[Low, white marble. Roughened and seamed.]

GEORGIANA, dau. of Nathaniel & Jane Burgess died Oct. 18, 1840, aged 7 yr's 3 mo.

No. 1939.

[Low, blue slate. Good condition. Symbol.]

To the memory of Elizabeth Barnes daughter of Mr Joseph Barnes & Mrs Elizabeth his wife who died Janry 12, 1796 aged 3 years 5 months & 22 days.

No. 1940.

[Low, blue slate. Good condition. Flaming urn.]

In memory of MR. JOSEPH BARNES who died Jan. 28, 1839, aged 75 y.rs.

No. 1941.

[Blue slate. Fair condition. Symbol.]

This Monument is erected to the memory of Mr Silvanus Dunham who died in Martinico Febry 1799 aged 29 years also in memory of Silvanus son of Mr Silvanus and Mrs Mary Dunham who died at sea Octr 9th 1799 in the 20th year of his age

> That manly virtue which adorn'd thy bloom
> Friendship recalls and weeps upon thy tomb
> There sad remembrance drops a silent tear
> And chaste affection stands a mourner there.

No. 1942.

[Blue slate. Good condition. Weeping willow and urn.]

In memory of MRS MARY COVINGTON Consort of CAPT THOMAS COVINGTON who died May 25, 1825 aged 65 years.

No. 1943.

[Blue slate. Good condition. Urn with flower on each side.]

In memory of Mrs SARAH COVINGTON. Consort of CAPT THOMAS COVINGTON. who Died Octbr 19th 1805 aged 51st years.

No. 1944.

[Blue slate. Good condition. Weeping willow and urn.]

This Stone is erected to commemorate CAPT THOMs COVINGTON who died October 24, 1825, aged 78 years.

No. 1945.

[White marble in freestone socket. Rough. Discolored.]

Father. BENJAMIN DILLARD Died Aug. 18, 1857, Aged 74 y,rs 8 mo,s.

Past away, but not forgotten.

No. 1946.

[Blue slate. Moss-covered. Flaming urn.]

In memory of Mrs POLLY DILLARD Consort of Mr BENJAMIN DILLARD who died March 1807 in the 22 year of her age.

No. 1947.

[Blue slate. Good condition. Weeping willow and urn.]

In memory of MRS Mercy Dillard. Consort of Mr Benjamin Dillard. who died March 28. 1824 aged 44 years.

No. 1948.

[Blue slate. Good condition. Urn.]

In memory of NANCY, wife of Benjamin Dillard, who died Dec. 22d 1849, in her 67 yr.

No. 1949.

[White marble in inclosure. Rough, discolored, inclined.]

DANIEL DOTEN died Feb. 6th, 1853. aged 80 yrs Also SALLY his wife died Feb. 7th, 1853. aged 77 y,rs.

Our flesh shall slumber in the ground,
Till the last trumpets joyful sound;
Then burst the bars in sweet surprise,
And in my Saviour's image rise.

No. 1950.

[Blue slate. Good condition. Urn.]

In memory of Mrs Sarah Tribbel widow to the late Joseph Tribbel deceas'd who died January 14th 1808 aged 75 years.

No. 1951.

[Blue slate. Fair condition. Drapery.]

This Stone Is Erected to the memory of Mr JOSEPH TRIBBEL who Died November 17th 1805 in the 76 year of his age

No. 1952.

[Blue slate. Good condition. Weeping willow and urn.]

In memory of Mrs Susannar Burgess, wife of Capt John Burgess Jur, who departed this life December 20, 1819, aged 33 years & 5 months.

Thou lovely chief of all my joys,
Thou sov'reign of my heart,
How could I bear to hear thy voice
Pronounce the sound depart!"

No. 1953.

[White marble. Gothic arch form. Four and one-half feet high· Rough, discolored. Foul anchor.]

CAPT. JOHN BURGESS, JR. born March 26, 1785. died May 4, 1850.

The anchor's dropt—the sails are furled!
Lifes' voyage now is o'er.
By faiths' bright chart he has gained that world
Where storms are felt no more.

No. 1954.

[Blue slate. Three and three-fourths feet high. Good condition. Urn.]

ERECTED to the Memory of SIMEON DIKE, who died June 4th 1843, aged 62 y.rs.

> Sleep dearest Husband, while above thee
> Flows the sad and silent tear;
> Oft at eve shall those that love thee,
> Weep and pray unnoticed here.

No. 1955.

[Blue slate. Good condition. Weeping willow and urn.]

To the memory of Capt NATHANIEL CARVER who Departed this life April 30 1815 aged 74 years

No. 1956.

[Blue slate. Four feet in height. Fair condition, but moss-grown. Weeping willow and urn.]

To the memory of Mrs Sarah Carver who Departed this life August 12. 1808 aged 64 years

No. 1957.

[White marble column. Discolored. In wooden inclosure. Freestone plinth. Granite base.]

(On west side:)

NATHANIEL CARVER, died Oct. 18, 1842, aged 78 yrs. JOANNA CARVER, died April 10, 1842, aged 76 yrs.

(On south side:)

Stephen died March 14, 1790, aged 45 ds. Nancy, died Sept. 24, 1798, aged 1 yr. & 8 mo. Nancy, died Nov. 27, 1814, aged 14 yrs. & 9 mo. Mary, died Nov. 10, 1811. aged 3 mo. Children of Nathaniel & Joanna Carver.

(East side, blank.)
(On north side:)

Nathaniel Carver, Jr. died Oct. 2, 1823, aged 32 yrs. Betsey, his wife, died Sept. 23, 1814, aged 27 yrs. Nancy, his wife died Feb. 22, 1826, aged 30 yrs. Nancy, dau. of Nathaniel & Nancy Carver, died Sept. 2, 1824, aged 13 mo.

No. 1958.

[Blue slate. Good condition. Weeping willow and urn.]

Sacred to the memory of MARGARET H. wife of Henry Robbins, died Dec,r 27, 1830 ; in the 31 yr, of her age.

"In her tongue was the law of kindness.

Also three of their Children Henry Augustus, aged 1, yr. 4 mo. Francis William, aged 3 yrs. 3 mo. Margaret Lewis, aged 1 yr. 5 mo.

No. 1959.

[Blue slate. Broken off at about one foot above the ground. Upper portion missing.]

in the 43 year of her age.

(Footstone reads:)

T   F

1800

M   F

No. 1960.

[White marble, in freestone socket. Fair condition.]

JOHN KING Jr. Died Feb. 4, 1873, Aged 63 y'rs. 7 mo's.

No. 1961.

[White marble. Moss-grown. Discolored.]

JOHN KING died June 1, 1860; Æ. 78 years & 5 mos. POLLY his wife died Jan. 10, 1847; Æ. 62 years & 9 mos.

No. 1962.

[Low, white marble. Discolored. Figure of lamb.]

AN INFANT son of Isaac B. & Harriet A. King died Aug. 27, 1857, aged 10 weeks.

No. 1963.

[Blue slate. Good condition. Weeping willow and urn.]

In memory of Mr Levi Whiting, who died May 20, 1821 in the 58 year of his age.

Death but entombs the body
Life the soul

No. 1964.

[Blue slate. Good condition. Weeping willow and urn.]

In memory of Mrs Mary Whiting Consort of Mr Levi Whiting, who died Sep. 28, 1818 aged 40 years.

Alas! and has she gone, and has she fled,
Gone to the silent mansions of the dead,
She is gone we trust to join the Joys on high,
With saints and angels o'er the starry sky.

No. 1965.

[Blue slate. Good condition. Weeping willow and urn.]

In memory of Miss Mary Bardan, Daughter of Mr Gershom Bardan and Mrs Mary his wife, died June 18, 1818 in the 19 year of her age.

Farewell bright Soul, a short farewell,
Till we shall meet again above
In the Sweet groves where pleasures dwell
And trees of life bear fruits of Love.

24

No. 1966.

[White marble. Four feet high. Rough. Moss-grown.]

Erected in memory of EPHRAIM PATY, who died Feb. 9, 1854, aged 70 y'rs & 10 mo's. Also his son GEORGE WINSLOW, who died at sea July 14, 1853, aged 19 y.rs & 5 mo.s.

Blessed are the dead who die in the Lord and their works do follow them.

[NOTE.—No. 1966 has fallen, and now lies prone on the ground,— Oct. 1896.]

No. 1967.

[Blue slate. Good condition. Weeping willow and urn]

In memory of Mrs Betsey Paty wife of Mr Ephraim Paty who departed this life December 31, AD. 1817 aged 30 years

> Of this vain world she took her last adieu,
> The promis'd land was now within her view;
> With pleasure she resign'd her mortal breath,
> And fell a willing sacrifice to DEATH.

No. 1968.

[White marble. Rough. Discolored. Moss-grown.]

Erected in memory of MARTHA, Wife of Ephraim Paty who died May 12, 1864 aged 69 y'r's 5 mos 16 days.

Asleep in Jesus.

No. 1969.

[Blue slate. Good condition. Four urns.]

In Memory of Four Children of Capt. Ephraim & Martha Paty, viz CORDELIA. died Dec. 14, 1833. Aged 2 y.rs 2 Mon. & 19 days.

SETH. died Dec. 23, 1833, Aged 4 y.rs 2 Mon. & 11 days.

ELVIRA. died Jan. 4, 1834, Aged 6 yrs. 4 Mon. & 24 days.

GEO. WINSLOW. died Jan 12, 1834, Aged 8 y,rs 3 Months.

No. 1970.

[Blue slate. Good condition. Weeping willow and urn.]

In memory of ESTHER wife of Otis Churchill, who died March 8th. 1837 ; in the 39th yr. of her age.

> The months of affliction are o'er
> The days and the weeks of distress
> We see her in anguish no more
> She has gained her happy release.

No. 1971.

[Blue slate. Good condition. Weeping willow and urn.]

Erected to the memory of MRS SALLY C. CHURCHILL wife of Mr Otis Churchill who died Feb.y 10, 1828 ; in

the 25 year of her age. Also their infant by her
side.

How soon these well wrought frames decay
How soon our pleasures fade away;
But at the LORD'S right hand on high,
Fair pleasures bloom that never die.

No. 1972.

[White marble. Rough. Discolored. Moss-grown. Weeping
willow and urn. Granite curbing around this and the next.]

IN MEMORY of THOMAS GOODWIN, was lost at
sea, Oct. 1831, Æ. 45 y'rs. HEVERLAND T. GOOD-
WIN his son died Jan'y 12, 1823, Æ. 6 mo. DESIRE
GOODWIN his dau. died April 30, 1823. Æ. 3 y'rs
HEVERLAND T. GOODWIN his son died June 10,
1830, Æ. 3 mo. CHARLES T. GOODWIN, his son
died Feb. 7, 1831, Æ. 10 mo.

No. 1973.

[White marble. Rough. Discolored.]

OUR MOTHER. ABAGAIL T. Widow of Thomas
Goodwin, died May 11, 1864; aged 77 years.

No. 1974.

[Blue slate. Good condition. Weeping willow.]

MARY, widow of Thomas Churchill, died July 12,
1835, aged 76 y.rs.

No. 1975.

[Blue slate. Good condition. Weeping willow and urn.]

Erected to the memory of THOMAS CHURCHILL,
Consort of Mary Churchill, formerly of Plympton who
departed this life February 26, 1826; aged 70 years.

No. 1976.

[Tomb—Granite, with iron door. Inscribed:]
PATY 1856.

No. 1977.

[Low, white marble. Inclosed.]

MARY EDWARDS, Daughter of William H. & Mary
S. Morton, died May 14, 1849. aged 2 y'rs. 6 mo. & 16
days.

No. 1978.

[Low, white marble. Inclosed.]

MARY ELLEN, Dau. of William H. & Mary S. Morton died June 23, 1843, aged 10 weeks.

No. 1979.

[Low, blue slate. Good condition. Symbol.]

In memory of 3 Children of John & Mary Goddard viz.
Mary died Augst 10, 1762 aged 6 years. Lydia died

Augst ɹ4, ɹ7G2 aged 2 years & 3 months. Polly died
June ɹ5, ɹ767 aged 2 years & 6 months.

No. 1980.

[Blue slate. Good condition, but inclined. Symbol.]

In Memory of Sarah Daughter of Mr Edward Morton
& Mrs Sarah his wife who died Nov.r 12, 1788 aged 7
years 9 months & 9 days.

No. 1981.

[Blue slate. Good condition. Urn with flower on each side.]

Here lies buried the body of CAPT EDWARD MORTON
who Died Nov'r 14 AD. 1804 in the 32 year of his Age
Likewise his late consort Mrs SARAH MORTON who Died
Feb. 21 AD. 1805. Aged 29 years

Healthful at dawn, soft slumber left his eyes,
I've rested well, he said, and in a moment dies.
Shocked with the scene with lingering grief opprest
His consort met him where the weary rest.

No. 1982.

[White marble block. Marble plinth. Granite base. Good condition.]

SARAH M. HOLMES Born Oct. 6, 1805, Died March
11, 1888.

No. 1983.

[Blue slate. Good condition. Urn and flowers.]

In memory of MRS EUNICE HOLMES who died Octr 16,
1824 aged 40 years.

When holy friendship drops the pious tear
And sacred garlands deck the hallowed bier,
Can bounteous heaven a greater solace give,
Than that which whispers "Friends departed, live.

No. 1984.

[Blue slate. Good condition. Urn and stars.]

MISS ELEANOR MORTON, Daughter of Edward & Sarah
Morton died March 6, 1835, aged 40 years & 1 Month.

No. 1985.

[White marble. Rough. Discolored.]

In Memory of LYDIA DELANO who died Mar. 22
1856, aged 52 y'rs 4 mo's & 22 days

To OUR SISTER.

A marble monument marks the spot,
And these words on it are graven,
Though her body lies here in the still churchyard
Our sister lives in Heaven.

No. 1986.

[White marble. Rough. Discolored.]

MARY EDWARDS, died June 2, 1838 : aged 2 y,rs
8 mo. & 2 ds. WILLIAM THOMAS. died May 10,

1838 : aged 3 weeks & 3 ds. Children of William & Susan
S Morey.

> See the lovely blooming flowers
> Fades and withers in an hour
> So our transient comforts fly
> Pleasure only blooms to die.

No. 1987.

[Blue slate. Good condition. Weeping willow and urn.]

In memory of ELLIS J HARLOW son of Cap Ellis
Harlow and Mrs Jerusha his wife who died November 24.
1826 ; aged 17 months.

No. 1988.

[Blue slate. Four and one-half feet high. Fair condition. Moss-
grown. Slightly inclined.]

Erected in memory of CAPT ELLIS J. HARLOW, who
Departed this life July 11, 1826 : aged 33 years.

> No nobler form has nature showed
> Then here has met an early blight,
> No fairer eye has ever glowed
> And beamed with intellectual Light.
>
> Yet scarce we mourn his manly form
> When once his nobler heart we view,
> In love so kind, in friendship warm,
> In honor and devotion true.
>
> O grave! thy triumph all shall be,
> To guard awhile this precious dust,
> The LORD of life is Lord of thee
> And thou shalt render back thy trust.

No. 1989.

[Low, blue slate. Good condition, save much inclined. Symbol.]

In memory of Osborn son of Mr Osborn Morton & Mrs
Patience his wife who died Sepr 18, 1790, aged 4 years &
10 months.

No. 1990.

[Blue slate. Good condition. Weeping willow and urn.]

In memory of Mrs Susanna Nichols wife of Moses
Nichols who died Aug 5 1822. in the 57 year of her age.

> Why do we mourn, why do we weep
> For a departed friend,
> For she has left a world of wo,
> And gone to a just friend.

No. 1991.

[Blue slate. Good condition. Flaming urn.]

Sacred to the memory of RIZPAH NICHOLS, wife of
Moses Nichols, who died March 4, 1841, aged 84 years.

No. 1992.

[Handsome granite block, polished; on granite plinth and base,—lot
in granite curbing.]

Capt. HARVEY WESTON died July 7, 1876, aged 84
years.

SALLY C. his wife died Oct. 21, 1883, aged 83 years.
SARAH E. their dau. died May 12, 1858, aged 18 years.

No. 1993.

[Blue slate. Good condition. Urn.]

REBECAH. Daug. of Simeon & Mary Dike, died Oct. 15, 1834, aged 8 years & 9 mon.

> She heard a voice we could not hear
> Which said, no longer stay,
> She saw a hand we could not see
> Which beckon'd her away.

No. 1994.

[Blue slate. Pyramidal. Good condition. Urn.]

In memory of Parney Young daughter of Simeon & Mary Dike who died Nov. 23 1813 aged 1 year & 9 months also an infant

> Sleep on, sweet babes,
> And take thy rest
> GOD call'd the home
> He thought it best.

No. 1995.

[Blue slate. Good condition, save a cleft near summit. Weeping willow, and an urn on which are the words "O, Death."]

In memory of WILLIAM P. G. DIKE son of Simeon & Mary Dike died April 13, 1830, aged 25 years.

> "Adieu a long adieu to all below
> To death and judgment I am call'd to go
> My days though few have like an arrow fled
> And now I'm numbered with the silent Dead
>
> Our God is love, his promises are sure,
> Great is his Power, none can his wrath endure.
> O! do not slight this Loud and solemn call,
> And while you mourn for me make Christ your all."

No. 1996.

[Granite block, on plinth and base of same.]

CAPT. GEORGE ALLEN Born Feb. 2, 1806, Died June 5, 1888.

No. 1997.

[Wooden slab.]

Henry S. Holmes, died Dec. 19th, 1862, aged 5 yrs. 1 mo. & 23 ds.

No. 1998.

[Blue slate. Good condition. Mausoleum.]

Erected to the memory of LUCY WESTON, Daughter of Seth & Lucy Weston late of Duxbury who died Oct. 22, 1831, aged 33 years

> Farewell, dear friends, a short farewell,
> Till we shall meet again above,
> Where endless joys and pleasures dwell
> And trees of life bear fruits of love.

No. 1999.
[White marble on marble plinth. Granite base. Good condition.]
CHARLES CHURCHILL Died Oct. 9. 1881 Aged 89 y'rs. 29 d'ys

No. 2000.
[Like preceding. Good condition.]
ABIGAIL, Wife of Charles Churchill Died Nov. 8, 1874, Aged 77 y'rs 5 mo's 3 days.

No. 2001.
[Low, white marble in freestone socket. Rose.]
Catharine Bridgham, daughter of Charles & Abigail Churchill age 11 years. December 31, 1850.

No. 2002.
[Purple slate. Good condition. Urn.]
REBECCA T. daughter of Charles & Abigail Churchill, departed this life May 12, 1835, aged 1 year 10 Months & 19 days.

No. 2003.
[Blue slate. Good condition. Figure of woman leaning on an urn inscribed "O! Death."]
Sacred to the memory of MARY ELIZABETH, dau. of Charles & Abigail Churchill, who died Sept. 13, 1819; aged 6 weeks & 4 days. Also NANCY (dau. of Thomas & Mary Churchill of Plympton) died Jan. 10, 1796; in her 16 year.

No. 2004.
[White marble. Discolored. Inclined.]
CAPT GEORGE SIMMONS died July 26, 1863; aged 81 years. MERCY SIMMONS his wife died Nov. 29, 1858; aged 75 years.

No. 2005.
[Blue slate. Pyramidal. Good condition. Weeping willow and urn.]
In memory of Lorenzo Simmons Son of Capt George Simmons, & Mrs Mercy his wife who died Septem 26, 1817 aged two years.

No. 2006.
[Low, blue slate. Pyramidal. Good condition. Urn.]
In memory of Joann White daughter of Capt George Simmons & Mercy his wife died June 21st 1825; aged 9 months and 11 days.

No. 2007.
[Low, white marble. Fair condition.]
MOSES SIMMONS died at sea March 15, 1834; aged 26 years.

AUGUSTUS F. SIMMONS died June 19, 1827; aged 14 years.

(NOTE.—Augustus F. Simmons was a frank, ingenuous and sincere youth, beloved by all his schoolmates,—one of whom was the writer of these lines. George W. Hosmer, our teacher, was much moved by the death of so promising a youth; and at Mr. Hosmer's suggestion many if not all the members of the school attended the funeral. Benjamin Drew was one of the eight bearers. White bands of cloth were secured about the casket containing the remains of our friend and schoolmate, and grasping these bands, we carried the precious burden from the house at the head of Water street to its final resting place. Those who knew young Simmons have never ceased to regret his early exit.)

No. 2008.

[Blue slate.   Four and one-half feet high.   Good condition.   Urn.]

In memory of CAPT. RICHARD BAGNELL, who died March 22, 1809, in the 56th year of his age.

Also BETHIAH, his wife who died Jan. 22, 1847, in the 90th y. of her age.

No. 2009.

[Low, blue slate.   Good condition.   Symbol.]

In Memory of Samuel West son of Mr Richard Bagnell & Mrs Bethiah his wife, who died Jany 12, 1786 aged 4 months & 24 days.

No. 2010.

[Low, blue slate.   Good condition.   Human face.]

In memory of Mary Simmons Goddard Daughter of Mr Daniel & Mrs Beulah Goddard who died Octr 19th 1798 aged 3 years 10 months & 19 days.

memento mori
Here lies the flower of our youth
Great God forgive our morning sin.

No. 2011.

[White marble.   Fair condition.   Hands clasped.]

Daniel Goddard, Died Oct. 30, 1844, Aged 73.   BEULAH, his wife Died Nov. 19, 1863. Aged 89. LEMUEL S. their son Died in South America in 1842.   Aged 37.

No. 2012.

[White marble.   Good condition.   In stone socket.]

BEULAH SIMMONS, Died Nov. 28, 1876, Aged 74 y'rs, 2 mo's, 28 days.

No. 2013.

[Blue slate.   Moss-covered, but compact.   Symbol.]

In Memory of Mrs Sarah Spinks wife of Mr Nicholas Spinks who departed this Life April ye 3d 1774. aged 38 years.

No. 2014.

[This and the next No. are white marble, inclosed. This stone is inclined to nearly 45 degrees.]

LEMUEL SIMMONS DIED Dec. 6, 1863 ; aged 73 years 4 months.

(He was universally beloved and respected; honest and upright with a cheerful and pleasant manner, and a kind benevolent heart. To know him was to love him.)

No. 2015.

PRISCILLA wife of Lemuel Simmons, died Mar. 1, 1835 ; in the 42nd year of her age. Also their infant son who died Jan. 26, 1823 ; aged 3 days.

No. 2016.

[Blue slate. Pyramidal. Good condition. Festoons.]

Sacred to the memory of Anna Hamblin Daughter of Hamblin Tillson and Susanna his wife who died July 4th 1812 aged 18 months 9 days.

So fades the lovely Blooming flower
frail Smiling solace of an hour
So soon our transient comforts fly
and pleasure only blooms to die.

No. 2017.

[Blue slate. Good condition. Seamed. Weeping willow and urn.]

In memory of Mrs Sally Burgis Consort of Mr Joseph Burgis who died Decr 29, 1824 aged 35 years.

No. 2018.

[Blue slate. Compact. Moss-grown. Weeping willow and urn.]

In memory of Fenelon T. Burgiss, Son of Joseph & Sally Burgiss, who died Oct 27, 1823, aged 15 months & 19 days.

He's left a world of sorrow, sin and pain
Wish not to call him back to life again
This lovely bud beginning to expand
Was soon transplanted to that happy land.

No. 2019.

[Blue slate. Good condition. Weeping willow and urn.]

In memory of Mr WILLIAM RICHMOND who died June 7 1815 in the 30 year of his age

My friends are gone my comfort fled
The sad remembrance of the dead
Recalls my wandering thoughts to mourn.

No. 2020.

[Blue slate. Good condition. Two urns.]

WILLIAM RICHMOND, died 1797, aged 56 y.rs. Also SALOMA wife of the above died June 8, 1836, in her 90th yr.

25

No. 2021.

[Blue slate. Fair condition. Weeping willow and urn.]

In memory of Mrs Hannah Bartlett the wife of Mr Nathaniel Bartlett who Departed this life July 28 1807 in the 40 year of her age Allso in memory of Four children of Mr Nathaniel Bartlett & Mrs Hannah Bartlett his wife

No. 2022.

[Blue slate. Good condition. Two weeping willows and urns.]

In memory of two children of Willm Morey and Polly his wife viz Cornelius died Decr 8, 1820 aged one month & 23 days Mary E. Morey died March the 20th 1823 aged one year 3 months & 7 days

No. 2023.

[Blue slate. Four feet high. Good condition. Urn.]

Erected in memory of MRS. MARY BARNES, wife of Capt Z. Barnes. who departed this life Oct.r 20, 1836, aged 38 y.rs.

The months of affliction are o'er
The days and the nights of distress,
We see her in anguish no more,
She's gained her happy release.

No. 2024.

[Blue slate. Good condition. Weeping willow and urn.]

Erected in memory of CAPT ZEACHEUS BARNES, who Departed this life December 26, 1832, aged 34 years.

Oft as the bell with solemn toll,
Speaks the departure of a soul,
Let each one ask himself, am I
Prepared should I be called to die ?

No. 2025.

[Blue slate. Good condition. Flaming urn.]

MARY W. Daughter of the late Zeacheus & Mary Barnes, died Dec. 11th, 1842, aged 14 years.

Think of that bright world where I
No more shall suffer pain,
And of that Heaven where all of us
May hope to meet again.

No. 2026.

[Blue slate. Good condition. Two urns.]

ERECTED to the memory of MR. LEMUEL SIMMONS, who died Dec. 11, 1833, in the 85 year of his age. And MRS. ABIGAIL, his wife died Oct. 2, 1817, in the 66 year of her age.

Their happy spirits o ward rise
To you blest world beyond the skies.
Come children view the place of rest
Prepare and be forever blest.

No. 2027.

[White marble. Rough. Discolored. Moss-grown.]

In memory of GEORGE STRAFFIN, who was kill'd with lightning in the Bay of Biscay Jan. 10, 1801, aged 32 y'rs. MARY S. widow of the above died March 30, 1843, aged 73 y'rs.

Also their two sons, GEORGE, died at sea July 7, 1824. in the 26th yr. of his age : ROBERT was lost at sea, Jan. 1821, aged 21 yrs.

No. 2028.

[White marble. Moss-grown.]

ALPHEUS RICHMOND died Aug. 30, 1858 ; Æ. 76 years 3 mos. Abbigal, his wife died Nov. 30, 1857 ; Æ. 73 years 6 mos. ALPHEUS RICHMOND Jr. was lost at sea, Mar. 18. 1854 ; Æ. 47 years 4 mos.

No. 2029.

[This and the following three Nos. are white marble, in the usual unhandsome condition of that material. They are set in granite sockets. The four are inclosed by a neat white fence.]

JOHN WILLIAMS, Born March 4, 1800 ; Died Nov. 23, 1852.

ELIZA ANN, Born June 30, 1829 ; Died April 6, 1830.

JOHN, Born July 3, 1831 ; Died Sept. 8, 1831 ; Children of John & Eliza Williams.

No. 2030.

ELIZA, Wife of JOHN WILLIAMS, Born Aug. 16, 1808, Died March 23, 1887.

No. 2031.

JOHN B. WILLIAMS, Died Oct. 9, 1872, Aged 35 years.

No. 2032.

ELIZA A. WILLIAMS Died May 5, 1878, Aged 45 y,rs. 9 mo,s.

No. 2033 a.

[Mottled marble, set in granite block. Good condition.]

SARAH F. BAGNELL Born January 29, 1833. Died February 27, 1892.

No. 2033 *b.*

[White marble. Fair condition.]

SAML. W. BAGNELL, died June 18, 1849; aged 62 years.

LOIS, his wife, died Dec. 30, 1820 : aged 32 years.

No. 2034.

[White marble. Good condition.]

MINERVA, Wife of Samuel W. Bagnell Died Dec. 8, 1877. Aged 82 y'rs, 4 mo's 8 days.

No. 2035.

[White marble in stone socket. Inclosed with wooden fence.]

PELHAM FINNEY, Died Feb. 12, 1868, Aged 56 y'rs 7 mo's.

WILLIAM H.

PELHAM W.

CLARA.

ALMIRA J.

Children of Pelham & Mary A. Finney.

No. 2036.

[This and the following three Nos. are inclosed by an iron fence. No. 2036 is over four feet long and was cemented in a stone socket. It has fallen and broken in two, but the inscription is still legible.]

FATHER & MOTHER. CAPT IGNATIUS PIERCE DIED Aug. 24, 1853, aged 68 years.   BETSEY his wife Died Nov. 30, 1859, aged 73 years.

Blessed are the dead who die in the Lord.

No. 2037.

[White marble in stone socket. Rough. Inclined.]

LUCY, Dau. of Ignatius & Betsy Pierce, died Oct ; 16, 1840, aged 18 years.

> My flesh shall rest beneath the ground,
> Till the great trumpets joyful sound;
> Then i'll awake in glad surprise,
> And in my Saviours image rise.

. No. 2038.

[White marble. Rough.]

SUSANNAH W. wife of Ignatius Pierce Jr. Died Aug. 24, 1840, Aged 22 years.   Their son died July 26, 1838.

> A husbands care, a husbands love,
> Could not save her from the grave,
> With thy child now sweetly rest,
> And learn the anthems of the blest.

No. 2039.

[White marble. Rough.]

WILLIAM NELSON, died Sept. 18, 1844, aged 8 mo.
WILLIAM NELSON, died Nov. 16, 1848, aged 3 yr's.
9 mo. Sons of I. & M. S. Pierce.

————o————

Dear little boys thy months were few
And suffering was thy lot below.
But Jesus' call thou hast obeyed.
And left this world of sin and wo.

No. 2040.

[This and the six following are inclosed by handsome iron fence,
and are in good condition, excepting the blue slate in the southwest
corner, which is weatherworn and moss-grown.]

GEN. JAMES WARREN died November 28, 1808;
aged 82. MERCY WARREN his wife, daughter of
James Otis of Barnstable, died October 19, 1814; aged
86.

No. 2041.

[Blue slate. Symbol. Inscription in capitals.]

Here lyes ye body of the Honourable JAMES WAR-
REN ESQR: who deceased June ye 29th, 1715, in ye
50th year of his age.

No. 2042.

[Blue slate. Defaced. Symbol.]

Here lyes   body of   WARREN   ge   t   who
dece Oct   29, 1707 in ye 48   year of his age.

No. 2043.

[Blue slate. Good condition. Symbol.]

Here lyes Buried the Body of Mrs ELIZABETH WARREN
Daughter of James Warren Esqr & Sarah His Wife Decd
Novr ye 5th 1744 Ætatis 33.

No. 2044.

[Blue slate. Good condition. Symbol. Inscription in capitals.]

Here lyes buried the body of Mrs MERCY WARREN who
died Janry the 17th 1745—6 in ye 42d year of her
age.

No. 2045.

[Blue slate. Good condition. Inscription in capitals. Symbol.]

Here lyes the body of Mrs PENELOPE WARREN the
wife of JAMES WARREN Esqr who departed this life
May the 25th 1737 in the 33d year of her age.

No. 2046.

[Blue slate. Fair condition. Symbol.]

Here lies buried the Body of Collo JAMES WARREN Esqr who departed this life JULY the 2d 1757 in the 58th year of his Age.

No. 2047.

[White marble. This and the following No. inclosed by wooden fence. This stone taken out of stone socket, and set in the ground.]

LUCIE S. Wife of Charles W. Johnson died Aug. 19, 1864 ; Æ. 21 yrs 6 mos & 6 d.

We shall meet with these our loved ones,
That were torn from our embrace,
We shall listen to their voices,
And behold them face to face.

Also JAMES H. GRACE D. & ELLA F. Children of James T. & Nancy G. Paulding.

No. 2048.

[White marble. Fair condition.]

JAMES T. PAULDING Co. B. 3 Mass. Regt. Died Aug. 19, 1880, Aged 59 y'rs.

No. 2049.

[Blue slate. Defaced and weatherworn. Going to pieces. Part of symbol.]

ye bod   Holmes   to Nathll   es ; who Decd July ye 6th 1740 in ye 39th year of her age.

No. 2050.

[Purple slate. Good condition.]

In memory of Mrs. POLLY BARTLETT wife of Ansel Bartlett, died June 23, 1878, Aged 95 y'rs 9 mo's.

No. 2051.

[Blue slate. Good condition.]

In memory of MR. ANSEL BARTLETT died May 26, 1836, aged 58 years. Also ANSEL BARTLETT son of the above died in Bremen Nov. 24, 1831, aged 24 years.

No. 2052.

[Blue slate. Weatherworn and moss-covered. Symbol.]

Here lyes ye body of Nathil King who decd Febry ye 7th 1734-5 in ye   th year   age.

No. 2053.

[Blue slate. Good condition. Mausoleum.]

In memory of NANCY D. PAULDING who died Aug. 27, 1840, aged 43 years.

Christ my Redeemer lives
And often from the skies
Looks down and watches all my dust
Till he shall bid it rise

No. 2054.

[White marble. Rough. Discolored.]

In memory of Mrs JEAN PATY wife of Capt Wm PATY Died Nov. 2, 1865, Æ. 68 Years.

No. 2055.

[Blue slate. Good condition. Weeping wlllow and urn.]

In memory of Hannah Curtis Paty Daughter of Capt William Paty & Mrs. Jane his wife who died Octr. 17, 1826 ; aged 4 years & 6 mo.

Of such is the kingdom of heaven.

No. 2056.

[White marble. Rough. Discolored.]

In memory of SUSAN H. ALLEN, wife of James H. Drew, who died May 22, 1815, aged 38 years.

No. 2057.

[Blue slate. Fair condition, but moss-grown. Flaming urn.]

To the memory of CAPT THOMAS POPE, who was born Novr. 1, 1770 Died July 6, 1820 in the 50 year of his age.

No. 2058.

[Blue slate, Originally about four feet by two and one-half. Broken across near the middle, the upper moiety leaning against the lower. Weeping willow and urn.]

In memory of Mr. Thomas Pope, who died July 20, 1832, aged 23 years.

Unveil thy bosom, faithful tomb,
Take this new treasure to thy trust ;
And give these sacred relics room
To slumber in thy silent dust.

No pain, no grief, no anxious fear
Invade thy bounds ; no mortal woes
Can reach the peaceful sleeper here,
While angels watch its soft repose.

No. 2059.

[Blue slate. Good condition. Weeping willow and urn.]

In memory of JOHN DAVIE ; who died June 27, 1841, aged 32 years 11 mos & 15 days.

No. 2060.

[Blue slate. Good condition. Weeping willow and urn.]

In memory of PRISCILLA, wife of John Davie ; who died Dec. 10, 1838, aged 19 years & 10 mos. JOHN L DAVIE, their son died Jan. 20, 1839, aged 5 mos & 20 days.

No. 2061.

[Blue slate. Good condition. Weeping willow and urn.]

In memory of DEBORAH C. DAVIE, who died July 13, 1838, aged 28 years, 5 mos & 27 days.

> She winged her way to realms above,
> Where all is light, and life, and love;
> Forever with her Savior blest,
> Her home His bosom, there to rest.

No. 2062.

[Blue slate. Good condition. Weeping willow and urn.]

In memory of LYDIA, wife of Ebenr Davie, who died June 29. 1840, aged 63 years. NATHANIEL C. DAVIE. their son, died at Amsterdam, Oct. 6, 1839, aged 19 years 10 mos & 6 days.

No. 2063.

[Blue slate. Good condition. Weeping willow and urn.]

In memory of Mr EBENEZER DAVIE, who died Feb. 10, 1832, aged 56 years & 11 mo's.

GEORGE DAVIE, son of the above, was drown'd at sea, Aug. 11, 1831, aged 18 years,

> Seize mortal seize the transient hour
> Improve each moment as it flies
> Life's a short summer, man a flower,
> He dies, Alas! how soon he dies.

No. 2064.

[Blue slate. Good condition. Weeping willow and urn.]

In memory of Mrs Sarah Harlow wife of Mr Seth Harlow who departed this life Feby 28, 1821 aged 82 years.

No. 2065.

[Blue slate. Fair condition. Symbol.]

To the memory of Mr SETH HARLOW, who Died June 30th 1802 in the 65th years of his age.

No. 2066.

[Blue slate. Cleft near summit. Moss-covered.]

In Memory of MISS MERCY HARLOW, died Nov. 9, 1837, in the 60 y,r of her age.

> She died in hope, She died in faith
> A life of suffering o'er
> She smiling met the shafts of death
> And lives to die no more.

No. 2067.

[Low, white marble. Fair condition. Rose.]

PHILLIP, Born Jan. 20, 1855, Died Sept. 22, 1859, Æt. 4 y's.

No. 2068.

[Low, white marble. Rough.]

HENRY, son of Phillip & Elizabeth Smith, died Jan. 30. 1850. aged 3 mon. & 8 days.

No. 2069.

[White marble. Rough, through disintegration of surface. Urn.]

In memory of CHARLES, son of Truman and Experience Bartlett who died July 22, 1826 : aged 6 years & 7 mon.

The beauteous flower that charms the eye
And decks the smiling plain,
With winter's blast shall fade and die,
But die to bloom again
Then why should sorrow wring thy brow
Say mourner say why weepest thou?

No. 2070.

[White marble, Weatherworn. Figure, a square structure, with radiations from upper surface ; above, and hanging at sides, draped curtains, with cords and tassels.]

SACRED to the memory of ANGELINE, dautr of Truman and Experience Bartlett died April 24, 1838 ; aged 20 yr,s.

Weep not for her, whom the veil of the tomb
In life's happy morning has hid from our eyes,
Ere sin threw a blight o'er the spirit's young bloom,
Or earth had profaned what was born for the skies.

No. 2071.

[White marble. Weatherworn and discolored.]

EXPERIENCE, wife of Truman Bartlett, Born April 5th, 1870 ; Died Jan. 11th, 1841.

STEPHEN, Son of Truman & Experience Bartlett, died at Buenos Ayres Dec. 16th, 1840 ; aged 38 years.

No. 2072.

[White marble. Condition like preceding.]

TRUMAN BARTLETT, Born March 10, 1776. Died August 18, 1841.

LUCIA, daughter of Truman and Experience Bartlett, Born July 4, 1813, Died October 3, 1841.

No. 2073.

[Blue slate. Pyramidal. Good condition.]

ERECTED in memory of MARY A. N. Daugh. of Joseph & Jane Barnes who died April 18, 1836, in her 7 year.

Sh's gone! I trust the GOD who gave,
Has laid this fair flower in the grave—
To pass beyond that narrow bourne :
And join the choir before His throne.

[Blue slate. Pyramidal. Good condition. Weeping willow and urn.]

In memory of Nancy C. Barnes, Daughter of Joseph Barnes, & Jane his wife who died Decr 5, 1825 ; aged 4 years & 5 months

Also Ellis Barnes, who Died Novr 27, 1816, aged 1 year & 7 months.

No. 2075.

[Blue slate. Pyramidal. Good condition. Figure of tree on left, bending over the inscription.]

To Roselia L. dau.r of Joseph & Jane Barnes, who died Febr. 2, 1832, in the 23 year of her age.

An affectionate child and sincere Christian.

No. 2076.

[Broken freestone socket. Headstone gone, footstone remains.]

J. B.

(The missing gravestone was to the memory of Mr. Joseph Barnes.)

No. 2077.

[White marble in freestone socket. Good condition. Weeping willow and urn.]

In memory of BETHIAH, wife of Henry O. Steward, who died Oct. 1, 1852, Æ. 35 y'rs 1 mo. & 25 days.

No. 2078.

[White marble in same base as preceding. Good condition.]

HENRY O. died July 27th. 1842, aged 4 mon. & 19 days. HENRY O. died Sept. 4th, 1843, aged 2 mon. & 5 days, CLARIBEL T. died Dec. 29th. 1844, aged 4 years & 17 days. Children of Henry O. & Bethiah Steward.

Jesus said, suffer little children, and forbid them not, to come unto me; for of such is the kingdom of heaven.

No. 2079.

[Purplish blue slate. Good condition. Symbol.]

In memory of Thomas Pope son of Cap Thomas Pope and Priscilla his wife who Died Augst 31st 1807 aged 7 years & 3 months

The work of god that beautious clay which here
In infant smiles so lovely did appear
As though in nature's nicest model cast,
Exactly polished wrought two fine to last
By the same powerfull hand again shall rise
To bloom more gay more lovely in the sky

No. 2080.

[Purplish blue slate. Good condition. Symbol.]

To the memory of Mrs Mary Pope wife of Mr Thomas Pope who died Janry ye 9th 1795 in the 27th year of her age.

No. 2081.

[Purplish blue slate. Good condition. Symbol.]

To the memory of Seth Luce son of Mr Ebenezer Luce & Mrs Sarah his wife who died Febry 14, 1796 in the 16 year of his age.

No. 2082.

[White marble. Fair condition, but discolored.]

TIMOTHY BARRY, died Feb. 5, 1856 ; Æ. 58 yrs. 2 mos. & 25 dys.

> Fare thee well; though woe is blending,
> With the tones of earthly love,
> Triumph high and joy unending,
> Wait thee in the realms above.

MARIA BARRY died Apr. 12, 1824 ; aged 2 dys.
TIMOTHY BARRY Jr. died Dec. 29, 1836 ; aged 7 wks. & 4 ds.

No. 2083.

[White marble. Rough.]

HATTIE S. daughter of Timothy & Maria Barry, died Dec. 30, 1858 ; Æ. 15 years 2 mo. & 19 days.

> Thy gentle spirit passed away
> Mid pain the most severe,
> So great we could not wish thy stay
> A moment longer here.
> Thou minglest now in that bright throng
> Around the eternal throne,
> And join'st the everlasting song
> With those before thee gone.

No. 2084.

[White marble in granite base. The whole mass inclined.]

FATHER AND MOTHER. JOB CHURCHILL, Died March 23, 1826, Aged 39 years. Hannah T. his wife died April 8, 1866, Aged 76 years.

No. 2085.

[Blue slate. Good condition. Weeping willow and urn.]

In memory of SALLY dau,r of Job & Hannah Churchill died Fe br,y 16, 1824 ; aged 1 year & 2 mon,s. Also In Memory of Sally, who died April 2, 1823 ; aged 1 year & 5 mo,s

[Blue slate. Good condition. Weeping willow and urn.]

In memory of LYDIA CHURCHILL wife of BARNABUS CHURCHILL died June 19, 1825 ; in the 65th year of her age.

No. 2087.

[Blue slate. Good condition. Weeping willow and urn.]

In memory of Mr Barnabas Churchill. who died August 29, 1821, in the 74 year, of his age.

No. 2088.

[Low, blue slate. Good condition. Symbol.]

To the memory of Mrs Sarah Churchill Wife of Mr Barnabas Churchill Who Died November 9th 1801 in the 48th Year of her Age.

No. 2089.

[Low, blue slate. Good condition. Symbol.]

In Memory of 2 Children of Mr Barnabas Churchill & Mrs Sarah his wife, Viz Barnabas died Sepr J4, J785 aged J0 months & J4 days. Barnabas died Decr 8, 1789 aged J0 months & 3 days.

No. 2090.

[White marble in granite socket. Good condition.]

OBED KEMPTON died February 24, 1839 ; Aged 24 years. OBED W. KEMPTON died June 17, 1855 ; Aged 16 years.

No. 2091.

[White marble. Like preceding, and in same base. Bears only the word:]

MOTHER.

No. 2092.

[White marble, in stone socket. Fair condition.]

HOMER BRYANT Co. E 23 Mass. Regt. Died June 6, 1864 Aged 45 y'rs.

No. 2093.

[White marble. Rough. Discolored. Weeping willows and obelisk.]

LUCRETIA, wife of John Pierce and consort of Cyrus B. Phillips, died Sept. 8, 1843. in the 46th. yr. of her age.

No. 2094.

[Low, white marble. Rough. Discolored. Inclined.]

CHARLES THOMAS, son of James M. & Phebe Atherton, died Aug. 7, 1846, aged 2 yr's & 4 mo.

. No. 2095.
[Row of tombs at foot of hill, bearing the names:]
WARREN
THOMAS
SPOONER
DAVIS
HEDGE

No. 2096.
[White marble in broken socket. Stone itself in fair condition.]
ALLEN HATHAWAY Co. K. 99 N. Y. Regt. Died
June 3, 1873 Aged 71 y'rs 20 d's.

No. 2097.
[Blue slate. Good condition. Symbol.]
To the memory of Mr Seth Churchill who died Jany
15th AD 1798 in the 44th year of his age.

Fresh as the grass our bodies stand
And flourish bright and gay
A blasting wind sweeps o'er the land
And fades the grass away.

No. 2098.
[Blue slate. Good condition. Weeping willow and urn.]
In memory of Mrs Elizabeth Churchill wife of Mr Seth
Churchill died Sepr 5 1814 in the 53 year of her age

No. 2099.
[Low, blue slate. Laminæ separating. Two symbols.]
In Memory of 2 Children of Mr Seth & Mrs Elizabeth
Churchill Viz Lucy died Sepr 2, 1793 aged 2 years & 2
months. David died Sepr 30 1793 aged 9 months & 3
days Also a 3d Seth died Sepr 24, 1795 aged 1 year 4
months & 5 days.

No. 2100.
[Handsome marble. Set in marble plinth, granite base. Good condition.]
BETSEY CROCKER, Dau. of Benj. & Lucy Bagnell,
Died Sept. 6, 1887, Aged 62 y'rs 7 mo's.

My trust is in the Lord.

No. 2101.
[Similar to preceding.]
LUCY EMILY, Dau. of Benj. & Lucy Bagnell, Died
Jan. 2, 1884, Aged 61 y'rs 4 mo's.

"He giveth his beloved sleep."

No. 2102.

[Similar to preceding, but inclined.]

ELIZABETH S. Dau. of Benj. & Lucy Bagnell, Died Dec. 21, 1869. Aged 32 y'rs 9 mo's.

No. 2103.

[Purple slate. Four feet high. Good condition. Weeping willow and urn.]

In memory of Mrs LUCY, wife of Benjamin Bagnell who left us Apr. 19, 1854, Æ. 61 yrs. & 9 ms.

"There shall be no more death, neither shall there be any more pain; for the former things are passed away."

No. 2104.

[Blue slate. Four feet high. Good condition. Flaming urn.]

ERECTED to the Memory of Mr BENJAMIN BAG-NELL who died March 8, 1839, in the 47 year of his age. Also ELIZABETH, dau. of Benjamin & Lucy Bagnell died Jan. 26, 1834, aged 4 years & 8 mon.

No. 2105.

[Low, blue slate. Good condition. Symbol.]

To the memory of Mr Joseph Mitchell who died December ye 30 ɉ791 Ætatis 54 Mrs Mary his wife died May 22d ɉ790 Ætatis 51.

No. 2106.

[Purplish blue slate. Pyramidal. Good condition. Symbol.]

To the memory of the amiable Mrs JANE DOGGET Consort of Mr SETH DOGGET who died May 31 1794 in the 26th year of her age   also an infant Daughter by her side

Come view the seen twill fill you with surprise
Behold the loveliest form in nature dies
At noon she flourish'd blooming fair and gay
At evening an extended corpse she lay.

No. 2107.

[Low, white marble, set in granite block.]

(On one side, the words:)

Our Father

[On obverse:]
Samuel Elliot June 12, 1801 Aug. 3, 1890.

No. 2108.

[Low, white marble block. Marble plinth. Granite base. Handsomely sculptured.]

(On the upper surface, the word:)

DARLING.

(In front, inscribed:)

Alma May, Daaghter of J. S. & M. D. Butler. Died Dec. 17, 1888. Aged 9 y'rs. 2 mo's.

Her heart was folded deep in ours.

No. 2109.

[Handsome granite block.]

Jane wife of Ellis T. Lanman, 1825—1891.

No. 2110.

[Handsome granite block.]

Rebecca H. Daughter of Ivory L. & Rebecca B. Harlow 1859—1887.

No. 2111 *a*.

[This and the two following are white marble, inclosed in handsome iron railing. A gate under an arched entrance has "D. Goddard 1854" cast upon it, in raised letters.]

In memory of DANIEL GODDARD, Jr. who died Aug. 1, 1849, in his 53 year.

No. 2111 *b*.

In memory of LYDIA, wife of Daniel Goddard, died Dec. 9, 1871, Aged 65 y'rs, 4 mo's

No. 2112.

In memory of Mary. wife of Daniel Goddard, who died Dec. 30, 1848, in her 52d yr. Also Daniel, their son who died Sept. 28, 1821, aged 16 Mon.

No. 2113.

[White marble, mottled. Cemented in marble socket, which is set in the ground. Good condition.]

CAPT THOMAS TRIBBLE. Died Sept. 15, 1864, Aged 63 y'rs.

CYNTHIA T. SHERMAN His wife Died Jan. 10, 1893, Aged 80 y'rs 10 m's.

No. 2114.

[White marble on marble base. Good condition. Inscription in capital letters.]

Mother. Elizabeth Ishmael Barnes
1824—1888

No. 2115.

[Like preceding.]

Father. Charles Elkanah Barnes 1820—1891

No. 2116.

[Small, marble tablet, by side of 2115.]

Charlie E. 1856—1859

No. 2117.

[Like 2116, and close by it.]

Charlie S. 1853—1855

No. 2118.

[Low, white marble. Good condition.]

Elkanah Barnes

No. 2119.

[Polished granite monument. Inscription in capitals.]

PATY.

Capt. Ephraim Paty   1806—1848
Sarah C. his wife   1806—1892

Sarah C.   1835—1858
William A.   1846—1847
Elizabeth F.   1848—1860   .
William A.   1849—1850

No. 2120.

[White marble. Granite base. Good condition.]

JOANNA A. wife of Reuben Hall. Died at Chelsea,
Mass. April 17, 1887, Aged 73 y'rs, 4 mo's.

Blessed are the dead who die in the Lord.

No. 2121.

[White marble. Granite base. Good condition.]

AUNT LOUISE.

Louisa Thompson Died Nov. 2, 1892, Aged 84 y'rs 23
days.   .

No. 2122.

[Like preceding.]

OUR FATHER.

Capt. THOMAS E. CORNISH Died May 20, 1880,
Aged 69 y'rs 6 mo's 4 days.

No. 2123.

[Polished granite, on granite base. Good condition. The first name
a duplicate of No. 1304, q. v. Inscription in capitals.]

Mary T. Bacon died Nov. 12, 1860, aged 50 yrs. 10
mos.

Betsey Bacon died Jan. 23, 1891, aged 82 yrs.

Rebecca Bacon died March 27, 1891, aged 78 yrs.

Daughters of Capt Geo. and Elizabeth Bacon.

No. 2124.

[White marble, on w. m. base. Good condition.]

ELIZA C. Wife of Asa Pierce died Feb. 1. 1890,
Aged 69 y'rs 6 m's 7 days.

At Rest.

No. 2125.

[Handsome granite block, on granite base. Good condition.]

Lieut. John B. Collingwood 1826—1863.

Susan, his wife 1829—1892.

Not changed, but glorified.

No. 2126.

[Granite block, on granite base. Good condition.]

Children of William and Eleanor Collingwood. William Jr. John Mary Robert S.

No. 2127.

[Fine marble. Marble plinth. Granite base.]

Charles Nelson Died March 19, 1893 Aged 88 y'rs 11 m'os

No. 2128.

[Handsome veined marble. Marble plinth. Granite base. Good condition.]

James Doten 1783—1859.

Lydia Doten 1799—1892.

No. 2129.

[Handsome marble block. Marble plinth. Granite base. In wooden paling.]

ASA N. KENDRICK Died Nov. 9, 1890, aged 75 yrs. 11 mos. 10 days.

No. 2130.

[Polished granite block. Good condition.]

David Diman 1794—1851

Abigail B. Diman 1800—1843

No. 2131.

[Like above No.; this and the above inclosed.]

Abigail N. Diman 1819—1860

Sarah N. Diman 1836—1861

No. 2132.

[Polished granite block. Good condition.]

Ellis D. Barnes 1831—1836.

No. 2133.

[Tall, blue slate, in freestone socket. Good condition.]

ABIGAIL T. SAVERY,

wife of Thomas Spinney of Boston Mass. Obit Nov. 7, A. D. 1839, Aged 42.

Also in memory of her son Robert Huntress Spinney, who died in New Orleans, on the 14 of August 1843, Aged 22.

No. 2134.
[Low, blue slate. Weatherworn. Symbol.]
In Memory of 2 Children Daughters of Mr. Judah Delano & Mrs. Penelope his wife. Viz 1st Salome died Sepr 6th 1785 Aged 1 year 5 Months   Days.   2d Penelope died April 9 1781 Aged 2 Days.

No. 2135.
[Low, thick, blue slate. Moss-grown. Symbol.]
In Memory of 2 Children of Mr Judah & Mrs Penelope Delano Viz. Henrey died Novr 4, 1790 aged 2 years & 4 months & 8 days died a Daughter Feby 4 1785 aged 1 day

No. 2136.
[Blue slate. Inclosed. Symbol. Fair condition.]
To the memory of Mrs. Abigail Sampson wife of Mr Stephen Sampson who died of the Small pox Janry ye 9 A. D. 1777 in the 45 year of her age.

No. 2137.
[Similar to No. 1236, by the side of which it is placed. Good condition.]
Mary W. Russell Wife of William S. Russell Born Dec. 24, 1798,   Died Apr. 30, 1890.

No. 2138.
[Low, blue slate. Symbol.]
Rebecca Cole Aged 18 years Died July ye 2d, 1714

No. 2139.
[Polished granite column. Granite plinth and base. Good condition. On the plinth the name:]
ROBBINS.
(On west side:)
Josiah A. Robbins 1823—1885
(On south side:)
John Briggs   1855—1856
Josiah Thomas   1857—1868
Walter Jackson   1870—1873
Sons of Josiah A. & R. W. Robbins.

No. 2140.
[Blue slate. Good condition. Urn.]
Erected to the memory of NATHAN G. CUSHING who died Jan. 22, 1854, in the 31st year of his age.

No—take me to your side, ye loved,
Ye lost, yet once again—
To bear no more what I have borne,
Nor be as I have been—
For rest, for rest, O give me room!
And give me rest within the tomb.

No. 2141.

[A copy of the original inscription of No. 430,—the gravestone now almost destroyed,—has been kindly furnished me by Edgar F. Raymond, Esq., who saw the monument when in fair condition. It read as follows:]

Here lyeth ten Children Viz three sons of Rev. Mr. John Cotton who Died in the Work of the Gospel Ministry at Charlestown in South Carolina Sept. 18th 1699. Where he had great success and 7 sons of Josiah Cotton Esq who deceased in their infancy

No. 2142.

[White marble block. Marble plinth, on granite base. Good condition.]

MARY L. CHURCHILL Died Jan. 22, 1889, Aged 72 years.

No. 2143.

[Low, blue slate. Pyramidal. Symbol. Fair condition. Is a few yards southeast of the Daniel Goddard Jr., iron fence near the fort outline.]

To the memory of Pricilla Davea Daughter of Capt Robart & Mrs Jerusha Davea who died Octr 11th 1802 aged 1 year 7 months & 11 days.

Babes rather caught from womb & breast
Claim right to sing above the rest
Becaus their found that happy shore
They never saw nor sought before.

No. 2144.

[Blue slate. Good condition. Weeping willow and urn.]

Erected In memory of Mrs. Harriot Davie, wife of Capt. Robert Davie who departed this life January 12, 1827; aged 28 years. Also their Daughter Harriot E. Davie, died Jany 20, 1827; aged 4 years & 21 days

Thus from thy kindred early torn
And to thy grave untimely borne
Vanish'd forever from my view
Thou partner of my youth adieu.
As in Adam all die even so in CHRIST
Shall all be made alive.

No. 2145.

[Blue slate, inscription scaled off: but standing close to Nos. 435 and 436, (q. v.) and to others of the Thomas family, it is probably at the grave of Nathaniel Thomas, the son of the Nathaniel Thomas who married Mary Appleton in 1694 (v. Davis' Ancient Landmarks of Plymouth, p. 261); and as Nathaniel and Mary had a second Nathaniel, b. in 1700, their first son bearing the father's name must have died before the close of the 17th century.]

No. 2146.

[White marble, similar to No. 509, by the side of which it stands. Inscription in capitals, save the epitaph.]

Our Mother. In memory of Eliza S. Harlow who died January 12, 1892, Æ. 86 years 3 mos 2 days.
At Rest.

No. 2147.
[Fine, white marble; plinth & base the same. Good condition.]
HARRIET WEBSTER Born Feb. 23, 1827, Died
Aug. 2, 1895.

Erected by her children.
No. 2148.
[Mottled marble, granite base. Good condition.]
Mary M Whiting 1894 March 26 79 years

There remaineth therefore a rest to the people of God.
No. 2149.
[A beautiful, polished stone. Mr. B. Dunham—a guide on Burial
Hill—calls it "Wesleyan marble." Good condition.]
Charles O. Churchill
1821—1891.
No. 2150.
[Material similar to preceding. Good condition.]
JAMES R. SHAW
1820—1891
No. 2151.
[Handsome granite block. Good condition.]

FATHER.	MOTHER.
Eliphalet Holbrook	Amelia Holbrook
1831—1886.	1834—1875.

No. 2152.
[Blue slate. Urn. Good condition.]
This Stone is erected to the memory of that unbias'd
Judge faithful Officer sincere Friend and honest Man Coll.
Isaac Lothrop who resigned this Life on the 26th day of
April 1750 in the 43 year of his age.
Had Virtues Charms the power to save
Its faithful Votaries from the Grave
This Stone had ne'er possess'd the Fame
Of being mark'd with LOTHROP'S name.
No. 2153.
[Blue slate. Good condition. Weeping willow and urn.]
Departed this Life June 23d 1796 in the 90th year of
her age Madam Priscilla Hobart Relict of the Revd Noah
Hobart late of Fairfield in Connecticut her third husband
her first and Second were John Watson Esq and Honble
Isaac Lothrop

No. 2154.

[White marble, on granite base. Good condition.]

Betsey E. Wife of William Finney
August 18, 1807.
June 29, 1888.

No. 2155.

. [White marble on granite base. Good condition.]

HARRIET A. Wife of ISAAC B. King. Died March
17, 1895, Aged 76 y'rs. 9 m's 14 days.

No. 2156.

[White marble. Good condition. Inclosed, by wooden fence, with
several gravestones bearing the same surname.]

Susan B. Morton   Born Dec. 25, 1832,   Died
March 9, 1894.

"So He giveth his beloved sleep."

No. 2157.

[Similar to 2156.]

William H. Morton   Born Aug. 20, 1832,   Died
April 7, 1895.

No. 2158.

[Elegantly polished and carved granite block. Granite plinth and
base. Height nearly six feet.]

PHINEAS PIERCE
1804—1841

DORCAS PIERCE
1809—1891

REBECCA JANE, THEIR DAUGHTER
1829—1833

(On the plinth:)

PIERCE

No. 2159.

[Polished granite block. Granite base. Inscription in capitals.]

Edwin F. Erland
Feb. 19, 1833,
July 13, 1896.

No. 2160.

[Veined marble. Good condition.]

(On the front:)

MOTHER
At Rest.

(On the reverse:)

LYDIA HOLMES
1805—1895.

No. 2161.

[This No. takes the place of No. 376, q. v. 2161 is a fine, beautiful block of slate, firm and compact. It is six inches in thickness, and about four feet high. This stone has been substituted for the former one in order to correct what Bradford's History of Plymouth Colony shows to have been an error. On the new stone a vessel under sail takes the place of the old-time symbol; and on the upper corners are sculptured representations of scallop shells.]

Here ended the Pilgrimage of JOHN HOWLAND who died February 23, 1672-3, aged above 80 years. He married Elizabeth daughter of JOHN TILLEY who came with him in the Mayflower Dec. 1620. From them are descended a numerous posterity.

"He was a godly man and an ancient professor in the wayes of Christ. He was one of the first comers into this land and was the last man that was left of those that came over in the Shipp called the Mayflower that lived in Plymouth."

Plymouth Records.

No. 2162.

[Erected to preserve the original stone No. 295 (Nathaniel Goodwin). No. 2162 is a tall handsome block of granite, from the face of which was scooped a cavity of right depth and dimensions to receive and protect No. 295,—which, fitted to and secured within said cavity, will, it is hoped, successfully resist the assaults of time and the elements for centuries to come.]

[At about a mile from the Town-house, on South street, was formerly a "pest-house," in which small-pox patients were treated. Near the site of the pest-house are several graves; two are marked by headstones,—only one however, has an inscription; this it seems to the author advisable to insert, although from the circumstances of the case the interment of Mrs. Mayhew was remote from Burial Hill:]

MARY MAYHEW wife of THOMAS MAYHEW, Esqr. who Decd Sept. 3d 1776 Aged 54 years.

[NOTE. If any errors or omissions are discovered in this work, the author would be glad to be informed thereof, that the proper corrections and insertions may be made in a third edition. But he requests his correspondents not to delay; for, being in his 85th year, he is perfectly aware that erelong the crossbones and hour-glass may decorate his own headstone. Address BENJAMIN DREW, 48 Summer street, Plymouth, Mass.]

www.ingramcontent.com/pod-product-compliance
Lightning Source LLC
Chambersburg PA
CBHW021123270326
41929CB00009B/1015